To Jane, my love, who has always supported and encouraged activities such as writing and has sacrificed nights and weekends for this book.

To Cory, my daughter, who is the light of my life.

Publishing Manager

Lloyd J. Short

Product Director

Karen A. Bluestein

Production Editor

Sandra Blackthorn

Editors

Jo Anna Arnott
Joseph P. Goodwin
Beth Hoger
Alice Martina Smith

Editorial Assistants

Fran Blauw
Stacie Lamborne

Technical Editors

Richard and Sally Clements

Indexed by

Sherry Massey

Book Design and Production

Dan Armstrong
Cheryl English
Lori A. Lyons
Jennifer Matthews
Joe Ramon
Dennis Sheehan
Peter Tocco

Composed in Times Roman and Excellent No. 47
by Que Corporation

D/L WA

lisher®

nd Traps

This book is to be returned on or before
the last date stamped below.

26. MAR 91
09. APR 91
23 APR E O
08. JUN 91
24. SEP 91
15. OCT 91
6 NOV 91 UD
29. NOV
28. DEC 91
24. JAN 92
24. NOV 92
02. FEB 94
19. MAR 94
12. April. 1P.
STORE

SUTTON LEISURE SERVICES

WALLINGTON LIBRARY
Shotfield, Wallington
SM6 0HY
081-770 4900

RENEWALS Please quote:
date of return, your ticket number and
computer label number for each item.

r, Jr.

Ventura Publisher® Tips, Tricks, and Traps

Copyright © 1989 by Que® Corporation

All rights reserved. Printed in the United States of America. No part of this book may be used or reproduced in any form or by any means, or stored in a database or retrieval system, without prior written permission of the publisher except in the case of brief quotations embodied in critical articles and reviews. Making copies of any part of this book for any purpose other than your own personal use is a violation of United States copyright laws. For information, address Que Corporation, 11711 N. College Ave., Carmel, IN 46032.

Library of Congress Catalog No.: 89-60241
ISBN 0-88022-413-4

This book is sold *as is*, without warranty of any kind, either express or implied, respecting the contents of this book, including but not limited to implied warranties for the book's quality, performance, merchantability, or fitness for any particular purpose. Neither Que Corporation nor its dealers or distributors shall be liable to the purchaser or any other person or entity with respect to any liability, loss, or damage caused or alleged to be caused directly or indirectly by this book.

92 91 90 89 8 7 6 5 4 3 2 1

Interpretation of the printing code: the rightmost double-digit number is the year of the book's printing; the rightmost single-digit number, the number of the book's printing. For example, a printing code of 89-1 shows that the first printing of the book occurred in 1989.

Ventura Publisher Tips, Tricks, and Traps is based on Ventura Publisher Version 2.0 and includes information on the Professional Extension.

WA

SUTTON LEISURE LIBRARIES

013332269

29 OCT 1990

686.2252

About the Author

Schuyler W. Lininger, Jr.

Schuyler W. Lininger, Jr., an Oregon chiropractor, has been a computer consultant and writer for the last seven years. He contributed several chapters to *Using WordPerfect 5*, *WordPerfect Tips, Tricks, and Traps*, 2nd Edition, and *WordPerfect Macro Library*, all published by Que Corporation, 1988.

Dr. Lininger uses desktop publishing to produce brochures, fliers, signs, and newsletters for his own clinic. In addition, with another doctor, he uses desktop publishing to produce *HealthNotes*, a newsletter distributed by natural foods stores.

Dr. Lininger serves as vice president of sales and develops products and product literature for a major food supplement company. He also teaches nutrition courses at Western States Chiropractic College in Portland, Oregon, and has lectured extensively on nutrition in the United States and abroad.

Contents at a Glance

Table of Contents

II Working with Text

IV Printing Ventura Documents

V Using Advanced Ventura Applications

ACKNOWLEDGMENTS

In everyone's life, there are a few teachers who help shape your life. I always promised myself that when I wrote a book, I would acknowledge those teachers: Miss Jones (first grade), Mr. McElhone (fifth grade), Mr. Weston (high school English), Dr. van der Elst (college anthropology), Dr. Frost (master's thesis committee chairperson), Dr. Carnes (chiropractic college anatomy), Drs. Bland and Wright (nutrition), and Barry Bevan (friend).

I would like to thank the public relations people and developers for all the companies mentioned in Appendix A. These people were uniformly helpful and gracious—often shipping beta and newly converted software to me overnight.

Finally, thanks to the terrific people at Que: Chuck Stewart, who recruited me electronically; Scott Flanders, Lloyd Short, and Karen Bluestein, who gave me the chance to do my own book; and all the editors, who are competent, dedicated, and professional. I can't imagine writing for a better publisher.

Trademark Acknowledgments

Que Corporation has made every effort to supply trademark information about company names, products, and services mentioned in this book. Trademarks indicated below were derived from various sources. Que Corporation cannot attest to the accuracy of this information.

1-2-3, Lotus, and Symphony are registered trademarks and Lotus Manuscript is a trademark of Lotus Development Corporation.

Apple, ImageWriter, LaserWriter Plus, Macintosh, MacPaint, and MacWrite are registered trademarks of Apple Computer, Inc.

Arts & Letters is a trademark of Computer Support Corporation.

AST TurboLaser is a registered trademark of AST Research, Inc.

AutoCAD is a registered trademark of Autodesk, Inc.

Bitstream is a registered trademark of Bitstream Inc.

CITIZEN is a registered trademark of Citizen America Corporation.

dBASE and dBASE III are registered trademarks and dBASE III PLUS and dBASE IV are trademarks of Ashton-Tate Corporation.

DESQview is a trademark of Quarterdeck Office Systems.

Diablo and Xerox are registered trademarks of Xerox Corporation.

DSOPTIMIZE is a trademark of Design Software.

EPSON and Graftrax are registered trademarks of Seiko Epson Corporation.

Fluent Laser Fonts is a trademark of CasadyWare, Inc.

FullWrite is a trademark of Ann Arbor Softworks, Inc.

GEM is a trademark of Digital Research Inc.

Hewlett-Packard, LaserJet Plus, and ThinkJet are registered trademarks and DeskJet, LaserJet, and ScanJet are trademarks of Hewlett-Packard Co.

IBM is a registered trademark and DisplayWrite is a trademark of International Business Machines Corporation.

JLaser is a registered trademark of Tall Tree Systems.

Microsoft, Microsoft Windows, Microsoft Word, and Windows/386 are registered trademarks of Microsoft Corporation.

MultiMate is a registered trademark of Multimate International, an Ashton-Tate company.

NEC is a registered trademark of NEC Information Systems Inc.

Norton Utilities is a trademark of Peter Norton Computing.

Okidata is a registered trademark of Oki America, Inc.

PageMaker is a registered trademark of Aldus Corporation.

PostScript is a registered trademark and Adobe Illustrator is a trademark of Adobe Systems Incorporated.

Publisher's Paintbrush is a trademark of ZSoft Corporation.

Quattro, SideKick, and SuperKey are registered trademarks of Borland International, Inc.

Ready! and ThinkTank are trademarks of Living Videotext, Inc.

SAMNA Word is a trademark of SAMNA Corporation.

SuperCalc is a registered trademark of Computer Associates International, Inc.

Tandy is a registered trademark of Tandy Corporation.

Ventura Publisher is a registered trademark of Ventura Software Inc.

Volkswriter is a registered trademark of Lifetree Software, Inc.

WordPerfect is a registered trademark of WordPerfect Corporation.

WordStar is a registered trademark of MicroPro International Corporation.

XyWrite is a trademark of XyQuest, Inc.

Conventions Used in This Book

The conventions used in this book have been established to help you learn to use the program quickly and easily. As much as possible, the conventions correspond with those used in the Ventura Publisher documentation.

Command and menu names are written with initial capital letters exactly as they appear on-screen. Names of dialog boxes are written in all capital letters. Options in dialog boxes and screen messages are written in a `special typeface` and capitalized exactly as they appear on-screen. Words and letters that the user types are written in *italic* or set off on a separate line.

Introduction

When I was in grade school, I had a teacher who suggested that I stop wasting my time trying to make a paper look better. As I recall, I was embellishing the margins, coloring in certain words for emphasis, and inserting small drawings to illustrate points.

I'm sure my teacher had my best interests at heart and was trying to suggest that I concentrate on content rather than form. The lesson was well taken; for years I concentrated on content and tried to make the form appealing without overdoing it and "wasting" my time.

For my master's thesis, obtained in 1973, I wrote a long paper about T.S. Eliot and his poem "The Wasteland." My nights were spent banging on a used portable Smith-Corona electric typewriter. I deleted words by backspacing and then holding the autorepeating X key. Sentences were double-spaced, not for legibility, but so additional thoughts, comments, or corrections could be written or typed between the lines. Pages were yanked from the typewriter and stacked into a pile, and a fresh piece of paper was immediately rolled into position. A thesaurus was at hand; a dictionary was available for meaning—proofing for correct spelling waited until later.

Random thoughts that didn't quite fit in with what was being written at the moment were inserted with rows of asterisks above and below or scrawled on a piece of lined yellow paper for later interpolation. References were penned on 3-by-5 cards and numbered sequentially. Where appropriate, the number on the reference card was scrawled above the text.

Once the initial draft was completed, all the typed pages, the notes on the lined yellow paper, and the 3-by-5 note cards were assembled on the floor. My technical writing instruments were at hand: a bottle of white glue, legal-sized white paper, and a pair of scissors.

Paragraphs were cut, edited, and glued into place on the legal-sized paper. The notes on the lined yellow paper were fleshed out into complete thoughts and then cut and pasted into place. As sections came together, transition sentences were written, and lines with arrows connected disconnected thoughts.

The collection of pages was then placed in order, and the references were double-checked. The endnote numbers were placed in order, and the 3-by-5 cards were marked to show to which endnotes they corresponded. Then the pages were numbered.

The entire pile of pasted pages and 3-by-5 cards was then taken to a typist I had located in a campus newspaper classified ad. She charged $1.50 per page and typed the thesis on an IBM Selectric typewriter. I sat in the room as she typed and proofed for spelling errors and omitted words as each page was completed. I made small pencil marks on mistakes and returned them to her either for whiting out and typing over or retyping.

Finally, the paper was completed and I had two photocopies made. The original was bound for permanent residence in the college library (where I doubt it has been widely circulated), one went to my thesis chairman, and one is on a bookshelf in my home.

This may seem an odd introduction to a book on desktop publishing, but many of you have had similar experiences writing your own school papers, designing newsletters, producing books or technical manuals, or preparing business documents.

With modern computers, you no longer need to struggle with old technology to produce your documents. Finally, I have been able to disregard my teacher's advice to spend less time "making it look good." With Ventura Publisher®, "good" is just exactly how it looks.

Word Processor or Page Layout Program?

A good word processor would have answered most of my prayers back in 1973. Word processing capabilities convinced me to make the investment, and I finally got a personal computer. The early days of word processing, however, meant dot-matrix printers with poor resolution. Not only that, you had to make complex modifications to get the printer to do simple things like underline or italicize text. The first article I wrote about computers explained how to master arcane printer codes.

If I wrote my thesis today using a word processor, I would have a dictionary and thesaurus at my fingertips. I would be able to cut and paste without a glue pot, number my footnotes automatically, and print the whole document with a simple command.

With the introduction of sophisticated word processors such as WordPerfect®, Microsoft® Word, MultiMate®, and XyWrite™ and the increasing availability of laser printers, not only is word processing easier, but the output is becoming indistinguishable from typeset documents.

The differences between high-end word processors and desktop publishing programs are becoming increasingly difficult to distinguish. Essentially, word processors excel at text handling; desktop publishers shine at page layout.

Text handling usually involves the following:

- Easy cursor movement to any point on a page and any point in a document.
- Fast, intuitive text manipulation. You can cut, paste, copy, search, replace, store, and retrieve text.
- Comprehensive font-attribute control with the capability to make text bold, italic, underlined, large, or small.
- Complete documentation capabilities including footnotes, endnotes, indexes, and tables of contents.
- Rapid and accurate proofing for spelling errors.

Page layout involves the following:

- WYSIWYG (what you see is what you get) display. The page on your monitor is a very close image of what the final printed page looks like.
- Easy column handling that allows multiple columns on a page. Pages may even be so complex that part of a page has three columns and another part of the page has two columns.
- Easily mixed and integrated text and graphics. Pictures, graphs, and drawings can be imported, cropped, resized, and moved anywhere on the page.
- Easily utilized graphics elements. Lines (called rules) of varying thicknesses and densities can be placed between columns, around pages, and under or over text. Squares, rectangles, circles, or

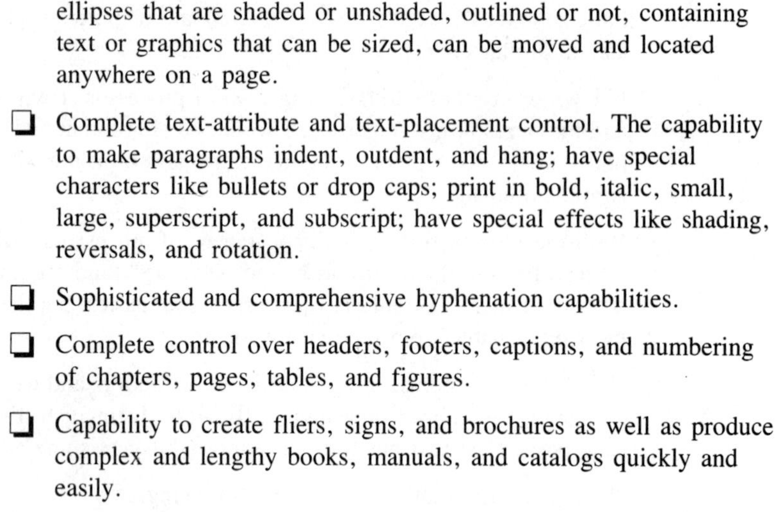

ellipses that are shaded or unshaded, outlined or not, containing text or graphics that can be sized, can be moved and located anywhere on a page.

- Complete text-attribute and text-placement control. The capability to make paragraphs indent, outdent, and hang; have special characters like bullets or drop caps; print in bold, italic, small, large, superscript, and subscript; have special effects like shading, reversals, and rotation.
- Sophisticated and comprehensive hyphenation capabilities.
- Complete control over headers, footers, captions, and numbering of chapters, pages, tables, and figures.
- Capability to create fliers, signs, and brochures as well as produce complex and lengthy books, manuals, and catalogs quickly and easily.

Today's word processors handle some of the chores of a desktop publishing program. Some word processors can manage columns and elementary graphics placement; some offer excellent font control. You can even use some word processors to create forms, newsletters, and reports that rival the output of desktop publishing programs.

Two caveats should be noted, however. Word processing programs are pushed to their limits when you use them to create sophisticated layouts, which means that you have to work hard to achieve your desired results. Additionally, as of yet, no word processing program allows graceful and sophisticated graphics placement in an interactive graphics environment where you can see what you create as you create it. What you get with desktop publishing is a powerful interactive environment in which to create documents.

A crystal ball may suggest that the word processing world is moving toward greater layout capabilities and that the desktop publishing world is moving toward greater text-processing capabilities. Until the two worlds become one, production of sophisticated documents of typeset quality requires the use of both a word processor and a desktop publishing program.

Investment in Equipment and Learning

Like any tool, and particularly any software tool, Ventura takes time to learn. Pundits have written that Ventura is difficult to learn to use. One purpose of this book is to help show you that Ventura is not overly hard to learn.

Probably the main force behind the belief that Ventura is hard to learn is the misunderstanding of the difference between ''learning'' and ''mastering.''

Chess is easy to learn but hard to master. Ventura is also easy to learn if you take a systematic approach to understand how Ventura assembles documents. Ventura is hard to master because hundreds of features are available, including document format and content; ways of viewing the document; style sheet and page control of formatting; editing and graphics-handling capabilities; graphic primitives including box text; automatic generation of tables of contents and indexes; and comprehensive print control. You may not use all the features, but no two people use the same features, so the completeness of the design unleashes terrific power.

Other desktop publishing programs may seem easier, but the complexity of Ventura shouldn't put you off. Instead, welcome the capabilities and the opportunity to grow with a program that most likely has the tools necessary to see you through your journey to mastery of Ventura.

Training issues aside, the hardware investment is a consideration. Although Ventura can run on an XT type of system (8088 processor), you lose productive time waiting for operations to complete. A better system is an AT or 386 system.

You need a hard drive. If you have a great deal of fonts for downloading to a printer and many graphic images, you need a *large* hard drive.

Although almost any graphics monitor works with Ventura, you will be happier with a higher resolution monitor. Experiment with monitors before you invest in one; the better the resolution, the less your eyes hurt at the end of a long work session. The larger the monitor, the more of your work you can see without scrolling. I have used a high-resolution, full-page Genius monitor from Micro Display Systems for the last two years and would never consider using less.

One measure of success in a software package is the degree to which other manufacturers have created add-on products to enhance the original program. Ventura has attracted a large number of developers who have created numerous products that make Ventura even better. In this book, I mention such products; in Appendix A, you find a list of suppliers of Ventura add-ons.

Types of Users

Because Ventura is such a powerful program, it appeals to a variety of users. For corporate work groups, a version of Ventura operates on a network, allowing your group to interact during the creation of a document.

Small businesses can benefit by using Ventura to create business cards, brochures, fliers, ads, signs, posters, and forms. Although any of these items can be produced by a local print shop, Ventura gives you interactive control and allows you to produce the types of documents *you* want.

For entrepreneurs, desktop publishing opens doors of opportunity. Many users of Ventura now make a living producing custom newsletters, forms, and brochures. Some people are in business producing custom catalogs and directories. Still others are involved with training business people in the use of Ventura. Desktop publishing in general—and Ventura in particular—has generated thousands of new and creative jobs in only a few years.

Although many graphics designers have become enamored of the Macintosh®, the time has come once again to take a serious look at the PC and the capabilities of programs like Ventura. No desktop publishing package for the Macintosh offers the degree of document and typographical control that Ventura provides. If you still have doubts about the new-found capabilities of the PC, read Chapters 7 and 9 to discover the incredible world of PC graphics and font handling.

Who Should Use This Book?

If you have used Ventura at all, even for a short time, this book is for you. As a beginner, you have begun to stretch and try to figure out how to make Ventura do something. This book helps you shorten the learning curve and incorporate advanced techniques into your next project.

If you are an intermediate or advanced user, you will find a great deal of useful, real-world information in this book to aid you in becoming a Ventura expert.

If you are an instructor of Ventura desktop publishing, you will find the organization and completeness of this book a valuable tool for your next class.

How This Book Is Organized

I wrote this book because no other book like it was available. I have read two types of books on Ventura. One type is a soup-to-nuts approach—essentially a rewrite of the Ventura manual. The other type of book does not explain how to use Ventura as much as it explains how to use Ventura to create a specific type of document; the book focuses on producing newsletters or brochures. Both types of books are useful, but this book is different.

Ventura Publisher Tips, Tricks, and Traps is a book of techniques broken down into logical areas of procedures. Because many Ventura books are essentially tutorials, procedures aren't grouped for easy access. This book groups topics in a refreshing and helpful new way that you will find useful and easy to refer to time and time again.

How To Use This Book

Part I of this book helps you understand the basics of Ventura Publisher. Chapter 1, "Getting Started: Setting Up and Starting Ventura," gives you information you will need to install and start the program.

Chapter 2, "Getting Oriented: Finding Your Way in Ventura," introduces you to Ventura's display screen, work area, commands, and modes. And you will become familiar with how to use Ventura's sidebar, layout area, and cursor.

In Chapter 3, "Understanding Ventura's File Management," you learn about how to work with Ventura "chapters." You are given information about style sheets and about text, graphics, publication, caption, and status files. In addition, you learn about the capabilities of DOS with Ventura Publisher.

In Part II of this book, you begin working with text. In Chapter 4, "Importing and Changing Text," you learn how to import text you have created with your favorite word processor, spreadsheet, or database. You learn how to tag text with your word processor for easier formatting and how to edit with Ventura's editing tools.

Chapter 5, "Understanding Style Sheets," introduces you to the concept of tags and other elements of the style sheet. You learn how to create, edit, and modify styles for text formatting.

Chapter 6, "Understanding Frames," leads you through the creation, placement, and modification of frames for holding text and pictures.

In Part III of this book, you begin working with graphics. In Chapter 7, "Importing and Changing Graphics," you learn that graphics can come from electronic or printed clip art, specialized graphics programs, or business programs such as spreadsheets that can produce graphic representations of data. Included are summaries of the capabilities of several graphics programs and samples of the art available from them.

Chapter 8, "Using Ventura's Graphics Tools," shows you how to use Ventura's built-in graphics tools to create lines, boxes, and circles. You also learn how to use the box text feature to create call outs for pictures.

In Part IV, you learn about printing Ventura documents. Chapter 9, ''Using Fonts,'' gives you an overview of the types of fonts available for a variety of printers as well as samples of what many of those fonts look like. Tips are included for users of dot-matrix as well as laser printers.

In Chapter 10, ''Proofing and Printing Your Chapter,'' you learn how to set up the printer for printing. You also learn more about the capabilities of different printers and the benefits and drawbacks of various types of laser printers.

Part V offers advice and tips for many of the sophisticated document controls available for Ventura and the Professional Extension. Chapter 11, ''Using Sophisticated Document Controls and Creating Large Publications,'' goes over many of the advanced capabilities of Ventura such as the program's capacity to print multiple chapters and create footnotes, headers, footers, indexes, and tables of contents.

In Chapter 12, ''Using the Professional Extension to Ventura Publisher,'' you gain experience in using the Professional Extension add-on to Ventura. You learn about the extensive hyphenation dictionary, expanded memory utilization, table creation, and equation editing.

And Appendix A gives you a listing of suppliers for Ventura-compatible products, instructions for installing Bitstream Fontware, and a table of decimal keyboard codes for various fonts.

Part

I

Understanding Ventura Basics

Includes

Getting Started:
Setting Up and Starting Ventura

Getting Oriented:
Finding Your Way in Ventura

Understanding Ventura's File Management

Chapter

1

Getting Started: Setting Up and Starting Ventura

Ventura is a large program and is demanding of your computer's resources. In exchange for Ventura's demanding nature, you get a desktop publishing program with tremendous power and flexibility.

Because this is a book for intermediate and advanced users of Ventura, you may have already installed Ventura on your system. Even if you have installed Ventura previously, some of the information in this chapter will be useful; just skip over the section titled ''Installing Ventura.'' If you have not yet installed Ventura, read this entire chapter before doing so.

Understanding System Requirements

Almost every software program lists the minimum computer system, monitor, and memory required for proper operation. Ventura is no exception. The following list itemizes the minimum system required for Ventura to work:

- An XT-class computer with a hard drive
- 3 to 6 megabytes of free hard drive space
- 640K of RAM (random-access memory)

- ❑ A graphics monitor and board
- ❑ A mouse or other input device such as a track ball
- ❑ A printer or access to a printer

Windows or GEM?

An *interface* is what the user of a piece of software sees. In 1-2-3®, for example, the user sees a grid and a simple command line; users access commands by pressing the slash (/) key. In WordPerfect®, users see an almost completely blank screen; they access commands by pressing function keys alone or in combination with other keys. In dBASE®, unless an application has been written, the user sees an essentially blank screen with a period in the lower left corner.

With such software, the user has to know how to input commands and also has to remember different ways of doing things for each software package. Little or no standardization exists. The lack of standards has made it hard for people to learn new software.

With the popularity of the Apple® Macintosh and the new graphics interface, users have begun to appreciate a more standardized approach to software. Using a Macintosh, you can be fairly confident that each software package—whether a spreadsheet or a word processor—works essentially the same. This is now becoming true for PC software applications running under Windows or GEM™.

The two major purposes of a graphics interface such as Microsoft® Windows or Digital Research's GEM are to offer a standard user interface and an accurate representation on the screen of what ultimately appears on the printed page. The two most popular desktop publishing packages for the PC have chosen different graphics managers. Aldus PageMaker® runs under Windows, and Xerox® Ventura Publisher runs under GEM. Although both "environments" have benefits, the choice of GEM by Ventura was a good one. GEM requires much less memory to run and, as a consequence, runs much faster.

1.1 Tip **Don't run Ventura under Windows.**

Although Microsoft Windows offers a much richer environment than GEM, unless you use Windows/386® on a 386 system, you will not find any benefits in running Ventura under Windows. Because Ventura has such huge memory requirements, you cannot access other programs using Windows while Ventura is running without extra RAM and a 386 system.

If you insist on running Ventura from Windows, copy the VP.PIF file found on disk 5 (if you are using 5 1/4-inch disks) or disk 3 (if you are using 3 1/2-inch disks) to the \WINDOWS\PIF subdirectory. Once you have loaded Windows, switch to the PIF subdirectory and click VP.PIF twice. When you quit Ventura, you return to the Windows Executive.

The version of GEM that comes with Ventura is a ''run-time'' version, capable of running only Ventura. For a complete GEM system, which has some added features, including a calculator and alarm clock, you need to purchase the GEM Desktop program.

System Options

Ventura operates on a minimum of an XT-class computer. As with most software packages, if you upgrade the computer, you upgrade the performance of the software. Ventura is no different. The amount of memory available for Ventura is also an important consideration in the speed of operation.

1.2 Tip Although Ventura can operate on an XT-class computer, use an AT or 386 system for better performance.

One of the reasons Ventura gained such wide initial acceptance was its capability of working on an XT computer. High-performance graphics software usually does not work quickly enough on an XT computer to be useful. The primary reason is that the microprocessor at the heart of an XT system is not powerful or fast enough to keep up with the demands of graphics-intensive software.

If you have an XT system, you can run Ventura; but the speed of operation may not always be tolerable. You will notice unsatisfactory speed performance when you have pages with a number of graphics and font changes. If the documents you produce are mainly text, you can get by with an XT system. If your documents use a great deal of graphics, consider upgrading your system to a faster and more powerful AT or 386 computer, especially if you use the Ventura Professional Extension.

1.3 Tip Learn the difference between extended and expanded memory.

If your computer has between 640K and 1,024K of memory, the 384K above the 640K can be either extended or expanded memory. Extended memory cannot be used by DOS to run programs or store data and is really useful only for RAM disks, disk caches, or print spoolers.

Memory above 1,024K is expanded memory and can be used by many programs to load larger amounts of data. You need to check the documentation of your software to see whether it supports expanded memory.

Some systems have special drivers that, in essence, convert the 384K of extended memory into expanded memory, making that memory more useful. To see whether your system supports this feature, consult your computer's documentation. The expanded memory standard supported by Ventura is called LIM (Lotus/Intel/Microsoft). You must have memory driver software compatible with LIM 3.2 or later for Ventura to be able to use the expanded memory (also called EMS).

Ventura requires 560K to 580K of conventional memory (the memory from 0-640K) in order to run. If you have up to 128K of EMS available, Ventura uses it to store some of the Ventura program (GEM.EXE and some Ventura screen buffers), which can free between 40K and 90K for Ventura to use for larger documents. If you have 256K or more of EMS memory, Ventura can use the extra memory for larger documents.

Depending on the amount of EMS memory available on your system, you can have documents up to 32 megabytes in size if you use EMS memory, the Professional Extension (see Chapter 12), and LIM 4.0 or later.

1.4 Trick

Look at the Ventura Publisher diagnostics screen to determine memory allocation.

An undocumented diagnostic feature exists in Ventura. This feature allows you to see how Ventura is using the available system memory for the various aspects of the program. To access the diagnostics screen, do the following:

1. Click Publisher Info from the Desk menu.

   Below the program name, the dialog box that appears lists the amount of EMS memory available. If you have a system without EMS memory, this number is zero. If you have a system with EMS memory, Ventura lists how much memory is allocated to the system (SYS) and how much is allocated to the application (APP). Use this information as a quick check of how much EMS memory Ventura thinks is available.

   The dialog box also lists the serial number of your software package. You must know this number if you need to call Ventura for telephone support.

2. Two outlined boxes are in the lower third of the dialog box. Move the cursor to the left box that reads `Ventura Software, Inc.` Point to the word `Ventura` and click.

The diagnostics box that appears lists how memory is allocated (see fig. 1.1 and table 1.1).

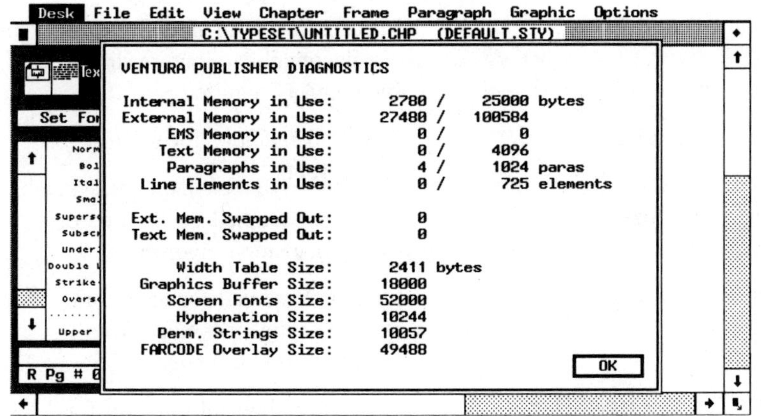

Fig. 1.1.
Ventura Publisher diagnostics screen.

Table 1.1
Ventura Publisher Diagnostics

Diagnostic Element	*Significance*
Internal Memory in Use	Memory used/memory reserved
External Memory in Use	Memory used by document/ memory available to document before disk swapping is required
EMS Memory in Use	EMS memory used/EMS memory available (if no EMS memory installed, both figures are zero)
Text Memory in Use	Text in use/maximum text buffer
Paragraphs in Use	Paragraphs in use/maximum number of paragraphs allowed
Line Elements in Use	Line elements in use/maximum number of line elements allowed
Ext. Mem. Swapped Out	Overflow of chapter file swapped to disk
Text Mem. Swapped Out	Text swapped to disk
Width Table Size	Size of width table: can accommodate up to 254 fonts in a single table

Table 1.1—*Continued*

Diagnostic Element	*Significance*
Graphics Buffer Size	Maximum size of graphic Ventura can accommodate before disk swapping is required
Screen Fonts Size	Reserved memory for storing screen fonts
Hyphenation Size	Memory occupied by the one or two hyphenation algorithms
Perm. Strings Size	Memory reserved for error and other essential messages from Ventura
FARCODE Overlay Size	Program coding information for Ventura

The diagnostics screen lets you know how Ventura is using your system's memory. As a user, you cannot affect certain parameters listed in table 1.1. You can, however, control certain memory allocations such as the complexity of the page (the more complex the page, the more paragraphs and line elements in use), the size of the width table (the more fonts installed, the larger the table), the screen fonts size (the more and the larger the screen fonts, the more memory is used), and the hyphenation size (use only one hyphenation file to reduce this value).

The purpose in knowing these figures is to let you release some memory if Ventura's performance becomes too sluggish. Reducing the complexity of a page, using only essential printer and screen fonts, and using only one hyphenation file improves Ventura's performance.

Although you can have chapters exceeding the size Ventura can hold in memory, Ventura stores data temporarily on the hard drive. Forcing Ventura to do excessive reading and writing to the hard drive takes time and slows your work. If you notice much disk access when you move from page to page in the chapter, consider reducing the complexity of the page (use fewer graphics, font changes, or paragraph tags) or splitting your chapter into two or more chapters.

Monitor Options

As listed in the system requirements, Ventura uses a graphics monitor and the appropriate board or card. When choosing a monitor, think about how it will be used: if you refer often to paper copy when using the monitor, you may be happier with a monitor that mimics the image of ink on paper. Of course, the higher the resolution of the screen, the easier on the eye.

1.5 Tip **Graphics monitors capable of a high-resolution, full-page, paper-white display save time and are easier on the eyes.**

Ventura requires a graphics monitor and card. You can use almost any graphics standard from low to high resolution. You can choose from many graphics monitor and card combinations. Some combinations are more satisfactory than others.

Paper-white displays are white displays with black characters (like the Macintosh). These displays are less stressful on the eyes than displays with a reverse image, such as green or amber on black. The reason is simple: the eye is used to viewing positive images (black on white). When you're laying out a page, you often will have to refer to documents or sketches, which are normally black ink on white paper. If you shift between a normal positive document and a reverse-screen image, your eyes are forced to refocus continually. Such refocusing is a source of eye strain and fatigue.

The quality of screen resolution varies dramatically. Screen resolution is measured in terms of *pixels* (picture elements). The initial graphics standard for the PC was low-resolution CGA (color graphics adapter), offering 640-by-200-pixel (horizontal-by-vertical) resolution. The Hercules company then offered a higher resolution monochrome graphics standard of 720 pixels by 348 pixels. IBM® then introduced the EGA (enhanced graphics adapter) standard, offering resolution of up to 640 pixels by 350 pixels.

To take advantage of programs such as Ventura, several companies such as Micro Display Systems (with the Genius monitor), Wyse, and Xerox began offering high-resolution, monochrome, full-page displays varying in resolution from 720-by-1,000 to 1,280-by-800—approaching 100 dpi (dots per inch) or one-third the resolution of a page printed on a 300-dpi laser printer.

The latest standard offered by IBM, and adopted by many other companies, is VGA (virtual graphics array), with resolution varying from 640-by-480 to 800-by-600. Many new VGA cards in conjunction with multisync types of monitors can show gray scale or color. (Multisync monitors can adapt to different resolutions.) The capacity to show gray scale is helpful for editing graphics images such as photographs stored in the TIFF (tagged image file graphics) format.

Besides resolution, the capability of a monitor to display a full page of text at once saves a lot of time. Standard monitors usually allow only 25 lines of data, whether in word processing, spreadsheets, or databases. In Ventura, if the font is small enough, more lines can be shown on such a monitor, but still about only one-third to one-half of the page is visible. To see the rest of a page in Ventura, you must either reduce the size of the page, making most of the text illegible, or use the scroll bars to move the page around the work layout area. Both changing views and scrolling require Ventura to redraw the screen; redrawing the screen can be time-consuming, especially if graphics are on the page. Neither resizing or scrolling is as satisfactory as being able to see an entire page (or two) at full size. Monitors such as Genius or those offered by Xerox or Wyse allow viewing of either one or two full pages at full size without scrolling. If your budget allows full-page monitors and you plan on doing serious desktop publishing, I recommend that you make the investment.

If a full-page monitor isn't in your budget, you will sacrifice some speed and convenience, but you can still produce first-class documents using Ventura.

1.6 Tip **If you don't have a full-page monitor but you do have either an EGA or VGA card and monitor, use the Soft Kicker to emulate a full-page monitor.**

The Soft Kicker from Aristocad, Incorporated, is an inexpensive alternative for those of you who either don't have or don't want to invest in a full-page monitor.

The Soft Kicker does three things. First, it creates a ''virtual page'' that stores an image of the entire page (not just the portion visible on the screen) allowing you to move quickly to any place on the page. You no longer need to use scroll bars to move around a page; instead, you move the mouse, and the screen image moves. Because the screen image is in memory, you don't need to wait for a screen update like you do when using scroll bars. Because the screen image moves with the mouse or cursor, if you are drawing a frame or typing text, the screen image moves with the frame drawing tool or text cursor.

Second, you can have the Soft Kicker emulate the reduced view by clicking the right mouse button. If you have an EGA card, the reduced view shows 75 percent of the page; if you have a VGA card, the reduced view shows the entire page. To return to normal view, click the right mouse button again.

Third, while you're in reduced view, the Soft Kicker has a small window that shows a normal view of the area around the cursor (useful for you to read menus at reduced view and see the effects of changes without having to return to normal view).

Pointing Device Options

Ventura supports any mouse, graphics tablet, touch pad, track ball, or other pointing device compatible with Microsoft, IBM PS/2, Mouse Systems, or PC Mouse standards.

1.7 Tip **Use a bus mouse instead of a mouse connected to the serial port if you plan to run Ventura from Microsoft Windows.**

If you don't already own a mouse, ask for a bus mouse rather than a serial mouse when you purchase one if you plan to run Ventura from Microsoft Windows.

Because of the way Ventura takes control of the mouse, when you quit Ventura and return to the Windows Executive, a serial mouse may not work correctly, whereas a bus mouse will.

Printer Options

Ventura allows you to print your documents on a variety of dot-matrix and laser printers. For detailed information about fonts, printers, and printing, read Chapters 9 and 10.

Modifying Your Computer for Ventura

Because of the intense memory requirements of Ventura, the way your computer is presently configured may not give Ventura all the tools it needs.

1.8 Tip **Remove all memory-resident programs from memory.**

Ventura requires most of the 640K of memory on your system. Memory-resident programs (often called "terminate and stay resident" or "TSR" programs), such as SideKick®, SuperKey®, Mirror, or other programs you are used to running in the background, "steal" memory needed by Ventura. If you try to use such memory-resident programs, Ventura posts a STOP message like the one shown in figure 1.2, informing you that not enough memory is available for you to run Ventura.

Fig. 1.2.

The STOP message, which is displayed because of lack of memory.

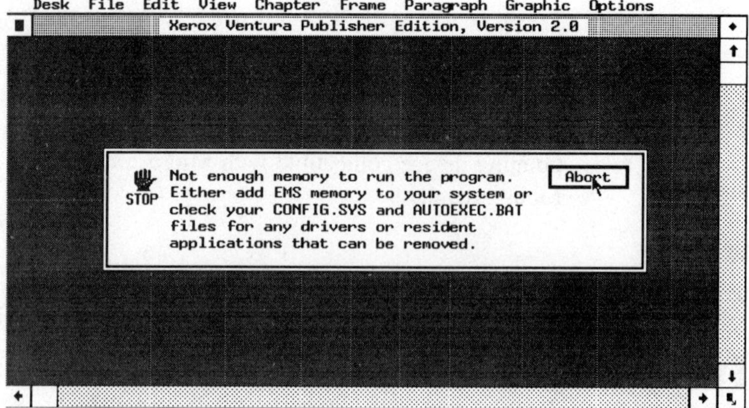

If you have a system with EMS memory, you may be able to use TSR programs that are capable of allocating themselves to EMS memory, keeping the lower 640K of memory relatively free. Programs such as DESQview™, a multitasking environment from Quarterdeck Office Systems, can use EMS and, therefore, can usually work with Ventura.

Be aware that even if you are able to run a TSR program, invoking it while running Ventura may corrupt Ventura's graphics screen. If screen corruption is a problem, remove the offending TSR program from memory before using Ventura.

Some disk caching, screen capture, and print spooling TSR programs and some Ventura add-ons will function if you have enough memory available for Ventura to run. You need to experiment to see which combinations work on your system.

Because most TSR programs can be unloaded from a command line, you may want to create a batch file that unloads your TSR software to free memory before you run Ventura and then create another batch file that reloads your memory-resident utilities after you quit Ventura.

1.9 Tip

Use the /A command line option switch to allow the use of memory-resident programs.

Ventura allows several command-line option switches. A command-line option (sometimes called a "switch") is a character or series of characters added to the command at the DOS prompt or included in a batch file. The command DRVRMRGR VP /S=SD_EGAHS.EGA, for example, tells DOS to load the GEM manager and run Ventura with an EGA screen driver (see Tip 1.19 for more examples). The /A= switch takes memory from the screen graphic and font buffers and reallocates it for use by Ventura documents. The reallocated memory is also available for resident programs or systems drivers.

In the preparation of this book, I needed to take electronic "snapshots" of the Ventura screens to show as examples. I was able to accomplish this task on a standard AT-class computer with only 640K of memory using the screen-capture utility from INSET Systems Inc. Because the screen-capture program uses about 48K of memory, I needed to "steal" some memory from Ventura's screen graphic and font buffers. I set the switch to */A=30* and was able to run Ventura as well as keep the screen-capture utility in memory.

Installing Ventura

Ventura Publisher comes on fifteen 5 1/4-inch or eight 3 1/2-inch disks. To begin the installation process, insert disk 1 into drive A and type *a:vpprep*. If you are installing Ventura from a drive other than drive A (for example, from drive B), insert disk 1 into drive B and type *b:vpprep b:*. Remember to type the second *b:* to let Ventura know where to look for the installation disk.

1.10 Tip

You need 3 to 6 megabytes of hard disk space to install Ventura—more if you use graphics or downloadable fonts.

Ventura uses between 1.5 and 3 megabytes of hard disk storage space for its programs and accompanying fonts. If, when you install Ventura, you select either an HP LaserJet Plus® or a Xerox 4045 printer, allow 3.5 megabytes of disk storage; if you install a JLaser®, dot-matrix, or Xerox 4020 printer, allow 2.5 megabytes of disk storage; if you install a PostScript® printer such as the Apple LaserWriter Plus®, allow 1.5 megabytes of storage space. If you install more than one printer, additional disk space is required.

If you have or plan to acquire a collection of electronic art or downloadable fonts, an additional 2 to 5 megabytes of memory are needed to store graphics and optional downloadable fonts. Remember that graphics and fonts require their own disk space for storage; even a small collection of art and fonts can fill a disk quickly.

1.11 Tip

After installing Ventura, you must have at least 2 megabytes of free disk space.

Ventura chapters do not need to fit into available memory because Ventura can swap overflow files either to a RAM disk, a disk cache, or other available disk space. In order for Ventura to work properly with chapters that do not fit entirely into memory, you must leave at least 2 megabytes of free disk space available for swapping. If this space is not available and you try to load a chapter that takes up more than the memory available, Ventura displays a warning message (see fig. 1.3).

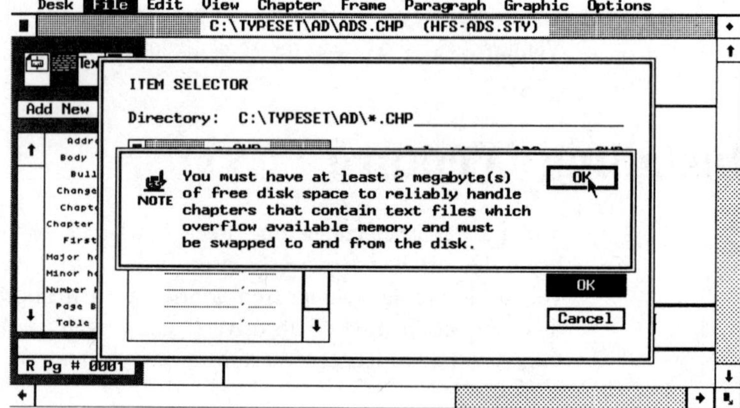

Fig. 1.3.

Warning message when less than 2 megabytes are available on hard disk.

1.12 Tip

Before installing Ventura, know your system.

During installation, Ventura prompts you for responses to the following questions. Research the answers before you begin the installation so that the installation is smooth.

1. `Is your hard disk drive C? Y`

   This question is slightly misleading because what is really being asked is, "Where do you want Ventura installed?" If you want Ventura installed on drive C, press Enter. If you want Ventura installed on another drive other than C, press N and then press Enter. You then see the prompt `Type your hard disk drive letter (A-Z)`? Type the letter of the drive on which you want Ventura installed and press Enter.

2. `Are you installing this version for the first time? Y`

   What is really being asked is whether you want to do a full installation or whether you are just making some changes to screen, input, or printer drivers. If you are installing Ventura for the first time, press Enter. If you are only making modifications, press N and then press Enter.

If you do a full installation, Ventura prompts you for the disks it needs. If you insert the wrong disk, Ventura lets you know and asks you to correct your mistake.

3. `Do you wish to install the EXAMPLE FILES? Y`

   Press Enter if you want to install the example files. Press N and then press Enter if you don't want to install the example files (see Tip 1.13 for more information).

4. `Which graphics card and display do you have?`

   From the list presented, find the name of your graphics card and monitor combination. (Some cards, such as the EGA cards, offer several monitor choices.) Make your choice based on your graphics card, memory available on the graphics card (if applicable), monitor type, and choice of color or monochrome display (if applicable).

5. `What mouse do you have?`

   From the list presented, choose the correct mouse type.

   You need to know whether your mouse runs from the serial port or whether it is a bus device.

6. `What communications port are you using for the mouse?`

   If you have a serial mouse, you need to tell Ventura whether the mouse is connected to communications ports #1 or #2. Names for these ports are COM1 and COM2 or serial 1 and serial 2. Note that even though your system may support more serial ports, Ventura doesn't allow you to use them for mouse support. If you have a bus mouse, this question will not appear.

7. `Which printer do you have?`

   From the list presented, choose the letter of the correct printer and press Enter. Additional choices are located on another screen; to see these selections, press PgDn and PgUp to toggle between the two menu screens.

   Ventura supports Epson FX/MX and LQ printers (they are listed separately on the menu screen) and other dot-matrix printers such as the Toshiba 24-wire. In addition, Ventura supports numerous laser printers. If your printer isn't listed, look in the printer manual to see whether your printer can emulate any of the printers on the list. Many printers emulate the Epson FX, for example; many laser printers emulate one of the Hewlett-Packard® (HP) printers; and any printer with PostScript capability works if you choose PostScript.

If you have a printer that isn't on the list and doesn't emulate any of the supported printers, contact Xerox and inquire whether new printer drivers are available for your printer. Look also at Chapter 9 for ways of using printers not directly supported by Ventura.

8. `Which printer port are you using?`

   From the list presented, choose the correct parallel or serial port used by your printer by pressing the appropriate menu letter. Then press Enter.

9. `Do you want to select another printer? N`

   If you want to install an additional printer, press Y and then press Enter. You will be prompted with questions 7 and 8 for the second printer. If you do not want to install a second printer driver, leave the default answer N and press Enter.

10. `Are these the correct screen and printer choices? Y`

    The next screen summarizes your screen, mouse (and serial port, if applicable), printer, and printer port selections. If everything is correct, press Enter; if not, press N and then press Enter. If you select N, the selection process begins again with question 4.

    If you answer Y to this question, Ventura then prompts you for the disks containing the appropriate drivers and fonts.

1.13 Tip **To save storage space, don't install the example files.**

The example files that Ventura may load at installation time require 338K of disk space. If you are an experienced Ventura user or if you don't plan to use any of the sample templates, answer N when the installation program asks whether you want to install the example files.

If you later decide you want the example files, just use the DOS COPY command to copy the contents of disk 4 (if you have 5 1/4-inch disks) or disk 2 (if you have 3 1/2-inch disks) into the TYPESET directory.

If you have already installed Ventura, you can delete the examples contained in the TYPESET directory. If you have your own chapters in the TYPESET directory, be sure to delete only the examples and not your own work.

1.14 Tip **When you change monitors, pointing devices, or printers, *reinstall* rather than *install* Ventura.**

To save time and avoid unnecessary work when all you are doing is changing a device such as monitor, pointing device, or printer, reinstall rather than install Ventura. To reinstall, follow the same steps for installation, but answer N to the question `Are you installing this version for the first time?`

1.15 Tip **If you are upgrading to Ventura 2.0 from Ventura 1.0, you first must delete certain files. If you are upgrading from Ventura 1.1, follow the procedure outlined in Tip 1.12.**

Ventura 1.0 occupied six directories that are not used by Ventura 1.1 or 2.0. After Version 1.0, Ventura consolidated all its files into the VENTURA directory. Both Versions 1.0 and 1.1 kept the example files in the TYPESET directory. Because Versions 1.1 and 2.0 use the single VENTURA directory for program files, if you are upgrading from 1.1 to 2.0, the Ventura installation program deletes any unnecessary files in the directory.

If you are upgrading from Version 1.0, you must delete files in certain directories and then remove the unused directories if you want to recover the disk space. To remove Version 1.0 from your disk, type the following commands in order at the DOS prompt and press Enter after each line:

```
CD \GEMSYS
DEL *.*
```

At the prompt `Are you sure (Y/N)?`, press Y.

```
CD \GEMBOOT
DEL *.*
```

At the prompt `Are you sure (Y/N)?`, press Y.

```
CD \GEMDESK
DEL *.*
```

At the prompt `Are you sure (Y/N)?`, press Y.

```
CD \GEMAPPS\VPSYS
DEL *.*
```

At the prompt `Are you sure (Y/N)?`, press Y.

```
CD \GEMAPPS
DEL *.*
```

At the prompt `Are you sure (Y/N)?`, press Y.

```
RD VPSYS
CD \
RD GEMAPPS
RD GEMSYS
RD GEMBOOT
RD GEMDESK
```

1.16 Tip

Modify the CONFIG.SYS file so that enough buffers and file handles are available for Ventura.

Usually located in the \ or root directory of your system is a file called CONFIG.SYS. The CONFIG.SYS file has configuration information that is read by your computer every time the system is either powered up or reset. A typical CONFIG.SYS file can read something like this:

```
DEVICE = ANSI.SYS
DEVICE = MOUSE.SYS
BUFFERS = 20
FILES = 20
```

Notice that besides device drivers (you may have more or less than the one shown in the example, depending on your system), a BUFFERS and a FILES statement exist. Examine your CONFIG.SYS file to see that BUFFERS and FILES statements are there and check that the values for these statements are at least 20. These values may be larger than 20, but larger values take up extra memory. A lower value in the BUFFERS statement slows performance (unless you are using a disk cache; see Tip 1.25). A lower value in the FILES statement may reduce the number of graphics and chapters that Ventura can accommodate.

To create or modify the CONFIG.SYS file, use your favorite word processor and save the file in plain ASCII format; check your word processor's manual for instructions on how to save a file as ASCII. You can create a CONFIG.SYS file from scratch without a word processor by typing the following commands at the DOS prompt (press Enter after each line):

```
COPY CON C:\CONFIG.SYS
BUFFERS = 20
FILES = 20
```

Then press Ctrl-Z (or F6). You will see the message `1 File(s) copied`.

The DOS COPY CON C:\CONFIG.SYS command overwrites any existing CONFIG.SYS file. Therefore, if other lines (such as DEVICE =

MOUSE.SYS) are in your CONFIG.SYS file, either use a word processor to edit the file or be sure to include these lines in the same way as you specified the BUFFERS and FILES lines if you create the file using the DOS COPY CON command.

1.17 Tip

Double-check your AUTOEXEC.BAT file to be sure that no memory-resident programs are automatically loaded that may make it impossible to load Ventura.

If you recall from Tip 1.8, memory-resident or TSR programs can reduce the amount of memory available to Ventura and make it impossible for Ventura to run correctly. Often, TSR programs are loaded automatically from an AUTOEXEC.BAT file each time the computer is powered on or reset. Check your AUTOEXEC.BAT file to see whether it contains any commands to load TSR programs. Delete those commands if they exist. Some brands of mice (for example, the Microsoft bus mouse) require that you run a program like MOUSE.COM to activate the mouse. If your mouse requires this, check the AUTOEXEC.BAT file to ensure that the program to load the mouse driver (usually called MOUSE.COM) is always loaded. To modify the AUTOEXEC.BAT file, make these changes using your word processor. Save the edited file as an ASCII file (see Tip 1.16). Alternatively, you may type the following commands at the DOS prompt (press Enter at the end of each line):

```
COPY CON C:\AUTOEXEC.BAT
MOUSE
```

Then press Ctrl-Z (or F6). You will see the DOS message `1 File(s) copied.`

1.18 Trick

Maintain two or more sets of CONFIG.SYS and AUTOEXEC.BAT files for different needs.

This trick is rather advanced, and the assumption is that you understand and can create batch files.

Assume that you have already set up an AUTOEXEC.BAT file that loads several TSR programs automatically. As mentioned previously, you cannot use this file with Ventura; you should use an AUTOEXEC.BAT file that doesn't include the TSRs. Instead of creating a new AUTOEXEC.BAT file each time you want to use Ventura, do the following:

1. Create a new AUTOEXEC.BAT file without the TSRs but name it AUTOEXEC.VP. (If for some reason you need a modified CONFIG.SYS file, create a special one for use with Ventura and

name it CONFIG.VP.) Rename the original AUTOEXEC.BAT file to AUTOEXEC.REG (and rename the original CONFIG.SYS file to CONFIG.REG, if necessary).

2. Create a batch file called VPBAT.BAT containing the following commands:

   COPY AUTOEXEC.VP AUTOEXEC.BAT
   COPY CONFIG.VP CONFIG.SYS (if necessary)

3. Create a second batch file called REGBAT.BAT containing the following commands:

   COPY AUTOEXEC.REG AUTOEXEC.BAT
   COPY CONFIG.REG CONFIG.SYS (if necessary)

4. Invoke the VPBAT file before running Ventura to create the correct AUTOEXEC.BAT and CONFIG.SYS files; invoke the REGBAT file to restore your system to normal for other work.

5. Remember to reset your system (press Ctrl-Alt-Del) to put the new AUTOEXEC.BAT and CONFIG.SYS files into effect.

Starting Ventura

Ventura creates a batch file called VP.BAT during installation. Unlike most software, Ventura uses a complex string of command line option switches to let the program know what screen and mouse drivers are available as well as how to handle some elements of memory. These switches are invoked automatically by the VP.BAT file, but you can modify them.

1.19 Tip

Learn the command line switches in the VP.BAT file for better memory control and quick modification of certain drivers.

When Ventura is installed, a batch file called VP.BAT is created and placed in the root directory (indicated by the backslash \). You invoke the file by typing *vp* and then pressing Enter. When the file is loaded, it in turn loads the GEM driver and the VP (Ventura) application. If you examine the VP.BAT file, you see something similar to the following:

```
DRVRMRGR VP %1 /S=SD_EGAH5.EGA /M=32
```

Following the command to load VP using the GEM DRVRMRGR, two switches are inserted during the Ventura installation process. A Ventura "switch" consists of a slash, a letter, an equal sign, and then a parameter (sometimes called an argument, as in a mathematical argument). In the preceding example, an /S= switch controls the screen and an /M= switch controls the mouse.

The *%1* in the example is a DOS command that allows you to specify a chapter for Ventura to load as soon as it starts up. If you have a chapter called EXAMPLE.CHP located in the TYPESET directory, for example, you can automatically load the chapter by typing *vp c:\typeset\example* on a DOS command line. If the TYPESET directory is not located on drive C, specify the correct drive. Also notice that you must specify the entire path of the chapter you want to load. If you always load the same chapter or use the same path, you can modify the command line in the batch file and replace the *%1* with the full name of the file you want loaded or precede the *%1* with a drive and path name.

You can modify the command line by adding or changing any of the switches listed in table 1.2.

Table 1.2
Command Line Option Switches for VP.BAT

Switch	*Parameter or Argument*
/S=	Screen driver setting. You can change this setting as long as the driver you are specifying is available in the VENTURA subdirectory. Because the driver setting is created automatically during installation, however, it is unlikely that you will need to change it.
/M=	Mouse driver. If you change mouse types or ports, you can change this setting without reinstalling Ventura. The argument consists of two numbers. The first number is the port; the second is the type of mouse used. The port options are *0* for COM1 (serial port 1), *1* for COM2 (serial port 2), and *3* for a bus connector. The mouse types of options are *0* for no mouse, *1* for Mouse Systems or PC mouse, *2* for any mouse (usually a bus mouse) using MOUSE.COM in your AUTOEXEC.BAT file or MOUSE.SYS in your CONFIG.SYS file, *3* for a Microsoft mouse using the serial port, and *:* for an IBM PS/2 mouse.
/A=	Screen graphic buffer. An error message about too little memory for running Ventura may appear if the CONFIG.SYS file has large numbers of device drivers or if you are running a TSR program such as a screen-capture utility. In such cases, you can gain a little memory by reducing the size of the graphic buffer. Enter any number

Table 1.2—*Continued*

Switch	*Parameter or Argument*
	between 1 and 32 for the /A switch to free between 1K and 32K of memory. In so doing, you may limit some of the file converters as well as the size of graphics and screen fonts that can be displayed and, in the case of graphics, printed. Setting this switch to 0 has a special meaning: 16K of memory is taken from the font buffer, but not from the graphics buffer, and reallocated for Ventura's use. The zero setting allows improved performance without slowing the redraw speed of the screen.
/E=	EMS memory. Used by only the Xerox Ventura Publisher Professional Extension, an add-on product discussed in Chapter 12. If you have the Ventura Professional Extension, you can limit the memory used by the Professional Extension by setting the /E switch to 0. If you use a JLaser or perhaps other printers that have memory which can be used as EMS memory (consult your printer manual), set the switch to 0.
/I=	INF file directory location. Ventura creates an INF file if none exists. If an INF file exists, Ventura uses the information in the file to control certain defaults such as the desired units of measure, the last view setting, preferences, the last mode setting, and the last style file used. If you want to return all these settings to Ventura's defaults, go to the VENTURA directory and delete the VP.INF file. If several people use the same copy of Ventura, each can have his or her own INF file stored in a different directory (the file *must* be called VP.INF). You can create several start-up files called TOM.BAT, JILL.BAT, and so forth, instead of VP.BAT. In the BAT file in each person's directory, set the /I switch to the VP.INF file in that directory (/I=C:JILL\VP.INF, for example). Now, when Tom and Jill load Ventura, their own settings are loaded.
/O=	Overflow files. If you have a RAM drive, specify its drive letter with this switch (for example, /O=D:). If you are using the Professional Extension and have EMS memory or if you are using a disk cache, you do not need this switch. If you specify a RAM disk and do not really have one, Ventura does not load properly.

Table 1.2—*Continued*

Switch	*Parameter or Argument*
/X=	Additional drives. Ventura automatically recognizes only drives A, B, and C. If you also have drives D and above, set this switch to let Ventura know about them. You must set this switch for each additional drive—for example, /X=D: /X=E:, if you have both drives D and E.

Setting Up Ventura

One of the strengths of Ventura Publisher is its capacity to hyphenate text. Producing high-quality output with the look of a typeset document is one of the main goals of desktop publishing. One characteristic of typeset material is proportionally spaced and justified text. For justified text to look good, longer words at the end of a line of text must be hyphenated correctly. Ventura accomplishes hyphenation by using a complex algorithm that inserts hyphens based on certain rules. If Ventura hyphenates words incorrectly or hyphenates words you don't want hyphenated at all, you can add them to an exception dictionary.

1.20 Tip

Look on the Loadable Filter disk 3 (if you are using 5 1/4-inch disks) or on disk 2 (if you are using 3 1/2-inch disks) for additional hyphenation modules.

Ventura supplies seven different hyphenation algorithms. See table 1.3 for a description of each module.

When Ventura is installed, only the fast U.S. English hyphenation module is copied to the Ventura directory. To use any of the other modules, you must insert disk 3 (if you are using 5 1/4-inch disks) or disk 2 (if you are using 3 1/2-inch disks) into drive A and copy the desired module. To copy the slower, more accurate U.S. English hyphenation module, for example, type the following command:

```
COPY A:USENGLS2.HY2 C:\VENTURA
```

The next time you load Ventura, you have two hyphenation modules available—the slow and the fast U.S. English versions. Chapter 5 gives more detailed information about hyphenation.

Table 1.3
Ventura Hyphenation Modules

Module Name	*Comments and Approximate Size of Module*
USENGLSH.HY1	Fast hyphenation of U.S. English (5K)
USENGLS2.HY2	Slower, more accurate hyphenation of U.S. English (14K)
UKENGLSH.HY2	British English (11K)
FRENCH.HY2	French (6K)
GERMAN.HY2	German (14K)
ITALIAN.HY2	Italian (5K)
SPANISH.HY2	Spanish (6K)

Changing Program Defaults

You can judge whether a program is friendly in two easy ways: One, does the software easily allow changes in default settings? Two, does the software remember the new defaults?

Ventura excels in both areas. When you learn about Ventura's file management in Chapter 3, you will gain an appreciation of Ventura's sophistication in remembering what kinds of files you like to keep and where you like to keep them.

Other default settings are as important. In this section, you will learn how to customize Ventura to suit your purposes. You will be delighted to discover that Ventura remembers exactly how you left your desktop—with the tools you like and where you like them.

1.21 Tip **Learn what kind of information is stored in the VP.INF file.**

Ventura stores the following information about the condition of the desktop and saves that information in a file called VP.INF, which is stored in the VENTURA directory for the next time you use the program:

- ❑ The measurement system used in dialog boxes that allow choices
- ❑ The measurement system you prefer for the rulers

- The last view setting (Normal, Reduced, Facing Pages, or Enlarged) you chose
- The last mode of operation (Frame, Paragraph, Text, or Graphic) you used
- File filters for text and graphics
- Directories to look in for text and graphics
- The last style file you loaded
- All the items you have set from the Options menu

1.22 Trick

Restore Ventura's default settings by deleting the VP.INF file.

If you want to restore all the factory default settings, delete the VP.INF file in the \VENTURA directory. The next time you load Ventura, a new VP.INF is automatically created; all the settings you may have changed are reset to the program's defaults. Some of the defaults are Normal view, Frame mode, and DEFAULT.STY style sheet.

1.23 Tip

Change the settings in the SET PREFERENCES dialog box to customize Ventura.

Click the Set Preferences command from the Options menu to access the SET PREFERENCES dialog box (see fig. 1.4). Examine table 1.4 for information about each setting in this dialog box.

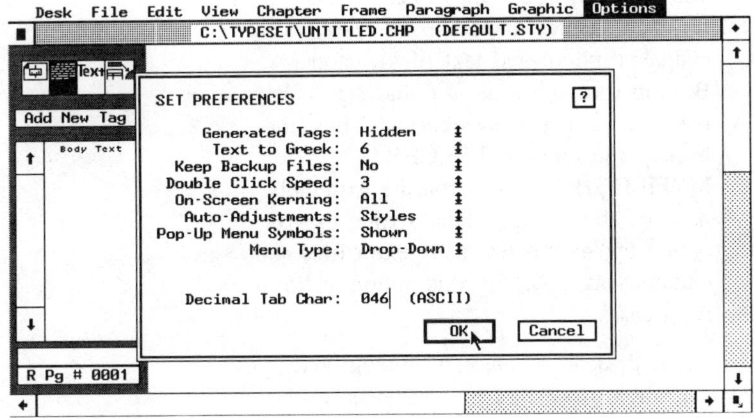

Fig. 1.4.

The SET PREFERENCES dialog box.

Table 1.4
SET PREFERENCES Dialog Box Options

Setting	*Options*
Generated Tags	Hidden or Shown. Footnotes, headers, footers, etc., are automatically created by Ventura with a paragraph tag (see Chapter 5). You decide whether you want the names of these tags displayed in the assignment list when you are in Paragraph mode (see Chapter 2). All generated tags begin with Z_. If you have a long list of tags, set this option to Hidden; otherwise, set the option to Shown.
Text to Greek	None, 2, 4, 6, 8, 10, or All. Displaying screen fonts takes time, especially when you choose the Reduced or Facing Pages views (see Chapter 2). If you choose None, all text is displayed—even if it is illegible. If you choose All, none of the text is displayed; it is represented by lines (this is called *greek* text). The number options refer to point sizes; depending on your selection, text in that point size and smaller is greeked. A good number to choose is 6 or 8.
Keep Backup Files	Yes or No. If you want to keep backup files for each chapter (including the style sheet, chapter caption, and text files), choose Yes. Backup files substitute a dollar sign ($) for the first letter of the extension. Thus, the backup file for MYFILE.CHP is MYFILE.$HP. Unless you are extremely nervous about losing data, setting this option to Yes creates many extra files and clutters your disk. Set this option to No in most cases.
Double Click Speed	Slow, 2, 3, 4, or Fast. In dialog boxes you can often make choices two ways: click the choice and then click OK or press Enter; or click twice rapidly on the choice. The speed you set for this option is a relative value

Table 1.4—*Continued*

Setting	*Options*
	relative value and determines how long Ventura waits for the second click. Unless you are very fast, setting the speed to Fast effectively disables the double-click capability. Select a speed that feels comfortable and works the way you expect.
On-Screen Kerning	None, 36, 24, 18, 14, 10, or All. If you set kerning on with the Chapter Typography command from the Chapter menu, and you have set the paragraph tag for kerning, you can choose to have kerning displayed on-screen with this option. On-screen kerning takes a great deal of processor time, and screen redraws are slower. Kerning is not crucial with small point sizes (nor is it very visible on-screen). The on-screen kerning setting does not affect printed output. Set this value to 18 or larger so only subheads or headlines are kerned on-screen. If a paragraph is set to be kerned, whether or not the kerning is shown on-screen does not affect printing. Thus, even if on-screen kerning is set to None, if the Chapter and Paragraph Typography settings have turned kerning on, kerning will take place at print time.
Auto-Adjustments	None, Styles, " and –, or Both. The Auto-Adjustments option refers to two very different items; listing them both in the same option is a bit confusing. Choosing Styles allows the interline spacing (see Chapter 5) to be adjusted automatically by Ventura whenever you make changes to font attributes by using the Set Font button in Text mode. Choosing " and – makes Ventura change all double hyphens (--) to em dashes (—) and text-style double quotation marks (") to typeset-style opening and closing double quotation marks (“”).

Table 1.4—*Continued*

Setting	*Options*
	Ventura makes these changes when you import a file. You can set Styles and " and – separately, but I recommend the setting Both.
Pop-Up Menu Symbols	Hidden or Shown. If you set this option to Hidden, you cannot tell which items in dialog boxes offer choices. If you set this option to Shown, all selectable items in dialog boxes have a vertical double arrow for you to click. Even if this option is set to Hidden, you can still make selections; but why make it challenging? Set this option to Shown.
Menu Type	Drop-Down or Pull-Down. If you're used to the Macintosh or Windows environment, set this option to Pull-Down. Pull-down menus require you to click the menu bar item before the menu appears. If you don't mind the menu popping up when you run the cursor over the menu bar item, select Drop-Down. This option is strictly a matter of choice and what you're accustomed to using.
Decimal Tab Char	Your choice of character in ASCII. The decimal tab forces alignment on a specific character. You can set decimal tabs with the Tab Settings command from the Paragraph menu or the Horz. Alignment option in the ALIGNMENT dialog box (accessed from the Paragraph menu). Choose the desired character from the list of Roman characters in Appendix A and type in the decimal code for the character you want.

1.24 Tip

Learn the on/off switches available on the Options menu.

Eight of the items available from the Options menu are just on/off switches. The first time you select them, you click them either on or off; the next time you select them, you reverse the option. Examine figure 1.5 to see which items are switches.

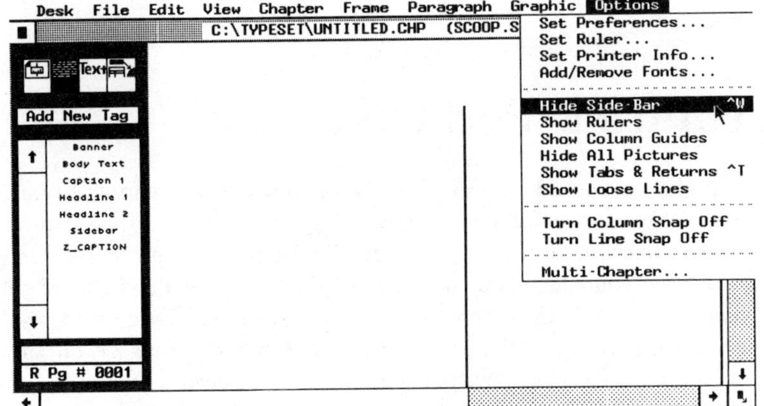

Fig. 1.5.

The Options menu.

All menu items with ellipses (...) following them open dialog boxes; those without ellipses are simple toggle switches. The following items are on/off switches:

- ❑ Hide/Show Side-Bar. See Chapter 2 to learn how to hide the sidebar to give you more working space in the layout area.
- ❑ Hide/Show Rulers. Ventura has both a horizontal and vertical ruler. See Chapter 2 for more information.
- ❑ Hide/Show Column Guides. When columns are created on a page, you can make the guides either visible or invisible. See Chapter 2 for more information.
- ❑ Hide/Show This/All Picture(s). Graphics take time to print and to be represented on the screen. You can hide or make visible all or individual graphics to the screen and printer. Chapter 2 tells you how.
- ❑ Hide/Show Tabs & Returns. Tabs, discretionary hyphens, nonbreaking spaces, line breaks, paragraph ends, and file ends all have special nonprinting symbols that Ventura either displays or hides. These symbols and their significance are discussed in Chapter 4.

- Hide/Show Loose Lines. *Loose lines* are lines of text with excessive space. See Chapter 4 to learn how to correct them.
- Turn Column Snap On/Off. You can force frames to align with column guides, as explained in Chapters 2 and 6.
- Turn Line Snap On/Off. You can force frames to line up with the interline spacing of paragraphs. See Chapters 2 and 6 for more information.

Improving Ventura's Performance

The faster and more advanced your system, the more responsive you will find Ventura. Don't let the fact you have an older XT system deter you from using the program. Just like a faithful old car, your XT—combined with the power of Ventura—will get you where you want to go. I used an XT with Ventura for most of a year and was able to launch a newsletter business and produce forms and other documents for my office. One way to improve performance on an XT system is with a turbo card that increases processing speed.

If you are fortunate enough to have a faster system with more than 640K of memory, you can use the following tips to increase performance even more.

1.25 Tip

A minimum of 640K of RAM is required for you to run Ventura. If you have additional memory, create a disk cache or RAM disk to speed up Ventura operations.

Ventura is demanding of RAM. If you have more than 640K of RAM, you can allocate some of the additional RAM to create a disk cache or a RAM disk.

A *disk cache* is created with utility software such as PC-CACHE from Central Point Software, Inc. (part of the PC Tools package), PC-Kwik from Multisoft, or Lightning from Personal Computer Support Group, Inc. Some 386 systems have hardware-caching built into the system, so consult your manual to see whether additional software caches are needed. Once installed, the cache program sets aside a certain amount of RAM memory to store the most recent information for which the computer calls. When another instruction is issued, the cache program looks first in the cache area (the area of set-aside RAM) for the information. If the cache contains the information, it is retrieved; if the cache does not contain the requested information, it is retrieved from the disk. Two things make caching work: one, usually more than half the time, the requested information is in the cache area; two, RAM speed is much faster than disk speed. Speed increases of more than 50 percent with cache software are the rule.

Although disk caching for other software can be used in systems with only 640K of memory, don't use any of the 640K for disk caching for Ventura.

Caching is especially helpful with long documents, complex pages, networks, and multiple screen fonts.

If you are using a cache, you may reduce or eliminate the BUFFERS statement in the CONFIG.SYS file (see Tip 1.16) because the cache serves the same function as the buffers.

Another use for more than 640K of RAM is a RAM disk. A RAM disk is not really a disk; it just acts like one. Ventura can use a RAM disk for its overflow files. If your system came with more than 640K of RAM, software was probably included to create a RAM disk; consult your system's documentation. Once the RAM disk has been created, you need to tell Ventura that the RAM disk exists. Do this by editing the VP.BAT file (see Tip 1.19 for more information) and including the command switch */O=n:*. (Note that this is the letter O, not a zero; substitute the letter of the RAM disk drive for the *n* in the command.)

A cache gives better performance to Ventura than a RAM disk. If you have a cache, you don't also need a RAM disk.

1.26 Trap **Set the /O switch only if you have a RAM disk.**

If you set the */O=n* switch in the VP.BAT file and you don't actually have a RAM disk, Ventura does not load properly. On some systems, you do not receive an error message, but Ventura does not function; on other systems, you may see an error message referring to inadequate file handles before Ventura refuses to load.

1.27 Trap **Don't fill up your directories.**

Although DOS allows you to keep hundreds of files in each directory, you pay a price in speed if the directories get too full (more than 128 files). Keep your directories compact—delete unused files, archive old chapters, remove backups if Ventura automatically makes backup files, and create additional directories for storage.

1.28 Tip **Optimize disk performance by compressing or defragmenting your files.**

As your hard disk fills up, and as you delete and add files, parts of the files are written to disparate sections of the hard disk. This fragmentation makes more work for Ventura. If the Ventura program is fragmented, it takes longer to load; if Ventura files (graphics or text) are fragmented, they take longer to retrieve.

Fortunately, several companies make defragmentation utilities. Some of the better known are PC-Compress from Central Point Software, Inc. (included with the PC Tools Deluxe package), Optimize from SoftLogic Solutions, Inc., and Speed Disk included in the Norton Utilities™ Advanced Edition from Peter Norton Computing. Use one of these utilities on a regular basis to keep your files together on the hard disk, improving performance.

Quitting Ventura

Quitting Ventura is easy. Just click Quit from the File menu. If you have made any unsaved changes to either a chapter or style file, Ventura stops you (see fig. 1.6). If you want to save your changes, click `Save` or press Enter. If you don't want to save any changes, click `Abandon`. If you have changed your mind and want to return to your project, click `Don't Quit`.

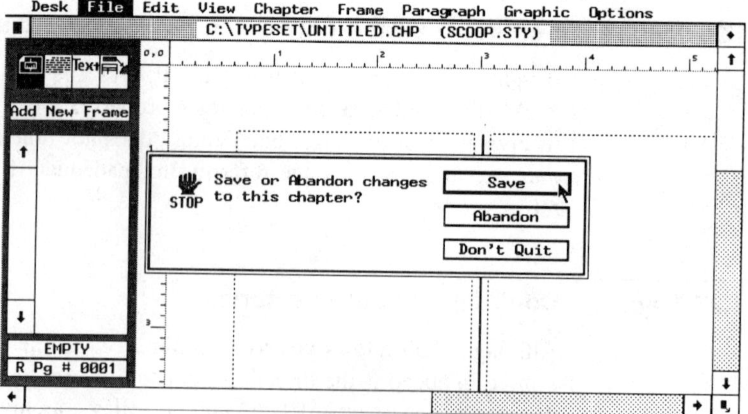

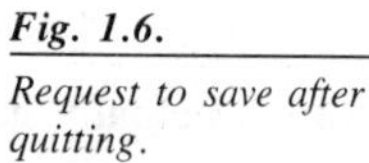

Fig. 1.6.

Request to save after quitting.

Chapter Summary

This chapter covered much material. If you have had previous experience with Ventura, you should be comfortable with the installation process. If you haven't had much prior experience with Ventura, the tips in this chapter have helped explain some of the more cryptic portions of the installation process.

You learned about the basic system requirements of Ventura. You examined the diagnostics screen and gained a better understanding of how Ventura allocates memory. You had a chance to review the various monitor and pointing device options. You also looked at the installation process in depth and explored the various command line option switches found in the VP.BAT file.

Finally, you were introduced to the various default options Ventura offers and some ways to modify them to suit your preferences.

In the next chapter, you will learn about the Ventura desktop and layout area. In future chapters, many of the options introduced in this chapter are explored in depth.

Chapter

2

Getting Oriented: Finding Your Way in Ventura

If you have used almost any software on a Macintosh or if you have used Microsoft Windows on a PC, you will feel right at home with Ventura. Unlike most software currently available for the PC, Ventura operates in a graphics environment with drop-down or pull-down menus. (However, more software for the PC is being written to run under Windows or Windows-like programs.)

Instead of Windows, Ventura uses the GEM interface from Digital Research, but the basic elements are the same. Both use icons (pictures representing functions), menus, dialog boxes, and a mouse. Together, these elements are called the user interface. The Ventura user interface is straightforward and logical.

In this chapter, you will learn your way around the Ventura work area, and you will learn about time-saving keyboard shortcuts, measurement options, and Ventura's different work modes.

Working in Different Modes

One of the most confusing things about computer software in general, and Ventura in particular, is the concept of working in modes. Ventura has four modes: Frame, Paragraph, Text, and Graphic. You choose a mode by clicking the icon for the mode you want, by clicking the mode you want from the View menu, or by using a keyboard shortcut.

Only certain things can be done in each mode, and even when you are in the correct mode to perform a task, you may need to perform a preliminary step. Suppose, for example, that you're in Paragraph mode and you want to change a font setting. If you don't first select a paragraph, you will not be able to access the Font option on the Paragraph menu.

Ventura helps you by graying menu choices that aren't available and by grouping logically the functions of the four modes. Be patient; working in modes takes time to get used to.

One way of looking at modes is as if each were a tool. A saw and a hammer, for example, have distinct capabilities. You don't hammer with a saw, and you cannot cut wood with a hammer. You also must put down the hammer before you can use the saw; you cannot use both at once. Modes are like the hammer and saw. You can only use them one at a time, and you cannot use one mode to do the work another mode is designed to do.

Each mode offers so many capabilities that each deserves its own chapter. Frame mode is discussed in Chapter 6, Paragraph mode in Chapter 5, Text mode in Chapter 4, and Graphic mode in Chapter 8.

Understanding Ventura's Work Area

Ventura's display area is similar to a desktop work area. On a desktop, you have one area for your tools, another for reference material, and still another for your work; the Ventura desktop also has separate areas for various activities. Look at figure 2.1 to see the entire Ventura desktop.

At the top of the screen is a menu bar with nine menu options. Below the menu bar is a shaded bar that displays the name of the subdirectory and document you're working on and the name of the active style sheet. In figure 2.1, the subdirectory (or path) of the document is C:\TYPESET\UNTITLED.CHP. Ventura refers to working documents as chapters and gives all chapters a CHP extension. The active style sheet is listed in parentheses, (DEFAULT.STY). Ventura gives all style sheets an STY extension.

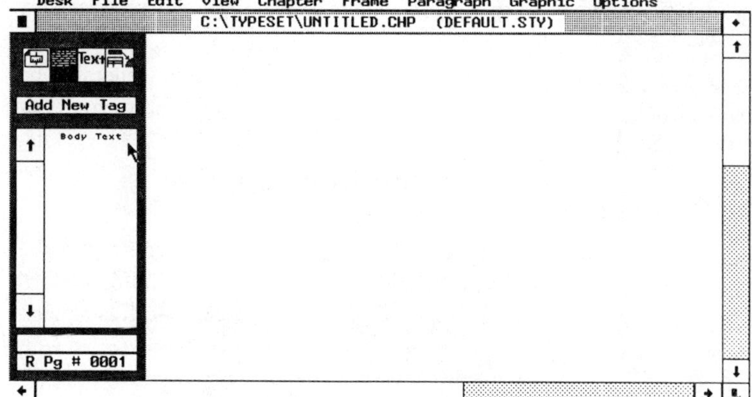

Fig. 2.1.

The Ventura desktop.

The large empty area is the layout area where your document takes shape. To the left of the layout area is the sidebar. This area contains the mode selectors (the four icons representing Frame, Paragraph, Text, and Graphic modes), the addition button (which displays either Add or Set, depending on the mode selected), the assignment list (a scrollable list of options), and the graphics tools (in Graphic mode only). At the bottom of the sidebar is a smaller box that lists the current selection and right or left page number.

2.1 Tip

Use different views to see different perspectives of your page.

Ventura has four different viewing sizes that allow you to look at the layout area from normal, reduced, enlarged, or facing-page perspectives. Switching among the different views changes only the magnification of the work area.

You can change views in two ways. You can choose the Reduced View, Normal View, Enlarged View, or Facing Pages View options from the View menu. (The Facing Pages View option is available only if the Chapter menu Page Size & Layout option has been set to double-sided.) Or you can use keyboard shortcuts to select different views: Ctrl-R for Reduced View, Ctrl-N for Normal View, and Ctrl-E for Enlarged View (Facing Pages View has no keyboard shortcut).

You will use the Normal View most of the time (see fig. 2.2). If you have a full-page monitor, you can see an entire 8 1/2-by-11-inch page; text characters appear about the same relative size as they will on the final printout.

You can use the Reduced View to see an entire page at a time regardless of your monitor's size (see fig. 2.3). Most of the text may not be legible, but you get an idea of what the layout will look like when the page is printed.

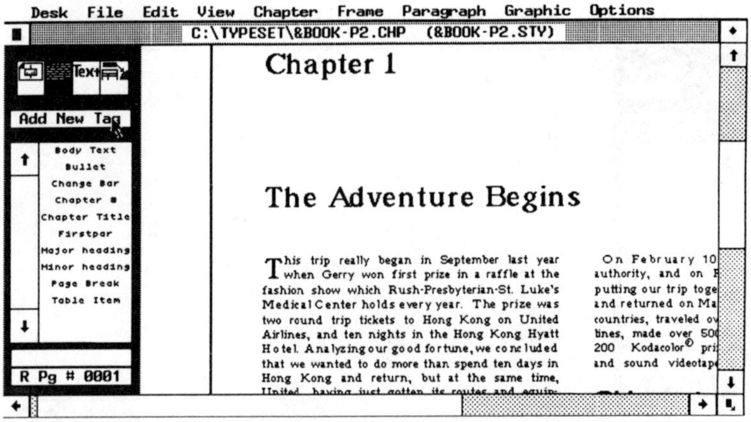

Fig. 2.2.

Normal View.

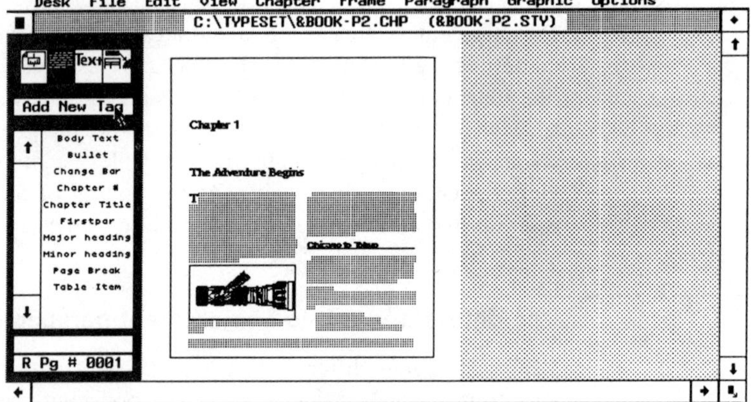

Fig. 2.3.

Reduced View.

Use the Enlarged View option to see a portion of a page magnified to twice its normal size (see fig. 2.4). You can use this view to make minor adjustments to text or graphics that would be hard to do in Normal View.

Use the Facing Pages View to see both the left and right pages (see fig. 2.5).

2.2 Trap

You cannot directly move objects or text across pages in the Facing Pages View.

When you're in Facing Pages View, you can see two pages at once. If a graphic is on the right page, you may assume that you can select and drag the image across the page to the left page, but Ventura will not allow you to do this.

Fig. 2.4.

Enlarged View.

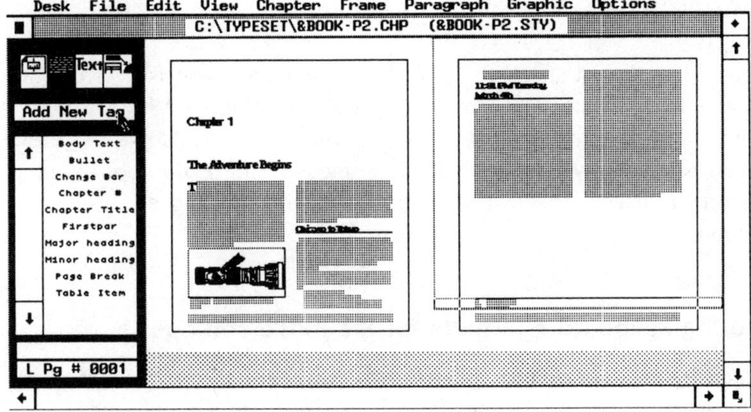

Fig. 2.5.

Facing Pages View.

2.3 Trick

Use Cut and Paste to move frames from one page to another.

How can you reposition frames if you cannot drag frames from one page to another while you're in the Facing Pages View? Just click the frame while you're in Frame mode and then press the Del key to cut the frame.

Once cut, the frame and its contents are transferred to an invisible Clipboard. Click the page you want to transfer the cut frame to and press the Ins key to paste the frame onto the page. The frame is transferred from the Clipboard onto the selected page in the same position it occupied on the page you cut it from. To reposition your newly transferred image, click it and drag it to where you want on the page.

Understanding the Sidebar

The sidebar, which is divided into five parts, is the area to the left of the work area. In the first part are four icons representing the four work modes of Ventura: Frame, Paragraph, Text, and Graphic. Below the icons is the addition button. The third part of the sidebar is the assignment list, and the last two parts are the current selection box and the page counter.

You can choose the mode icons and the addition button with either the mouse or keyboard shortcuts. You can select the assignment list only by using the mouse. The last two parts report status information. The current selection box reports the contents of a frame, page, or attribute, and the page counter gives the current page number.

Using Keyboard Shortcuts

Ventura has 44 keyboard shortcuts, which are commands you issue from the keyboard, not from the menus. Pressing Ctrl-N (for Normal View) is faster than moving the mouse to the View menu, moving the mouse down the View menu to the Normal View option, clicking the mouse, and finally repositioning the cursor on the page. You can save much time by learning and using the most common shortcuts.

2.4 Tip **Memorize the keyboard shortcuts for the mode settings.**

Ventura makes it easy for you to remember the keyboard shortcuts for the four modes. The shortcuts for the Frame, Paragraph, Text, and Graphic modes are Ctrl-U, Ctrl-I, Ctrl-O, and Ctrl-P. These letters are the last four letters on the top row of the keyboard, and they correspond to the four mode icons from left to right. To choose the different modes, hold down the Ctrl key and press the appropriate letter.

2.5 Tip **Use keyboard shortcuts whenever possible to save time and eliminate the need to reposition the mouse.**

Shortcuts are divided into two groups: command shortcuts and typographical shortcuts. Typographical shortcuts are discussed in Chapter 4. Table 2.1 lists the keyboard command shortcuts.

Table 2.1
Keyboard Command Shortcuts
and the Modes in which They Are Available

Command Shortcut	*Command (Mode)*
Ctrl-2	Addition or set button (All)
Ctrl-A	Bring to front (Graphic)
Ctrl-B	Renumber chapter
Ctrl-C	Insert special item (Text)
Ctrl-D	Edit special item (Text)
Ctrl-E	Enlarged View, 2× (All)
Ctrl-F	Fill attributes (Graphic)
Ctrl-G	Go to page *n* (All)
Ctrl-I	Paragraph mode
Ctrl-K	Update tag list (All)
Ctrl-L	Line attributes (Graphic)
Ctrl-N	Normal View (All)
Ctrl-O	Text mode
Ctrl-P	Graphic mode
Ctrl-Q	Select all graphics (Frame or Graphic)
Ctrl-R	Reduced View (All)
Ctrl-S	Save (All)
Ctrl-T	Show or hide tabs and returns (All)
Ctrl-U	Frame mode
Ctrl-W	Show or hide sidebar (All)
Ctrl-X	Recall last dialog box or cancel button (All)
Ctrl-Z	Send to back (Graphic)
Home	Go to first page (All)
PgUp	Go to preceding page (All)
End	Go to last page (All)
PgDn	Go to next page (All)
Ins	Paste what's on Clipboard (Frame, Text, Graphic)
Del	Cut and store on Clipboard (Frame, Text, Graphic)
Shift-Del	Copy and store on Clipboard (Frame, Text, Graphic)
Esc	Redraw screen
F1 to F10	Assign paragraph tags (Paragraph)

Using the Addition Button

The addition button is active in all four Ventura modes. In the Frame and Graphic modes, the addition button adds frames. In the Paragraph mode, selecting the addition button calls up the ADD NEW TAG dialog box. In the Text mode, you use the addition button to modify text attributes for selected text.

2.6 Tip

Save time by using the keyboard shortcut to select the addition button.

When you perform a function by using a keyboard shortcut, you save time because you don't need to move the mouse from its working location to a selection box or menu and then back to the work area. You can choose the addition button in all four modes by pressing Ctrl-2. Figure 2.6 shows an example of adding a frame.

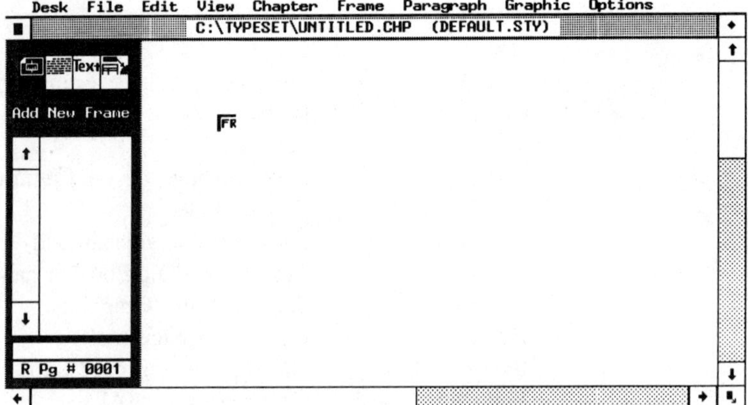

Fig. 2.6. *The addition button selected to add a frame.*

2.7 Tip

If you want to add more than one frame, press the Shift key when you select the addition button.

Sometimes you will want to add more than one frame at a time. You can avoid having to reselect the addition button by pressing Shift before selecting the addition button. You can continue to add frames until you release the Shift key, after which you can add one more frame. You cannot use the Ctrl-2 keyboard shortcut while you are pressing the Shift key.

2.8 Trick **If you accidentally press the addition button, immediately use Del to remove unwanted frames, or you can choose another function to deactivate the addition button.**

If you press the addition button accidentally or hold down the Shift key too long, Ventura will not let you turn off the addition button by simply clicking the addition button to deselect it. Instead, you must do one of two things to turn off the addition button.

You can click once in the work area of Ventura. This procedure creates a small frame, which you can immediately remove by pressing Del. You also can choose a mode other than the one you're currently in. Selecting another mode deactivates the addition button. Then you can reselect the mode you want to work in.

Using the Assignment List

Depending on the mode you're in, the assignment list either lists files, paragraph tags, or text attributes. (In Graphic mode, the assignment list is replaced by graphics tools.) You select options in the assignment list by using the mouse pointer to highlight the option and then clicking.

2.9 Tip **To avoid confusion in the assignment list while in Frame mode, use standard extensions on your file names.**

Perhaps more than any other software, Ventura rewards you for using standard file name extensions. DOS limits file names to eight letters, followed by a period, followed by three more letters. The three letters following the period are the file name extension. To function properly, some files require specific extensions, such as COM, EXE, or BAT. Ventura establishes file name extension conventions for text and graphics files.

If you examine figure 2.7, you can see three files listed in the sidebar area. Two of the files have TXT extensions, which indicates that they are ASCII text files. The other file has a GEM extension, which means that it is a graphics file in GEM format.

2.10 Tip **Learn and use the extensions Ventura recommends so that when you import files, Ventura will automatically screen for the file you're looking for.**

Importing text and graphics is discussed in detail in Chapters 4 and 7. When you tell Ventura to load a text or graphics file, Ventura asks about the program

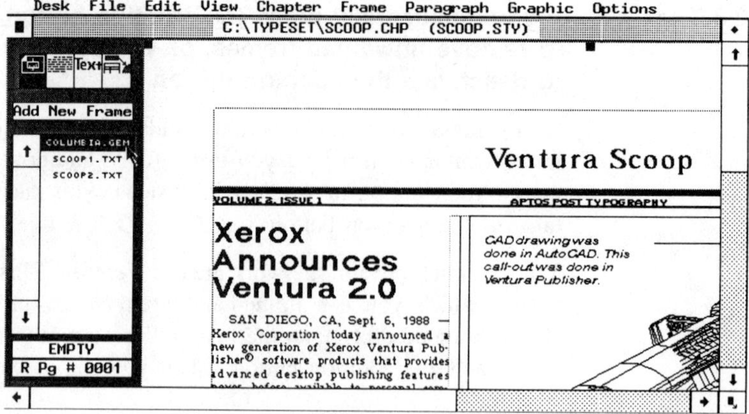

Fig. 2.7.

The assignment list.

that created the file. Ventura supports many word processors and graphics programs but needs to be told which program created the file you're trying to import. Most graphics programs automatically add the proper extension to files they create. Other programs, such as WordPerfect and WordStar®, don't. Develop the habit of adding the proper extension to your files when you create them.

Table 2.2 lists common file extensions and the programs that create them.

2.11 Trap

Unused files in the assignment list waste time when you open a chapter. Remove from the assignment list files (text and graphics) that you're no longer using.

Each time you open a chapter, Ventura hyphenates every text file. The more text, the more time it takes to hyphenate. Graphics files that require conversion are converted into IMG files each time Ventura loads a chapter.

As you create your chapter, if you decide not to use a particular graphic or article, don't just remove it from a frame. Removing a text or graphics file from a frame or page doesn't remove it from the chapter. Ventura wastes time hyphenating and converting unused files each time you load the chapter.

Removing a file from the assignment list does not erase the file.

You can remove a file from the assignment list in two ways. First, you can click the frame containing the text or graphics file you want to remove. To use the second way, you need to know the exact name of the file. Then you follow these steps:

1. Select the Edit menu from the menu bar.
2. Click the Remove Text/File option.

3. If you have selected a frame previously with text or graphics, Ventura enters the file name in the REMOVE FILE dialog box; if you have not selected a frame previously, type the name of the file you want to remove. Remember to include the file name extension if one exists.
4. The `Remove from` line displays `List of Files`. You don't need to change this setting.
5. Click OK or press Enter.
6. If you left the `File Name` line blank or entered an incorrect file name, you see a NOTE dialog box, which tells you that no file by the name you typed exists. Check the file name again and repeat steps 1 through 4.

Table 2.2
File Extensions and the Software that Created Them

Extension	*Software*
Word Processors	
DOC	Microsoft Word and MultiMate
TXT	ASCII, Xywrite, or WordStar UK
RFT	DCA
WP	WordPerfect
WS	WordStar
XWP	Xerox Writer
ASC	WordPerfect ASCII, Leading Edge ASCII, etc.
Graphics Programs	
CGM	CGM format
EPS	Encapsulated PostScript
GEM	GEM line art
HPG	Hewlett-Packard plotter files (HPGL)
IMG	GEM image
PCT	PICT format (Macintosh)
PCX or PCC	PC Paintbrush and Publisher's Paintbrush™
PIC	Lotus 1-2-3 graph, Video Show
PNT	MacPaint® (Macintosh)
P*	Mentor Graphics
SLD	AutoCAD®
TIF	TIFF
WMF	Windows Metafile

The TIFF format is produced by some graphics and most scanning software.

2.12 Tip

Use meaningful names for files and tags.

Don't use meaningless file names like TEXT1 or GRAPHIC1 for text or graphics files; instead, use names that describe the contents of a file. The file names SEPT_RPT.TXT and SEPT_SLS.PIC, for example, let you know not only what type of files they are (remember the tip on using file name extensions), but also what's in the files. Meaningful file names make the job easier when you import or place text or graphics files.

You should give all files associated with a specific chapter a common prefix. Prefixes can be one or two letters followed by an underline or nonalphabetic characters (except for asterisks and question marks—characters that have specific meanings reserved for DOS). The files AN_MAIN.TXT and AN_GRAPH.PCX, for example, can both be associated with the same chapter about animals. Or you can use a nonalphabetic prefix such as @ or # to distinguish files for a specific chapter (@FIRST.TXT and @LOGO.CGM, for example).

Your tags also should have meaningful names that include information about what sort of paragraph the tag is for or some sort of shorthand that reveals a tag's characteristics. A tag name such as Headline 36 Pt could indicate a 36-point headline. A tag for a centered paragraph with a 24-point Times bold font might be Tms B 24 Cntr.

Tag names can be up to 13 characters long, and you can use characters such as spaces, question marks, and asterisks, which are not allowed in file names.

2.13 Trick

Use nonalphabetic characters to force files or tags to appear in a certain order in the assignment list.

Files or tags appear in alphabetical order in the assignment list. If you want files of the same kind grouped together in the assignment list, you can force them together by using a nonalphabetic first character. If you give names such as @SEPT.PIC and @OCT.PIC to all files containing sales graphs, for example, these files will appear together in the list.

You can use a similar strategy to group tags together. Instead of using tag names such as Lg Point Para and Sm Point Para, you could use Para Lg Point and Para Sm Point. Keeping similar tags together on the assignment list helps you remember what the tags do and helps you locate tags for rapid assignment.

Finding a Page

Once you have created a large chapter, you need a quick way to move from one page to another without scrolling through the entire chapter. Ventura has several shortcuts for moving through a chapter.

2.14 Tip

Use the PgUp, PgDn, Home, and End keys to move through a chapter.

Use the special keys PgUp and PgDn to move backward or forward through a chapter. Use the special keys Home and End to move to the beginning or end of a chapter. In a long chapter, it may take much time to move forward (either one page at a time with PgDn or jumping to the end with End). Once you reach the end of the chapter, moving backward by using PgUp or Home takes less time.

2.15 Tip

Use the Go to Page command to move to a specific or relative point in the chapter.

If you know the page number you want to go to, you can use the Go to Page command by following these steps:

1. From the Chapter menu, click Go to Page. This menu choice is active in all modes.

   or

   Press Ctrl-G, the keyboard shortcut for Go to Page.

2. On the `Selected Page` line of the GO TO PAGE dialog box, enter the page number you want to go to.
3. Click OK or press Enter.

If you want to go to a relative point in the chapter, you can use the pop-up menu at the `Which Page` option in the GO TO PAGE dialog box and choose `First`, `Prev`, `Next`, or `Last`. These choices, however, duplicate the functions of Home, PgUp, PgDn, and End; you should use the keyboard shortcuts for faster operation.

2.16 Tip

If your chapter has several text files, use Go to Page to find the first, last, next, or previous part of the file.

In newsletter and magazine formats, an article often begins on one page and continues on another. In a large chapter, it's easy to get confused remembering which page contains the continuation of an article. Ventura solves this problem by helping you locate text files that have been broken up across several pages. To move to another part of the chapter containing a specific text file, follow these steps:

1. You must be in either Frame or Graphic mode. Click the frame or page containing the text file you're interested in.

2. From the Chapter menu, click Go to Page or use the keyboard shortcut Ctrl-G.

3. The selection on the `Relative to` line will be `File`. Select the pop-up menu for `Which Page` (see fig. 2.8).

4. From the Which Page pop-up menu, choose `First` or `Last` to go to the first or last page of the file; choose `Prev` or `Next` to go to the page before or after the current page.

5. Click OK or press Enter.

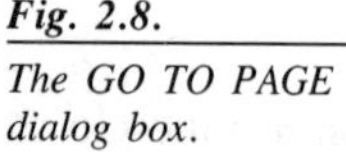

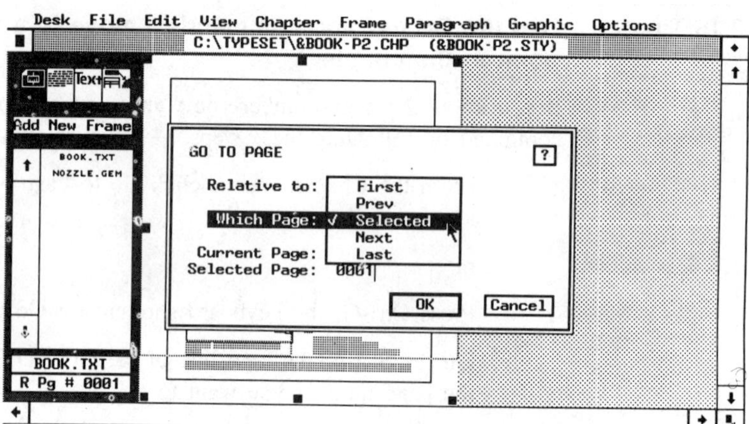

Fig. 2.8.

The GO TO PAGE dialog box.

If you didn't select a frame or page, the `Relative to` line displays Document. If you look at the pop-up menu for `Relative to`, you see that the File option is grayed; you cannot select it. In this case, "document" really means "chapter." The terminology is inconsistent in Ventura, so be aware of what the word "document" means in this dialog box.

Understanding the Layout Area

The chapter you create takes shape in the layout area of the Ventura desktop. If you're used to traditional methods of producing newsletters, brochures, reports, presentations, financial statements, catalogs, fliers, or even graphic design, think of the layout area as an electronic pasteboard.

On this pasteboard, you have great flexibility in placing text and graphics, and with Ventura, you control the typography—the way letters and words look on a printed page. By having an accurate electronic representation of your final document (what you see is what you get, or WYSIWYG), you have greater control over your work.

Scrolling Shortcuts

Unless you have a full-page monitor that can display the entire page in Normal View or you are using the Soft Kicker (see Chapter 1), you need to move the page around the work area with scroll bars. Most monitors are not designed to show an entire page. If you use WordPerfect as a word processor, for example, you know you can see a maximum of 24 lines of text at a time. Depending on the size of your page and your choice of font in Ventura, you may see only 25 percent of your document at a time. You need to learn good scrolling techniques to allow you to use Ventura efficiently.

2.17 Tip **Use the scroll bars instead of the "scroll one line at a time" arrow.**

In the corners of the Ventura desktop are arrows. Depending on which arrow you select, clicking an arrow causes the layout area to shift one line up, down, left, or right. You should use the arrows if you want to move the work area just a little.

If graphics are on the page or if you're using a slower computer such as an XT, you will notice that Ventura pauses after each scrolling increment to redraw the screen. Redrawing makes this method of scrolling tedious and frustrating.

You can move around the page faster by using the scroll controls located in the scroll bars. The scroll bars are the bottom and right borders of the layout area. The white blocks in the scroll bars are the scroll controls. You activate a scroll control by pointing at it with the mouse, clicking, and holding down the mouse button. You move the horizontal scroll control left or right and the vertical scroll control up or down. When you release the mouse button, your page in the layout area shifts according to how you moved the scroll control.

2.18 Tip

Turn off graphics when you're scrolling to save more time.

If you have a page containing an image, hide the graphic. When a graphic is hidden, Ventura doesn't have to redraw it each time you scroll to a new location on the page. You can hide a single image or all graphics in a chapter. To hide a single graphic, use the following procedure:

1. Select the graphic by clicking the frame that contains the graphic. You must be in either Frame or Graphic mode to do this procedure. (You can select multiple graphics by holding down the Shift key and clicking another graphics frame.)
2. From the Options menu, click Hide This Picture. (To turn off all graphics, do *not* select any individual graphic; from the Options menu, click Hide All Pictures.)

The frame containing the image turns opaque (see fig. 2.9 for examples of both visible and hidden graphics). To make one graphic visible again, select the graphic in either Frame or Graphic mode and, from the Options menu, click Show This Picture. To make all graphics in the chapter visible again, click Show All Pictures.

You can select more than one graphic on a page by holding down the Shift key while you select multiple graphics.

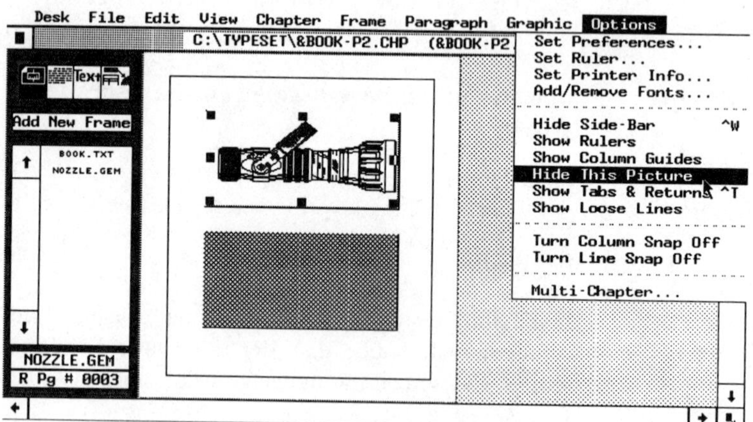

Fig. 2.9.

Layout area with one graphic visible and one graphic hidden.

2.19 Trap

Remember to redisplay graphics before printing.

Hidden pictures not only don't display, they don't print. Although you can speed printing time by hiding images when you print rough drafts, remember to redisplay the graphics before your final printing.

If you forget to redisplay the graphics, Ventura reminds you at print time that some graphics are still hidden and asks whether you want to print the hidden graphics.

2.20 Trick

To position the page quickly, position the cursor in the layout area before selecting either Normal or Enlarged View.

When you're in Normal View and want to change to Enlarged View, or when you're in Reduced or Facing Pages View and want to change to Normal or Enlarged View, you can force the positioning of the new view.

Assume you're in Reduced View and want to change to Normal View. Position the mouse cursor over the area you want centered in the layout area when you change to Normal View and then press Ctrl-N to choose Normal View. You can be in any mode and you don't have to select anything on the page such as a frame, paragraph, text, or graphic. Simply positioning the mouse cursor over the area tells Ventura how you want the new view centered. Obviously, you must use the keyboard shortcuts for Normal (Ctrl-N) or Enlarged (Ctrl-E) View for this trick to work.

This trick also works from Facing Pages View, but you must perform an extra step. Because Ventura doesn't know which of the facing pages you want centered in the layout area, you need to select something first. If you're in Frame mode, choose the page; if you're in Paragraph mode, select a paragraph. If you're in Text mode, click some text to activate the text cursor, and if you're in Graphic mode, select either the page or a frame before positioning the cursor and changing views.

2.21 Trap

Only if you have the GEM Desktop from Digital Research should you use the Size Box or the Full Box features of the Ventura desktop. These features are not fully implemented.

In the lower right corner of the Ventura desktop is a box with an arrow pointing down and to the right; a diamond is in the upper right corner. These are icons for sizing and then restoring the size of the Ventura desktop.

In Windows for the PC and in programs that run on the Apple Macintosh, the window in which many programs run can be resized. The GEM operating environment in which Ventura runs also has that capability, but it has not been fully implemented in the run-time version of GEM that is provided with Ventura. You can click and drag the box with the arrow to resize the Ventura desktop and then click the diamond icon to restore the desktop to its maximum size. Unless you have other software that operates under GEM, such as the GEM Desktop, these features have no use.

2.22 Tip

Increase the working layout area by hiding the sidebar.

You can hide the sidebar by selecting Hide Side-Bar from the Options menu or with the Ctrl-W keyboard shortcut (see fig. 2.10). Although the sidebar is hidden, the keyboard shortcuts for selecting the four modes or the addition button are still functional. The only thing you cannot do without restoring the sidebar is access the assignment list.

To restore the sidebar, choose Show Side-Bar from the Options menu or press Ctrl-W.

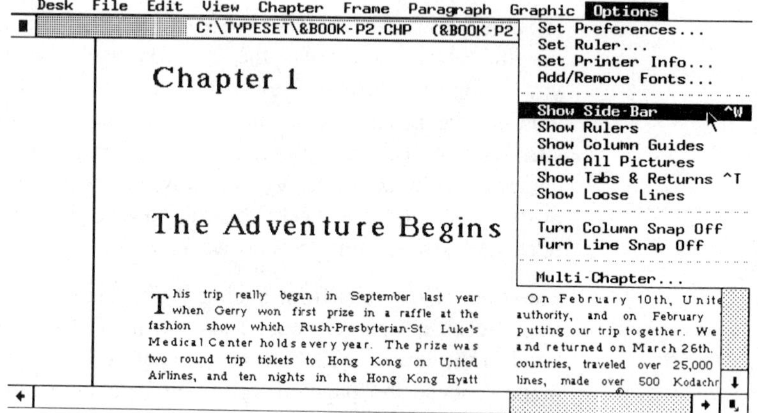

Fig. 2.10.

The Ventura desktop with the sidebar hidden.

2.23 Tip

To decrease screen redrawing time, change the Text to Greek option to a lower number.

It takes time for Ventura to create a graphic display of text. In character-based software like WordPerfect or WordStar, less computing power is needed because the PC character set is generated quickly. In a graphic environment like GEM or Windows, more computing power is required to give an accurate representation of what the printed page will look like.

When you reach the point in your production where you want to see how only the layout looks, you can use Ventura's greeking feature.

Greeking means showing a representation of what the text will look like. Ventura allows you to select the point size of text you want to greek. From the Options menu, select Set Preferences. The SET PREFERENCES dialog box has a pop-up menu at the `Text to Greek` option (see fig. 2.11). You can choose from six choices ranging from `None` (meaning no text is greeked) to `All` (meaning all text is greeked).

If you select None, then even small type is portrayed accurately even in Reduced or Facing Pages View, which slows screen redrawing time significantly. If you choose All, then all type, even headlines, is greeked in Reduced and Facing Pages Views. A better strategy is to select a middle range for normal work and then choose 10 for your final layout examination. Most text (except headlines in Reduced or Facing Pages View) is greeked if you choose 10.

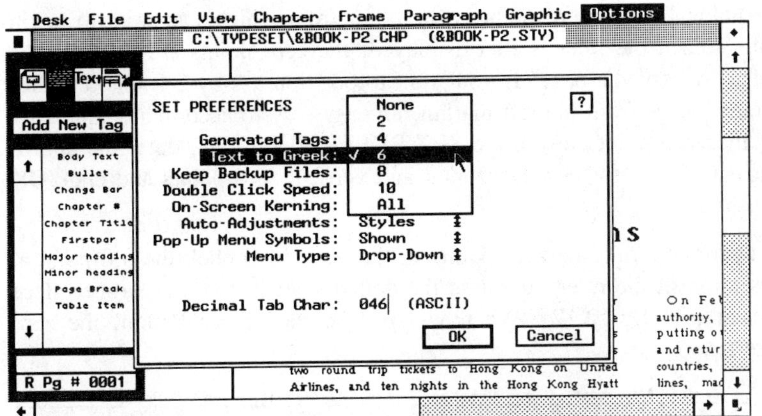

Fig. 2.11.

The Text to Greek pop-up menu from the SET PREFERENCES dialog box.

Using Invisible Snap Grids, Guides, and Rulers

One benefit to working with hard copy layout in the traditional manner is that you can use layout paper with blue grid lines to position text and graphics precisely. Ventura offers similar capabilities electronically and without getting any glue on your hands.

2.24 Tip **Turn on the ruler display during layout in order to position frames of text and graphics accurately.**

Ventura has a ruler that runs along the top and left side of the layout area. To display the ruler, choose Show Rulers from the Options menu. To hide the ruler, choose Hide Rulers from the Options menu.

The rulers can be adjusted in two ways. First, the horizontal and vertical rulers can be set independently in inches, centimeters, or picas. For example, you can set the horizontal ruler to measure in inches and the vertical ruler to measure in picas. You make these choices from the SET RULER dialog box (accessed when you choose Set Ruler from the Options menu).

Once the rulers are displayed, you can see dotted lines that move along the rulers. These dotted lines cross-reference the position of the cursor on the page.

2.25 Tip

Set the horizontal and vertical zero points to position frames of text or graphics accurately.

The horizontal and vertical zero points also can be changed from the SET RULER dialog box. A zero point is the point from which you want to begin measuring. When the ruler is first displayed, the zero points are set from the upper left corner of the page. If you want to position a 2-by-2 frame 3 inches down and 3 inches from the left margin, an easy way to accomplish this is by resetting the zero points. From the SET RULER dialog box, enter the appropriate measurements for new horizontal and vertical zero points and click OK or press Enter.

A shortcut for resetting the zero points of the ruler is to click the 0,0 point at the intersection of the rulers and drag the dotted ruler lines to the proper place on the page (see fig. 2.12). When you release the mouse button, the zero points are reset.

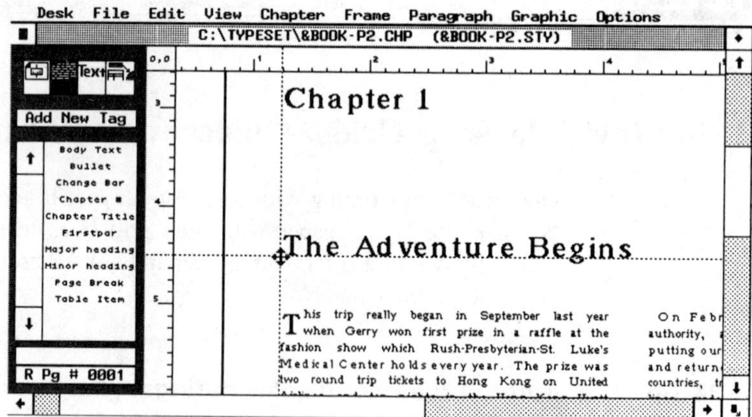

Fig. 2.12.

Visually setting the zero point.

2.26 Tip

For greater control during layout, make the column guides visible.

Both pages and frames can have their own column widths and margins. Columns and margins are discussed in detail in Chapter 6. Once the columns and margins have been set, they serve as invisible constraints for any text. Much like a mold determines the shape of whatever is poured into it, columns and margins control the shape of text flow. Ventura keeps track of column and margin settings automatically and will not display them after you select the Show Column Guides option from the Options menu. The guides then show as little dotted lines and define the boundaries of the columns (see fig. 2.13).

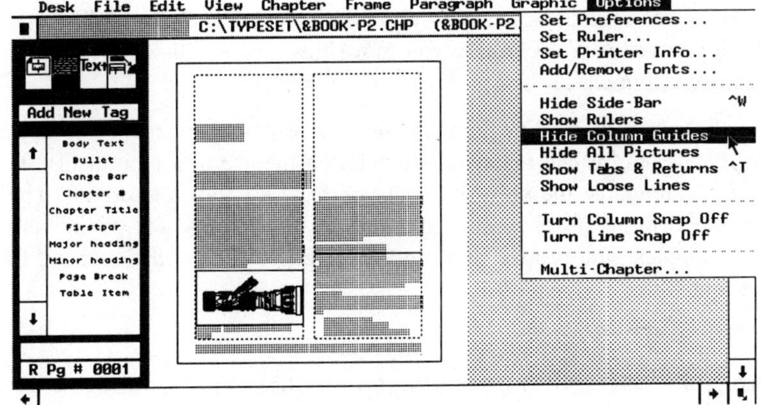

Fig. 2.13.

Column guides displayed as dotted lines.

To hide the column guides, click Hide Column Guides from the Options menu. The column guides don't print, so they don't need to be hidden at print time.

2.27 Tip

To have frames line up perfectly with column guides, choose Turn Column Snap On. To have frames line up perfectly with the tops or bottoms of columns, choose Turn Line Snap On.

Once the columns and margins have been set, Ventura gives you the option of having the borders of newly created or resized frames snap to or line up with the column guide. Frames that are being resized snap to a column guide on the side that is being resized.

To force frames to line up with either the top of bottom of a column, turn line snap and resize or move the frame toward the top or bottom of the column. As you resize or move the frame, you will notice the frame jump in increments. The increment the frame jumps is determined by the body text's interline spacing.

Column and line snap are turned off and on at the Options menu.

Understanding the Cursor

The cursor is the entry point for a computer. If you are accustomed to working with character-based software such as WordPerfect, you're used to seeing a blinking rectangle or underscore cursor on the screen. The cursor lets you know where you are in a document; you move the cursor with arrow keys or other keyboard commands.

In graphics-based programs like Ventura, the cursor does not respond to keyboard commands but instead is moved around with the use of a mouse. (To be accurate, you can enable the keyboard, but you have no reason to do so.) The mouse cursor positions itself within the document for placing text or drawing frames and graphics; you use the mouse to make menu choices and respond to dialog box queries.

2.28 Tip **Learn what the different cursor shapes mean so that you know at a glance what effect an action will have.**

Ventura has 13 different mouse cursor shapes (see fig. 2.14) that fall into three categories (see table 2.3). Mode cursors distinguish the four basic modes of operation in Ventura—Frame, Paragraph, Text, and Graphic. Graphics cursors function only in Graphic mode. Frame manipulation cursors let you add, move, and resize frames as well as move an image that has been placed in a frame.

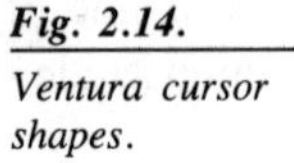

Fig. 2.14.

Ventura cursor shapes.

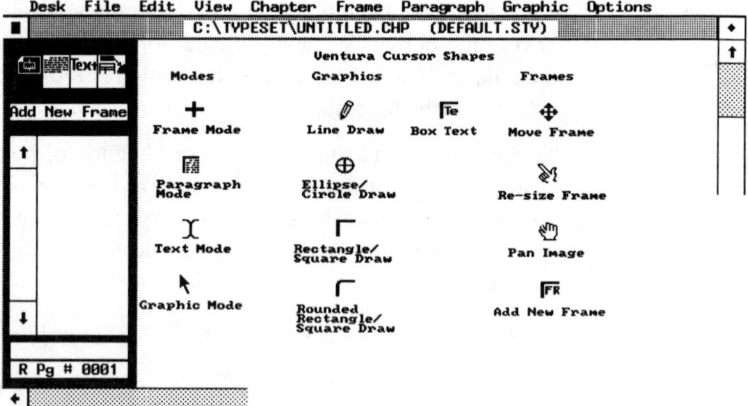

Table 2.3
Mouse Cursor Shapes

Mode Cursors
Frame Mode (cross)
Paragraph Mode (corner with text)
Text Mode (I-beam)
Graphic Mode and Selector (arrow)
Graphics Cursors
Box Text (corner with Te)
Line Drawing (pencil)
Ellipse/Circle Drawing (circle with cross)
Rectangle/Square Drawing (corner)
Rounded Rectangle/Square (rounded corner)
Frame Manipulation Cursors
Add New Frame (corner with FR)
Resize Frame (finger pointing)
Move Frame (cross with four arrows)
Pan Image (hand)

2.29 Trap **When clicking a frame handle to resize, be sure that the cursor shape changes to the pointing finger.**

When you want to resize a frame while you are in Frame mode, click the frame to choose it and reveal the eight resizing handles. You resize your frame by clicking and dragging a resizing handle.

Be careful, however. If the cursor is a cross with four arrows, the frame isn't resized but moves instead. This frame movement is frustrating, and it creates extra work for you because it can cause other elements, such as text and graphics, to reflow in response to the relocated frame.

Resizing is discussed in more detail in Chapter 6.

Understanding Measurement Options

If you have experience with manual methods of prepublication, you already know several different systems of measurement, such as inches and centimeters. If you handle typography, you also are familiar with the traditional printer's measures picas and points. If you don't have experience in this area, don't worry. All you need to know is that an inch contains 72 points and a pica is 12 points. That means a pica is 1/6 of an inch.

2.30 Tip **Change the units of measurement in the dialog boxes to units you're familiar with and that seem most appropriate for what you're measuring.**

Many of the dialog boxes allow you to change options, such as margins or widths, that are entered in a unit of measure. If a dialog box presents measures in inches, you can easily change to another system of measure by clicking the word `inches`. Ventura cycles from inches to centimeters to picas, and from points to fractional points. In addition, all the numbers in the dialog box recalculate immediately to reflect the new measure. If the numbers become too large to fit, you see tildes (~) rather than numbers. Ventura remembers the numbers but doesn't display them.

A few dialog boxes have two or more places where the units of measure can be changed. In these dialog boxes, you can, for example, set one unit of measure to inches and another to centimeters.

Once you have changed the units of measure in a particular dialog box, Ventura remembers your preference and stores it in the VP.INF file. The next time you use the same dialog box, your preferred units of measure are waiting for you.

Using Commands

Ventura offers such complete control over the final printed page and so many formatting features that your access needs to be organized in a logical way. Before desktop publishing programs like Ventura were written, you had to master cryptic coding languages or resort to manual pasteup to format your pages as comprehensively as Ventura does.

2.31 Tip **Study the menu choices to gain an understanding of how Ventura is organized.**

The menu bar contains eight options (not counting the Desk option), and each menu offers many choices. The choices are grouped functionally, and each group is separated by a dotted line. The most used functions have keyboard shortcuts listed on the menu. If a dialog box is associated with the menu option, the option is followed by an ellipsis (...). A list of the menu bar options and their functions follows:

Menu Option	*Types of Functions*
File	Open or begin a chapter
	Save or abandon a chapter
	Load text or graphics, and retrieve or save style sheets
	Print, manage files, and quit
Edit	Cut, copy, and paste
	Special item insertion and editing
	Text and graphics file management
View	Facing pages
	Reduced, normal, and enlarged
	Mode selection
	(Note that you can select all options except Facing Pages View from the View menu with keyboard shortcuts. No dialog boxes are associated with this menu.)
Chapter	Page layout and typography settings
	Number and anchor frames and pages
	Headers, footers, and footnotes
	Page insert and delete, and Go to Page
Frame	Frame layout, typography, positioning, and scaling
	Frame anchors, captions, and repeating frames
	Vertical rules and other frame rules
	Control over image files
Paragraph	Paragraph tag control
	Rules around, below, and above paragraphs
	Color control and style sheet control
Graphic	Show graphics on all pages and position control of graphics on page
	Line and fill attributes

Menu Option	*Types of Functions*
	Graphics selection and grid control
Options	Preferences, ruler, printer, and font settings
	Hide and show sidebar, rulers, column guides, pictures, tabs, returns, and loose lines
	Column and line snap off and on
	Multichapter operations

Getting Help

Ventura comes with a comprehensive reference manual, and you have this book, so what more could you need? How about on-line help?

2.32 Tip **Click and hold the question mark in the dialog boxes to see a list of topics for which help is available.**

Every dialog box in Ventura has a question mark box. Click and hold the box to see a list of topics. Drag the cursor until the topic you're interested in is highlighted and then release the mouse button. A special NOTE dialog box appears with a brief explanation. Although these explanations are not comprehensive, they are sufficient to jog your memory if you're already familiar with the function. Click OK or press Enter to return to the dialog box.

Don't overlook the PUBLISHER INFO dialog box available from the Desk menu. It has 11 topics in its help box that cover topics not covered elsewhere.

Chapter Summary

In this chapter you have been exposed to the way Ventura does things. You learned about the sidebar and the sidebar's different functions, including the mode selection icons, the addition button, and the assignment list.

You learned how to find a page, how to scroll a page on the layout area, and how to change views. You also learned how to use column guides, use the rulers and measurement options, and make frames line up with the column guides. You also learned about the cursor shapes and what each one signifies. Finally, you gained some understanding of modes and commands and the way Ventura is organized to make its power accessible.

Chapter

3

Understanding Ventura's File Management

With Ventura, you can create documents that look as if they were produced by a printer using traditional methods. To produce professional-looking documents with Ventura, you can incorporate text, graphics, and design elements electronically rather than mechanically.

When a printer or designer works on a document using traditional technology, many disconnected elements are connected to create the final result. The printer opens one file folder with typeset text, another with drawings of photographs, a third with captions for the graphics, and perhaps a fourth with rules to separate columns and dingbats to add interest. The printer then pastes the text, graphics, captions, and design elements onto a master page. A plate is made of the master page and used in an offset or regular press.

You do the same thing in Ventura, but you do it electronically. You open several file folders, one containing your text, another holding your graphics, a third with graphics captions, and another containing design elements, and you assemble these file folders onto the Ventura desktop. Once everything is on the desktop, you electronically cut and paste until the document suits you.

If you understand that nothing is inherently different about what you are doing electronically compared with what the printer does manually, you will have a better grasp of what Ventura helps you accomplish.

This chapter will help you understand the elements of a document and how Ventura stores the information you create. You will learn how to manage a complex array of files in a sensible and logical way, how to move chapters and publications on your hard drive and from system to system, and how to name your files and save your work.

In Ventura, the *chapter* is the basic unit that you work with. A chapter is composed of *files*: text, information, and graphics. If you have several chapters and link them, the linked chapters are called a *publication*. If you can remember files, chapters, and publications, you are on your way to managing your Ventura documents.

Few concepts in Ventura are more confusing than file management. One cause of confusion is that Ventura uses many kinds of files. Another cause of confusion is that when you import a file (such as a graphic or text file) with some desktop publishing programs and word processors, the added file is incorporated into the document you are working on. Ventura, however, does not actually incorporate a file; instead, Ventura *links* the file to the document. Linking rather than merging can be confusing, but linking has distinct advantages (discussed later in this chapter). And a third cause of confusion is that the linked files comprising a document—or a chapter, in Ventura terminology—can be located anywhere on your hard disk. Ventura remembers where you have stored the text or graphic file, but if you move any files without letting Ventura know (by using regular DOS commands), Ventura will not be able to locate needed files.

Using multiple files, linked rather than merged and in multiple directories rather than a single directory, requires both understanding and planning. This chapter will help you understand how Ventura organizes the components of a chapter so that you can plan and organize you work and feel confident rather than confused.

Understanding Chapters

A chapter has two types of files: files you create and files Ventura generates. The files you create can be stored anywhere on your hard disk. The files Ventura creates are stored together in the subdirectory that you designate for the chapter.

In Chapter 2, you learned about file name extension conventions for text and graphics files. The files generated automatically by Ventura also have certain conventions.

3.1 Tip

Learn the file name extensions for files Ventura creates.

Ventura creates or manages several kinds of files. Table 3.1 lists the extensions of generated files and what those files contain. The generated file names for CAP, CHP, CIF, VGR, and other special Ventura files are always the same as the chapter name; only the extension is different. Some generated files can be edited carefully and saved as ASCII text files; others cannot be edited.

Table 3.1
Ventura Files and Their Contents

Extension	*Contents (editable or noneditable)*
CAP	Caption file (editable). Contains all ''loose'' text—text not associated with imported text files. All captions, box text, and text entered into empty frames in the edit mode, for example, are found in this file.
CHP	Chapter file (noneditable). Contains pointer information so Ventura can find the files associated with the chapter.
CIF	Chapter information file (noneditable). Stores additional information associated with the chapter.
CNF	Printer configuration file (editable). There are CNF files for Hewlett-Packard and PostScript printers. Contains information about the location and type of downloadable fonts (see Chapter 9 for more information).
C00	Print to disk files (may be editable). If you choose to print a chapter to a file rather than to a printer, when you issue the print command, Ventura will prompt you for a file name and automatically supply the C00 extension.
FNT	Font file extension used by Ventura (noneditable). Downloaded (soft) fonts from other companies may have other extensions.
GEN	Generated file (editable). When Ventura creates a table of contents or index, the text is inserted into a GEN file. Also, when you request the printing of style sheet information, Ventura puts that information in a GEN file.

Table 3.1—*Continued*

Extension	*Contents (editable or noneditable)*
INF	Information file (noneditable). Ventura stores information about your preferences and the state of the desktop (last style sheet, view, and mode selected) in a special VP.INF file. If you want to restore the original Ventura defaults, delete the VP.INF file. Ventura creates a new one with the original defaults intact. Ventura also creates INF files with information about screen fonts.
PUB	Publication file (noneditable). If you use the Multi-Chapter command from the Options menu either to move chapters or create publications, a PUB file is created to store the Multi-Chapter information.
STY	Style sheet files (noneditable). Each chapter has an associated style sheet containing information about tags and page layout.
VGR	Ventura graphics file (noneditable). Any time you create graphics by using the tools available in the Graphic mode, a file containing information about the lines, boxes, ovals, circles, rectangles, or squares is created.
WID	Printer width table (noneditable). Ventura provides width tables for the printers and fonts it supports. Many font vendors also supply width tables to allow their fonts to work with Ventura. The width table contains information about the type and size of available fonts.

3.2 Trap **When naming files, use extensions other than the reserved extensions that Ventura uses.**

You should find no reason to name files with any of the reserved extensions Ventura uses for its own files. Always use other file name extensions.

Managing Chapters

Two basic organizational strategies are available, each with pluses and minuses, for managing Ventura chapters.

3.3 Tip

For each new chapter, create a separate subdirectory to store all files associated with a single chapter or publication.

Here is the first strategy: Each time you create a chapter, create a new subdirectory in the TYPESET directory to store the chapter. Use the same name for the subdirectory that you plan to use for the chapter. Before loading Ventura, copy all the chapter files—text and graphics—into the new subdirectory.

To prepare a subdirectory for a chapter called REPORT, for example, do the following:

1. Type *cd \typeset* to move to the TYPESET directory created by Ventura during installation.
2. Type *md \report* to create a subdirectory of TYPESET called REPORT. The REPORT subdirectory is where you will store all files related to the REPORT chapter.
3. Copy all text files (created by your word processor) and all graphics files (scanned images, 1-2-3 PIC files, or paint or draw files) to the \TYPESET\REPORT subdirectory.

The benefits to using this strategy follow:

- ❑ All files associated with one chapter are in one place. You don't have to hunt all over your hard disk to find scattered files.
- ❑ You are working only with *copies* of text and graphics files. The originals are still in their original directory. If you alter or damage a file, you easily can restore the original.
- ❑ If you decide to delete a chapter and all its associated files, you easily can do so without worrying about whether a style sheet or graphics file is shared by other chapters.

And here are the drawbacks to using this strategy:

- ❑ Each text or graphics file exists in duplicate. If you have a large number of duplicate files on your hard drive, disk space is used up more rapidly, resulting in less storage capacity.
- ❑ Each time you change chapters, you need to reteach Ventura where things are stored. Each chapter and associated files are in

their own discreet directory. But Ventura's file retrieval system expects file elements to be in their *own* directories—all text files in the same text directory, all graphics files in the same graphics directory, all style sheets in the same style sheet directory, and so on. If you keep all the chapter directories as subdirectories of TYPESET, the problem is minimized because you easily can use the backup button to move one level up to view all the chapter directories' subdirectories.

3.4 Tip

Store each file type in a separate directory; keep all your chapters grouped by subject or category.

The second strategy is to store all ''like'' elements in a categorized directory or subdirectory. As an example, store all chapters and their generated elements in a CHAPTER subdirectory of TYPESET, all graphics in a GRAPHICS directory or subdirectory, all text in a TEXT directory or subdirectory, and so on.

To prepare a subdirectory for text files, for example, do the following:

1. Type *cd \typeset* to move to the TYPESET directory created by Ventura during installation.
2. Type *md \text* to create a subdirectory of TYPESET called TEXT. The TEXT subdirectory is where you will store all text files.
3. Copy all text files (regardless of the type) to the \TYPESET\TEXT subdirectory.

The benefit to using this strategy follows:

- ❑ If you create subdirectories for each file type, Ventura remembers where each file type is located from session to session—saving time in searching for files when you use the Load Text/Picture command from the File menu. (If, however, you create a different subdirectory for each graphic and text type, you need to show Ventura where items are stored each time you try to load a file.)

The drawbacks to using this strategy follow:

- ❑ Files associated with one chapter are scattered. You may have to hunt several places on your hard disk to find all the files you are looking for. Deleting all elements of obsolete chapters is also difficult.
- ❑ If you decide not to create special subdirectories but use the original file location, you are working with original text and graphics files. If you alter or damage a file, you may have to redo the work.

- ❑ If you decide to delete a chapter and all its associated files, you will have to be absolutely sure that the file is not also used by another chapter. If a file is shared by two or more chapters and you delete the shared file, the undeleted chapter will be incomplete without the deleted file.

You can subdivide file types further if you have several graphics or text sources. You can have a PIC subdirectory for 1-2-3 PIC graphic files, a PCX subdirectory for files created with Publisher's Paintbrush from ZSoft, a TXT subdirectory for ASCII text files, a WP subdirectory for WordPerfect files, and so on. However, Ventura remembers only one directory each for chapters, style sheets, text, line art, and images. Therefore, keeping all "like" files in one directory is simpler.

3.5 Trap

If you link your files haphazardly rather than use one of the two suggested strategies, you will have a difficult time identifying all files associated with chapters.

When I first began using Ventura after it was first published, I did not try to keep the files associated with a chapter in their own directory; nor did I try to keep all "like" files together. The result? Any time I wanted to recover disk space by deleting or archiving old files, I wasn't sure whether the file I was deleting was linked to some other Ventura chapter.

Meantime, because the TYPESET directory was the Ventura default for all generated files, TYPESET was filling up with a great deal of files. Because many of those files came as part of the examples, I had trouble telling which files needed to be kept and which files could be erased or archived.

At other times, I was completely done with a chapter and wanted either to remove or archive it to free up disk space. With all the elements of the chapter spread out in a disorganized way, removing a chapter involved a great deal of extra detective work.

To minimize work and confusion, follow one of the two chapter organization strategies detailed earlier in this section. If you have followed the "old" haphazard procedure in the past and now want to reorganize your Ventura files, see the tips in this chapter on using Desktop Manager and VP Tools.

Understanding Paths and Filters

Using Ventura, more than most software, requires an understanding of paths and file filters. DOS stores files (program or otherwise) in directories. All directories branch off of a root directory (\). You are allowed to name a directory with up to eight letters, and naming directories something meaningful is best.

3.6 Tip

Learn where Ventura initially keeps its files.

Ventura stores all its program files in a directory called VENTURA. In addition, Ventura stores the example files and the DEFAULT.STY style sheet in the TYPESET directory. When Ventura is loaded for the first time, it looks at the TYPESET directory for all chapter, style, text, line art, and image files as well.

When you select either Open Chapter or Load Diff. Style from the File menu, Ventura presents you with a dialog box called the ITEM SELECTOR (see fig. 3.1). When you select Load Text/Picture from the File menu, before you see the ITEM SELECTOR dialog box, you see the LOAD TEXT/PICTURE dialog box, from which you select either `Text`, `Line-Art`, or `Image` (see fig. 3.2). Depending on which option you select, you choose the specific file format of the file you want to open.

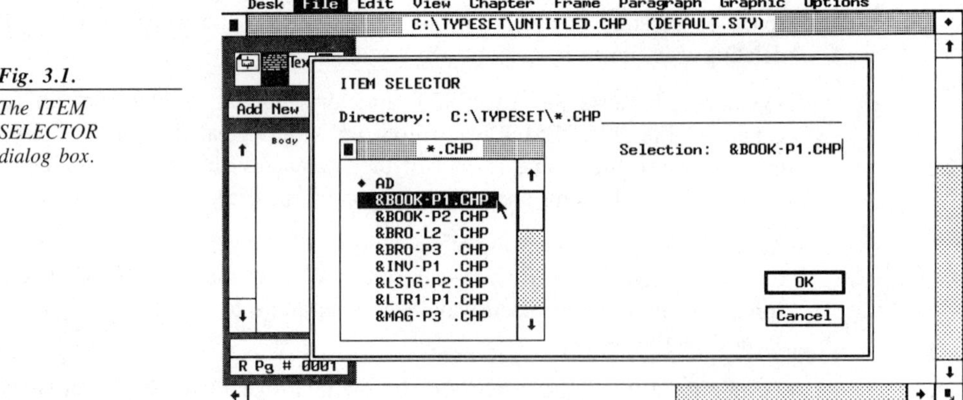

Fig. 3.1.
The ITEM SELECTOR dialog box.

3.7 Tip

Change directories from the ITEM SELECTOR dialog box to locate files you want to open and move to directories where you want a file to be saved.

You often will see the ITEM SELECTOR dialog box when using Ventura. Any time you want to open, load, or save a file or chapter, you are presented with this dialog box.

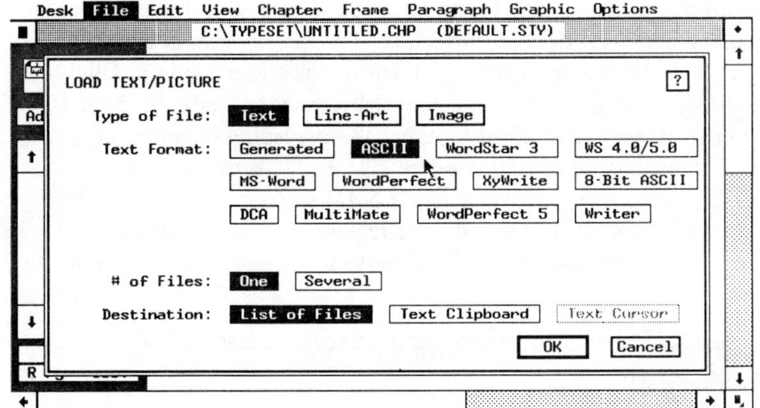

Fig. 3.2.

The LOAD TEXT/ PICTURE dialog box.

Examine figure 3.1 carefully and notice the following features of the ITEM SELECTOR dialog box:

- The `Directory` line shows you the current path and file filter. In the figure, the path name is C:\TYPESET, which means that the TYPESET directory is on drive C. The file filter is looking for any files with the CHP extension. You can edit this line by pressing the up-arrow key or clicking the path name to reposition the cursor. You can move through the path name by using the left- or right-arrow key. You can delete individual letters with either the Backspace or Del keys. If you want to delete the entire path name, press Esc.
- The file name box shows up to nine subdirectories or file names. If more than 100 files match the `Directory` line file filter request, you hear a beep. Only 100 files are loaded into the file name box, so not all files matching the filter appear.
- Click the up or down arrows or use the scroll bar to move through the file list. Click an arrow to move up or down one file at a time; click and drag the scroll bar to move quickly through the list.
- The `Selection` line is initially blank. You can type the path and file you want or scroll through the file list and click to select the file you want. Click OK or press Enter to confirm your choice. Double-clicking the file name has the same effect as selecting the file and then clicking OK or pressing Enter. After you select the file but before you click OK, you can edit the name of your selection the same way you edit the `Directory` line.

- The *directory diamond* is the small black diamond to the left of directory names in the file name box. The *backup button* is the larger black rectangle in the upper left of the file name box. Click the directory diamond to move into that directory; click the backup button to move back a level to either the preceding directory or a list of the available disk drives (see fig. 3.3). To change drives, click the drive letter. If you select a 5 1/4-inch or 3 1/2-inch disk drive that has no disk inserted, you receive an error message informing you to insert a disk and retry or to cancel the operation.

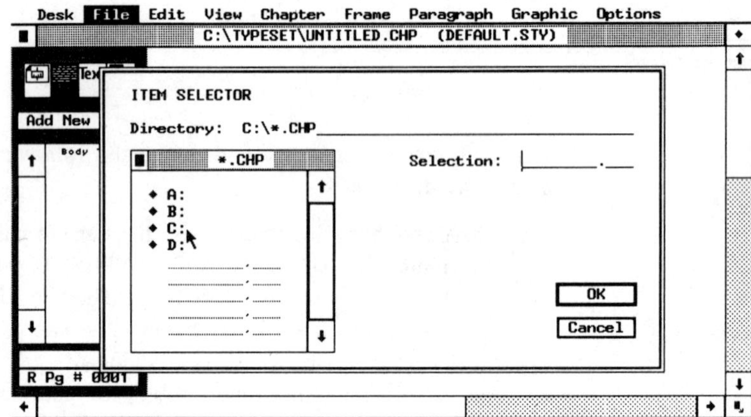

Fig. 3.3.
The ITEM SELECTOR dialog box displaying available drives in the file name box.

3.8 Tip

Save time in selecting files by using file filters.

DOS offers you a distinct advantage: you can filter for files. If you have a directory that contains a large number of files, screening a few files is much easier than scrolling through everything in the directory. By using file filters, you can locate quickly the files you are looking for.

With DOS, files can have names of up to eight characters, followed by a period and an extension of up to three characters. Here is an example:

12345678.123

By modifying the `Directory` line in the ITEM SELECTOR dialog box, you can filter for specific files or specific types of files. Two kinds of filters are available in DOS. One is the question mark (?), which replaces a single letter; the second is the asterisk (*), which replaces any number of letters.

If you are looking for WordPerfect files and systematically named all Word-Perfect files with the extension WP, you can filter for WordPerfect files by specifying *.*WP*. Translated, the asterisk requests all files (regardless of the number of characters in their file names) with the extension WP.

In figure 3.4, the only files shown in the file name box have the extension WP. Look at the `Directory` line in the dialog box. Notice the filter C:\WP50\RENTAL*.WP. This filter specifies all files with a WP extension in the RENTAL subdirectory of the WP50 directory on the C drive.

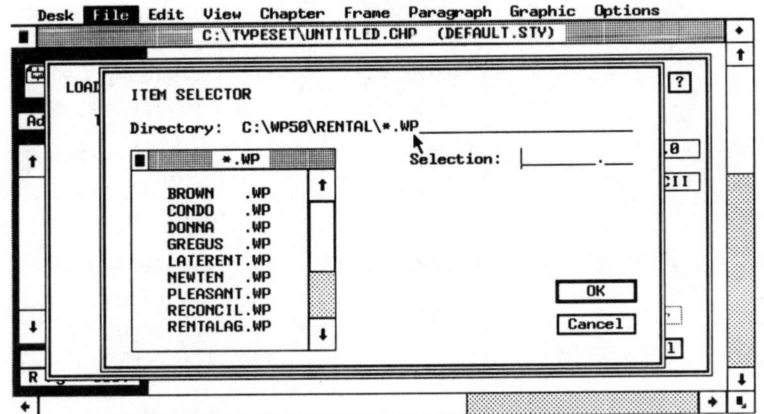

Fig. 3.4.

*The ITEM SELECTOR dialog box with *.WP filter.*

3.9 Tip **Ventura has preset 28 filters that you can modify. If you modify the filters, Ventura remembers the new filter.**

Ventura has preset 28 filters. Table 3.2 lists these filters.

Table 3.2
Default Filters and Associated Menu Command and File Type

Default Filter	*Menu Command*	*File Type*	*Comments*
CHP	Open Chapter	Chapter	Extension automatically given to all chapters by Ventura
GEN	Load Text/ Picture (Text)	Generated	Tables of contents, style sheets, and indexes

Table 3.2—*Continued*

Default Filter	*Menu Command*	*File Type*	*Comments*
TXT	Load Text/ Picture (Text)	ASCII, XyWrite, 8-bit ASCII	Different buttons for ASCII and XyWrite
WS	Load Text/ Picture (Text)	WordStar 3, 4, 5	Different buttons for different versions of WordStar
DOC	Load Text/ Picture (Text)	Microsoft Word, MultiMate	Different buttons for Word and MultiMate
WP	Load Text/ Picture (Text)	WordPerfect 4, 5	Different buttons for different versions of WordPerfect
RFT	Load Text/ Picture (Text)	DCA	Some word processors such as DisplayWrite save in DCA format
XWP	Load Text/ Picture (Text)	Xerox Writer	
GEM	Load Text/ Picture (Line-Art)	GEM Applications	Ventura converts some graphics line-art formats to GEM files
SLD	Load Text/ Picture (Line-Art)	AutoCAD	
PIC	Load Text/ Picture (Line-Art)	1-2-3, Symphony®, VideoShow	Lotus and VideoShow have separate buttons
P*	Load Text/ Picture (Line-Art)	Mentor Graphics	

Table 3.2—*Continued*

Default Filter	*Menu Command*	*File Type*	*Comments*
PCT	Load Text/ Picture (Line-Art)	Macintosh PICT files	Must be transferred from Macintosh; not the same as MacPaint files
EPS	Load Text/ Picture (Line-Art)	Encapsulated PostScript	Actually an ASCII file of a PostScript program; chapters printed to disk with PostScript driver are importable as EPS files; change filter to C00 to find them
CGM	Load Text/ Picture (Line-Art)	Various applications	
HPG	Load Text/ Picture (Line-Art)	Applications that save data in Hewlett-Packard Graphics Language format	
WMF	Load Text/ Picture (Line-Art)	Windows applications that save or export data in Windows Metafile format	Windows Clipboard files can be converted to WFN with the Ventura-supplied utility CLIP2VP.EXE (found on disk 5 for 5 1/4-inch disks or disk 3 for 3 1/2-inch disks)

Table 3.2—*Continued*

Default Filter	*Menu Command*	*File Type*	*Comments*
IMG	Load Text/ Picture (Image)	GEM or HALO DPE	Ventura converts many graphics image file formats to IMG files
PCX	Load Text/ Picture (Image)	ZSoft or compatible PCC applications such as Publisher's Paintbrush	Clips may have extension; PC* filter will find both file types
PNT	Load Text/ Picture (Image)	MacPaint format	Must be from Macintosh; transferred not the same as PICT files
TIF	Load Text/ Picture (Image)	Tagged image file format	
STY	Load Diff. Style	Style sheets	

3.10 Trap **Although Ventura can remember up to 28 different file filters for opening files, only five different directories are remembered.**

Although you can change filters to search for different file types, Ventura only remembers the last directory location for broad categories. Directories are recalled for chapter, style, text, line art, and image files.

If you change the directory to look for one kind of text, all subsequent searches for text take you to that directory even if you are looking for a different type of text with a different filter.

Therefore, if you don't immediately find the file you know is in a specific directory, double-check the directory you are currently in and, if necessary, move to the correct directory.

Transferring Chapters to a Floppy Disk

At times, you will want to archive or transfer chapters or publications to or from a floppy disk. Because chapter elements are often scattered throughout a hard disk and because Ventura places pointers to those elements in the CHP file, you must use special Ventura commands for your copying instead of the usual DOS COPY command.

3.11 Trap

Avoid using DOS COPY to move files to new directories or to copy files to a floppy disk for archiving or transferring to a new system.

Because Ventura links files, you cannot move files around without letting Ventura know where the new files are. When copying is done within Ventura, the CHP file is updated. When copying is done outside of Ventura, no updating of the CHP file occurs; when you later try to load the chapter, Ventura may not be able to find the style sheet, text or graphic files, Ventura-generated files, or width table.

3.12 Tip

Use the Multi-Chapter command to move or transfer chapters or files.

To move chapters or publications to another location on your hard drive or to copy a chapter or publication to a floppy disk for archiving or transferring to another system, use Ventura's Multi-Chapter command. Copying a single chapter is obviously not really a multiple-chapter operation, but no other way is available for you to copy a chapter with Ventura. Just remember that the chapter-copying function is with the Multi-Chapter menu choice.

To use the Multi-Chapter command to copy a chapter to a floppy disk, do the following:

1. Click Multi-Chapter from the Options menu.
2. Click New to clear any previous selections.
3. Click Add Chapter to get to the ITEM SELECTOR dialog box.
4. Click the chapter of your choice and then click OK. (If you prefer, you can double-click the chapter of your choice.)
5. If you accidentally select a chapter you don't want, highlight it by clicking the chapter name and then click Remove Chap.
6. Click the chapter to highlight it.
7. Click Copy All (see fig. 3.5).

   The COPY ALL dialog box appears. The `SOURCE` area has a `PUB` or `CHP` line that lists the name of the chapter you want to copy. The `DESTINATION` area has five possible destinations that you can edit.

8. If you want to copy the chapter to drive A, type *a:* on the PUB & CHPs line. Remember the backslash, or you are prompted to insert the name of a directory.

9. Click the Make All Directories the Same As the First option, and all the directories are changed to A:\ (see fig. 3.6).

   A message box informs you of the progress of copying all the files to the floppy disk.

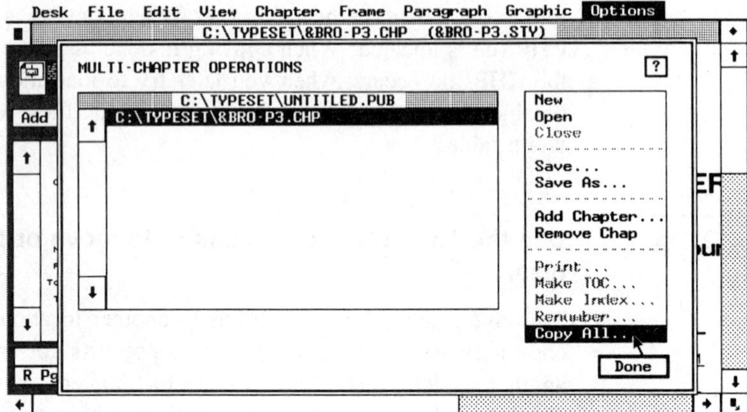

Fig. 3.5.
Selecting the Copy All command.

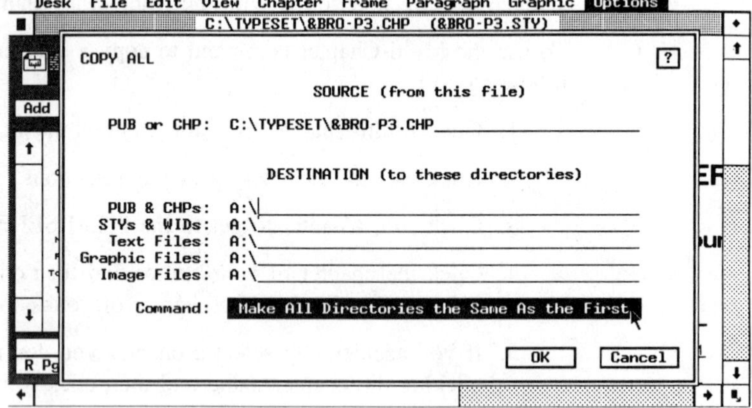

Fig. 3.6.
The COPY ALL dialog box.

3.13 Tip **When using the Copy All command, make sure that your destination has enough room for all the files to fit.**

If your hard disk does not have enough room, not all the files will be copied. Ventura does not check beforehand to make sure that enough room is available, so you will need to determine ahead of time the amount of space available or take a chance that you have enough space.

If you are trying to copy a chapter to a floppy disk for archival purposes, Ventura prompts you for additional disks if a single disk does not have enough room for all the files. Be sure to number the disks so you will be able to reverse the process easily.

3.14 Tip **Use VP Toolbox to delete or copy files from the DOS prompt.**

VP Toolbox from SNA, Inc., is a utility that works outside of Ventura (unlike Desktop Manager from New Riders, which is a memory-resident utility). VP Toolbox has powerful capabilities for editing style sheets; these capabilities are discussed in Chapter 5. VP Toolbox also allows you to delete or copy (not move) files, chapters, or publications from the DOS prompt.

DOS Capabilities from within Ventura

Most software packages offer poor DOS capabilities from within the program. Unfortunately, Ventura is no exception.

3.15 Tip **DOS operations within Ventura are limited. Learn the limitations and perform other necessary operations outside of Ventura.**

Ventura DOS operations that you can perform are limited to making a directory, removing a directory, and deleting files. To access the DOS FILE OPERATIONS dialog box (see fig. 3.7), click the DOS File Ops selection from the File menu.

Clicking the `Select Different File Specification` option takes you to the ITEM SELECTOR dialog box (see Tip 3.8 to learn how to change file specifications from this dialog box). You also can specify the directory and file filter of your choice on the `File Spec` line in the DOS FILE OPERATIONS dialog box.

By typing a new directory name and clicking the `Make Directory` option, you create a new directory by that name. By typing an empty existing directory name and clicking the `Remove Directory` option, you delete the directory you named. (You cannot remove a directory that contains files.)

If you want to delete files, type the full path and file filter (*.* for all files); then click the `Delete Matching File(s)` option. Ventura warns that you

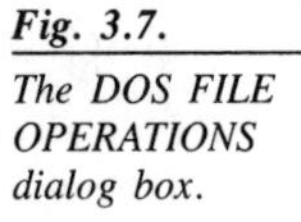

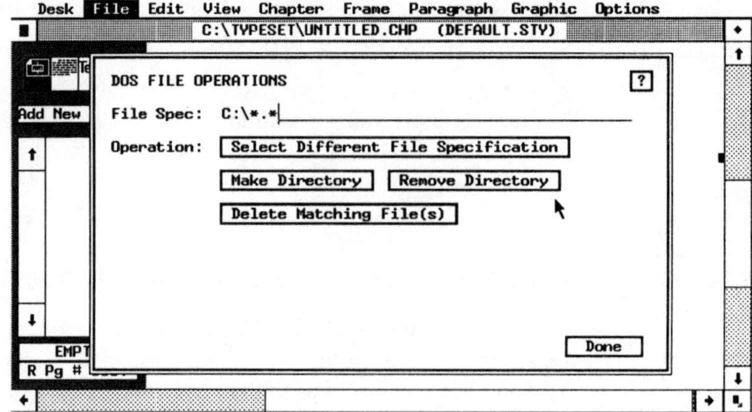

Fig. 3.7.

The DOS FILE OPERATIONS dialog box.

have requested it to delete files before proceeding. If you want to delete the specified files, click `Delete`; otherwise, click Cancel. (Pressing Ctrl-X, which usually triggers the Cancel button, does not work in the delete files warning box.)

Although you can delete files with the DOS File Ops command, you cannot move or copy files.

3.16 Tip

To obtain extensive DOS file capabilities from within Ventura, use Desktop Manager.

Desktop Manager is a Ventura add-on product from New Riders Publishing. Once installed, Desktop Manager is available for use at all times from inside Ventura. Desktop Manager has the following capabilities:

- ☐ Document control allows you to track a chapter's status. You can determine what the chapter is about and when it was written and last revised. You also can tell at a glance what the revision, printing, and archiving history is (see fig. 3.8).

- ☐ File information allows you to see at a glance all the files associated with a chapter, the type of file each is, the creation date, the file size, and the total size of all files associated with a chapter (see fig. 3.9).

- ☐ Style sheet information gives a listing of all tags in a style sheet. You can see at a glance the tag name, alignment, number of tabs, font face, size, style, and whether any special effects such as bullets are used (see fig. 3.10). Although you can view this information, you cannot edit it with Desktop Manager.

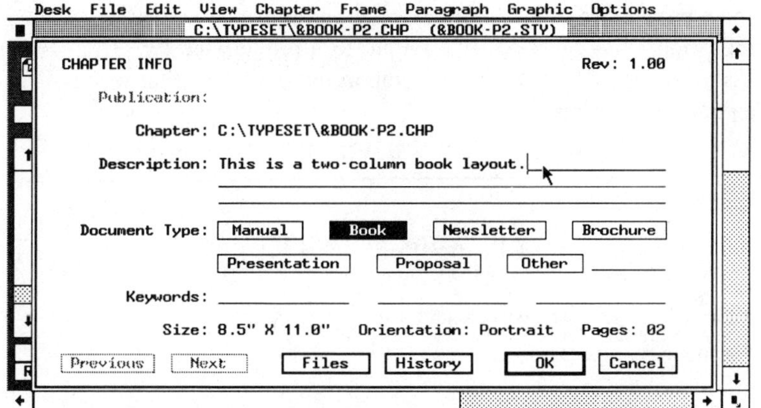

Fig. 3.8.

The Desktop Manager CHAPTER INFO dialog box.

Desk File Edit View Chapter Frame Paragraph Graphic Options

C:\TYPESET\SCOOP.CHP (SCOOP.STY)

FILE SIZES

Filename	Type	Date	Time	Size
SCOOP.CHP	CHAPTER	11/25/88	2:02 PM	2K
SCOOP.CIF	INFO	11/26/88	4:17 PM	1K
SCOOP.STY	STYLE	11/25/88	2:02 PM	2K
OUTPUT.WID	WIDTH	11/26/88	5:48 PM	132K
SCOOP.VGR	GRAPHICS	11/25/88	2:02 PM	1K
SCOOP.CAP	CAPTION	11/25/88	2:02 PM	1K
SCOOP2.TXT	TEXT	9/06/88	2:52 PM	1K
SCOOP1.TXT	TEXT	9/06/88	2:52 PM	3K
COLUMBIA.GEM	LINE ART	9/06/88	5:09 PM	13K

Total Size: 158K

File Name File Info Done

Fig. 3.9.

The Desktop Manager FILE SIZES information box.

Desk File Edit View Chapter Frame Paragraph Graphic Options

C:\TYPESET\SCOOP.CHP (SCOOP.STY)

STYLE SHEET INFO

Style Sheet: C:\TYPESET\SCOOP.STY

Tag Name	Size	Face	Style	Alignment	Tabs	Effects
Banner	9	Helvetica	Bold	Left	2	
Body Text	10	Times	Normal	Justified	8	
Caption 1	10	Helvetica	N-Italic	Left	2	
Headline 1	72	Times	Bold	Centered	2	
Headline 2	24	Helvetica	Bold	Left	2	
Sidebar	12	Times	B-Italic	Justified	2	
Z_BOXTEXT	10	Times	Normal	Left	8	
Z_CAPTION	8	Times	Normal	Justified	2	
Z_LABEL CAP	10	Helvetica	Normal	Centered	2	

Done

Fig. 3.10.

The Desktop Manager STYLE SHEET INFO dialog box.

- Report production prints information about a chapter or publication. You can direct the output to a printer (see fig. 3.11), a disk file, or a Ventura file (for importing and formatting within Ventura before printing).

Fig. 3.11.

A manager report produced by Desktop Manager.

3:52 PM 11/26/88

VP Manager Report

PUBLICATION:
CHAPTER: C:\TYPESET\SCOOP.CHP
STYLE SHEET: C:\TYPESET\SCOOP.STY
WIDTH TABLE: C:\VENTURA\OUTPUT.WID

DESCRIPTION: This is a sample newsletter which illustrates basic techniques for merging text and graphics into a document using frames

DOCUMENT TYPE: NEWSLETTER

KEYWORDS:

SIZE: 8.5" X 11.0" ORIENTATION: Portrait PAGES: 02

REVISIONS: PUB: 00 CHAPTER: 01.00

DATES -	LAST REV:	4/06/87	8:05 AM
	LAST PRINT:	6/12/87	9:37 AM
	LAST ARCHIVE:	6/12/87	9:37 AM
	CREATED:	6/12/87	9:37 AM

STAGE: FINAL DRAFT STATUS: ACTIVE

OUTLINE: 1/01/80 1ST DRAFT: 1/01/80 2ND DRAFT: 1/01/80 FINAL: 1/01/80

WRITER:
ILLUSTRATOR:
EDITOR:
MANAGER:

FILES:

C:\TYPESET\SCOOP.CHP	CHAPTER	11/25/88	2:02 PM	2K
C:\TYPESET\SCOOP.CIF	INFO	11/25/88	2:02 PM	1K
C:\TYPESET\SCOOP.STY	STYLE	11/25/88	2:02 PM	2K
C:\VENTURA\OUTPUT.WID	WIDTH	11/19/88	4:21 PM	33K
C:\TYPESET\SCOOP.VGR	GRAPHICS	11/25/88	2:02 PM	1K
C:\TYPESET\SCOOP.CAP	CAPTION	11/25/88	2:02 PM	1K
C:\TYPESET\SCOOP2.TXT	TEXT	9/06/88	2:52 PM	1K
C:\TYPESET\SCOOP1.TXT	TEXT	9/06/88	2:52 PM	3K
C:\TYPESET\COLUMBIA.GEM	LINE ART	9/06/88	5:09 PM	13K

- Backups can be done automatically every 5, 10, 15, or 30 minutes.
- File management is greatly enhanced. You can move or delete parts of or complete chapters and publications. Other features already available within Ventura, such as copying a chapter or publication, renaming a chapter or style sheet, and creating or deleting a directory, are consolidated into one dialog box (see fig. 3.12).

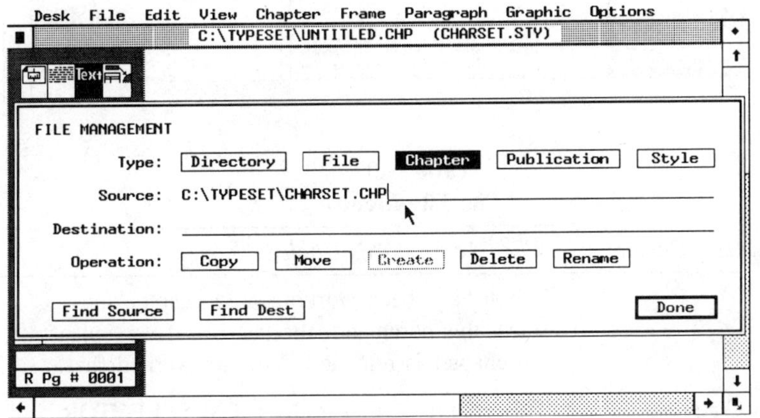

Fig. 3.12.
The Desktop Manager FILE MANAGEMENT dialog box.

If you are a frequent user of Ventura and have watched your chapters and their associated files grow over time, Desktop Manager will help you organize your existing files.

Using the File Menu

The File menu contains commands concerning file operations, including opening and saving chapters and style sheets, and loading text and graphics files.

3.17 Tip **Use the Ventura File menu for opening and saving files.**

From the menu bar, you can choose the File menu, which offers 11 selections (see fig. 3.13). Nine selections are discussed here. Table 3.3 provides information on when to use each option.

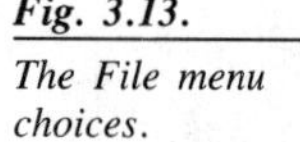

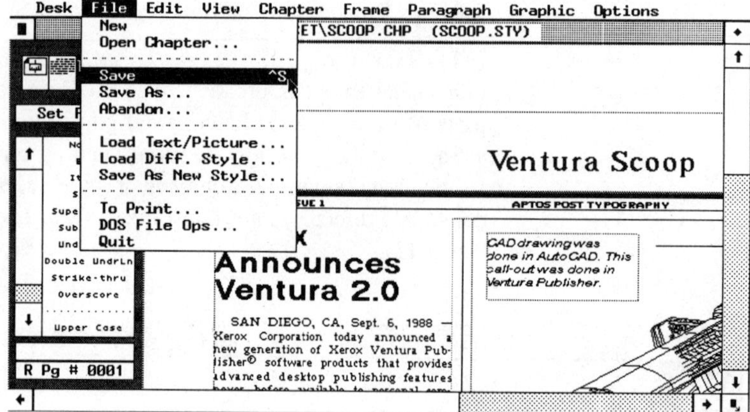

Fig. 3.13.

The File menu choices.

Table 3.3
The File Menu

File Menu Choice	*When To Use This Choice*
New	If you have been working on a chapter and select this command, the last saved version of the chapter is reloaded. You are warned first.
Open Chapter	This command makes the ITEM SELECTOR dialog box appear with the file filter *.CHP. Whatever chapter you select is loaded. If you are currently working on a chapter that has not been saved, you are given the opportunity to save your work.
Save ^S	This command (or the keyboard shortcut Ctrl-S) saves your chapter, including all associated files that have been modified, and the style sheet. Use this command often while working on a chapter, to avoid losing your work if the computer loses power or Ventura crashes. Better yet, use Desktop Manager to back up your work automatically at timed intervals. If you have not named the chapter previously, issuing this command is the same as issuing the Save As command.

Table 3.3—*Continued*

File Menu Choice	*When To Use This Choice*
Save As	This command makes the ITEM SELECTOR dialog box appear to allow you to save the current chapter under a new name. You may want to use this command if you are making changes to a chapter but want to retain the original intact. If you plan to retain the original work, issue this command as soon as you open the chapter so you don't forget and lose previous work.
Abandon	This command invokes a prompt, asking whether you want to save or abandon the current work to restore the last saved version of the chapter. If you click Abandon, Ventura loads the last saved version of the chapter you are working on.
Load Text/Picture	This command allows you to load text, line art, or images into the current chapter.
Load Diff. Style	This command makes the ITEM SELECTOR dialog box appear with the file filter *.STY to allow you to apply another style sheet to the current chapter.
Save As New Style	This command works the same as Save As but concerns only the style sheet.
Quit	This command quits Ventura. Before leaving, you are given the chance to save the chapter and style sheet you are working on if they were previously unsaved.

3.18 Trick

Use the File Type/Rename command on the Edit menu to rename text files from within Ventura.

You can rename files from within Ventura if you follow a few rules. First, you can only rename files that are on the assignment list—files that already have been loaded by Ventura. Second, the file must be in a frame. Third, only text files are eligible. To rename a text file, follow these steps:

1. Click the frame that contains the file you want to rename. The file name should appear in the current selection box on the sidebar.

2. Click the File Type/Rename command from the Edit menu.
3. Change the path and/or name on the New Name line of the FILE TYPE/RENAME dialog box (see fig. 3.14). Notice that you also can change the file format from this dialog box. (Changing the file format is discussed in Chapter 4.)
4. Click OK or press Enter.

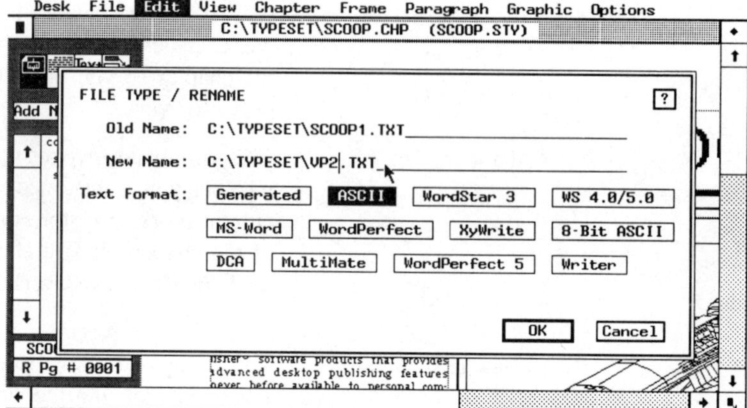

Fig. 3.14.
The FILE TYPE/ RENAME dialog box.

The file name is now changed, and the change should be reflected in both the current selection box and the dialog box.

You cannot change the names of graphics files by using this method.

Using Style Sheets

Any time you create a document—whether with a word processing, spreadsheet, or desktop publishing program—you carefully determine how you want the final product to look. In many cases, each time you create similar documents, you have to redo all the margins and reselect the fonts—essentially recreate the format. In Ventura, using style sheets, you do not need to redesign similar documents once you have determined the way you want a specific type of document to look. Comprehensive understanding of style sheets is the key to saving time with Ventura. Chapter 5 offers comprehensive information about style sheets.

Chapter Summary

Many topics were examined in this chapter. You learned several ways to create a manageable filing system for the files you create and the files Ventura generates. You also learned all the file extensions Ventura uses for files it creates and what those files are for. You learned to use file filters to locate rapidly the file you want to load into Ventura. You gained expertise in moving up and down directory levels by using the ITEM SELECTOR dialog box.

The limitations of Ventura DOS operations were discussed, and several ways around those limitations with Ventura utilities, such as VP Tools and Desktop Manager, were examined. You also learned about the options on the File menu bar and when to use each one. And you learned how to copy, move, and delete chapters and their associated files for archiving or to free up disk space.

Up to this point, you have spent time learning about the basics of Ventura. In the following chapters, you will examine text handling, style sheets, and frames.

Part II

Working with Text

Includes

Importing and Changing Text

Understanding Style Sheets

Understanding Frames

Chapter

4

Importing and Changing Text

Ventura is the consummate desktop publishing program; Ventura is not a word processor. What is the difference?

With the introduction of full-bodied word processors such as FullWrite™ on the Macintosh and WordPerfect 5.0 on IBM-compatible PCs, word processing has taken a step in the direction of desktop publishing—but only a first step. With the introduction of desktop publishing programs such as Ready, Set, Go! for the Macintosh that offer word processing features such as search and replace and spell checking, desktop publishing has taken a small step in the direction of word processing. In the opinion of many experts, this trend of word processors embodying more desktop publishing features and vice versa will continue until the two types of software are merged.

Currently, however, word processors don't even begin to offer the advanced typographic and layout control of Ventura. Ventura's graphical interface allows you to see on the monitor what the document will look like when printed—the so-called WYSIWYG (what you see is what you get) interface—and is far ahead of similar features on word processors.

On the other hand, no desktop publishing programs even begin to offer the advanced editing capabilities and cursor handling of even inexpensive word processors. The makers of Ventura recognized this lack of word processing capability and made it easy for you to use a word processor to create text to import later for design and layout with Ventura. At the same time, Ventura offers limited editing capabilities for adding to, deleting, and modifying text.

Then, realizing that you may want to take a last look at the text with your word processor (perhaps for spell checking), Ventura saves any modifications you make to your originally imported file.

Finally, acknowledging that you may want to use information from databases or spreadsheets as the basis for or as enhancements to documents, Ventura allows you to import data from almost any other type of program. Not only does Ventura allow you to import data, but if you choose, the spreadsheet, database, or word processor can embed formatting information directly into the text before importing into Ventura. This feature automates much of the formatting effort and saves you time, especially with frequently produced reports.

This chapter discusses creating and importing text from a variety of sources, including word processors, database programs, and spreadsheets. You also learn about Ventura's Text mode and how to mark, insert, delete, move, copy, and modify text. Finally, you will see how to insert special items such as box characters and fractions in Ventura.

Creating Text in a Word Processor

Words are one-third of what Ventura is all about; the other two-thirds are graphics and formatting. Interestingly, although Ventura has some basic editing capabilities, it relies primarily on text produced by word processors such as Microsoft Word, XyWrite, and WordPerfect.

On the positive side, you will not have to learn another word processor to use Ventura. On the negative side, you *will* have to move between your word processor and Ventura during the production of your final product.

This section helps you understand the relationship between Ventura and your word processor. "Working in the Text Mode" later in this chapter deals with editing within Ventura.

4.1 Tip **Use your regular word processor to create text to import later into Ventura.**

Ventura can accept text from virtually any word processor on the market. For some of the popular word processors, many formatting attributes such as underline and boldface transfer directly; for some less widely used word processors, although formatting commands may not transfer, the text imports without difficulty.

Word processors such as Lotus Manuscript™, DisplayWrite, Volkswriter®, Office Writer, WordStar 2000 (not WordStar 3, 4, or 5), and SAMNA Word™

are not directly supported by Ventura. You must first convert the files created by these word processors into DCA Version 2.0 Revisable Form Text files. Refer to the documentation for the specific word processor to learn how to make this conversion.

Word processors such as Microsoft Word, MultiMate, WordPerfect (including Version 5.0), WordStar (including Version 5.0), Xerox Writer, and XyWrite (including Versions II and III) are directly supported by Ventura. You can import files from these programs without additional conversion.

Other word processors may be able to save files or convert them to DCA Version 2.0 Revisable Form Text or one of the formats of the directly supported word processors. If not, most all word processors allow you to save, convert, or print to disk in plain ASCII format. Ventura can import ASCII files.

4.2 Trap

Ventura modifies the text file you import. Use a copy of the file instead of the original.

Ventura does not actually incorporate your text file into a chapter; instead, the text file is ''linked'' to the chapter. Any editing done in Ventura modifies the text file. If you add or delete any text, the text file you loaded into the chapter has text added or deleted.

A good practice is to use one of the strategies for file organization described in Chapter 3. If you follow one of those strategies, you load a copy of your text file—keeping the original in unmodified form.

Keeping an original in unmodified form is good for at least two reasons: One, if anything should happen to the file used by Ventura, you have a backup so you can begin again. (Yes, Ventura has been known to crash and damage files—another reason to back-up your work frequently.) Two, if you want to print the text file using a word processor, the unmodified file is not cluttered with Ventura codes.

Figure 4.1 is a printout of a document originated in WordPerfect. Notice that no formatting codes are in the text; the document is what you are accustomed to either creating or receiving from a word processor. Figure 4.2 is another story altogether. After formatting in Ventura, several paragraphs have been tagged with @ formatting commands (paragraph tags inserted by Ventura are discussed later in this chapter). Quotation marks, double dashes, and ellipses have been replaced by numbers surrounded by less-than and greater-than signs (< >). The book title *Laurel's Kitchen Cookbook* in the sixth paragraph is also surrounded by codes so that the title will be italicized.

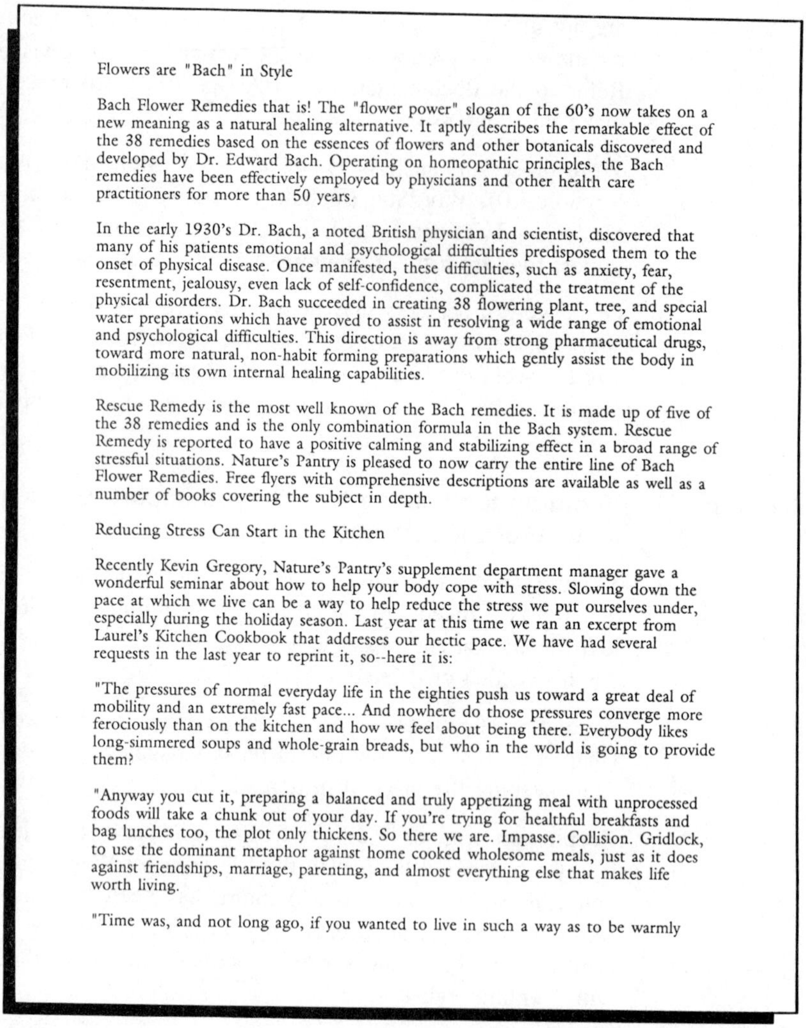

Fig. 4.1.

Unformatted original text file.

Flowers are "Bach" in Style

Bach Flower Remedies that is! The "flower power" slogan of the 60's now takes on a new meaning as a natural healing alternative. It aptly describes the remarkable effect of the 38 remedies based on the essences of flowers and other botanicals discovered and developed by Dr. Edward Bach. Operating on homeopathic principles, the Bach remedies have been effectively employed by physicians and other health care practitioners for more than 50 years.

In the early 1930's Dr. Bach, a noted British physician and scientist, discovered that many of his patients emotional and psychological difficulties predisposed them to the onset of physical disease. Once manifested, these difficulties, such as anxiety, fear, resentment, jealousy, even lack of self-confidence, complicated the treatment of the physical disorders. Dr. Bach succeeded in creating 38 flowering plant, tree, and special water preparations which have proved to assist in resolving a wide range of emotional and psychological difficulties. This direction is away from strong pharmaceutical drugs, toward more natural, non-habit forming preparations which gently assist the body in mobilizing its own internal healing capabilities.

Rescue Remedy is the most well known of the Bach remedies. It is made up of five of the 38 remedies and is the only combination formula in the Bach system. Rescue Remedy is reported to have a positive calming and stabilizing effect in a broad range of stressful situations. Nature's Pantry is pleased to now carry the entire line of Bach Flower Remedies. Free flyers with comprehensive descriptions are available as well as a number of books covering the subject in depth.

Reducing Stress Can Start in the Kitchen

Recently Kevin Gregory, Nature's Pantry's supplement department manager gave a wonderful seminar about how to help your body cope with stress. Slowing down the pace at which we live can be a way to help reduce the stress we put ourselves under, especially during the holiday season. Last year at this time we ran an excerpt from Laurel's Kitchen Cookbook that addresses our hectic pace. We have had several requests in the last year to reprint it, so--here it is:

"The pressures of normal everyday life in the eighties push us toward a great deal of mobility and an extremely fast pace... And nowhere do those pressures converge more ferociously than on the kitchen and how we feel about being there. Everybody likes long-simmered soups and whole-grain breads, but who in the world is going to provide them?

"Anyway you cut it, preparing a balanced and truly appetizing meal with unprocessed foods will take a chunk out of your day. If you're trying for healthful breakfasts and bag lunches too, the plot only thickens. So there we are. Impasse. Collision. Gridlock, to use the dominant metaphor against home cooked wholesome meals, just as it does against friendships, marriage, parenting, and almost everything else that makes life worth living.

"Time was, and not long ago, if you wanted to live in such a way as to be warmly

4.3 Trap

Ventura does not understand all of your word processor's formatting. Avoid formatting that Ventura does not understand.

Ventura is smart about translating some formatting codes from your word processor into identical formatting instructions for itself. Many word processor formatting codes, however, are not handled well and are lost. To save yourself extra work, avoid formatting that Ventura does not understand.

Ventura supports the following text attributes: bold, underline, superscript, subscript, strike-through, discretionary hyphen, and nonbreaking space. Other

```
@SUBHEAD = Flowers are <169>Bach<170> in Style

@DROPCAP PARA = Bach Flower Remedies that is! The <169>flower power<170>
slogan of the 60's now takes on a new meaning as a natural healing alternative. It
aptly describes the remarkable effect of the 38 remedies based on the essences of
flowers and other botanicals discovered and developed by Dr. Edward Bach.
Operating on homeopathic principles, the Bach remedies have been effectively
employed by physicians and other health care practitioners for more than 50 years.

In the early 1930's Dr. Bach, a noted British physician and scientist, discovered that
many of his patients emotional and psychological difficulties predisposed them to
the onset of physical disease. Once manifested, these difficulties, such as anxiety,
fear, resentment, jealousy, even lack of self-confidence, complicated the treatment
of the physical disorders. Dr. Bach succeeded in creating 38 flowering plant, tree,
and special water preparations which have proved to assist in resolving a wide
range of emotional and psychological difficulties. This direction is away from
strong pharmaceutical drugs, toward more natural, non-habit forming preparations
which gently assist the body in mobilizing its own internal healing capabilities.

Rescue Remedy is the most well known of the Bach remedies. It is made up of
five of the 38 remedies and is the only combination formula in the Bach system.
Rescue Remedy is reported to have a positive calming and stabilizing effect in a
broad range of stressful situations. Nature's Pantry is pleased to now carry the
entire line of Bach Flower Remedies. Free flyers with comprehensive descriptions
are available as well as a number of books covering the subject in depth.

@SUBHEAD = Reducing Stress Can Start in the Kitchen

@DROPCAP PARA = Recently Kevin Gregory, Nature's Pantry's supplement
department manager gave a wonderful seminar about how to help your body cope
with stress. Slowing down the pace at which we live can be a way to help reduce
the stress we put ourselves under, especially during the holiday season. Last year
at this time we ran an excerpt from <MI>Laurel's Kitchen Cookbook<D> that
addresses our hectic pace. We have had several requests in the last year to reprint
it, so<197>here it is:

<169>The pressures of normal everyday life in the eighties push us toward a great
deal of mobility and an extremely fast pace<193> And nowhere do those pressures
converge more ferociously than on the kitchen and how we feel about being there.
Everybody likes long-simmered soups and whole-grain breads, but who in the
world is going to provide them?

<169>Anyway you cut it, preparing a balanced and truly appetizing meal with
unprocessed foods will take a chunk out of your day. If you're trying for healthful
breakfasts and bag lunches too, the plot only thickens. So there we are. Impasse.
Collision. Gridlock, to use the dominant metaphor against home cooked wholesome
meals, just as it does against friendships, marriage, parenting, and almost
everything else that makes life worth living.
```

Fig. 4.2.

Text file after insertion of Ventura formatting codes.

attributes such as italics or font changes are not supported unless you insert special formatting codes. Ventura's special codes are discussed later in this chapter.

Ventura does not support some attribute combinations, centering, flush right, or tabs other than left tab. Footnotes, page numbers, indexes, or tables of contents automatically generated by your word processor aren't supported by Ventura. See Chapter 11 to learn how to create footnotes, page numbers, indexes, or tables of contents with Ventura.

4.4 Trap

Some tabs inserted by WordStar may not act like tabs in Ventura.

Some tabs created by WordStar are not really tabs; they are spaces. In WordStar, it doesn't matter whether tabs are tabs or whether tabs are spaces. But in Ventura, using proportional type, space-tabs don't do the same job as tabs that push text an absolute distance. To ensure that WordStar inserts real tab characters, be sure that the Vari-Tab command in WordStar is turned off.

4.5 Trap

Tabs work differently in Ventura than in most word processors. Insert tabs rather than spaces. Don't insert spaces or tabs to indent paragraphs and don't use more than one space after a period or colon.

If you are accustomed to using typewriters, you know there's no difference between setting a tab of five and pressing the space bar five times. With Ventura, there's a big difference between spaces and tabs, and in most cases you use both differently than you may be used to doing. Here are some pointers regarding the way spaces and tabs are treated by Ventura:

- ❑ Ventura measures *absolute* rather than *relative* horizontal distance. If you insert five spaces expecting them to behave as a tab stop of five, proportional type does not align the space-tabs correctly. In proportional type, each letter width is different. Unless you use a monospace type such as Courier, space-tabs don't work.
- ❑ Many word processors measure horizontal lines by the number of characters. More advanced word processors allow you the option of measuring in characters or inches. Set your word processor measurements in inches and use the same tab-stop measurements for paragraph tags in Ventura. That way, the formatting in your word processor closely approximates what Ventura produces, saving you time and effort in reformatting.
- ❑ Ventura usually *justifies* lines; the right edge of text lines up with the right margin and the left edge of text lines up with the left margin. Justification takes precedence over tab settings. If a paragraph in Ventura is justified, the tab settings are ignored and tabs do not work.
- ❑ Ventura can automatically indent paragraphs. Set `First Line` to `Indent` on the ALIGNMENT dialog box, which you access from the Paragraph menu, instead of inserting spaces or tabs to indent a paragraph.

- Regardless of what your ninth-grade typing instructor told you, when you create text with a typeset look, insert only one space after periods, question marks, and colons. If you leave two spaces and use proportional type, too much of a gap results. If you have already created text with two spaces after terminal punctuation, do a search for two spaces and replace with one space with your word processor (if it has search and replace capability).

4.6 Trap

Extra carriage returns in your original document create too much space between paragraphs when imported into Ventura.

Commonly, people press Enter twice after each paragraph. Although the extra space between paragraphs makes a document more readable, Ventura provides more precise controls over interparagraph spacing, making the insertion of two carriage returns unnecessary.

Fortunately, you can continue to insert two returns after each paragraph, if that is the way you are used to writing, and then let Ventura know you want the second carriage return ignored. To have Ventura filter the extra returns, type the following at the beginning of your document:

@PARAFILTR ON =

Note the spelling of this text. For some reason, Ventura omits the *E* in the word *FILTER*. If you misspell this tag, the tag will not work.

Remember to type this filter tag into the document with your word processor; the filter will not work if you try to add it after you have loaded the file into Ventura.

To have Ventura recognize some double carriage returns in your document, even if you have set the filter on, press Enter, press the space bar once, and press Enter the second time.

4.7 Tip

Learn the formatting commands that can be embedded into the text before it is imported into Ventura.

One of the great strengths of Ventura is its capacity to import "preformatted" text. *Preformatting* is the insertion of codes into the text before importing that text into Ventura. Two types of preformatting can be employed, both of which are done with the word processor:

- Paragraphs can be tagged with @*TAG NAME* =. Use an at sign (@), followed by the name of a tag (up to 13 characters long, with or without spaces), followed by an equal (=) sign. Precede and follow the equal sign with a space. If tag names already exist in a style sheet when you import the document into Ventura, the tagged paragraphs assume the attributes of the tags. If no tags by those names exist in the style sheet, the tags are assigned, but the attributes of the tags are those of the Body Text tag and the tag names appear in all capital letters in the assignment list.

- ❑ Embedded codes are enclosed by angle brackets, also called the less-than and greater-than symbols (< >). Embedded codes allow you to set text attributes, insert nonkeyboard characters, and set special Ventura controls. Refer to Appendix A for the charts of symbols and dingbats. On that chart, under ''Roman,'' you can find the decimal equivalents of nonkeyboard characters—typographical symbols you cannot type in directly from the keyboard. To insert a degree sign, for example, type *<198>* into your text file with your word processor. When you load the file into Ventura, the <198> is converted into a degree sign (°). (If you want to include the angle brackets, type <<>>, <<>, or <>>.)

4.8 Trap

If you embed a tag command into your text file, be sure that the tag name is identical to the tag defined in Ventura.

Ventura treats tags you insert into your document using the @ command as undefined tags if those tags are not spelled *exactly* the same as in the style sheet. Undefined tags are treated the same as Body Text tags. Be sure that you spell and space the tag name correctly; capitalization doesn't matter.

If you want to add a tag when entering text with your word processor and that tag has not been previously defined in Ventura, do the following:

1. Type the tag name into the document with your word processor (for example, *@NEW TAG =*).
2. Load the file into Ventura. In Paragraph mode, you see the tag name `NEW TAG` in the assignment list.
3. Click the paragraph that you tagged with the NEW TAG tag. You see `NEW TAG` in the selection box. Now you can assign to the tag any paragraph attributes you desire. Once assigned, all paragraphs tagged with the NEW TAG tag reflect those attributes.

4.9 Tip — You can set text attributes by preformatting.

Ventura has a series of codes that can be used for preformatting. Some of these codes can be used regularly. Other codes are used less often in preformatting and should be set transparently in Ventura.

You should preformat text attributes when you want specific words or phrases to have different characteristics than those specified by the paragraph tag. If you want the word *one* to be italicized in a paragraph of unitalicized text, for example, preformat the attribute in your word processor by placing the proper format codes around the word: <I>one<D>.

Here are a few notes about the use of text attribute commands: First, several attributes can be combined within a single set of angle brackets. *<BIP14>*, for example, specifies bold italic type in 14-point size. Second, all attributes are turned off at the end of a paragraph or when you type *<D>*. Third, all attributes are turned off as soon as another attribute command is encountered, and only the new attribute command has any effect.

Table 4.1 lists preformatting codes that you will use regularly.

Table 4.1
Regularly Used Preformatting Codes

Code	*Attribute*
< B >	Boldface (also can be set by most word processors)
< U >	Underline (also can be set by most word processors)
< ^ >	Superscript (also can be set by most word processors)
< v >	Subscript (also can be set by most word processors)
< X >	Strike-through (also can be set by most word processors)
< M >	Medium-weight type (Roman)
< I >	Italics
< = >	Double-underline
< O >	Overscore
< S >	Small type
< D >	Resume normal (not needed at end of paragraph where all text attributes are turned off automatically)

Table 4.1—*Continued*

Code	*Attribute*
< P*n* >	Changes point size to the size specified by *n*
< - >	Discretionary hyphen (for words that may not be hyphenated properly by Ventura)
< N >	Nonbreaking space (treats the space as a character so names like ''John Smith'' remain on the same line)
< $!text >	Hidden text for notes that don't display in Ventura. Use hidden text to write notes, comments, or reminders that will not appear in Ventura.
< R >	Line break. Does not insert a paragraph return but forces a new line (useful in database applications)
< $F*text* >	Footnote text that appears at the bottom of the page referenced by the footnote
< $ >	Creates fractions. Insert the <$> code followed by *numerator/denominator* or *numerator* over *denominator* (for example, <$>1/2 or <$>1 over 2 produces ½).

Table 4.2 lists codes that are not used regularly but may be useful to you at times. These codes are inserted in text with your word processor.

Table 4.2
Rarely Used Preformatting Codes

Code	*Attribute*
< $B() >	Hollow box
< $B1 >	Filled box
< _ >	Em space
< ~ >	En space
< + >	Figure space
< | >	Thin space
< F*n* >	Changes typeface, where *n* represents one of the Font ID numbers recognized by Ventura. See Appendix K of your Ventura manual for a list of the Font ID numbers.

Table 4.2—*Continued*

Code	*Attribute*
< C*n* >	Changes color, where *n* represents one of the eight colors available to Ventura (with PostScript printers, the colors may be set for special text effects rather than colors; see Chapter 9). Colors are white (0), black (1), red (2), green (3), blue (4), cyan (5), yellow (6), and magenta (7). Reset color to the tag default with <255>.
< J*n* >	Base line jump by *n* points. This can be set after you mark text in Edit mode by clicking the Set Font button and using the `Shift Up/Down` option. If you must use this command, calculate jumps up using the following formula: n=256−(4.17*pt. size); calculate jumps down using the following formula: n=(4.17* pt. size). To jump up 10 points, for example, the calculation is 256−(4.17*10)=214, so the command is <J214>. To jump down 10 points, the calculation is (4.17*10)=42, so the command is <J42> (round to the nearest whole number).
< B%*n* >	*Kerning*, or increasing or decreasing the space between letters, can be done visually on-screen. If you want to kern with this command, specify *n* in em spaces (positive or negative values are acceptable).
< $R[C#] >	Chapter number. Replace # with the chapter number (see Chapter 11 for more information).
< $R[P#] >	Page number. Replace # with the page number (see Chapter 11 for more information).
< $&*n*[*x*] >	Anchor reference. Replace *n* with the name of the anchor. Replace *x* with the anchor position: use *v* for below, ^ for above, and − for automatic. If you omit the brackets, the anchor is fixed on the same page. *<$&Graph7[^]>*, for example, places the frame named "Graph7" in the line above the text containing the anchor reference.

Table 4.2—Continued

Code	*Attribute*
< $I*P*[*PS*];*S*[*SS*] >	Index reference. Replace *P* with the primary entry and *S* with the secondary entry. Replace *PS* and *SS* with the primary and secondary sorting keys. Replace *$I* with *$S* or *$A* for *See* or *See Also* references (see Chapter 11 for more information on indexing your publication).

4.10 Tip

Use keyboard shortcuts to insert special typographical characters.

Producing documents that look typeset is the reason that you use Ventura. In ‘‘real’’ typesetting, you can access many typographical symbols not available to users of personal computers in the past. Ventura allows keyboard input of many typographical symbols.

Examine table 4.3 to see what special typographical characters you can enter directly into text using Ventura.

Table 4.3
Special Text Characters and Keyboard Shortcuts

Special Character	*Keyboard Shortcut*
Copyright mark ©	Ctrl-Shift-C
Trademark (circle) ®	Ctrl-Shift-R
Trademark (TM) ™	Ctrl-Shift-2
Em space	Ctrl-Shift-M
En space	Ctrl-Shift-N
Figure space	Ctrl-Shift-F
Thin space	Ctrl-Shift-T
Nonbreaking space	Ctrl-Spacebar
Open quotation mark ‘‘	Ctrl-Shift-[(can be automatically converted)

Table 4.3—*Continued*

Special Character	*Keyboard Shortcut*
Close quotation mark ”	Ctrl-Shift-] (can be automatically converted)
Em dash —	Ctrl-]
En dash –	Ctrl-[
Discretionary hyphen	Ctrl -
End of line	Ctrl-Enter

4.11 Trap

Certain typographical symbols such as en dashes, registered trademarks, and copyright symbols cannot be entered directly with your word processor. Learn Ventura's embedded commands to get these symbols.

Although Ventura allows keyboard input of many typographical symbols, it does not allow for all possibilities. Two ways are available for you to indirectly enter special characters not available from keyboard shortcuts:

- Enter the decimal code of the special typographical character between angle brackets using your word processor. Look at the character set charts under "Roman" in Appendix A for a listing of the characters and their decimal-code equivalents. If, for example, you want to enter the British pound sterling sign, (decimal 156), type *<156>*. When the file is imported into Ventura, the embedded <156> code automatically converts to £.

- If you are in Ventura and want to insert a special character, look up the character set decimal equivalent of the symbol you want in Appendix A. Press and hold the Alt key and type the decimal value using the numeric keypad (do not use the numbers at the top of the keyboard). To get the British pound sterling sign, hold the Alt key and type *1 5 6*. The correct symbol appears on the screen.

You can use either of these techniques for any of the special typographical characters available in the Ventura character set. Figure 4.3 gives examples of special characters entered either with keyboard shortcuts or with the Alt key and the numeric keypad.

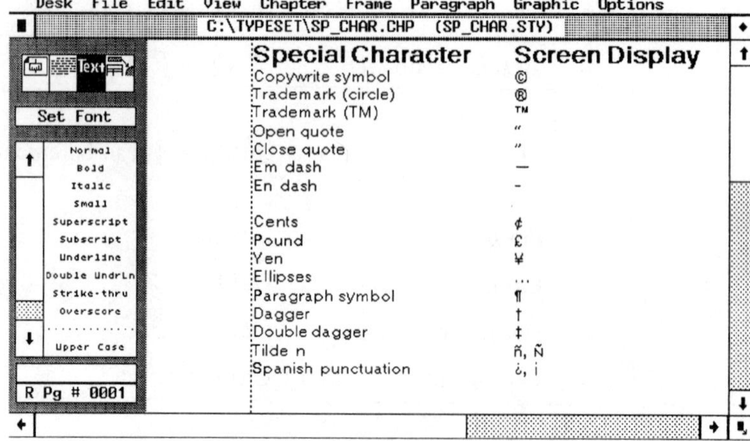

Fig. 4.3.

Special characters and Ventura screen display.

4.12 Tip

Either embed codes for typographical quotation marks (“smart” quotation marks) and em dashes or tell Ventura to handle the conversion automatically.

One distinct difference between the material produced by personal computer software in the past and the material produced by sophisticated layout programs such as Ventura is the capacity to have typographical or ‘‘smart’’ quotation marks and em dashes.

In the past, quotation marks and apostrophes were of the straight up and down variety (see fig. 4.4). With Ventura, you can insert typographical quotation marks in one of three ways:

- ❑ Use the keyboard shortcut in Ventura when entering text to insert open (Ctrl-Shift-[) or close (Ctrl-Shift-]) quotation marks.
- ❑ Use your word processor to insert the decimal codes inside angle brackets into your text file for open quotation marks (<169>) and close quotation marks (<170>). You can create a macro by using a word processor (if it has macro capability) or a program such as SuperKey to search for and replace regular quotation marks with the Ventura-embedded codes.
- ❑ Use Ventura’s capacity to convert quotation marks and double dashes automatically into smart quotation marks and em dashes. Select Set Preferences from the Options menu and set the `Auto-Adjustments` option to `''` and `--` or `Both` (see fig. 4.5). Then, whenever you load a text file, Ventura automatically converts straight up and down quotation marks and double dashes to smart quotation marks and em dashes.

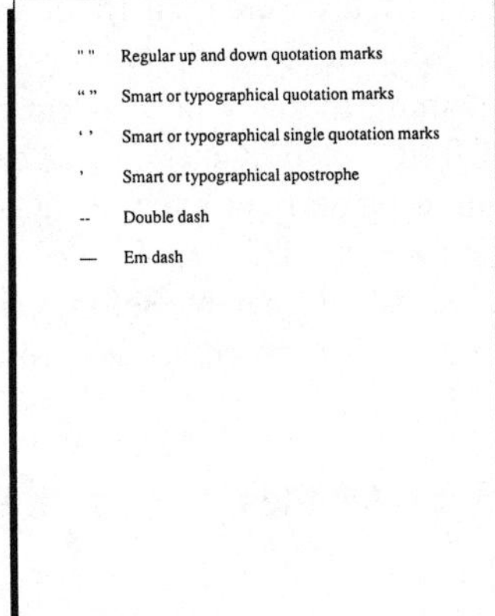

Fig. 4.4.
Typographical punctuation printed on a laser printer.

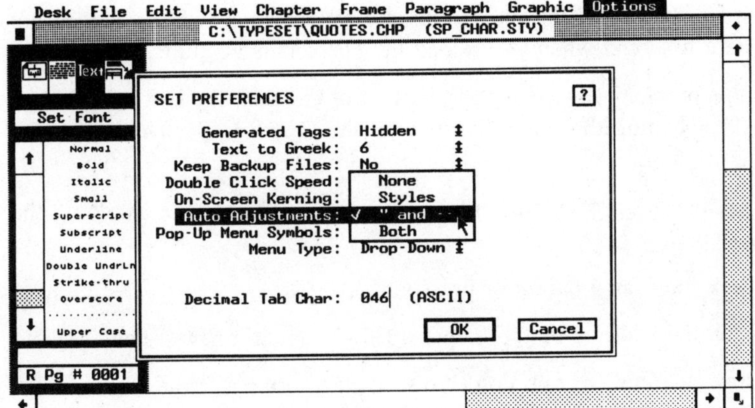

Fig. 4.5.
The Auto-Adjustments *option in the SET PREFERENCES dialog box.*

4.13 Tip

Use your word processor's spell checking feature to check for spelling errors in text you enter with Ventura's text editor.

Ventura is not a full-featured word processor and cannot check documents for spelling errors. Most word processors such as WordPerfect, WordStar, and Microsoft Word come with built-in spelling checkers. Be sure to verify spelling before importing your files into Ventura. Following are some suggestions to help you avoid spelling errors in text you enter by using Ventura:

- ❑ If you use Ventura to add to existing text files, use your word processor to recheck the edited file for errors before printing a final copy.

- ❑ If you need to add a block of text, create a frame and enter the text into the new frame. Ventura saves the text in a CAP file. If you click the frame containing the new text and then use the File Type/Rename command from the Edit menu, you can give the block of text in the frame a name (and even designate your preferred word processor format). Trap 4.14 gives details on this procedure. Make a note of the file name. Before printing a final copy, load the file into your word processor and run a spell check.

4.14 Trap

You can spell check and edit CAP files, but don't alter the spacing in the CAP file.

The Caption file (CAP file) contains text you enter for either box text, captions, or text entered into empty frames in Edit mode. You can load the CAP file as an ASCII text file into your word processor, run a spell check, and do *minor* editing. If any of the paragraphs are altered in length, text does not appear where it should when you reload the chapter in Ventura.

To avoid this problem, always make a backup of the CAP file before running a spell check or editing the file. That way, if the CAP file is altered, you can restore the original.

Better yet, save the text entered into a frame as a separate file by doing the following steps:

1. Click the Frame button or press Ctrl-U.
2. Click the addition button or press Ctrl-2 to add a new frame.
3. Draw a frame. (If you don't know how to draw a frame, see Chapter 6.)
4. Click the Text button or press Ctrl-O.
5. Enter the text into the empty frame.
6. Click the Frame button or press Ctrl-U.
7. Select the frame into which you just entered text by clicking it. Notice that the selection box says `FRAME TEXT`.
8. Click the File Type/Rename command from the Edit menu. You see the FILE TYPE/RENAME dialog box (see fig. 4.6).
9. In the space next to the `New Name` prompt, type the path where you want the file stored followed by what you want to name the file. You also can save the file in the format of your favorite word

processor—the file need not be saved as an ASCII file. (The Old Name line is empty because the file you are naming was originally frame text and didn't have a name.)

10. Click OK or press Enter.

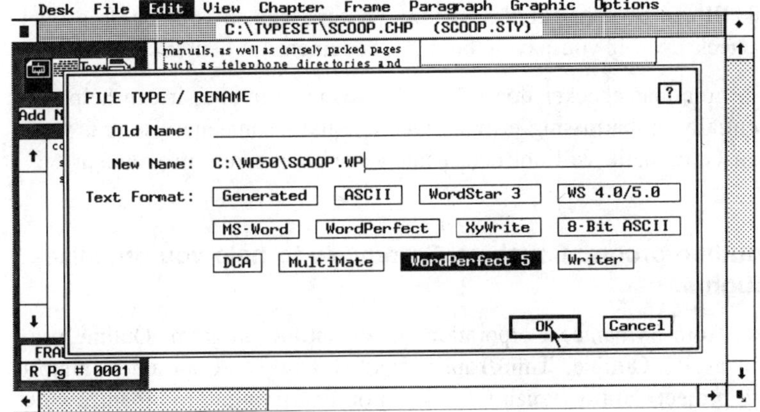

Fig. 4.6.
The FILE TYPE/RENAME dialog box.

The assignment list now shows the name of the new file. The new file is independent, not "tied" to any frame like CAP text is. Now you can spell check and edit the text file without worrying that altering size or spacing will damage the file.

If you change the length of the text, you may have to resize the frame if all the text is to fit correctly.

4.15 Tip

Limit your use of Ventura for text entry to short paragraphs. Use your word processor for longer additions.

Use your word processor for text entry longer than a few sentences. Ventura's text-editing capabilities are limited and best used for text generated within Ventura, such as headers, footers, and captions.

4.16 Tip

Use a grammar checker such as Grammatik III to proof your text.

A temptation with powerful formatting programs like Ventura is to allow the appearance of your text to become more important than what the text says. Although presenting your work in as pleasing and professional a way as possible is certain to have a positive effect on the reader, poorly written or ungrammatical prose will cause your reader's interest to wander faster than poor typography.

Using artificial intelligence techniques, programs such as Grammatik III from Reference Software check your document for common grammatical errors such as vague adverbs, cliches, archaic phrasing, and passive voice.

In addition, Grammatik III looks for unmatched punctuation (for example, an open parenthesis without a matching close parenthesis) and double words.

Grammatik III can be configured to ignore Ventura tags so you can do a final grammar check even if you have edited the document in Ventura.

Although a grammar checker doesn't do the writing for you, it can help you avoid potentially embarrassing errors. Even so, have someone else read your work. Even Grammatik will not detect many common errors in grammar.

4.17 Tip

Use an outline program such as Grandview to help you organize your thoughts.

Grandview, from Symantec Corporation, is an outline program. Outline programs such as PC Outline, ThinkTank™, and Ready!™ are an aid to almost any writing project. Not only can you use an outline program to organize your ideas, you can export the outline and load it into Ventura for printing (see fig. 4.7).

I used Grandview extensively to help organize material for this book. Grandview is an extremely capable "thought organizer." You can use outline programs to help prepare charts and presentations that can be copied or printed on acetates for use with overhead projectors.

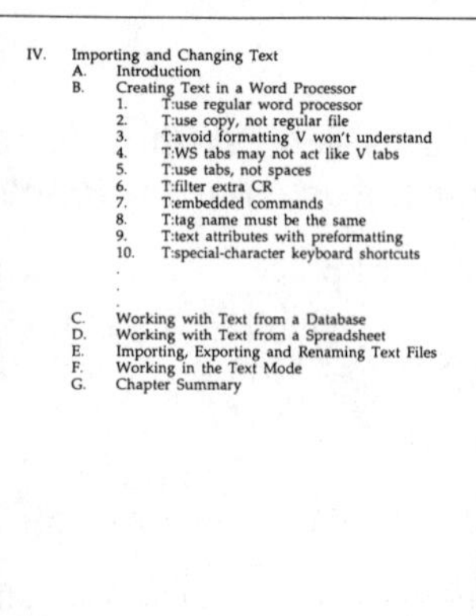

IV. Importing and Changing Text
  A. Introduction
  B. Creating Text in a Word Processor
    1. T:use regular word processor
    2. T:use copy, not regular file
    3. T:avoid formatting V won't understand
    4. T:WS tabs may not act like V tabs
    5. T:use tabs, not spaces
    6. T:filter extra CR
    7. T:embedded commands
    8. T:tag name must be the same
    9. T:text attributes with preformatting
    10. T:special-character keyboard shortcuts
    .
    .
    .
  C. Working with Text from a Database
  D. Working with Text from a Spreadsheet
  E. Importing, Exporting and Renaming Text Files
  F. Working in the Text Mode
  G. Chapter Summary

Fig. 4.7.

A portion of the outline of a current chapter produced by Grandview and formatted by Ventura.

Working with Text from a Database

One of the newest areas of interest in desktop publishing is publishing the data contained in databases in a near-typeset form. Ventura offers exciting formatting possibilities and even opens the way for new businesses such as directory and catalog publication. To get the most out of your database data, you must extract and massage the data into a form Ventura understands. To do the extraction, you may need to write a program in the language of the database. If you have a database of customer names and phone numbers, for example, and you want to create a directory for Ventura to publish, you must export the name and phone data into a file Ventura can use because Ventura cannot directly use the data in a database structure.

Once you have mastered the extraction and preparation of the data, you can produce directories, lists, and catalogs that are indistinguishable from the work of professional publishers.

4.18 Tip **Learn to extract information from your database program for database publishing.**

Database publishing is exciting. If your business maintains price, catalog, or customer lists in a database like dBASE IV™, you can easily "publish" the information by using Ventura to format the data. Database publishing consists of four steps:

- ❑ Set up a style sheet in Ventura (see Chapter 5).
- ❑ Output the data from your database.
- ❑ Load the data into Ventura.
- ❑ Print the data.

For Ventura to use the information stored in your database, the data must be put into a form understandable by Ventura. All database programs like dBASE can output data in ASCII format, which Ventura understands. How you extract the data depends on the program. Databases like dBASE require a program; other databases may be simpler or more complex. Because dBASE and programs like dBASE are the most popular, chances are you can extract all or part of the data from your database with a simple program.

Figure 4.8 shows the code for a dBASE program that works with dBASE III®, dBASE III® Plus, or dBASE IV and compatible files. You can easily modify the program, substituting the names of your own database and fields (see fig. 4.9 for an illustration of the database structure of the example given in this tip).

Fig. 4.8.

Sample dBASE program to extract data.

```
*dBase database publishing program
*(c)1983-1988 Schuyler Lininger
USE
SET HEADING OFF
SET BELL OFF
SET SAFETY OFF
SET TALK OFF
SET ECHO OFF
CLEAR ALL
CLEAR
RELEASE ALL

? "Type 'X' to eXit, any other key to continue."
SET CONSOLE OFF
WAIT TO mgo
SET CONSOLE ON

IF UPPER(mgo) = "X"
 RELEASE ALL
 CLEAR
 ? "Cancelling program, returning to dBase III+ command level."
 CANCEL
ENDIF

IF .NOT. FILE ("mstore.ndx")
  CLEAR
  ? "Creating index, please be patient."
  USE address
  INDEX ON store TO mstore
  USE
ENDIF

*Change the name of the datafile "address" to suit your needs

USE address INDEX mstore

CLEAR

STORE DTOC(DATE()) TO mdate
 @ 6,0 SAY "File will be saved as 'ADRSBOOK.'  Type any key to
continue."

*Change the path and filename to suit your needs

 SET ALTERNATE TO C:\typeset\adrsbook
 SET CONSOLE OFF
 WAIT
 SET CONSOLE ON

CLEAR

*Sets current alphabetical letter
STORE ASC(store) TO mtest

SET ALTERNATE ON
?? "@ALPHA = "
?? CHR(mtest)
? "@BODY TEXT = "
DO WHILE .NOT. EOF()

 IF DELETE()
  SKIP
 ENDIF

 STORE TRIM(store)+ ', ' +TRIM(attention)+ ". " + TRIM(address);
 + ", " + TRIM(city)+ ", " + state +". " + zip + "." + "<R>";
 to mline

*check for alphabetical letter change
 IF ASC(mline) <> mtest
  STORE ASC(mline) TO mtest
  ?
 ?? "@ALPHA = "
 ?? CHR(mtest)
  ? "@BODY TEXT = "
 ENDIF

??mline

 SKIP

ENDDO WHILE .NOT. EOF

?
store "rev "+mdate to rev
?? "@REVISION = "
?? rev
 SET ALTERNATE OFF
 USE
 RELEASE ALL
 CLEAR ALL
 SET TALK ON
 SET ECHO ON
 CLEAR
```

Fig. 4.9.

Sample database structure.

```
. display structure
Structure for database: C:address.dbf
Number of data records:      104
Date of last update   : 12/03/88
Field  Field Name  Type       Width    Dec
    1  STORE       Character     35
    2  ATTENTION   Character     15
    3  ADDRESS     Character     30
    4  CITY        Character     15
    5  STATE       Character      2
    6  ZIP         Character      5
** Total **                     103

.
Command Line  |<C:>|ADDRESS          |Rec: 1/104    |    |Num

                 Enter a dBASE III PLUS command.
```

4.19 Tip

Preformat the database with tags and line breaks.

Figure 4.10 illustrates the output of a database as produced by the dBASE program in figure 4.8. Notice the lack of returns between the lines of data; also notice that line breaks (<R>) are inserted at the end of each line of data; in addition, the tags @ALPHA = and @BODY TEXT = are inserted by the program in figure 4.8.

By inserting tags before the text is imported, you avoid having to tag text in Ventura—saving a great deal of time, especially with complex databases.

By inserting a line break (<R>) rather than a carriage return at the end of lines, all the data appears to Ventura as a single paragraph. If you had 100 records in a database and output them with a carriage return between each record, Ventura sees 100 paragraphs when it loads the file. Loading many paragraphs takes time. If the number of paragraphs is too large (too many line

```
Advanced Nutrition, Seattle, Rick. 321 NE 72 Street, Seattle, WA. 98115.<R>Alpin
e Health Haus, Jennifer. 7611 SE 27th, Mercer Island, WA. 98040.<R>
@ALPHA = B
@BODY TEXT = Bay Street General Store, Susan. 1255 Bay Street, PO 1333, Florence
, OR. 97439.<R>Brownsville General Store, Tony or Marty. 421 Main, Brownsville,
OR. 97327.<R>Burien Special Foods, Rob or Joyce. 148 SW 152nd, Seattle, WA. 9816
6.<R>Burliman's Whole Foods Co., Nancy or Bill. 140 E 5th, Eugene, OR. 97401.<R>

@ALPHA = C
@BODY TEXT = Camas Health Foods, Bill or Jung He. 407 NE 4th, Camas, WA. 98607.<
R>Canby Nutrition, Tom. 319 SE 1st, Canby, OR. 97013.<R>Central Coop, Jean. 1835
 12th Avenue, Seattle, WA. 98122.<R>Coast Health Foods, Manager. 2140 NE Highway
 101, Lincoln City, OR. 97367.<R>Cornucopia General Store, Candy. Wagner Square,
 Redmond, OR. 97756.<R>Country Cooks Coop, Cara. 4706 Erickson Road, Longbranch,
 WA. 98351.<R>Country Store Health Foods, Betty or Harry. 228 NE Greenwood, Bend
, OR. 97701.<R>Country Vitamins, Pat. 919E NW Circle, Corvallis, OR. 97330.<R>
@ALPHA = D
@BODY TEXT = Daily Grind Natural Foods, Maryann. 4026 SE Hawthorne, Portland, OR
. 97202.<R>
@ALPHA = E
@BODY TEXT = East Hill Nutrition, Sally. 25814 102nd Pl. SE, Kent, WA. 98031.<R>

Command        <C:> ADDRESS          Rec: 23/104        Ins   Num

                 Enter a dBASE III PLUS command.
```

Fig. 4.10.

Database output prepared for Ventura.

or paragraph elements), you may not be able to load the database into Ventura at all. In the example given, lines are broken with a <R> code until a new letter of the alphabet is begun. The new letters are formatted in a different typeface with a different tag (ALPHA).

Here are some guidelines for you to follow when formatting database information before importing it to Ventura:

- ❑ Use <R> to break lines carrying the same tag in large databases.
- ❑ Use carriage returns to begin lines requiring a new tag.
- ❑ Use carriage returns to keep a single paragraph from going beyond the 4K to 8K limit imposed by Ventura.
- ❑ Use carriage returns or line breaks (<R>) to publish small databases that do not overstep the paragraph or line element limitations of Ventura.

Once generated, the output from the database can be imported into Ventura. Tags can be set for each formatting variation (see Chapter 5 for more information on tags and style sheets). Figure 4.11 is an example of a simple database publication.

Fig. 4.11.

Sample database publication of an account contact.

A to Z Natural, Carolyn. 3028 SW Hawthorne, Portland, OR. 97214.
Advanced Nutrition, Seattle, Rick. 321 NE 72 Street, Seattle, WA. 98115.
Alpine Health Haus, Jennifer. 7611 SE 27th, Mercer Island, WA. 98040.

Bay Street General Store, Susan. 1255 Bay Street, PO 1333, Florence, OR. 97439.
Brownsville General Store, Tony or Marty. 421 Main, Brownsville, OR. 97327.
Burien Special Foods, Rob or Joyce. 148 SW 152nd, Seattle, WA. 98166.
Burliman's Whole Foods Co., Nancy or Bill. 140 E 5th, Eugene, OR. 97401.

Camas Health Foods, Bill or Jung He. 407 NE 4th, Camas, WA. 98607.
Canby Nutrition, Tom. 319 SE 1st, Canby, OR. 97013.
Central Coop, Jean. 1835 12th Avenue, Seattle, WA. 98122.
Coast Health Foods, Manager. 2140 NE Highway 101, Lincoln City, OR. 97367.
Cornucopia General Store, Candy. Wagner Square, Redmond, OR. 97756.
Country Cooks Coop, Cara. 4706 Erickson Road, Longbranch, WA. 98351.
Country Store Health Foods, Betty or Harry. 228 NE Greenwood, Bend, OR. 97701.
Country Vitamins, Pat. 919E NW Circle, Corvallis, OR. 97330.

Daily Grind Natural Foods, Maryann. 4026 SE Hawthorne, Portland, OR. 97202.

East Hill Nutrition, Sally. 25814 102nd Pl. SE, Kent, WA. 98031.
Edan Nutrition, Ed. 2075 NW Buchanan, Corvallis, OR. 97330.
Evergreen Nutrition, Eugene, Marc or Dorothy. 1653 Willamette, Eugene, OR. 97401.

First Alternative Food Coop, Barbara. 1007 SE 3rd, Corvallis, OR. 97333.
Food Front Cooperative, Joe. 2375 NW Thurman, Portland, OR. 97210.
For Your Health, Ray or Dennis. 13215 SE 240th, Suite A, Kent, WA. 98031.
Fred Meyer Nutrition (AB), Judy. 2520 S. Santiam Blvd, Albany, OR. 97321.
Fred Meyer Nutrition Centers, Stefani Stout. 3800 SE 22nd, Portland, OR. 97202.
Fred Meyer Nutrition, B'verton, Sharon or Deb. 11425 SW B-H Highway, Beaverton, OR. 97005.

4.20 Trap

The amount of data or the way it is formatted can affect Ventura's capabilities.

You can use tabs and carriage returns to separate database fields, but know that each tab and carriage return uses memory. If too many tabs or carriage returns are used, you may encounter a "frame too complex" error message. In such cases, you must reduce the complexity of the text you are loading by splitting the file into smaller files or using less complex formatting.

4.21 Trap **Changes made to your database are not automatically reflected in the Ventura chapter.**

When you make changes to your database, you must "republish" your work to reflect the changes. Ventura does not maintain a "hot-link" to your data (maybe someday), and changes are not automatically incorporated into your chapter.

Working with Text from a Spreadsheet

You cannot load information directly from a spreadsheet into Ventura. You can, with effort, incorporate data from a spreadsheet into Ventura. My advice, however, is to use spreadsheet data only if it is necessary as part of a chapter. Do not try to use Ventura as a regular tool for creating spreadsheet reports unless you have the Professional Extension (see Chapter 12). (The Professional Extension can directly convert PRN files produced by programs such as 1-2-3 into tabular data.) The latest generation of spreadsheets, such as Lotus 1-2-3 with publishing add-ons and Microsoft® Excel, are much more capable—with less blood and tears—of creating typeset-quality reports.

4.22 Trap **Spreadsheets printed to disk use spaces rather than tabs. If imported into Ventura for use with a proportional font, they do not align correctly.**

Spreadsheets created by programs such as 1-2-3 cannot be directly read by Ventura. You must first print the file to disk. (In 1-2-3, the command is /Print; then select File rather than Printer.) When you print a spreadsheet to a disk file using 1-2-3, the file is given the extension PRN and can be loaded into Ventura as a WordStar 3 file (not as an ASCII file).

When 1-2-3 prints a file to disk, the columns of data are separated by spaces, not tabs. After loading the PRN file into Ventura, you will notice that the columns don't line up correctly. If you print the spreadsheet using a proportional font, the output is a spreadsheet not properly aligned and therefore difficult to read (see fig. 4.12).

4.23 Tip **Use Ventura's Edit function to replace spaces with tabs for correct spreadsheet formatting.**

To have properly aligned output from a spreadsheet using proportional type, do the following:

Fig. 4.12.

Improperly spaced spreadsheet printed with proportional font.

October, 1988 RENTAL SUMMARY

****

House No.	#1	# 2/D	# 3/D	# 4	# 5	# 6
Partner	0	1	1	0	2	2
Address	18025	40020	40030	39875	39710	18175
	Seaman	Hall Ct	Hall Ct	Gary	Gary	Van Fleet

****

DEPOSITS (damage, pet)						
Prev Month	775.00	615.00	750.00	1,050.00	900.00	695.00
This Month	0.00	0.00	475.00	0.00	0.00	0.00
(Deposit Refunds)	0.00	0.00	0.00	0.00	0.00	0.00
(Chgs Against Dep)	0.00	0.00	0.00	0.00	0.00	0.00
Sub-total	775.00	615.00	1,225.00	1,050.00	900.00	695.00

IMPOUNDS (T&I)	(T&I)					
Prev Month	1,154.10					
This Month	115.41	0.00	0.00	0.00	0.00	0.00
(Taxes Pd from Imp)	0.00	0.00	0.00	0.00	0.00	0.00
(Ins Pd from Imp)	0.00	0.00	0.00	0.00	0.00	0.00
Sub-Total	1,269.51	0.00	0.00	0.00	0.00	0.00
TOTAL CASH BALANCE	2,044.51	615.00	1,225.00	1,050.00	900.00	695.00

1. Load the spreadsheet PRN file into Ventura. All the paragraphs are tagged with the Body Text tag.
2. Switch to Paragraph mode and click one of the paragraphs.
3. Click Alignment from the Paragraph menu and change the `Horz. Alignment` option to `Left`.
4. Select Tab Settings from the Paragraph menu and set the tabs to correspond to your spreadsheet columns.
5. Change to Edit mode and replace all spaces between columns with a single tab.

4.24 Tip

Use a nonproportional font to print the spreadsheet. This is easier than reformatting as described in Tip 4.23.

If you would rather not reformat the spreadsheet as extensively as described in Tip 4.23, select a nonproportional font such as Courier for all the text. Fixed or monospace fonts give each character and space the same horizontal width. Printing with a fixed-space font produces a properly aligned spreadsheet without any conversion or reformatting (see fig. 4.13).

October, 1988 R E N T A L   S U M M A R Y

House No.	#1	# 2/D	# 3/D	# 4	# 5	# 6
Partner	0	1	1	0	2	2
Address	18025	40020	40030	39875	39710	18175
	Seaman	Hall Ct	Hall Ct	Gary	Gary	Van Fleet
DEPOSITS (damage, pet)						
Prev Month	775.00	615.00	750.00	1,050.00	900.00	695.00
This Month	0.00	0.00	475.00	0.00	0.00	0.00
(Deposit Refunds)	0.00	0.00	0.00	0.00	0.00	0.00
(Chgs Against Dep)	0.00	0.00	0.00	0.00	0.00	0.00
Sub-total	775.00	615.00	1,225.00	1,050.00	900.00	695.00
IMPOUNDS (T&I)	(T&I)					
Prev Month	1,154.10					
This Month	115.41	0.00	0.00	0.00	0.00	0.00
(Taxes Pd from Imp)	0.00	0.00	0.00	0.00	0.00	0.00
(Ins Pd from Imp)	0.00	0.00	0.00	0.00	0.00	0.00
Sub-Total	1,269.51	0.00	0.00	0.00	0.00	0.00
TOTAL CASH BALANCE	2,044.51	615.00	1,225.00	1,050.00	900.00	695.00
EXPENSES						
Mortgage	263.68	684.00	0.00	633.10	789.17	765.56
Impounds	115.41	0.00	0.00	0.00	0.00	0.00
Other	0.00	0.00	5.00	0.00	0.00	0.00

Fig. 4.13.

Spreadsheet printed with Courier (a monospace font).

4.25 Trick

Use conversion programs such as Tabin to convert spreadsheet data into a format that helps you avoid extensive reformatting in Ventura.

Tabin from Corel Systems Corporation converts the spaces in PRN files produced by spreadsheets into tabs separating each column.

Once in Ventura, you change the paragraph alignment and tabs to align the data properly. Tabin offers some options such as the positioning and adding of dollar signs to the output. Tabin creates tag names for differently formatted rows of spreadsheet data and produces a separate file with tab information for each of the tags. You then set the tabs in Ventura according to the tab information provided by Tabin (see fig. 4.14).

4.26 Trap

Changes made to your spreadsheet are not automatically reflected in the Ventura chapter.

When you make changes to your spreadsheet, you must "republish" your work to reflect the changes. Ventura does not maintain a "hot link" to your spreadsheet, and changes to the original spreadsheet are not automatically incorporated into your chapter. Remember also that Ventura is not a spreadsheet. If you use Ventura to change any numbers in the data, subtotals, totals, or other numbers that depend on the changed figures are not recalculated. Either recalculate the figures manually or do the math in your spreadsheet program and then export and reformat the data in Ventura again.

Importing, Exporting, and Renaming Text Files

Once you have created a text, database, or spreadsheet PRN file, load it into Ventura for formatting. After you load the file, the fun starts!

4.27 Tip

Text files created on an Apple Macintosh computer can be used by Ventura.

Many word processing software packages for the Apple Macintosh can save files in formats that can be loaded by Ventura. Microsoft Word for the Macintosh, for example, can save files as Microsoft Word for DOS; WordPerfect for the Macintosh can save files as WordPerfect IBM 4.2. Other word processors are capable of saving documents as text files, which are generally ASCII files that can be imported into Ventura.

October, 1988	RENTAL SUMMARY					
**						
House No.	#1	# 2/D	# 3/D	# 4	# 5	# 6
Partner	0	1	1	0	2	2
Address	18025	40020	40030	39875	39710	18175
	Seaman	Hall Ct	Hall Ct	Gary	Gary	Van Fleet
**						
DEPOSITS (damage, pet)						
Prev Month	775.00	615.00	750.00	1,050.00	900.00	695.00
This Month	0.00	0.00	475.00	0.00	0.00	0.00
(Deposit Refunds)	0.00	0.00	0.00	0.00	0.00	0.00
(Chgs Against Dep)	0.00	0.00	0.00	0.00	0.00	0.00
Sub-total	775.00	615.00	1,225.00	1,050.00	900.00	695.00
IMPOUNDS (T&I)	(T&I)					
Prev Month	1,154.10					
This Month	115.41	0.00	0.00	0.00	0.00	0.00
(Taxes Pd from Imp)	0.00	0.00	0.00	0.00	0.00	0.00
(Ins Pd from Imp)	0.00	0.00	0.00	0.00	0.00	0.00
Sub-Total	1,269.51	0.00	0.00	0.00	0.00	0.00
TOTAL CASH BAL	2,044.51	615.00	1,225.00	1,050.00	900.00	695.00

Fig. 4.14.

Spreadsheet printed with proportional font after being formatted with Tabin from Corel Systems Corporation.

If your Macintosh word processor can save files in a format that Ventura can load, you can transfer the file from your Macintosh by using one of the following methods:

- ❑ Connect your Macintosh to your PC with a modem cable and use a program such as MacLink Plus from DataViz Incorporated or xFer! from Messenger Software to transfer files. MacLink Plus can also convert MacWrite®, Excel, Jazz, Multiplan, and Microsoft Word files into files that can be read on the PC by 1-2-3, dBASE, and WordStar.

- ❑ Use the PC Option Board from Central Point Software if you have a 3 1/2-inch drive. The Option Board connects to the 3 1/2-inch drive and allows it to read and write to Macintosh disks. You can use your 3 1/2-inch drive as a regular PC drive as well as use its new capacity to emulate a Macintosh disk drive.
- ❑ Use a DaynaFile disk drive as an external drive for your PC. This drive allows Macintosh data to be read by your PC.
- ❑ Use your network to transfer files back and forth between the PC and the Macintosh. If you are on a local area network (LAN) connecting both Macintosh and PC computers, convert the Macintosh files into files that Ventura can load and transfer the files directly by using the LAN.
- ❑ Use the disk drives built into the new Macintosh computers that can read and write DOS disks.

4.28 Tip Use the Load Text/Picture command to load text files into Ventura.

Loading text files into Ventura is easy (remember, the text file is only linked not actually incorporated into a Ventura file). To load a file, do the following:

1. Click the Load Text/Picture command from the File menu.
2. At the LOAD TEXT/PICTURE dialog box, click the Text button.
3. Click the file format of the text file you want to load. If you want to load several files at once, click `Several`. If you are importing a text file created with Microsoft Word, for example, click `Word`.
4. Select the location in Ventura where you want to load the file. You can load the file to one of the three `Destination` choices: `List of Files`, `Text Clipboard`, or `Text Cursor`.

   `List of Files` links the file to the current chapter. The file name appears on the assignment list.

   `Text Clipboard` loads the file to the Clipboard. The name of the file does not appear on the assignment list. To incorporate the file, go to Text mode and place the text cursor where you want the text to begin. Press the Ins key to flow the new file into your chapter.

   `Text Cursor` works the same as `Text Clipboard`, but you place the cursor before you call the LOAD TEXT/PICTURE dialog box. The name of the file does not appear in the assignment list unless you are inserting the file into an empty page or frame. If this is the case, the file name in the assignment list is `UNTITLED`.

5. Click OK or press Enter. If you selected `Several` for `# of Files`, keep selecting files to load by using the steps presented here. When you are done, click OK or press Enter one last time without selecting a file.

Note: If you have installed the Professional Extension but have loaded only the Ventura base product (see Chapter 12), the `PRN-to-Table` option will appear in the LOAD TEXT/PICTURE dialog box. This filter will correctly load a PRN file, but the table will not appear unless you are actually using the Professional Extension.

4.29 Trick

Use Ventura's renaming function to convert files from one word processing format to another.

You can convert text files from any format Ventura supports to any other format. WordStar files, for example, can be converted to WordPerfect 5.0 files.

You may want to covert a file, for example, if a friend or fellow worker wrote an article in WordStar 5 for your newsletter or magazine. You may want to edit the article and proof it for spelling or grammatical errors but don't use WordStar 5 yourself. Instead, you use WordPerfect 5.0. Unfortunately, no conversion utility yet comes with WordPerfect for converting a WordStar 5 file to WordPerfect 5.0. To solve the problem, use Ventura's built-in conversion capability.

Another situation may be that you receive articles from many sources in many different file formats. For convenience and simplicity, you may want to keep all the files in the format of the word processor you use. Convert all foreign file formats into your preferred format by using the built-in conversion capabilities of Ventura.

To convert a file from one format to another, do the following:

1. Load the file into Ventura with the Load Text/Picture command from the File menu.
2. Flow the text onto a page or into a frame.
3. While in Frame mode, click the page or frame containing the text you want to convert.
4. Choose the File Type/Rename command from the Edit menu.
5. Change the path and the name of the file, if you want. Select the text format to which you want to convert the file. Click OK or press Enter when you're done.
6. Save the chapter by using the Save or Save As command from the File menu.

Note: Until you save the chapter, format changes in the text file are not made. Also, the conversion capabilities of Ventura apply only to text files. You cannot convert one type of graphic file to another type of graphic file by using the procedure in this trick.

4.30 Trap

The WordPerfect 5.0 filter in the original release of Ventura 2.0 is faulty. Save your WordPerfect 5.0 file as a 4.2 file and don't use the WordPerfect 5.0 filter.

The Xerox support group has sent a warning to Ventura users. The filter used to load WordPerfect 5.0 files into Ventura is defective under certain circumstances. If you enter any embedded codes or use the Alt-keypad technique to enter codes above decimal 128, saving the text file as a WordPerfect 5.0 file can corrupt the file, causing the text to be lost or damaged the next time the chapter is opened in Ventura.

Here are two possible workarounds:

- Delete the WordPerfect 5.0 filter by going to the VENTURA directory and deleting the file called WPERF5.LOD. Save all your WordPerfect files as WordPerfect 4.2 files (by using the Text In/Out function) and load them into Ventura by using the WordPerfect filter.
- Load your WordPerfect 5.0 files into Ventura but then use Ventura's FILE TYPE/RENAME dialog box to change the file to either a WordPerfect 4.2 or ASCII text file before saving the chapter.

No doubt this bug will be corrected in a later version of Ventura. Check with your dealer or Xerox support to determine whether the bug has been corrected in your version of Ventura.

4.31 Trick

Rename the hyphenation modules so you can easily tell them apart. Change the extension of the hyphenation modules so you can use the faster module during editing and the slower, more accurate module for final output.

The USENGLSH.HY1 hyphenation module that was loaded to your hard disk at installation time is fast but not as comprehensive as USENGLS2.HY2. Ventura looks at the extension (HY1 or HY2) to determine which module to use. The module with the HY1 extension is the first module Ventura uses; the HY2 module is used as a secondary source. The `Hyphenation` option on the ALIGNMENT dialog box (which you access from the Paragraph menu) allows you to choose whether the tagged paragraph will be hyphenated with the HY1 or HY2 module—or not hyphenated at all if set to `Off`. The HY1 module is listed first at the `Hyphenation` choice. Only one module should have the extension HY1; only one module should have the extension HY2. Only one module can be active per tag.

Because you can easily forget which module is which, rename the USENGLSH.HY1 module to FAST with the DOS command

```
RENAME USENGLSH.HY1 FAST
```

Rename the USENGLS2.HY2 module to SLOW with the DOS command

```
RENAME USENGLS2.HY2 SLOW
```

Only one U.S. hyphenation module should have the HY1 or HY2 extension at a time for two reasons: first, two modules slow down Ventura's speed; second, two modules consume more memory.

Use only the FAST module for preliminary editing and layout; use only the SLOW module for final editing and output where greater accuracy is important. You can create two batch files to automate the renaming of these files. To activate the desired module, rename the file to add the HY1 extension. To activate the FAST module, use this DOS command:

```
COPY FAST FAST.HY1
```

If you have other modules with the HY1 extension, be sure to delete or rename them.

Type the following DOS commands to create a batch file called FAST that renames the FAST module so that Ventura uses that module when hyphenating (press Enter at the end of each line):

```
COPY CON C:\FAST.BAT
DELETE C:\VENTURA *.HY1
COPY C:\VENTURA\FAST C:\VENTURA\FAST.HY1
```

When you are done, press Ctrl-Z or F6.

Type the following DOS commands to create a batch file called SLOW that renames the SLOW module so that Ventura uses that module when hyphenating (press Enter at the end of each line):

```
COPY CON C:\SLOW.BAT
DELETE C:\VENTURA *.HY1
COPY C:\VENTURA\SLOW C:\VENTURA\SLOW.HY1
```

When you are done, press Ctrl-Z or F6.

To use either batch file and rename the desired hyphenation module, type *fast* or *slow* on the DOS command line before loading Ventura. Notice that the batch files first delete all HY1 files in the VENTURA directory to ensure that you always start with only the new HY1 file module.

Once you have loaded Ventura, double-check to see whether you have loaded the fast or slow hyphenation algorithm by tagging a paragraph and clicking Alignment on the Paragraph menu. Figure 4.15 shows that only the fast hyphenation module is available.

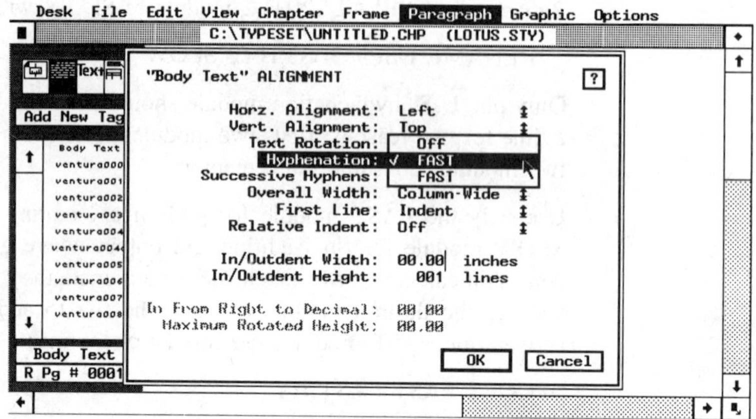

Fig. 4.15.

The ALIGNMENT dialog box with the fast hyphenation module activated.

4.32 Tip

If you are creating a document in two languages, you can have two different language hyphenation modules available at the same time.

Ventura offers hyphenation modules in five languages besides American English. The other languages are British English, French, German, Italian, and Spanish. All these modules are on disk 3 (if you are using 5 1/4-inch disks) or disk 2 (if you are using 3 1/2-inch disks). All these modules have the extension HY2. Change the extension to HY1 and delete or rename other HY1 modules if you want one of these other language modules to be the primary hyphenation module.

If you want to hyphenate in two languages, place the desired hyphenation module (with the HY2 extension) in the VENTURA directory. Remember, don't have two modules with the HY2 extension. Load the chapter and tag the foreign-language paragraphs. Then select the Alignment command from the Paragraph menu and change the `Hyphenation` option to the desired foreign language hyphenation module. In this way, some tags will use the foreign language module, and other tags will be hyphenated with the English module.

4.33 Trap

Only the first seven letters in a word are examined by the hyphenation algorithm modules.

The hyphenation modules supplied by Ventura are excellent. Not only are the algorithms used accurate, but words are hyphenated quickly. One reason the speed is so good is that only the first seven letters of any word are examined for hyphenation. Longer words are not hyphenated after the seventh letter. As an example, Ventura sees the word *hypertension* as *hy-per-tension* and not *hy-per-ten-sion*.

4.34 Tip

Add long words or words you don't want hyphenated to the HYPHUSER.DIC.

Ventura hyphenates words after the seventh letter if the word has been entered into the user hyphenation dictionary called HYPHUSER.DIC. Following are the rules for using your text processor for entering words into HYPHUSER.DIC:

- ❑ Save the file HYPHUSER.DIC as an ASCII file. If you save the file in any other format, incorrect hyphenation may result.
- ❑ Enter words in lowercase letters only.
- ❑ Enter words without hyphens if you want to keep Ventura from hyphenating the word. You may want to prevent your name from being hyphenated; if your name is Bob Williams, enter *williams* into the HYPHUSER.DIC file.
- ❑ Add asterisks between any letters after the seventh to force Ventura to keep looking for hyphenation opportunities. You would enter *hypertension* as *hy-per-t*e*n-*sion*.

4.35 Tip

For dictionary hyphenation rather than algorithm hyphenation, use the Profession Extension's complete hyphenation dictionary.

The Professional Extension for Ventura offers an extensive hyphenation dictionary rather than an algorithm for hyphenating. For critical applications, consider the Professional Extension option. You need expanded memory to take advantage of the 130,000-word hyphenation dictionary (see Chapter 12 for more information about the Professional Extension and its capabilities).

Working in the Text Mode

Once you have loaded your text file into Ventura and placed it on the page or in a frame (see Chapter 6), you may want or need to edit the text. The following tips discuss how to mark, insert, move, delete, copy, and modify text attributes. Actual formatting of text with tags is covered in depth in Chapter 5.

4.36 Tip

Position the cursor in Text mode.

In order to edit text, you must be in Text mode. To get into Text mode, either click the Text mode icon or use the keyboard shortcut Ctrl-O. In Text mode, the cursor changes to an ''I-beam'' shape. Position the cursor by moving the mouse and clicking. A blinking vertical line representing the cursor is inserted into the text. You cannot insert text without first positioning the text cursor.

4.37 Tip

To see the ends of paragraphs, fixed spaces, and end of file markers, turn on Show Tabs & Returns.

You may find it handy to know where the paragraphs end with a carriage return, where discretionary hyphens or fixed spaces are, where tabs are located, where a line break is, and where the end of the file occurs. You can display the characters that indicate these conditions with the Show Tabs & Returns command.

Press Ctrl-T or select the Show Tabs & Returns command from the Options menu to display the hidden characters. Leave the hidden characters visible when editing so you don't inadvertently delete them (see fig. 4.16).

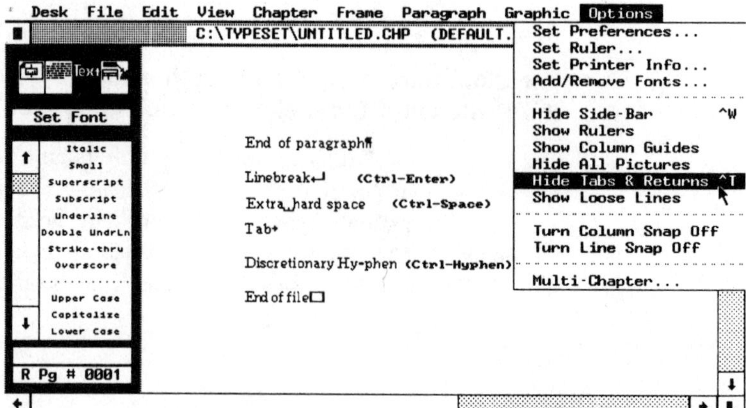

Fig. 4.16.

Hidden characters made visible.

4.38 Tip

Click and drag with the mouse or click twice while holding down the Shift key to mark text.

Once you have loaded a file into a frame or onto a page in Ventura, you can delete, copy, or alter the attributes on blocks of text. You can select a block of text in one of two ways:

- ❑ Click at one end of the block you want to mark and hold down the mouse button while dragging the I-beam pointer to the other end of the block. Release the button, and the selected text is highlighted (see fig. 4.17).
- ❑ Click at one end of the block and then hold down the Shift key and move the I-beam pointer to the other end of the block and click again. Everything between the two clicks is highlighted (see fig. 4.17).
- ❑ Extend the selection of text in either of the two ways discussed by holding down the Shift key and then clicking where you want the selection extended. All text after your last click, including the new text, will be highlighted.

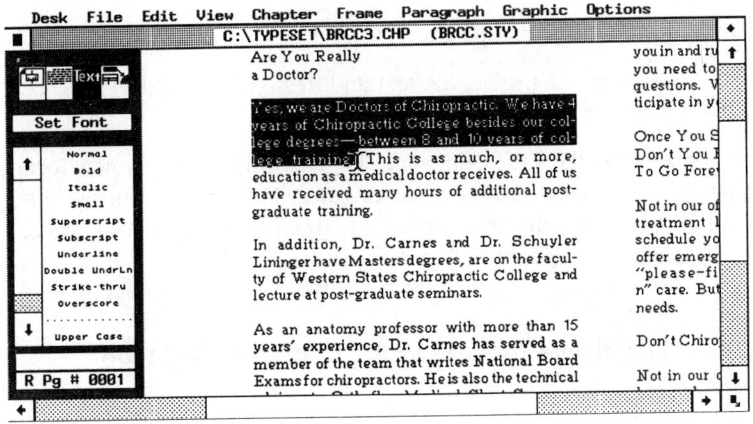

Fig. 4.17.

Selected text, highlighted.

4.39 Tip

To insert text, place the cursor in the text and begin typing.

Ventura always operates in the Insert mode. Most word processors allow you to either insert or overwrite text. Ventura only allows you to insert text. Deleting text is a separate operation.

4.40 Tip

To delete single letters of text, use either the Backspace or Del key. To delete a block of text, select the block and press Del.

To delete single letters or small amounts of text, position the cursor in front of the letter you want deleted and press the Del key. If you want to delete text to the left of the cursor, press the Backspace key.

If you want to delete blocks of text, first select the text and then press the Del key or choose Cut Text from the Edit menu.

Note: Unlike Macintosh programs and most Windows software, typing while text is selected does not replace the selected text with what has just been typed. Pressing any key other than Del has no effect on the selected text.

The most recently selected and deleted text is stored on the Clipboard and can be recovered if you press the Ins key. Newly deleted or copied text overwrites whatever was on the Clipboard; new text is not added to old text on the Clipboard. Text that you delete by pressing the Del key (without first selecting it) or Backspace key is not stored on the Clipboard. Ventura does not have an "undo" function, although you can go back to the last version of the chapter that you saved by selecting Abandon from the File menu.

4.41 Tip

To copy text, first select it and then copy it.

If you want to copy text, first select the text and then press Shift-Del or select Copy Text from the Edit menu.

Copied text is placed on the Text Clipboard. To insert the text in its new location, position the text cursor and press Ins or select Paste Text from the Edit menu. Pasted text assumes the style of the paragraph into which it is pasted unless some text attributes are copied along with the text.

4.42 Tip

To move text, first delete the text to the Clipboard and then reinsert the text.

Moving text is similar to copying text. First select the text to move and then delete it from its old position by pressing the Del key or selecting Cut Text from the Edit menu. To complete the move, position the text cursor where you want the text to reappear and press the Ins key or select Paste Text from the Edit menu.

4.43 Trap **You must be in the same mode for pasting as you were for cutting or copying, or the paste function does not work correctly.**

When you cut or copy something, what you have cut or copied is transferred to an invisible Clipboard. Unfortunately, you cannot examine the Clipboard to see what has been transferred there. Also, only the last item you cut or copied is on the Clipboard all other items are discarded.

Ventura maintains three Clipboards: one for frames, one for text, and one for graphics. Because three Clipboards exist and you cannot view them, you must be sure that you are in the correct mode when you paste from the Clipboards.

One way to see whether the current Clipboard has anything on it is to look at the Paste Text command on the Edit menu. If you are in Text mode and text is on the Clipboard (you have selected and either cut or copied something to the Text Clipboard), the Paste Text menu item is black; if nothing is on the Clipboard at the time, the menu item is gray (see fig. 4.18).

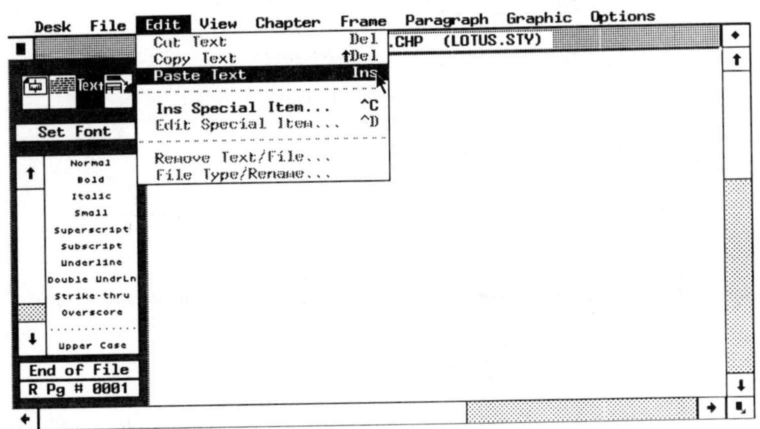

Fig. 4.18.
The Edit menu's Paste Text command indicating that some text is on the Clipboard.

If you try to cut or copy and then paste text in the Frame mode, the Edit menu lists the Paste Frame command; in the Graphic mode, the Edit menu lists the Paste Graphic command.

4.44 Tip **Text attributes for a paragraph are set with the paragraph tag (see Chapter 5), but individual letters, words, or sentences within a paragraph can have their own text attributes.**

Ventura offers wonderful control over the appearance of your text. In addition to the comprehensive control offered by paragraph tags and style sheets, you can mark letters, words, or sentences and apply special attributes to them.

When you are in the Text mode, the assignment list displays 13 text attributes. To set attributes for a block of text while in Text mode, select the block of text and then click the desired attribute or attributes from the assignment list. You also can click the Set Font button (or press Ctrl-2) for control over font selection, point size, color, and positioning. Clicking the Set Font button (or pressing Ctrl-2) while text is selected accesses the FONT SETTING FOR SELECTED TEXT dialog box. You can use the kerning and letter spacing capabilities of the dialog box or visually kern by using the shifted right- or left-arrow keys to loosen or tighten the space between letters and words. Look at figure 4.19 for an idea of how each text attribute affects the printed result; note that some attributes cannot be combined. Small and subscript, for example, both make the font smaller, but combining them doesn't make the font smaller yet.

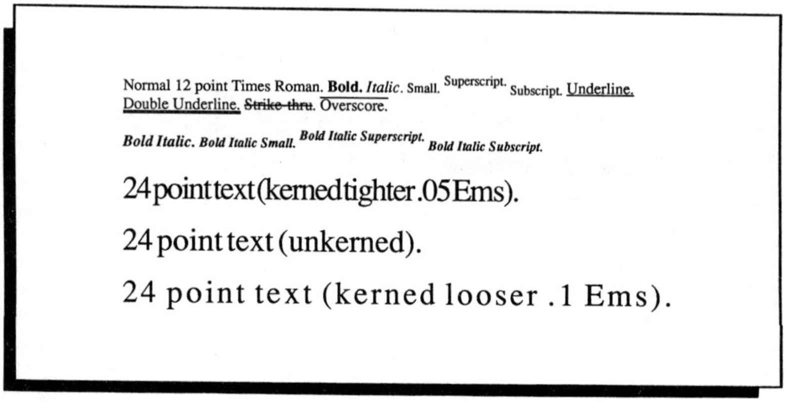

Fig. 4.19.

Printed examples of the effect of text attributes.

Normal 12 point Times Roman. **Bold.** *Italic.* Small. Superscript. Subscript. Underline. Double Underline. ~~Strike thru~~. Overscore.

Bold Italic. Bold Italic Small. Bold Italic Superscript. Bold Italic Subscript.

24pointtext(kernedtighter.05Ems).

24 point text (unkerned).

24 point text (kerned looser .1 Ems).

The first part of table 4.4 lists the 13 attributes in the Text mode assignment list and what each does. The second part of the table lists the options on the FONT SETTING FOR SELECTED TEXT dialog box and what each does. To open the FONT SETTING FOR SELECTED TEXT dialog box, click the Set Font button or press Ctrl-2 (see fig. 4.20).

Table 4.4
Text Attributes

Assignment List Attributes	*Effect on Selected Text*
Normal	Removes any attributes applied and restores the paragraph tag defaults
Bold	Makes bold those fonts capable of being made bold
Italic	Italicizes those fonts capable of showing italics
Small	Reduces the size of the selected text
Superscript	Reduces the size of the text and shifts it up
Subscript	Reduces the size of the text and shifts it down
Underline	Underlines the text (including spaces)
Double-UndrLn	Double-underlines the text (including spaces)
Strike-thru	Draws a single line through the text
Overscore	Draws a single line above the text
Upper Case	Converts the selected text to all capital letters
Capitalize	Converts the first letter of every word of selected text to a capital letter
Lower Case	Converts the selected text to all lowercase letters

FONT SETTING Dialog Box Attributes	*Effect on Selected Text*
Face	Changes the selected text to a new typeface; the current face is highlighted.
Size	Changes the selected text to a new size (if a PostScript font is used, you can set a Custom Size); setting the size of a font also can be done interactively on-screen (use the shifted up- and down-arrow keys).
Style	The available styles of text appear in black with the current style highlighted.

Table 4.4—*Continued*

Attributes	*Effect on Selected Text*
Color	If your printer is capable of printing color, you can change the color of the print with this option; if you have a PostScript printer, changing colors may create a special effect (see Chapter 9).
Overscore	Draws a line over the selected text; can be set `On` or `Off`; also can be set from the assignment list.
Strike-Thru	Draws a line through the selected text; can be set `On` or `Off`; also can be set from the assignment list.
Underline	Draws a line under the selected text; can be set `On` or `Off`; also can be set from the assignment list.
Double Underline	Draws two lines under the selected text; can be set `On` or `Off`; also can be set from the assignment list.
Shift	Text can be shifted `Up` or `Down` a specified amount; you can change the measurement units by clicking the desired unit.
Kern	Text can be kerned `Tighter` or `Looser` a specified amount; measurement units are always in 1/100's of an em (an *em* is the width of the character @ in the selected font); kerning can also be done interactively on-screen (use the shifted left- and right-arrow keys).

4.45 Trap **Do not accidentally delete attribute settings.**

When any of the attribute settings are applied to text, an attribute setting is placed before and after the affected text. Although the attribute codes are not visible and cannot be made visible, they act as an extra character when you move the text cursor across them with the arrow keys. When you encounter an attribute setting, the current selection box displays `Attr. Setting`. Be careful

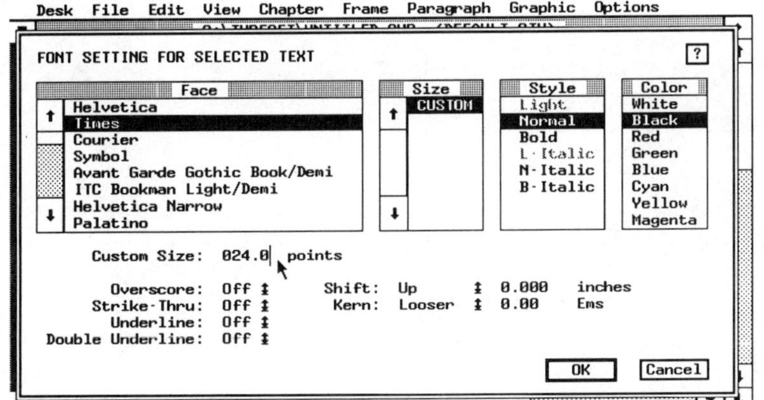

Fig. 4.20.

The FONT SETTING FOR SELECTED TEXT dialog box.

when editing not to delete one of these codes. If you do delete an attribute setting code, the effect is the same as if you had marked the text and selected Normal. All attributes are canceled, and the text is reset to the paragraph tag settings.

If you accidentally delete an attribute setting code, you can restore it immediately by pressing Ins.

Chapter Summary

In this chapter, you learned about preparing text for use by Ventura. You learned how much of your word processor's formatting is used by Ventura and how Ventura interprets carriage returns, spaces, and tabs. You also learned how to embed formatting codes and tag names directly into your text for interpretation by Ventura. Keyboard shortcuts were examined as well as the entry of decimal codes for special characters such as em dashes and "smart" quotation marks.

You learned how to export data from database and spreadsheet files for importation into Ventura and how to add tags and set up tabs for proper formatting of these types of files.

You also learned how to import text from the Apple Macintosh computer and how to load text into Ventura for formatting. You examined the different hyphenation modules and how to make hyphenation more efficient in Ventura.

You learned all about text editing—from inserting and deleting to moving and copying. Finally, you learned to apply text attributes such as bold and italic characteristics.

Chapter 5 begins to look at style sheets and paragraph tags—the real power of Ventura.

Chapter

5

Understanding Style Sheets

The heart of the Ventura desktop publishing system is the style sheet. A *style sheet* is a collection of information that tells Ventura how you want the document to appear.

When you first load a text file into Ventura, the document appears unremarkable. No text attributes appear, and there is no special placement of text.

In the process of formatting the document to prepare it for printing, you develop a style sheet. This chapter concentrates on what style sheets are, how you can create style sheets, and how style sheets are applied to your documents.

Creating a Style Sheet

Whenever you start Ventura, the line under the menu bar gives you certain information about the current chapter and style sheet. In figure 5.1, the chapter name is UNTITLED.CHP in the TYPESET subdirectory of disk drive C. The style sheet is shown in parentheses; in figure 5.1, the style sheet is named DEFAULT.STY. No path name is shown for the style sheet.

The DEFAULT.STY style sheet contains no tags other than the Body Text tag. You have three options when creating a style sheet:

- Load the DEFAULT.STY style sheet (if it is not already loaded), immediately rename it by using the Save As New Style command from the File menu, and create your own style sheet by adding formatting information to the newly named style sheet.
- Modify one of the many sample style sheets provided with Ventura.
- Purchase professionally designed style sheets and use them with or without modification. New Riders Publishing has issued several excellent collections of style sheets.

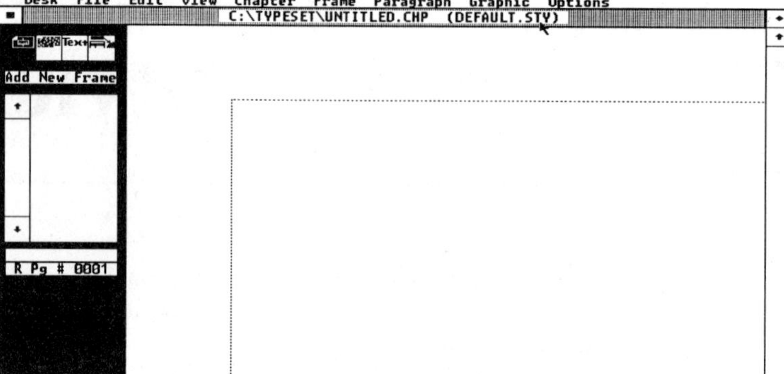

Fig. 5.1.
Chapter and style sheet status line.

5.1 Tip

Understand the concept of the tag.

Tags are a collection of stylistic and typographical attributes that can be applied to a paragraph. Tags are the center of the style sheet and give a style sheet power. If you look at the Paragraph menu (see fig. 5.2), you see eight items dealing with style and typography: Font, Alignment, Spacing, Breaks, Tab Settings, Special Effects, Attribute Overrides, and Paragraph Typography. These eight items offer almost 70 options that can be set for a given paragraph. Don't be overwhelmed by all the choices. Instead of trying to master all the tag possibilities, learn the most important and frequently used tag settings. Glance at the dialog boxes so you know what is available but don't get bogged down.

Besides the first eight items on the Paragraph menu, three additional choices are available; they deal with ruling lines and boxes. The Paragraph menu also offers the options Define Colors and Update Tag List. You can use all these items to help define the style of a paragraph.

Once you have decided on the way you want a paragraph to look, Ventura remembers all your specifications and saves them in a tag. The tag can easily be applied to other paragraphs in the current chapter; if the same style sheet is used, the tag can be applied to paragraphs in other chapters.

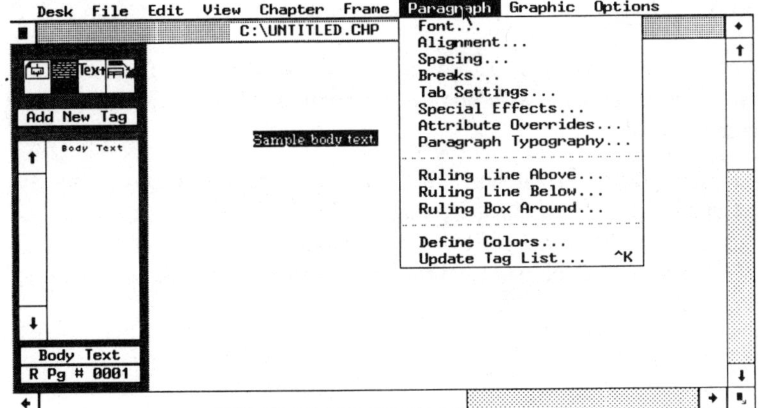

Fig. 5.2.

The Paragraph menu.

5.2 Tip

Understand the concept of the style sheet.

A *style sheet* is the way Ventura remembers how you want a document to look. A style sheet is composed of four major components. When a new style sheet is selected or an existing style sheet is modified, the following four items may change:

- ❏ Tags controlled by the Paragraph menu
- ❏ Layout controlled by the Chapter menu (Page Size & Layout, Chapter Typography, Auto-Numbering, and Footnote Settings commands)
- ❏ Frame settings controlled by the Frame menu
- ❏ The selected printer width table

A style sheet holds all the paragraph tags that you define for the various areas of text in your document. Style sheets can be identified in the current directory by the extension STY. Only one style sheet may be active for a chapter at a time.

5.3 Tip

Apply tags in one of three ways.

Tags are applied to text in one of three ways:

- ❏ In Paragraph mode, click a paragraph to highlight it. Then click an existing tag name in the assignment list.

- In the word processing stage of text development, preface paragraphs with a special code using the desired Ventura tag name. This code is in the format

  @ TAG NAME =

  where TAG NAME can be any tag in your style sheet. (If no tag exists, one is created with body text attributes when the text file is loaded into Ventura.)

- In Paragraph or Text mode, either select a paragraph or insert the text cursor somewhere in the paragraph. Then press one of the function keys F1 through F10. If the function key has been assigned to a tag, the assigned tag is applied to the selected paragraph.

This chapter provides tips for applying tags in each of these ways.

5.4 Tip

Understand the information that style sheets contain.

Style sheets hold a tremendous amount of information. The information is organized fairly clearly. Refer to table 5.1 for the menus and the commands that affect settings in the style sheet. Don't let the terminology and diversity and number of settings frustrate you; most of the settings and terminology will be clear to you by the end of this chapter (other information is explained in other chapters in this book). Until you are familiar with style sheets, refer to table 5.1.

Table 5.1
Settings Affected by Style Sheets

Menu and Options	*Option Selected and Comments*
Paragraph Menu	
Font	This choice sets the font for the paragraph. The font consists of Face, Size, Style, and Color options. You can also turn on or off Overscore, Strike-Thru, Underline, and Double Underline options for the selected paragraph.
Alignment	This option sets horizontal (Left, Center, Right, Justified, or Decimal) and vertical (Top, Middle, or Bottom) alignment of text.

Table 5.1—*Continued*

Menu and Options	*Option Selected and Comments*
	The alignment option allows you to set the overall width of the document to Column-Wide or Frame-Wide. You can also Indent or Outdent the first line of a paragraph, specify the width and height of the indent or outdent, and set Relative Indent on or off. You can specify the hyphenation dictionary to be used and define the number of successive hyphens to be allowed. If Horz. Alignment is set to Decimal, you can define the distance you want the decimal alignment In From Right to Decimal (to decimal align without having to use tab settings—In From Right to Decimal sets the alignment point from the right margin). Finally, you can set Text Rotation and the Maximum Rotated Height.
Spacing	This choice sets Above, Below, Inter-Line, and Inter-Paragraph spacing. You can set an entire paragraph to indent from the left or right. You can indent the paragraphs whether the spacing for the Above option is always added or added only when the paragraph is at the top of a column. You can have separate settings depending on whether the paragraph is on a right or left page.
Breaks	This choice sets page, column, and line breaks. With this option you can set Next Y Position for vertical columns. You can define whether or not you want breaks within paragraphs. The Keep With Next option forces a paragraph such as a heading to appear in the same column or page as the next paragraph.
Tab Settings	This option sets up to 16 tabs in left, center, right, or decimal orientation. You can specify leader characters to be any character with any spacing. You can enable the Auto-Leader option to insert automatically the leader

Table 5.1—*Continued*

Menu and Options	*Option Selected and Comments*
	character at the end of a paragraph and continue to the right margin. (No tab needs to be set for Auto-Leader to work.)
Special Effects	This choice controls the Big First Char (drop-cap) and Bullet options. You can define the big first character with this command using the same options found in the FONT dialog box. You also can set the spacing for the big first character by defining on which line you want the bottom of the first character to rest. Fifteen choices for bullets are offered, or you can choose your own bullet character and set the indent spacing after the bullet.
Attribute Overrides	This option allows customizing of the position and size of the Overscore, Strike-Thru, Underline, Superscript, Subscript, and Small Cap attributes set in Text mode. This option allows you to specify whether some attributes (such as underline) apply only to text or from margin to margin even if only a few characters are selected.
Typography Setting	This choice controls kerning, letter spacing, tracking, and whether the interline spacing for the paragraph expands to accommodate font changes made to selected text in Text mode. Minimum, normal, and maximum space width values for letter spacing can be defined.
Ruling Lines	Ruling lines can be set above or below the paragraph. You can set the width (None, Text, Margin, Column, Frame, or Custom) of the line, choose its color and pattern, and decide whether you want dashes. You can set up to three rules and control their thicknesses and spacing. You can also define the rules to overlap text. You can indent the rules and specify the width and spacing of dashes.

Table 5.1—*Continued*

Menu and Options	*Option Selected and Comments*
Ruling Box Around	You can define a box to surround the selected frame, text, margin, column, or custom setting using the same settings used with the Ruling Lines commands.
Define Colors	This choice configures the screen to display colors or shades of gray. You can define colors for text, frames, or graphics by choosing one of seven settings, naming the color, and mixing the custom color using a CMYB (cyan, magenta, yellow, and black) palette.
Update Tag List	This option allows you to print a style sheet, remove a selected tag from a style sheet, save a style sheet with a new name, rename a tag, and assign up to 10 tag names to function keys to speed up the tagging process.
Chapter Menu	
Page Size & Layout	This choice sets orientation of a page to `Portrait` or `Landscape`. You can select the paper type and dimension from seven choices, set the page as either single- or double-sided, and decide whether to start on a right or left page.
Chapter Typography	This choice allows you to specify the number of lines for widows and orphans (1 to 5 lines) and set `Column Balance On` or `Off`. You can select `Move Down To 1st Baseline By` and align the first line of a paragraph using the height of the tallest capital letter or the `Inter-Line` setting. You can set `Pair Kerning` to `On` or `Off`, but if you set it `Off`, Ventura does not kern even if the PARAGRAPH TYPOGRAPHY dialog box has set kerning on.
Auto-Numbering	This option allows you to turn on or off automatic numbering of paragraphs and selects the style and text (if any) of the generated numbers.

Table 5.1—*Continued*

Menu and Options	*Option Selected and Comments*
Footnote Settings	This option sets the usage and format of footnotes. You can change the starting footnote number, change the position and the appearance of the numbering system, use separator lines, and determine the width, height, and spacing of the lines.
Options Menu	
Set Printer Info	This choice sets the width table of the printer (see Chapter 9 for more information about printer width tables).

5.5 Tip **Information about frames is stored in the CHP file, not the STY file.**

Frame settings are not stored with style sheet information, but with the chapter file. See Chapter 6 for more information about frames.

5.6 Trick **Good designers use fewer rather than more tags.**

Ventura allows up to 128 tags to be set at one time. Good designers don't use that many tags. Mixing too many fonts or design elements in a single document is distracting. Practice good design and use as few tags as possible.

Starting with Ventura's Supplied Style Sheets

Ventura comes with 20 style sheets that supply excellent examples of how to design books, brochures, newsletters, reports, manuals, overheads, database publications, and miscellaneous forms.

The appendix of your Ventura manual lists the 20 style sheets and gives a description of each. Sample printouts of the chapters associated with the style sheets are also provided.

If you do not yet have the confidence to build a document design from scratch, use the style sheet examples as starting places. The following sections provide information about loading, modifying, and saving style sheets.

Loading Style Sheets

Whether you use a Ventura-supplied style sheet or a style sheet that you have developed yourself, you must load that style sheet and apply it to the current chapter before any of the design elements held by the style sheet can be implemented.

5.7 Tip Learn how Ventura loads chapters.

Load a chapter into Ventura by doing the following:

1. Click the Open Chapter command from the File menu.
2. From the ITEM SELECTOR dialog box (notice the *.CHP filter) you can either type the name of the chapter you want or select it from the list by scrolling and then clicking the chapter name.
3. Click OK or press Enter. (If you prefer, use the mouse shortcut and double-click rapidly on the chapter name to select it.)

A message box appears notifying you that Ventura is `Loading Chapter`. As the chapter is being loaded, Ventura keeps you posted about the style sheet, text, and graphics files being loaded. During the loading of text files, Ventura also lets you know that hyphenation of the text is taking place. The larger the file, the more time it takes to hyphenate. If you have a large file, be patient.

If Ventura cannot find a file where it should be, you are notified. Ventura cannot find files if you have renamed them by using the DOS command, if you have deleted the file, or if you have copied the file to a new directory or disk by using the DOS COPY command and then deleted the original file.

Always use the Multi-Chapter command on the Options menu to copy chapters and their associated files from one disk or directory to another.

5.8 Tip Learn how Ventura loads style sheets.

Using Ventura, you can load a style sheet in one of two different ways:

- ❑ Ventura automatically loads the style sheet associated with that chapter whenever you load a chapter.

- ❑ Choose the Load Diff. Style command from the File menu to load a new style sheet. This function works the same way the Open Chapter command does (described in Tip 5.7).

Modifying Style Sheets

If you use a Ventura-supplied style sheet to format your document, you may want to make some modifications to the tag descriptions to customize the format to your specifications. If you are using a style sheet developed for a previous document, you may want to change some of the tag descriptions to fit your current publication.

5.9 Trap

If you modify a style sheet, save the modified style sheet under a new name before modifying. If you do not, you may unintentionally affect other documents.

Whenever you create a new document by using a style sheet that is also used by another chapter, rename the style sheet with the Save as New Style command on the File menu.

If you don't get into the habit of saving modified style sheets under new names, the time will come when you will load an old chapter and be surprised that it doesn't look the same as it used to look. Its unexpected and unwanted new appearance is because you modified the style sheet when you used it with another chapter, didn't remember that the style sheet was shared by more than one chapter, and didn't rename the style sheet.

5.10 Trap

If you reinstall Ventura, you may overwrite modified style sheets.

Whenever you reinstall Ventura (or install the Professional Extension—see Chapter 12), you are given the option of installing the example files. If you answer *Yes*, all the example files are reinstalled in the TYPESET directory. This can create a problem if you have used some of the Ventura-supplied style sheets, modified them, but haven't renamed them. When you reinstall Ventura, the modified style sheets are replaced by the originals from the Ventura disk.

To guard against this, answer *No* when asked whether you want to install the example files. Better yet, whenever you modify a style sheet, give the style sheet a new name.

Saving Style Sheets

When you save a chapter, the associated style sheet is automatically saved. But, if you try to exit Ventura, you are prompted to save or abandon the modifications made to the style sheet. If you choose Abandon, none of the changes you made to tags or page margins and settings are saved. If you choose Save, an Item Selector dialog box appears. You can choose the existing name to save the style sheet under to type a new name.

5.11 Tip **When you assign a chapter, give the same name to the style sheet, text files, and printer width table if it is customized.**

The names of the text file and the associated style sheet are much easier to remember if they have the same name as the chapter. If you have multiple text files, consider naming them the same as the chapter and replacing the last letter of the file name with an incremental number.

If you customize the printer width table by adding or deleting fonts for a specific job, rename the printer width table with the name of the chapter.

Graphic files should not be renamed unless the graphics you use are specific to a particular job and will not be used by other documents. The reason for this is that graphics are often shared by different chapters (as in the case of a corporate logo). Renaming a graphics file used by a previous chapter causes a Not Found message when you try to reload the previous chapter.

Using this suggested naming convention makes it easy to "clean up" projects later because you can easily identify the files associated with a chapter. You cannot rename a graphic from within Ventura.

Controlling Chapter Elements

Some fundamental design decisions are made at the chapter level and cannot be changed for individual pages within a given chapter. Examples are page size, orientation, and single- or double-sided pages. Defaults for widows, orphans, and column balance, where text appears at the top of a column and kerning occurs, are set from the Chapter menu and can be overridden for a frame from the Frame menu. Kerning can be overridden from the Paragraph menu.

5.12 Tip

Before beginning to lay out a document, verify the chapter settings that you want.

On the Chapter menu are two commands that you should set before beginning to lay out a document. These commands are Page Size & Layout and Chapter Typography.

From the PAGE LAYOUT dialog box, you control four options:

- Orientation. Set this option to Portrait or Landscape. Select Portrait if the pages are to be laid out the long way; that is, the document is taller than it is wide. Select Landscape if the document is wider than it is long.
- Paper Type & Dimension. Set this option to Half (5 1/2 by 8 1/2 inches), Letter (8 1/2 by 11 inches), Legal (8 1/2 by 14 inches), Double (11 by 17 inches), B5 (17.6 by 25 centimeters), A4 (21 by 29.7 centimeters), or Broad Sheet (18 by 24 inches). Select the dimensions of the paper you will use. Not all printers can handle all sizes of paper. Check your printer documentation and also read about broad-sheet handling in Chapter 10.
- Sides. Set this option to Single or Double. If you are printing a newsletter, book, or report requiring a different page offset for left and right pages, choose Double. If you are printing a flier, calendar, or document not requiring different offsets for left and right pages, choose Single. If you choose Single, you cannot select Facing Pages View from the View menu. If you want different headers, column and margin settings, and other features for left and right pages, you must select Double.
- Start On. Set this option to Right Side or Left Side. Using this option, you specify whether the first page is to start on a left or right page.

From the CHAPTER (DEFAULT) TYPOGRAPHY SETTINGS dialog box, you control five options that become the defaults for the chapter. You can override these settings for a frame from the FRAME TYPOGRAPHY SETTINGS dialog box.

- Widows (Min Lines at Top). Choose a value between 1 and 5. *Widows* are isolated lines of text at the top of a column or page. If a paragraph doesn't quite fit on a page or in a column, Ventura breaks the paragraph and leaves a minimum of the specified number of lines at the top of the new page or column. A single can force from 2 to 5 lines with this option. A suggested setting is 2 or 3.

- Orphans (Min Lines at Bottom). Choose a value between 1 and 5. *Orphans* are similar to widows except they are lines at the bottom of a page or column. If a paragraph begins on one column or page and flows to the next, a single line at the bottom doesn't look good. The single line moves to the next column or page if not enough room is available for the specified minimum number of orphaned lines. A suggested setting is 2 or 3.

- Column Balance. This option can be set to Off or On. When multiple columns on a page don't fill the page, one column is shorter than the others (see fig. 5.3). Set Column Balance: On to force the columns to the same length (see fig. 5.4). Column balance can be affected by Widows, Orphans, and Keep With Next (from the BREAKS dialog box) settings. The Column Balance option does not guarantee perfect columns; you may need to use empty frames (see Chapter 6) or the vertical justification feature included in the Professional Extension (see Chapter 12) to balance the columns perfectly.

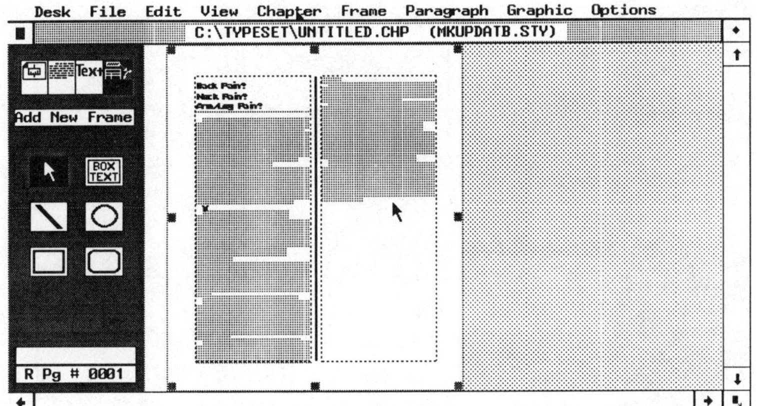

Fig. 5.3.

Column Balance set to Off.

- Move Down To 1st Baseline By. This option can be set to Cap Height or Inter-Line. When a line begins at the top of a column, the line can begin in one of two places. If you specify Cap Height, the baseline of the line moves below the column top the height of the tallest capital letter in the current font (see fig. 5.5). If you select Inter-Line, the baseline of the line begins down from the top of the column the amount specified for the interline spacing for that paragraph tag (see fig. 5.6).

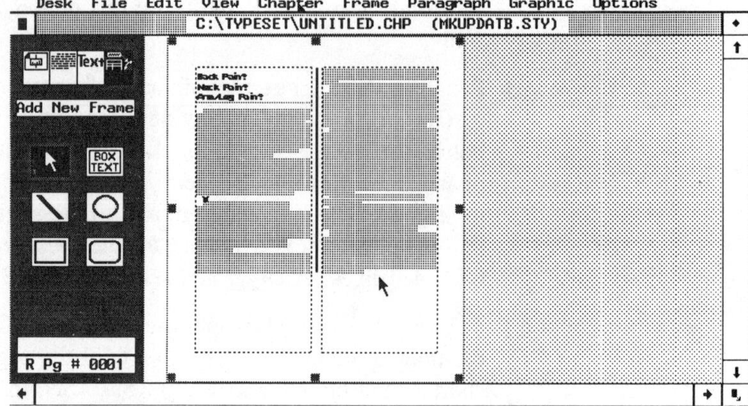

Fig. 5.4.

Column Balance set to On.

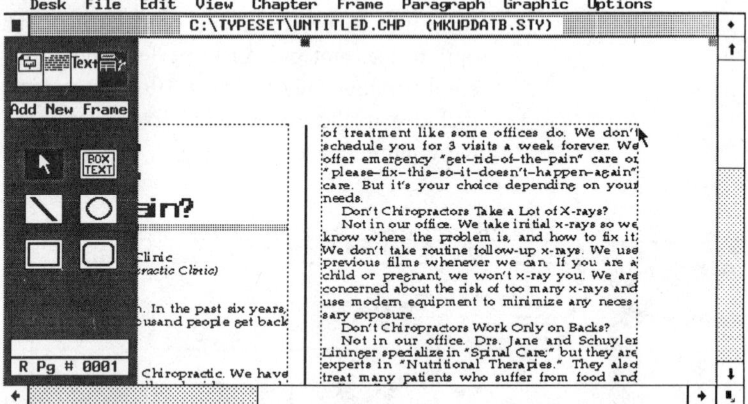

Fig. 5.5.

Text moved down from top of column by cap height.

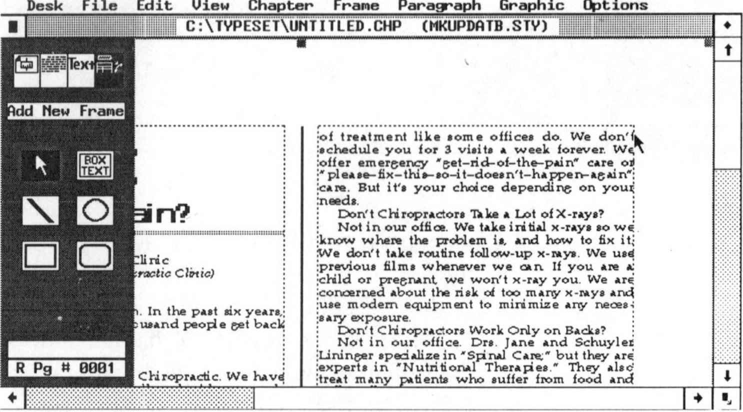

Fig. 5.6.

Text moved down from top of column by interline spacing.

- Pair Kerning. This option can be set to On or Off. This option turns kerning on for the entire chapter, overriding any tag settings you specified with the Paragraph Typography command from the Paragraph menu. When letters are kerned, the screen takes longer to be redrawn and the printer slows down. If you get in the habit of turning Pair Kerning: Off for the chapter, you can work more quickly. Remember to set Pair Kerning: On from the Chapter menu before printing the final document, or nothing is kerned.

Controlling Style Sheet Elements

The next two sections of this chapter deal with the fine details of style sheet and tag control. Because Ventura is such a tightly integrated program, and because design decisions from the style sheet, frame, graphic, and font levels can have impacts that ripple across an entire publication, the tips in this section should be coordinated with tips in other sections and chapters.

Many areas of style and tag control will not meet your needs or apply to your document. In such cases, skim quickly over the tip so you know about it and skip to the next tip or section. Don't try to memorize all the information provided in this book. Just familiarize yourself with it so you know where to look for it when the need arises.

Using the Printer Width Table

Fonts are discussed in-depth in Chapter 9. For now, you need to know that each printer has its own set of fonts. In some cases you can add extra fonts; in other cases you can use only the ones originally provided with the printer.

Some printer fonts are wider or taller than the fonts of another printer. To accurately represent on the screen what is to appear on the printed page, Ventura needs to know the width and height of each character in a specific printer's set of fonts.

Ventura (or the manufacturer of your printer or fonts) provides font information in a printer width table for each supported printer. The width table gives Ventura information about the shape, width, height, and kerning pairs of characters in the font set for a specific printer.

5.13 Trap

If you use a printer with one width table for proofing and another printer with a different width table for final output, your final document probably will not match the proof.

If you print to a dot-matrix printer for proofs by using a dot-matrix printer width table, for example, and print to a laser printer by using a laser printer width table for final copy, the two documents will not match.

Because the width tables for the two printers are so different, font shapes, widths, and heights aren't interchangeable. This can lead to unexpected alterations in formatting, such as the appearance of headings and the beginning and ending of articles.

5.14 Tip

Use the final printer width table all the time—even for proofs.

If you use a dot-matrix printer to proof your work before sending the final document to a typesetter or a laser printer, learn to make the final copy correspond to the proof.

If you use a PostScript printer such as the Apple LaserWriter for final output but use an Epson LQ for your copies and proofs, do the following to keep draft and final copies comparable:

1. For the draft copy, select Set Printer Info from the Options menu.
2. From the SET PRINTER INFO dialog box, click `EPSON LQ` as the printer you want to use for draft copies.
3. Also in the SET PRINTER INFO dialog box, click the command box `Load Different Width Table (i.e., Font Metrics)`.
4. From the list of width tables, point to `POSTSCPT.WID` and double-click, click once and then click OK, or click once and press Enter to select this file (see fig. 5.7). Click OK or press Enter to exit the SET PRINTER INFO dialog box.
5. Choose To Print from the File menu.
6. From the `Which Pages` option on the PRINT INFORMATION dialog box, choose `All`, `Selected`, `Left`, `Right`, or `Current` depending on which pages you want printed. If you choose `Selected`, enter the `From Page` and `Through Page` information (see Chapter 10 for more information on printing).
7. Click OK or press Enter to begin printing.
8. When you are ready to print the final copy, repeat steps 1 through 3 but select `POSTSCRIPT` as the type of printer to use. Leave the width table as POSTSCPT.WID.

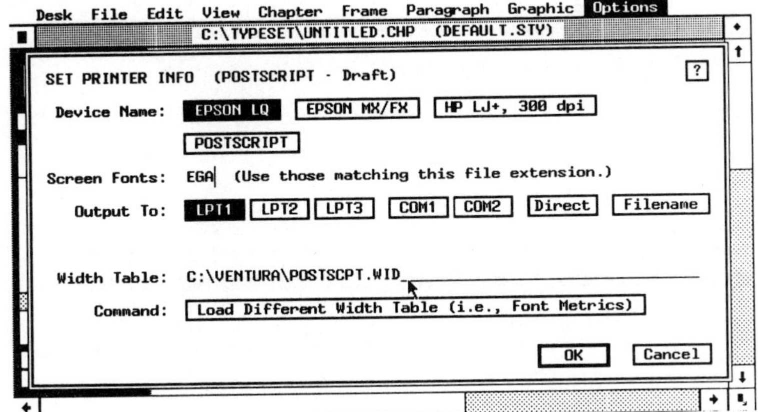

Fig. 5.7.

The SET PRINTER INFO dialog box with dot-matrix printer (EPSON LQ) and POSTSCPT.WID width table selected.

Use this same procedure for any combination of printers. The output on the dot-matrix printer may not look exactly right (see fig. 5.8), but the overall placement of the characters is what appears on the final laser or typeset copy (see fig. 5.9).

5.15 Trap

If you transfer chapters between systems and don't transfer the width table at the same time, documents produced on different systems may look different.

When you copy a chapter, use the Multi-Chapter command from the Options menu to automatically copy the width table associated with the style sheet.

If you use the DOS COPY command and neglect to include the appropriate width table, Ventura uses the default width table OUTPUT.WID. This file may not be the correct width table for your printer and may not include all the fonts used in the document.

5.16 Trap

Just because the name of a font appears in a width table doesn't mean the font is available.

Included in the POSTSCPT.WID table provided by Ventura are the built-in fonts usually found on PostScript printers. Also included, however, are 31 other Adobe fonts that must be purchased separately. Figure 5.10 shows some of these fonts. If you specify fonts not available to your printer, your printer substitutes another font. PostScript printers substitute Courier for unavailable fonts (see fig. 5.11). Adding, removing, and downloading fonts is discussed in Chapter 9.

Fig. 5.8.

Printout using dot-matrix printer and POSTSCPT.WID width table.

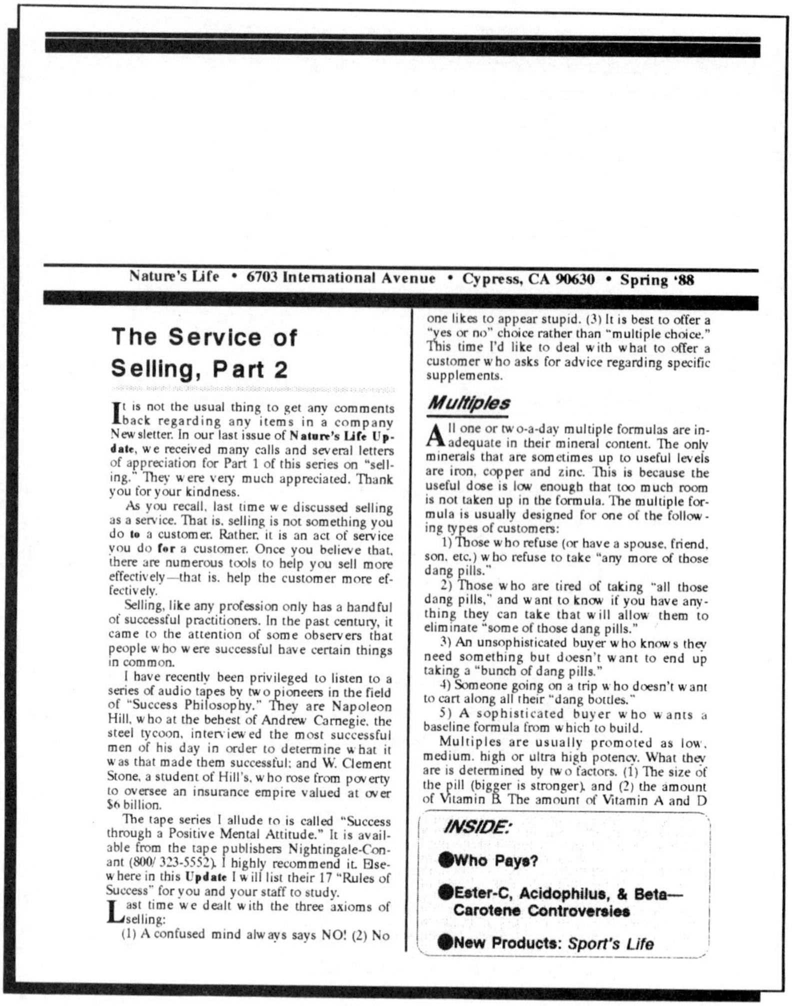

Nature's Life • 6703 International Avenue • Cypress, CA 90630 • Spring '88

The Service of Selling, Part 2

It is not the usual thing to get any comments back regarding any items in a company Newsletter. In our last issue of **Nature's Life Update**, we received many calls and several letters of appreciation for Part 1 of this series on "selling." They were very much appreciated. Thank you for your kindness.

As you recall, last time we discussed selling as a service. That is, selling is not something you do **to** a customer. Rather, it is an act of service you do **for** a customer. Once you believe that, there are numerous tools to help you sell more effectively—that is, help the customer more effectively.

Selling, like any profession only has a handful of successful practitioners. In the past century, it came to the attention of some observers that people who were successful have certain things in common.

I have recently been privileged to listen to a series of audio tapes by two pioneers in the field of "Success Philosophy." They are Napoleon Hill, who at the behest of Andrew Carnegie, the steel tycoon, interviewed the most successful men of his day in order to determine what it was that made them successful; and W. Clement Stone, a student of Hill's, who rose from poverty to oversee an insurance empire valued at over $6 billion.

The tape series I allude to is called "Success through a Positive Mental Attitude." It is available from the tape publishers Nightingale-Conant (800/ 323-5552). I highly recommend it. Elsewhere in this **Update** I will list their 17 "Rules of Success" for you and your staff to study.

Last time we dealt with the three axioms of selling:

(1) A confused mind always says NO! (2) No one likes to appear stupid. (3) It is best to offer a "yes or no" choice rather than "multiple choice." This time I'd like to deal with what to offer a customer who asks for advice regarding specific supplements.

Multiples

All one or two-a-day multiple formulas are inadequate in their mineral content. The only minerals that are sometimes up to useful levels are iron, copper and zinc. This is because the useful dose is low enough that too much room is not taken up in the formula. The multiple formula is usually designed for one of the following types of customers:

1) Those who refuse (or have a spouse, friend, son, etc.) who refuse to take "any more of those dang pills."

2) Those who are tired of taking "all those dang pills," and want to know if you have anything they can take that will allow them to eliminate "some of those dang pills."

3) An unsophisticated buyer who knows they need something but doesn't want to end up taking a "bunch of dang pills."

4) Someone going on a trip who doesn't want to cart along all their "dang bottles."

5) A sophisticated buyer who wants a baseline formula from which to build.

Multiples are usually promoted as low, medium, high or ultra high potency. What they are is determined by two factors. (1) The size of the pill (bigger is stronger), and (2) the amount of Vitamin B. The amount of Vitamin A and D

INSIDE:

- **Who Pays?**
- **Ester-C, Acidophilus, & Beta—Carotene Controversies**
- **New Products:** ***Sport's Life***

Working with Columns and Margins

One of the first things you do when designing a Ventura chapter is set the margins of the page and determine the number of columns for each page. You can specify different margins and numbers of columns for various pages in the chapter by adding frames. The tips in this section help you understand how to set margins and columns for your document.

Nature's Life • 6703 International Avenue • Cypress, CA 90630 • Spring '88

The Service of Selling, Part 2

It is not the usual thing to get any comments back regarding any items in a company Newsletter. In our last issue of **Nature's Life Update**, we received many calls and several letters of appreciation for Part 1 of this series on "selling." They were very much appreciated. Thank you for your kindness.

As you recall, last time we discussed selling as a service. That is, selling is not something you do **to** a customer. Rather, it is an act of service you do **for** a customer. Once you believe that, there are numerous tools to help you sell more effectively—that is, help the customer more effectively.

Selling, like any profession only has a handful of successful practitioners. In the past century, it came to the attention of some observers that people who were successful have certain things in common.

I have recently been privileged to listen to a series of audio tapes by two pioneers in the field of "Success Philosophy." They are Napoleon Hill, who at the behest of Andrew Carnegie, the steel tycoon, interviewed the most successful men of his day in order to determine what it was that made them successful; and W. Clement Stone, a student of Hill's, who rose from poverty to oversee an insurance empire valued at over $6 billion.

The tape series I allude to is called "Success through a Positive Mental Attitude." It is available from the tape publishers Nightingale-Conant (800/323-5552). I highly recommend it. Elsewhere in this **Update** I will list their 17 "Rules of Success" for you and your staff to study.

Last time we dealt with the three axioms of selling:

(1) A confused mind always says NO! (2) No one likes to appear stupid. (3) It is best to offer a "yes or no" choice rather than "multiple choice." This time I'd like to deal with what to offer a customer who asks for advice regarding specific supplements.

Multiples

All one or two-a-day multiple formulas are inadequate in their mineral content. The only minerals that are sometimes up to useful levels are iron, copper and zinc. This is because the useful dose is low enough that too much room is not taken up in the formula. The multiple formula is usually designed for one of the following types of customers:

1) Those who refuse (or have a spouse, friend, son, etc.) who refuse to take "any more of those dang pills."

2) Those who are tired of taking "all those dang pills," and want to know if you have anything they can take that will allow them to eliminate "some of those dang pills."

3) An unsophisticated buyer who knows they need something but doesn't want to end up taking a "bunch of dang pills."

4) Someone going on a trip who doesn't want to cart along all their "dang bottles."

5) A sophisticated buyer who wants a baseline formula from which to build.

Multiples are usually promoted as low, medium, high or ultra high potency. What they are is determined by two factors. (1) The size of the pill (bigger is stronger), and (2) the amount of Vitamin B. The amount of Vitamin A and D

INSIDE:

- **Who Pays?**
- **Ester-C, Acidophilus, & Beta—Carotene Controversies**
- **New Products: *Sport's Life***

Fig 5.9.

Same printout but using PostScript printer and POSTSCPT.WID width table.

5.17 Tip

Although Ventura uses the term *frames*, think in terms of *pages* and *boxes*.

Remember two things about Ventura to simplify your work and help you understand how Ventura ''thinks.'' Ventura manuals use the terms *underlying page* and *frame*, and so will I in this book. Even so, my suggestion is that you think in terms of *pages* and *boxes*. These terms are defined in the following paragraphs.

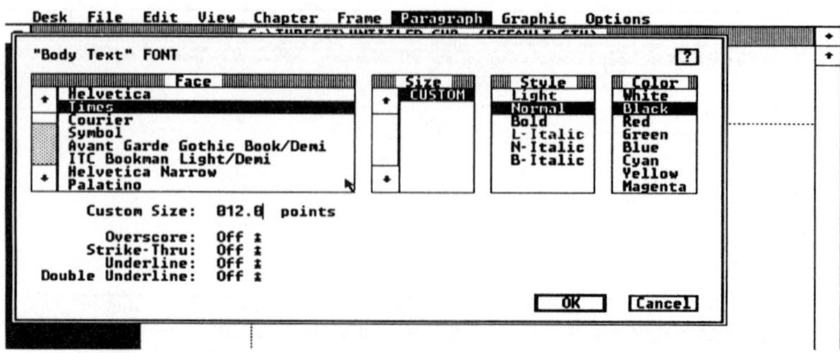

Fig. 5.10.

Examples of Adobe PostScript fonts listed in the width table but available only as downloadable fonts.

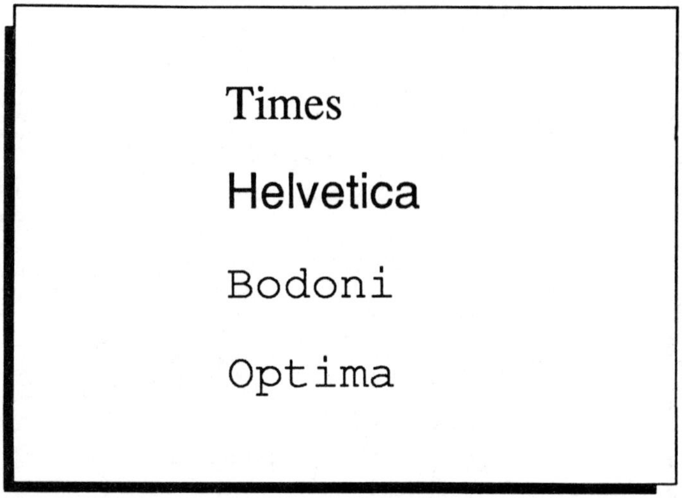

Fig. 5.11.

Courier being substituted for Bodoni and Optima, which weren't available to the PostScript printer.

Times

Helvetica

Bodoni

Optima

- A *page* (the Ventura term is *underlying frame* or *underlying page*) is what you see when you load Ventura. You can flow an entire document onto a page and Ventura creates enough pages to hold all the text. From this perspective, Ventura acts much like a word processor. Settings for the margins and columns for the page are stored with the style sheet.

- A *box* is what Ventura calls a *frame*. I use the term *frame* in this book, but *box* more clearly explains the concept of frame. A box holds something (text, pictures, graphics, or captions) and can be placed on something (a page or another box). Boxes can hold only so much information. If you put more in a box than the box can hold, you must either make the box bigger or create another box for the overflow. If you don't like the position of a box, you can pick it up and move it somewhere else. Boxes can go on top of pages or on top of other boxes. Boxes, or frames, can have their own column and margin settings just as a page can. The margin and column settings for frames are not stored with a style sheet. Because the settings for frames are unique for each chapter, the frame settings are stored in the CHP file. Frames often confuse users of Ventura. If you understand the concepts in this paragraph, you shouldn't be confused any longer.

Using the definitions just given, you can substitute the terms used by Ventura. Pages are the bottom level, or underlying frame. Only text can flow onto a page. Graphics, captions, or additional text must be placed inside a frame. The frame goes on top of the page or another frame. Users of PageMaker may find the concept of boxes or frames a little unsettling. Don't make frames complicated or constricting; you will soon find the way Ventura organizes and places text and graphics to be logical, straightforward, flexible, and more powerful than you can imagine.

5.18 Tip

Use the Margins & Columns command from the Frame menu to set margins and columns for a page or frame.

Set the columns and margins of a clean page with no frames by changing to Frame mode and selecting Margins & Columns from the Frame menu. Set the columns and margins of a frame by selecting the frame before selecting Margins & Columns from the Frame menu.

If you have created frames and placed them on the page, setting columns and margins is a bit more complex. After switching to Frame mode, you must select the page before setting the margins and columns. If you don't select the page first, you may accidentally set margins and columns for one of the frames on the page.

To set margins and columns for a page or frame, do the following:

1. Change to Frame mode and select the desired page (by clicking anywhere on the page) or frame (by clicking in the frame). When you have selected the page or frame, eight little black boxes (called *handles*) surround the page—one box at each corner and one in the middle of the sides (see fig. 5.12).

2. Choose Margins & Columns from the Frame menu (see fig. 5.13). Don't be confused; if you are setting columns and margins for a *page*, you must use the *Frame menu*. If it doesn't confuse you, consider the page to be one big frame. If it does confuse you, just remember to set the columns and margins for the page or frame from the Frame menu.

3. From the MARGINS & COLUMNS dialog box, choose the number of columns. Click a number from 1 to 8.

4. Set the four margins for the page—top, bottom, left, and right. Text and graphics are not placed in the space that you designate as margins space.

5. The number of columns you select is divided into the actual frame width of the page, minus the left and right margins, to produce columns of equal width. If you want columns of unequal width, edit the widths manually. (Do not specify widths that are more than the width of the page.) If you decide to have columns of equal width, click `Make Equal Widths` and Ventura recalculates equal column widths.

6. Set `Gutters` (the space between columns) to the amount you want.

7. Click OK or press Enter.

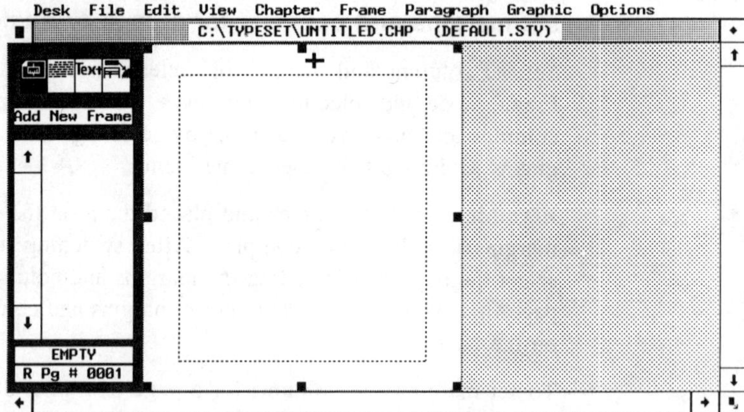

Fig. 5.12.
Reduced view of selected page showing all eight handles.

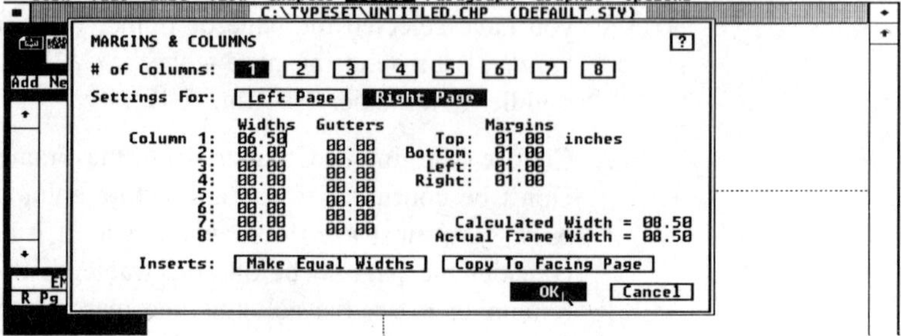

Fig. 5.13.
The MARGINS & COLUMNS dialog box.

5.19 Trap

Ventura does not always warn you if the sum of column widths is greater than the actual width of the page.

As you enter values on the MARGINS & COLUMNS dialog box, notice the `Calculated Width` and `Actual Frame Width` values. These numbers change as you modify the layout of the page and give you an idea of the amount of space left to assign to a column.

You may possibly exceed the actual page width. If you do, your design won't be as planned. If the numbers get too out of line, Ventura issues a warning.

5.20 Tip

Set Sides to Double from the PAGE LAYOUT dialog box to have different column and margin settings for facing pages.

If you are creating a double-sided document, decide whether you want columns and margins the same or different on facing pages. If you want them different, enter the settings for either the left page or right page; then click the button for the other page and enter new values for the other page. If you want facing pages to have the same specifications, click `Copy To Facing Page`.

Controlling Tag Elements

In Ventura, one of the most difficult tasks to keep up with is managing paragraph tags. Not only can the names of the tags be cryptic, but keeping track of all the settings for each tag can be a major job. When you move between projects, each with its own layout and set of tags, the job becomes overwhelming. This section offers some suggestions for tag organization.

5.21 Tip

Develop a system for keeping track of tags.

You can keep track of tags in three basic ways:

- ❑ Use a utility such as Desktop Manager from New Riders Publishing, or VP Toolbox 3.0 from SNA, Incorporated. Such utilities developed for Ventura (with or without the Professional Extension) can tell you what tags are contained in a style sheet and what the settings for each tag are. Desktop Manager works within Ventura as a memory-resident utility and produces reports that can be printed by Ventura. VP Toolbox 3.0 works as a stand-alone utility and has much more power for modifying and consolidating tags and style sheets. VP Toolbox also tells you which tags aren't being used so those tags can be deleted easily.

- ❑ Use the catalog capability in Ventura. When in Paragraph mode, press Ctrl-K or select Update Tag List from the Paragraph menu. Click `Print Stylesheet` from the UPDATE TAG LIST dialog box to produce a file of generated text with your choice of name and the GEN extension. This file contains a log of the major settings, including tag settings, for your chapter (see fig. 5.14). Load the style sheet STYLOG.STY in the TYPESET directory and load the generated text file so that you can read or print it.

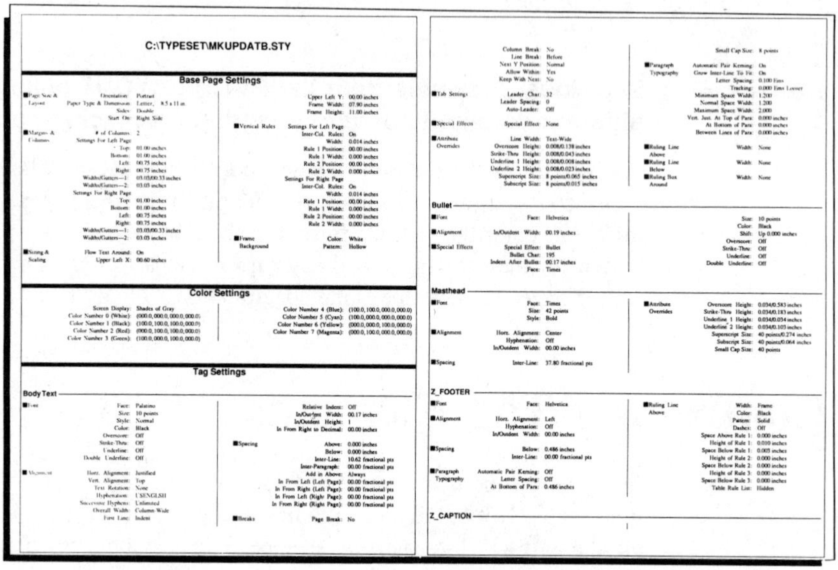

C:\TYPESET\MKUPDATB.STY

Base Page Settings

Color Settings

Tag Settings

Fig. 5.14.

The first two pages of a style sheet report prepared and printed by Ventura.

- ❑ Use a written log to keep track of settings for each chapter and tag. In the workbook provided with your Ventura program is a page planning and tag content form. Copy this form before filling it in.

Each of the three methods of managing tags has its good and bad points. My suggestion is to use Desktop Manager and periodically produce reports on chapter and tag content with either Desktop Manager or with Ventura's built-in Print Stylesheet function. For more precise control over tags, use VP Toolbox 3.0.

Naming, Renaming, and Removing Tags

Part of managing tags used to format your documents is the maintenance of lists of tag names. As you become more familiar with Ventura, you will find yourself naming and renaming tags, and removing them from the style sheet altogether. Tag names can be up to 13 characters long, including spaces and capital or lowercase letters. (Ventura doesn't distinguish between case in tag names.) The tips in this section help you to simplify this process.

5.22 Tip **Keep the same tag names in various style sheets to allow quick modification of documents by switching style sheets.**

Flexibility is a built-in benefit of Ventura. Any time it is possible, make maximum use of that flexibility. Switching from one style sheet to another is a powerful and efficient way to quickly modify the look of an entire document.

As an example, assume that you are heading a new newsletter project. One of your groups is responsible for developing text and graphics—the content. Another group is responsible for how the newsletter will look—the design. Within the design group are several competing layouts, and you, as project coordinator, have not yet decided which layout you prefer.

In your initial instructions to the design group, provide a list of tag names to use: all headings are tagged *Heading*, all subheadings are tagged *Subheading*, all bylines are tagged *Byline*, and so on (these same tag names are given to the content group for inclusion in text files). The design group then creates a series of mock newsletters with different designs. The designs are controlled by the style sheets; the style sheets use the same tag names, but the tags have different specifications.

To make your decision, load the text and graphics. Then switch from one style sheet to another to examine the different designs, print out samples, and make a decision. Because the content group used the same tag names as the design group in developing text, you do not have to change or apply tags; swapping style sheets does all the work for you.

Figures 5.15 and 5.16 are examples. Figure 5.15 uses Adobe Palatino as the body font and Adobe Helvetica for the heading, subheading, and table of contents. Figure 5.16 uses Adobe Helvetica for the body text and Adobe ITC Franklin Gothic Demi and Heavy for the heading, subheading, and table of contents. A simple switch from one style sheet to another accomplished the transformation.

Fig. 5.15.

Newsletter using the Palatino and Helvetica fonts.

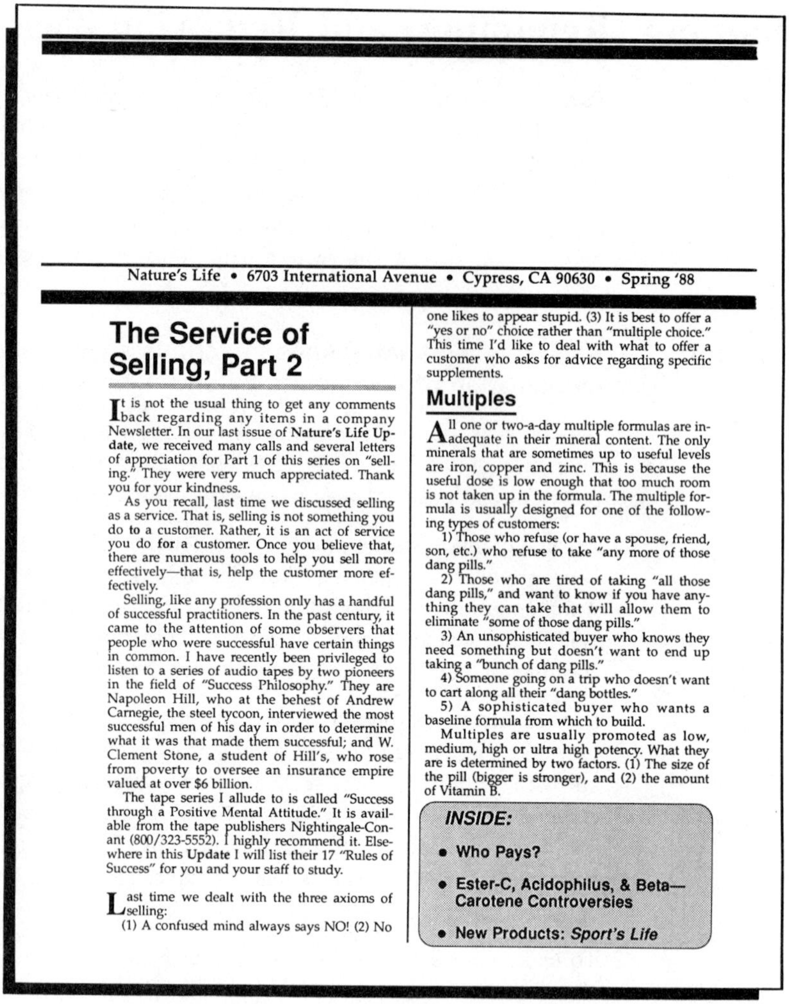

Nature's Life • 6703 International Avenue • Cypress, CA 90630 • Spring '88

The Service of Selling, Part 2

It is not the usual thing to get any comments back regarding any items in a company Newsletter. In our last issue of **Nature's Life Update**, we received many calls and several letters of appreciation for Part 1 of this series on "selling." They were very much appreciated. Thank you for your kindness.

As you recall, last time we discussed selling as a service. That is, selling is not something you do **to** a customer. Rather, it is an act of service you do **for** a customer. Once you believe that, there are numerous tools to help you sell more effectively—that is, help the customer more effectively.

Selling, like any profession only has a handful of successful practitioners. In the past century, it came to the attention of some observers that people who were successful have certain things in common. I have recently been privileged to listen to a series of audio tapes by two pioneers in the field of "Success Philosophy." They are Napoleon Hill, who at the behest of Andrew Carnegie, the steel tycoon, interviewed the most successful men of his day in order to determine what it was that made them successful; and W. Clement Stone, a student of Hill's, who rose from poverty to oversee an insurance empire valued at over $6 billion.

The tape series I allude to is called "Success through a Positive Mental Attitude." It is available from the tape publishers Nightingale-Conant (800/323-5552). I highly recommend it. Elsewhere in this **Update** I will list their 17 "Rules of Success" for you and your staff to study.

Last time we dealt with the three axioms of selling:

(1) A confused mind always says NO! (2) No one likes to appear stupid. (3) It is best to offer a "yes or no" choice rather than "multiple choice." This time I'd like to deal with what to offer a customer who asks for advice regarding specific supplements.

Multiples

All one or two-a-day multiple formulas are inadequate in their mineral content. The only minerals that are sometimes up to useful levels are iron, copper and zinc. This is because the useful dose is low enough that too much room is not taken up in the formula. The multiple formula is usually designed for one of the following types of customers:

1) Those who refuse (or have a spouse, friend, son, etc.) who refuse to take "any more of those dang pills."

2) Those who are tired of taking "all those dang pills," and want to know if you have anything they can take that will allow them to eliminate "some of those dang pills."

3) An unsophisticated buyer who knows they need something but doesn't want to end up taking a "bunch of dang pills."

4) Someone going on a trip who doesn't want to cart along all their "dang bottles."

5) A sophisticated buyer who wants a baseline formula from which to build.

Multiples are usually promoted as low, medium, high or ultra high potency. What they are is determined by two factors. (1) The size of the pill (bigger is stronger), and (2) the amount of Vitamin B.

INSIDE:

- **Who Pays?**
- **Ester-C, Acidophilus, & Beta—Carotene Controversies**
- **New Products: *Sport's Life***

Other examples where you may want to switch style sheets to modify designs are for correspondence, catalogs (or other database publishing), forms, and fliers.

Develop a list of tag names that you want to use in different types of documents. Let members of design teams know the tag names that are standard for the document they are working on. Keep tag names simple and descriptive: *Heading* is easier to understand than *HL fnt H12B*, although Ventura accepts both names.

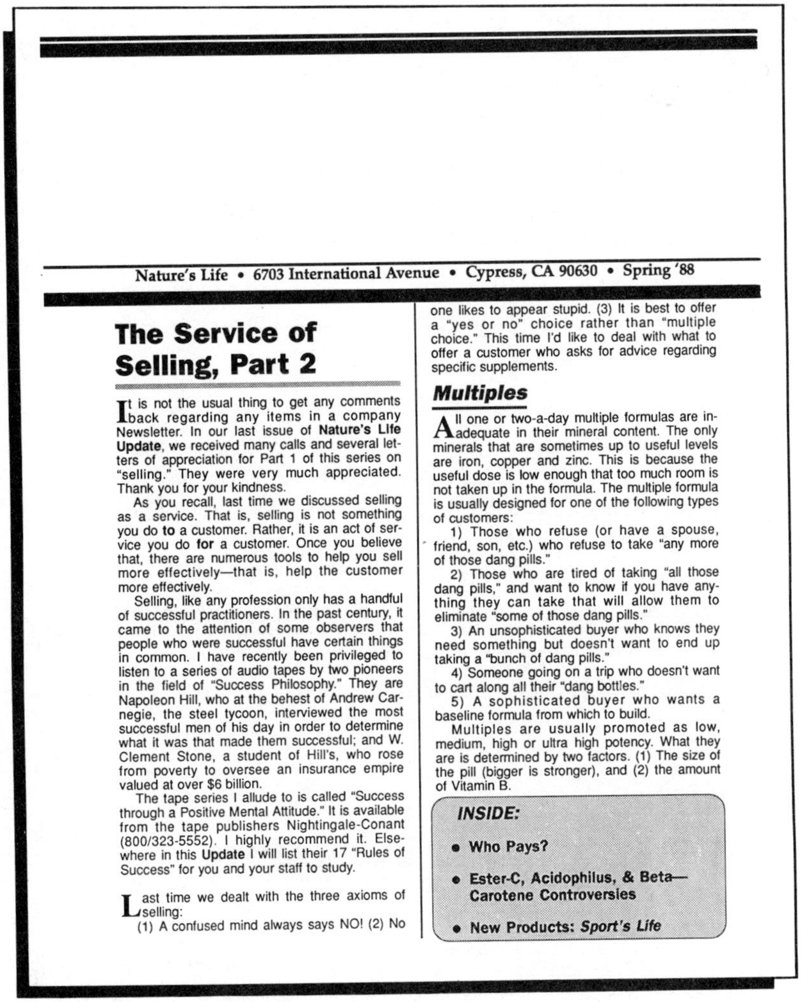

Nature's Life • 6703 International Avenue • Cypress, CA 90630 • Spring '88

The Service of Selling, Part 2

It is not the usual thing to get any comments back regarding any items in a company Newsletter. In our last issue of **Nature's Life Update**, we received many calls and several letters of appreciation for Part 1 of this series on "selling." They were very much appreciated. Thank you for your kindness.

As you recall, last time we discussed selling as a service. That is, selling is not something you do **to** a customer. Rather, it is an act of service you do **for** a customer. Once you believe that, there are numerous tools to help you sell more effectively—that is, help the customer more effectively.

Selling, like any profession only has a handful of successful practitioners. In the past century, it came to the attention of some observers that people who were successful have certain things in common. I have recently been privileged to listen to a series of audio tapes by two pioneers in the field of "Success Philosophy." They are Napoleon Hill, who at the behest of Andrew Carnegie, the steel tycoon, interviewed the most successful men of his day in order to determine what it was that made them successful; and W. Clement Stone, a student of Hill's, who rose from poverty to oversee an insurance empire valued at over $6 billion.

The tape series I allude to is called "Success through a Positive Mental Attitude." It is available from the tape publishers Nightingale-Conant (800/323-5552). I highly recommend it. Elsewhere in this **Update** I will list their 17 "Rules of Success" for you and your staff to study.

Last time we dealt with the three axioms of selling:

(1) A confused mind always says NO! (2) No one likes to appear stupid. (3) It is best to offer a "yes or no" choice rather than "multiple choice." This time I'd like to deal with what to offer a customer who asks for advice regarding specific supplements.

Multiples

All one or two-a-day multiple formulas are inadequate in their mineral content. The only minerals that are sometimes up to useful levels are iron, copper and zinc. This is because the useful dose is low enough that too much room is not taken up in the formula. The multiple formula is usually designed for one of the following types of customers:

1) Those who refuse (or have a spouse, friend, son, etc.) who refuse to take "any more of those dang pills."

2) Those who are tired of taking "all those dang pills," and want to know if you have anything they can take that will allow them to eliminate "some of those dang pills."

3) An unsophisticated buyer who knows they need something but doesn't want to end up taking a "bunch of dang pills."

4) Someone going on a trip who doesn't want to cart along all their "dang bottles."

5) A sophisticated buyer who wants a baseline formula from which to build.

Multiples are usually promoted as low, medium, high or ultra high potency. What they are is determined by two factors. (1) The size of the pill (bigger is stronger), and (2) the amount of Vitamin B.

INSIDE:

- **Who Pays?**
- **Ester-C, Acidophilus, & Beta—Carotene Controversies**
- **New Products: *Sport's Life***

Fig. 5.16.

Newsletter using the Helvetica and Franklin Gothic fonts.

5.23 Tip **If you want to remove or rename a tag, use the UPDATE TAG LIST dialog box.**

To keep the assignment list uncluttered and to avoid confusion in assigning tags, when no paragraphs are assigned to a specific tag, remove the tag from the assignment list. You can tell which tags are assigned and in use by clicking a paragraph while in Paragraph mode and noting the tag name in the current selection box. The VP Toolbox utility has an option that tells you which tags are unassigned and not in use. You also may want or need to rename a tag at some point. To remove or rename a tag, follow these steps:

1. Select Paragraph mode by clicking the Paragraph icon or pressing Ctrl-I.

2. Click Update Tag List from the Paragraph menu or use the keyboard shortcut Ctrl-K.

3. If you have not already saved the chapter, you are prompted to save or abandon changes. Click `Save` or press Enter. (If the chapter is untitled, you are prompted to enter the name of a chapter.)

4. Scroll through the `Tag` list on the UPDATE TAG LIST dialog box (see fig. 5.17). Click the tag you want to remove.

5. Click `Remove Selected Tag`.

6. The REMOVE TAG dialog box appears (see fig. 5.18). The tag you are removing appears on the `Tag Name to Remove` line. The `Tag Name to Convert to` line lists `Body Text`. (You also can change the conversion name to any existing tag name.) Click OK or press Enter.

Fig. 5.17.
The UPDATE TAG LIST dialog box.

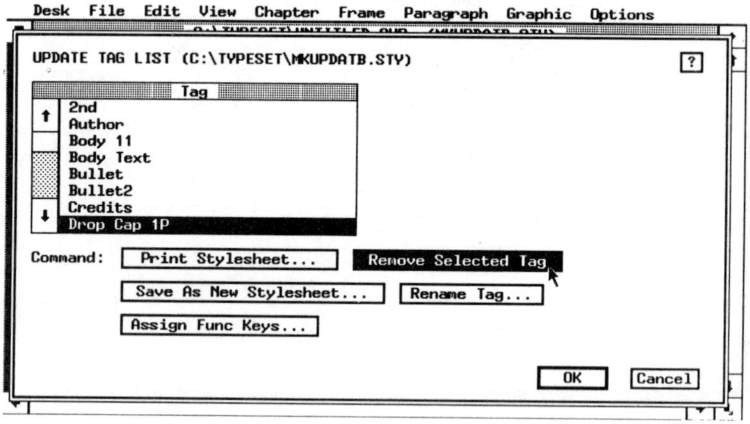

The tag name you removed or renamed is no longer on the `Tag` list on the UPDATE TAG LIST dialog box or in the assignment list. All paragraphs associated with that tag are retagged with the specified conversion tag name.

5.24 Trap

Be careful about removing tags from shared style sheets.

If you remove a tag from a style sheet used by other chapters and then load one of those chapters, the assignment list shows the name of the deleted tag, but the tag has the attributes of the Body Text tag.

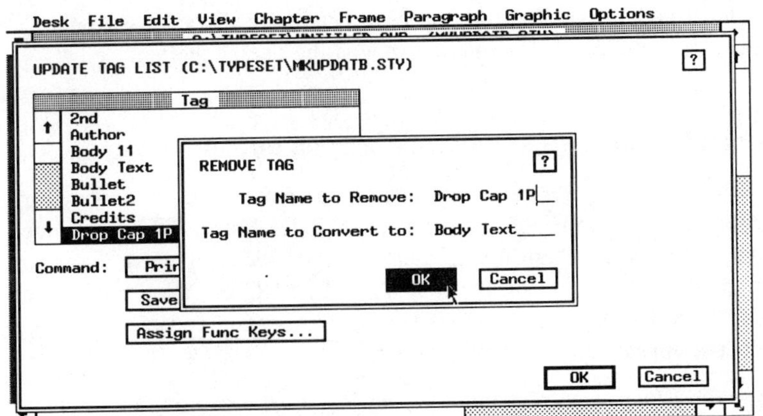

Fig. 5.18.

The REMOVE TAG dialog box.

If you rename your style sheets so that each document has a unique style sheet, you do not have the problem of deleting tags used by other documents.

5.25 Trick Develop a system for naming tags.

Because a tag name can be 13 characters long, you have a great deal of flexibility in naming tags. Unfortunately, cryptic and unhelpful tag names are all too common. Although this may not be too great a problem if you are the only person using the chapter, if others work with you or edit your chapters, you make life easier by developing a system of naming tags. Tags appear in the assignment list in alphabetical order, regardless of when they were created. Tags beginning with numbers appear before tags beginning with letters.

You can name tags by using one of several strategies:

- Name by hierarchy. For example, name all tags dealing with headers *Heading 1*, *Heading 2*, *Heading 3*, and so on. Do not name the tags *1 Heading* and *2 Heading* because the tags are placed in the assignment list in alphabetical order. If you have other tags with leading numbers, the tags are ordered according to number instead of by function.
- Name by type. Use the same name for the first part of the tag and distinguish the tag by the rest of the name so that all tags of the same type appear together on the assignment list. The names *Text Times 12* and *Text Times 14*, for example, distinguish between two tags whose primary difference is 12-point text and 14-point text.
- Name by group. If you have a sidebar in the document, you may want to use different fonts in that area than in the rest of the article. Name the tags for the sidebar *SB Heading*, *SB Text*, *SB*

Author, and so on. The tags are associated with the sidebar by the letters *SB*; the rest of the name explains the use of the tag.

5.26 Tip

Z_ tags can be modified in the same way as any other tag.

Ventura automatically creates a tag whenever you create a header, footer, caption, section number, and table of contents or index entry. These generated tags are preceded by the characters Z_ and appear on the assignment list if you set `Generated Tags: Shown` on the SET PREFERENCES dialog box (which you access from the Options menu). If you set `Generated Tags: Hidden`, the Z_ tags do not appear in the assignment list.

You can modify (and even rename) a Z_ tag just as you can any other tag.

5.27 Tip

Ventura requires a tag named Body Text.

You cannot remove or rename the Body Text tag. If you try, Ventura does not allow it and issues a warning.

Assigning Tags to Paragraphs

Ventura allows you several ways to assign tags to text. You can assign a tag name to a function key and, while in Paragraph mode, select a paragraph. Or while you're in Text mode, insert the cursor anywhere in a paragraph and then simply press the function key to tag the current paragraph. Alternatively, you can use your word processor to insert tag names in text, as explained in Chapter 4. When loaded into Ventura, Ventura assigns the correct tags. The tips in this section explain how to speed up the process of tagging paragraphs.

5.28 Tip

For increased speed in tagging, assign up to 10 tags to function keys.

Pressing Ctrl-K in any mode except Paragraph gives you a shortcut to the ASSIGN FUNCTION KEYS dialog box (see fig. 5.19). If you press Ctrl-K or select Update Tag List in Paragraph mode, you first encounter the UPDATE TAG LIST dialog box from which you click `Assign Func. Keys` to reach the ASSIGN FUNCTION KEYS dialog box. You can assign up to 10 tag names to the function keys. Ventura does not support the F11 or F12 function keys, and unfortunately you cannot use Alt, Shift, or Ctrl in combination with the function keys to add more tags.

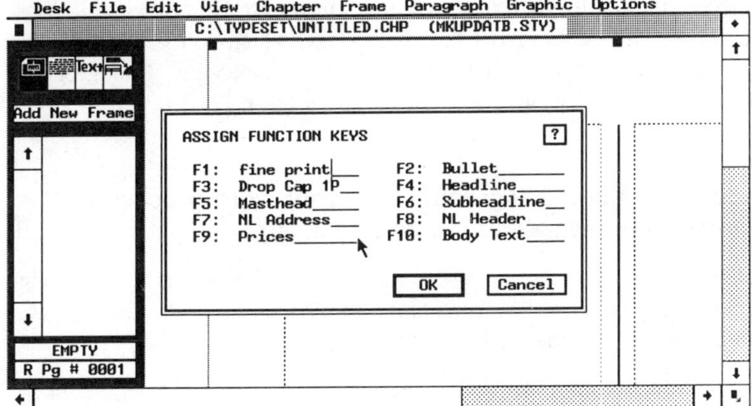

Fig. 5.19.
The ASSIGN FUNCTION KEYS dialog box.

Although it doesn't matter whether you capitalize a tag name in the same way as it was created, you must spell and space the tag name exactly the same as in the assignment list. If any tag names are spelled or spaced incorrectly, Ventura notifies you as you exit the ASSIGN FUNCTION KEYS dialog box. Function keys with incorrect tag names either stay unassigned or, if previously assigned to another tag, revert to the previous tag name.

Once assigned, you can tag a paragraph with a function key in one of two ways:

- ❑ In Paragraph mode, select the paragraph and then press a function key. The tag assigned to the function key is applied to the selected paragraph. This method also works if you have selected multiple paragraphs.
- ❑ In Text mode, press a function key. Whatever paragraph the cursor is in at the time you press the function key has the tag assigned to the function key applied.

5.29 Tip **In the word processing stage of development, you can assign tags that do not exist, but when you load the text file into Ventura, the unassigned tags appear in all uppercase letters in the assignment list.**

If you tag paragraphs in your word processor with tags that do not exist in the style sheet to be used with the file, these tag names appear in all uppercase letters in the Paragraph mode assignment list when the file is loaded to Ventura. Ventura creates a corresponding tag and assigns the tag the characteristics of the Body Text tag.

After modifying the tag to your specifications, rename the tag (use the Rename Tag option on the UPDATE TAG LIST dialog box, which you access from the Paragraph menu) so that the letters are no longer uppercase. Changing the name reminds you that you have already modified the tag.

5.30 Trap

If you incorrectly enter a tag name with your word processor, Ventura treats the misspelled tag as a new tag.

Be careful when you type tag names in your word processor. If you accidentally misspell a tag name, Ventura treats the misspelled tag as a new tag. The new, unidentified tag has the characteristics of the Body Text tag.

Use a keyboard macro program (such as SuperKey from Borland) or the macro capabilities of your word processor (if your word processor has one) to assign common tag names to macro keys to avoid spelling errors in tag names.

5.31 Tip

Use a utility such as PubStar I to assist you when assigning tags with your word processor.

PubStar I is a utility from Metroplex Digital Corporation developed to help Ventura users easily tag paragraphs while using their word processors. Load PubStar I before starting your word processor. While typing text in your word processor, you can bring up the PubStar I menu, which displays all the tags in the style sheet you designate. Other features allow you to examine the main attributes of a tag, create a new tag, modify an existing tag, remove a tag, and even insert special characters (like copyright symbols) and index entries.

If you plan to pretag most of your text, PubStar I can save you a great deal of time and prevent you from making errors in tag names.

Understanding Font Attributes

The topic of fonts is covered in detail in Chapter 9. Fonts are in many ways the most interesting aspect of desktop publishing. Each font has a history and a purpose. Some fonts *shout* at you with their boldness or design. Some fonts quietly inform; others insist. Some fonts try to attract attention and others try to hide information (like the warnings on cigarette packs or the fine print on a contract). After using fonts for a time, you find yourself noticing the fonts used on street signs compared with the fonts used in a brochure for a hotel chain. As you become "font aware," the world of printed words never seems the same.

In Ventura style sheets, fonts are associated with tags: each tag has a specific font. You change fonts either with a tag or by setting a font attribute. Within a paragraph, an attribute (such as underlines, subscripts, or even a complete font change) can affect all or part of a word, sentence, or paragraph. The specified attributes override the font setting of the tag. Attribute settings do not affect the tag setting although they do override the tag setting.

5.32 Tip **The Set Font addition button really means "Set Font Attribute for the Tagged Text."**

In Text mode, you can change selected text in one of two ways:

- ❑ You can click the Set Font addition button (or use the keyboard shortcut Ctrl-2). When you click the Set Font button, the same dialog box appears as if you had selected Font from the Paragraph menu, but the dialog box is called FONT SETTING FOR SELECTED TEXT (see fig. 5.20).

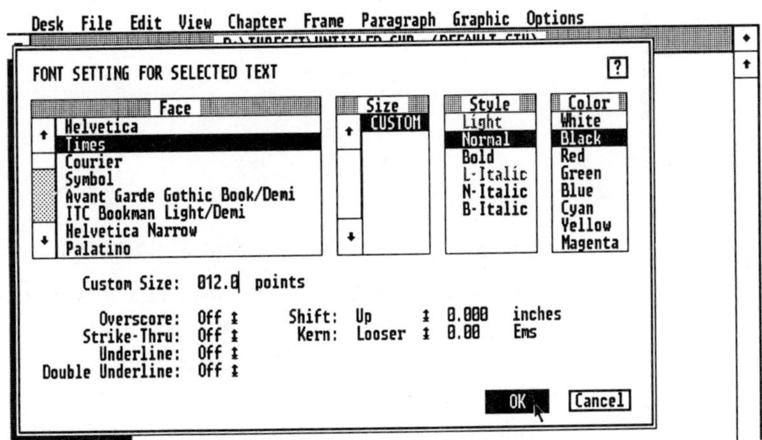

Fig. 5.20.
The FONT SETTING FOR SELECTED TEXT dialog box.

Only the selected text is affected by the specifications made in this dialog box (whether you have selected one letter or all the text on a page) unless you have changed the `Line Width` setting to `Margin-Wide` on the ATTRIBUTE OVERRIDES dialog box from the Paragraph mode (in which case, some attributes extend from margin to margin). You can change fonts; alter font size, style, and color; turn overscore, strike-through, underline, or double-underline on or off; shift text up or down; and kern or spread text by using the FONT SETTING FOR SELECTED TEXT dialog box.

Whatever attributes you set in the dialog box override the attributes previously set for the text by the paragraph tag.

If you change your mind later about the attributes you have set for text, reselect the text, click the Set Font button, and use the FONT SETTING FOR SELECTED TEXT dialog box to change the specifications.

- You can click any of the 10 options in the assignment list that affect appearance; there are also 3 options (uppercase, capitalize, and lowercase) that determine whether lowercase or uppercase letters are used (see fig. 5.21). You can choose more than one option, but some, like superscript and subscript, override each other.

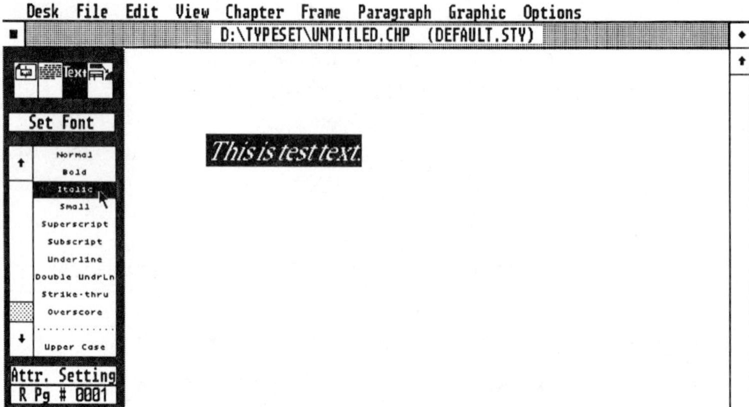

Fig. 5.21.
Text attributes listed in the assignment list.

5.33 Trap

Attributes set in Text mode are not stored with the style sheet.

Remember that attributes set in the Text mode become embedded codes in the text file and are not part of a style sheet. Attributes set with the Paragraph menu in Paragraph mode become part of a tag stored in a style sheet.

5.34 Trick

Click Normal to reset selected text to tag settings.

If you have set a number of attributes and decide you want to restore the text to its tag settings, reselect the text and then click `Normal` in the assignment list. All the attributes are removed whether they were set from the FONT SETTING FOR SELECTED TEXT dialog box or applied from the assignment list.

5.35 Trap

Clicking Capitalize capitalizes all words.

If you are trying to capitalize the title of a book or phrases in which some words (such as *of* or *the*) are not normally capitalized, don't use the `Capitalize` option on the whole phrase. If you do apply the `Capitalize` option to an entire block of text, you must edit the words that are incorrectly capitalized.

5.36 Tip **You can set the typeface for individual characters.**

At times you may want to change the typeface for individual characters or words in a paragraph. (If you want to alter the typeface for an entire paragraph, select the paragraph in Paragraph mode and use the Font command from the Paragraph menu to alter the tag specifications.)

Following are several examples of situations in which you may want to change the typeface of a single character or word (see fig. 5.22).

- ❑ Dingbats. If you have a PostScript printer or if dingbat types of characters are available on your printer, you can add a dingbat for emphasis.
- ❑ Symbols. Mathematical symbols and special alphabets are available.
- ❑ Emphasis. A different typeface can be used for special effect or emphasis.

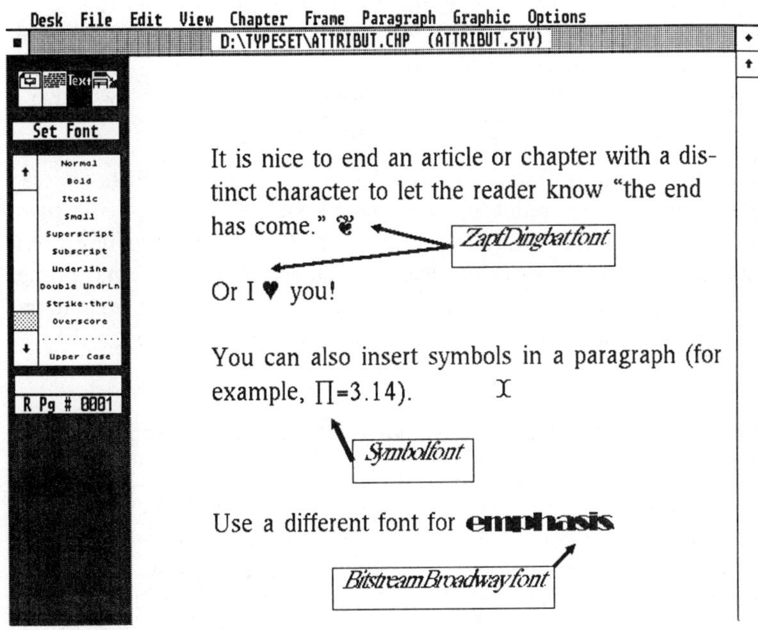

Fig. 5.22.
Examples of font changes within a paragraph.

5.37 Tip

You can set font sizes interactively.

Ventura gives you three ways to change font size:

- Paragraph mode dialog box. Change the point size of text by selecting a paragraph and then selecting Font from the Paragraph menu. Make the desired changes to the `Size` option on the FONT dialog box.
- Text mode dialog box. Select the desired text and change the point size by clicking the Set Font addition button or using the shortcut Ctrl-2. Make the desired changes to the `Size` option on the FONT SETTING FOR SELECTED TEXT dialog box.
- Text mode interactive. Select the desired text; instead of accessing the FONT SETTING FOR SELECTED TEXT dialog box, hold down the Shift key and press the up- or down-arrow key. Press Shift-down arrow to decrease the point size one point at a time; press Shift-up arrow to increase the point size one point at a time.

If you have a printer with only a few point sizes (for example, an Epson LQ with seven point-size choices), to change from 14 to 18 points, press shift-up arrow four times. The fourth time you press the up arrow, the screen font changes size. Pressing Shift and one of the arrows cannot decrease or increase point sizes beyond the sizes available in the dialog boxes.

If you have a PostScript printer or a printer that allows font scaling, you can change the point sizes one point at a time interactively (or in one-tenth point increments from the FONT SETTING FOR SELECTED TEXT dialog box). Because all printer font sizes are not usually installed as screen fonts, printer font sizes without corresponding screen font sizes look ragged on your monitor. This ragged appearance does not affect the final printed output.

5.38 Tip

Learn the distinction between pair kerning, letter spacing, and tracking.

On the TYPOGRAPHY SETTINGS dialog box, which you access from the Paragraph menu, are settings for `Automatic Pair Kerning`, `Letter Spacing`, and `Tracking`. Definitions for these three options are given here so that you can use them more efficiently while in Paragraph mode. To reach this dialog box, select a paragraph and then choose Paragraph Typography from the Paragraph menu.

- `Automatic Pair Kerning`. This option moves specific letter pairs closer together for easier reading. Usually, kerning is more important with large font sizes than with small font sizes. Kerning is done automatically with Ventura using information in the printer width tables. Depending on your printer and the manufacturer of the font (generally the provider of the width table information), kerning information for a range of 100 to 500 font pairs is available. The arrows in figure 5.23 show where pair kerning has taken place. Notice how the pairs of letters have moved closer together to create a more pleasing visual image. In small point sizes, such subtleties are lost and Ventura spends unnecessary time formatting and printing.

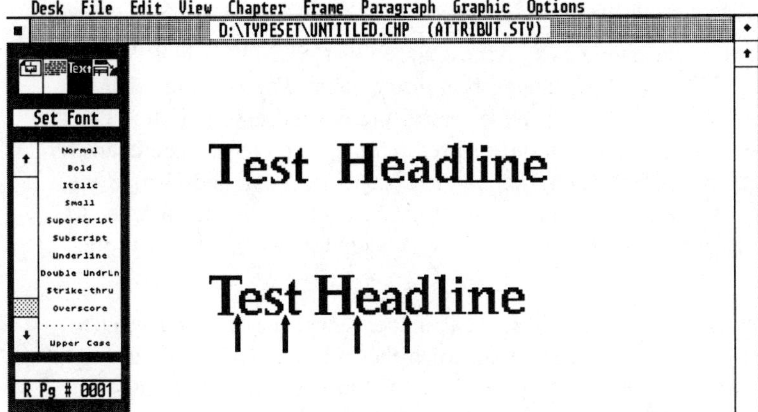

Fig. 5.23.

Kerning larger font sizes.

- ❑ `Letter Spacing`. This option justifies a line of text by adding space not just between words, but between letters. If no hyphenation point exists in a long word at the beginning of a line, that word cannot be split to help "fill in" the space on the preceding line, making the preceding line look loose (too much space between words). Ventura highlights loose lines if you click Show Loose Lines from the Options menu. If you set `Letter Spacing: On` in the TYPOGRAPHY SETTINGS dialog box, you can specify the amount of space allowed between letters by using the `space width` options.

- ❑ `Tracking`. This option controls whether every letter is closer together or farther apart in an entire paragraph. You can tighten or loosen this spacing. You may want to change the tracking value to tighten a heading or to fit an extra line on a page. The more you tighten the text, the more text fits in the same space (sort of like cramming an extra box into the trunk of your car).

5.39 Tip

You can set intercharacter font spacing interactively.

You can change the space between characters in a number of ways.

- Paragraph mode dialog box. In Paragraph mode, select a paragraph and then choose Paragraph Typography from the Paragraph menu to access the TYPOGRAPHY SETTINGS dialog box. If you turned `Pair Kerning: On` in the CHAPTER TYPOGRAPHY dialog box from the Chapter menu, you can set `Automatic Pair Kerning: On` in the TYPOGRAPHY SETTINGS dialog box from the Paragraph menu.
- Text mode dialog box. Access the FONT SETTING FOR SELECTED TEXT dialog box in the same way you did when setting fonts: in Text mode, select the desired text and click the Set Font addition button (or press Ctrl-2). To change intercharacter spacing, select `Kern: Looser` or `Kern: Tighter` and change the `Ems` value appropriately. An *em* is the width of a capital letter M (although Ventura uses the @ character for better results) in the selected font.
- Text mode interactive. In Text mode, select the text you want to kern tighter or looser. Hold down the Shift key and press the right arrow to increase the space (by 0.02 em each time you press the arrow) between the characters; press the left arrow to decrease the space (by 0.01 em each time you press the arrow) between the characters. As you press the arrows, the spacing between the letters changes on-screen.

One sophisticated use of this interactive spacing capability is increasing the space between letters of an entire headline to make the headline spread across the width of the page.

5.40 Tip

Learn how to shift text up or down from the baseline.

You can make minute changes in interline spacing by selecting the text you want to adjust and clicking the Set Font addition button or pressing Ctrl-2. Set `Shift: Up` or `Shift: Down` in the FONT SETTING FOR SELECTED TEXT dialog box and enter the amount of space you want to shift the selected text. Click OK or press Enter. Any changes are immediately reflected on the screen.

If you shift text too much, one line of text may overlap another line of text, making both lines illegible.

Using Underline, Overscore, and Strike-Through

You can emphasize text by using the underline, overscore, and strike-through options offered by Ventura. As with other text attributes, you can assign these options in one of two ways. If the attribute is to affect the entire paragraph, use the Paragraph menu's Font command to access the FONT dialog box. If the attribute is to affect a portion of text within a paragraph, select text while in Text mode and choose the desired attribute from the assignment list.

5.41 Tip **Unless you want an entire paragraph affected, use Text mode and select only the words you want to underline, double-underline, strike-through, or overscore.**

In Text mode, select the text to which you want to apply an attribute and click `Underline`, `Double UndrLn`, `Strike-thru`, or `Overscore` on the assignment list. You can apply one of the underline attributes and the strike-through and overscore attributes to the same text.

In Text mode, you can select the text to which you apply attributes; in Paragraph mode, the attributes are applied to entire paragraphs.

5.42 Trap **Underlining also underlines spaces.**

Ventura does not offer the option of whether spaces in text are underlined. When you tag text and turn on `UnderLine` or `Double UndrLn`, words *and spaces* are underlined. If you want to underline only text, you must select individual words and apply the `Underline` attribute to each word (see fig. 5.24).

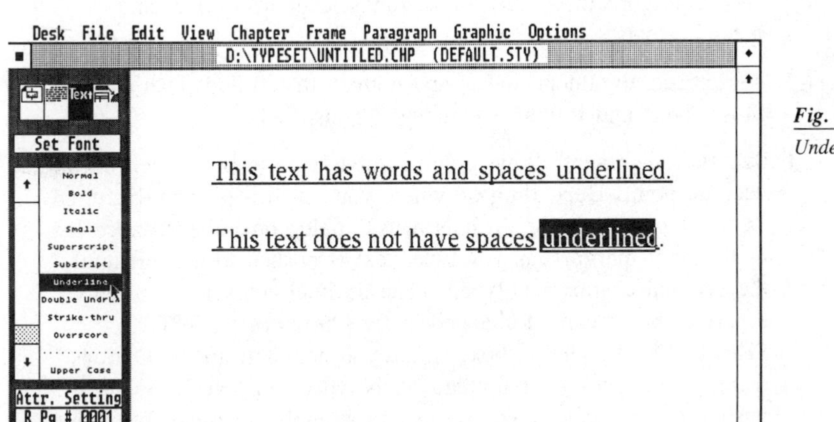

Fig. 5.24. *Underlined text.*

5.43 Trap **If both underline and double-underline features are applied to the same text, the double-underline takes precedence.**

Obviously, you cannot have text that is both underlined and double-underlined. If you try to set both these text attributes, double-underlining takes precedence.

Selecting Alignment Options

You can change the alignment of text in a paragraph on a page with the Alignment command on the Paragraph menu. The ALIGNMENT dialog box is straightforward. Whenever you create a tag, you should glance at this dialog box. The options you may commonly change are Horz. Alignment, Vert. Alignment, and Indent or Outdent. Text Rotation is rarely used (discussed in Chapter 9); once set, the Hyphenation option should remain constant.

5.44 Tip **Set horizontal alignment from the ALIGNMENT dialog box.**

The Horz. Alignment option on the ALIGNMENT dialog box sets text so it can be aligned Left, Center, Right, Justified, or Decimal (see fig. 5.25). Each of these types of alignment is described next:

- Left alignment makes text flush left with a ragged or unjustified right margin.
- Right alignment makes text flush right with a ragged left margin. As you type, you begin at the right margin and text is pushed to the left.
- Center alignment is used for headings, captions, verse, and special effects.
- Justified alignment makes text both flush left and flush right. Most books and formal documents are justified.
- Decimal alignment allows columns of figures to be aligned on the decimal point. Depending on where you set the In From Right to Decimal option on the ALIGNMENT dialog box (the distance left of the right margin), as you type, text is pushed to the left until the decimal character is typed. (The decimal character is usually a period, but it can be changed in the Option menu SET PREFERENCES dialog box, which you access from the Options menu.) After the decimal character is typed, all text following it is pushed to the right. If you need more complex decimal formatting, you must set decimal tabs.

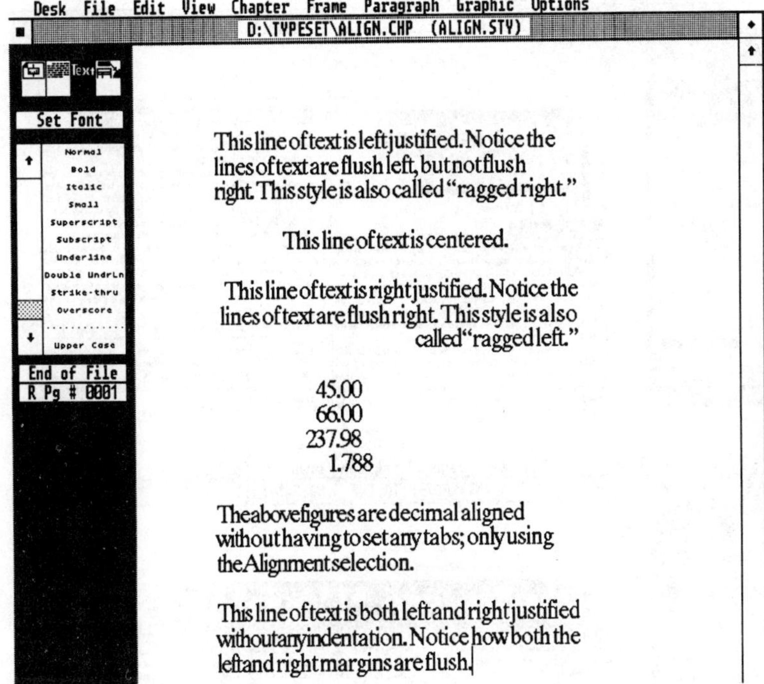

Fig. 5.25.

Examples of various text alignments.

5.45 Tip

Change the Overall Width setting to Frame-Wide to override the page or frame column settings.

Once you have set up columns, text (including headlines) respects the column boundaries. When you want text to extend past column boundaries and spread across an entire page or frame, you must override the column settings. In figure 5.26, a heading is restricted to the width of the column. By changing the `Overall Width` option on the ALIGNMENT dialog box to `Frame-Wide` (remember, this can mean Page-Wide), the heading overrides the column barrier and extends across the entire page (see fig. 5.27).

5.46 Tip

Don't use tabs to indent the first line of a paragraph. Use the Indent option instead. Because Ventura doesn't have a margin release feature, use the Outdent option to put text outside of the margin boundaries.

If you like to indent the first line of a paragraph, don't use tabs to achieve the effect. Instead, set `First Line: Indent` and specify a value for `In/Outdent Width` on the ALIGNMENT dialog box. If, for example, you want all body

Fig. 5.26.

Heading set to column-wide width.

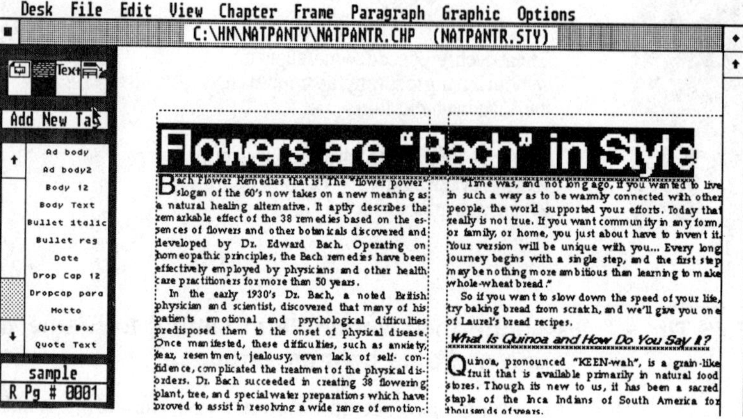

Fig. 5.27.

Heading set to frame-wide width.

text paragraphs to be indented one-quarter inch, change In/Outdent Width to 0.25 inch.

You can achieve a margin-release effect for the first line of a paragraph (sometimes called a *hanging paragraph* or *hanging indent*) by setting First Line: Outdent and specifying an In/Outdent Width value.

If you want to indent or outdent more than one line in a paragraph, change the In/Outdent Height to the number of lines you want affected. Figure 5.28 gives examples of indented and outdented text.

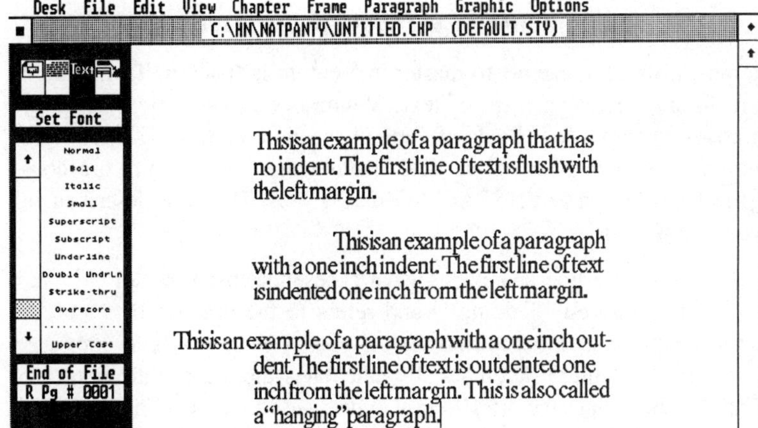

Fig. 5.28.

Examples of text with 1-inch indent and outdent.

Selecting Hyphenation Options

Hyphenation strategies are discussed in detail in Chapter 4. This chapter gives an additional tip for controlling hyphenation from the Paragraph menu.

5.47 Tip **Set the number of successive hyphens to be allowed from the ALIGNMENT dialog box.**

When a number of sentences in a row end in hyphens, the excessive hyphens are distracting. To control the number of successive hyphens allowed, click Alignment from the Paragraph menu in Paragraph mode. Set the `Successive Hyphens` option on the ALIGNMENT dialog box to a value from 1 to 5; you may also set this option to `Unlimited`. If you choose 2, only two successive lines of text are hyphenated. If you choose `Unlimited`, there is no limit to the number of successive lines of text that can end with hyphens.

Making Vertical and Horizontal Spacing Adjustments

Ventura allows you to control vertical and horizontal spacing of text. You are already familiar with some horizontal spacing control techniques such as kerning, tracking, indenting, outdenting, and paragraph alignment. The tips in this section provide additional information about spacing.

5.48 Tip **Learn the four measurements of vertical spacing used in Ventura.**

One of the most difficult concepts to master in Ventura is spacing. To maintain a consistent distance between lines of text, Ventura controls vertical spacing. Confusion arises when the four kinds of vertical space do not always apply to a given situation. The four types of vertical spacing used by Ventura are controlled by the Paragraph menu's SPACING dialog box. They are described in the following paragraphs:

- `Inter-Line`. Interline spacing is what typesetters used to call *leading* (pronounced ''ledding'') and refers to the practice of placing strips of lead between lines of type to make the final copy more legible. Ventura automatically calculates the leading at about 1.2 times the point size. If 10-point type is used, the leading is about 12 points. You can change this value, but this is not generally done. Some designers recommend more leading if a reader's eye has to travel a long horizontal distance or if only one column is on a page.

- `Above`. The default value for space above text is set by Ventura to the same value as the leading. When you press Enter, the value in the `Above` option is added to the paragraph leading, resulting in vertical white space equal to two lines of leading (as if you had pressed Enter twice). If you don't want extra white space between paragraphs, you can either change the `Above` value to zero or press Ctrl-Enter (for a line break) between paragraphs. If you insert a line break instead of pressing Enter, features like indent and outdent, which depend on new paragraphs, do not function. If you want additional space between paragraphs, such as before or after a heading, increase the `Above` or `Below` options on the SPACING dialog box.

  You can suppress `Above` at the tops of columns and pages (so that the paragraph begins at the top of the column without leaving the extra space above it) by setting `Add in Above` to `When Not at Column Top`. If `Add in Above` is set to `Always`, the value indicated for `Above` is always added, regardless where the paragraph falls.

- `Below`. The `Below` option works similarly to the `Above` option except that it adds space after a paragraph.

  If you have specified values for both the `Above` and `Below` options, only the larger of the two values is used.

  If you have added either a ruling line above or a ruling line below to a paragraph, the total height of the ruling line is added to the

Above or Below value to calculate which value is larger and therefore which value to use after pressing Enter.

- Inter-Paragraph. Inter paragraph space is calculated only if both the Above and Below values are identical. Otherwise, the Inter-Paragraph value is ignored. Unless you have a special reason for wanting additional space between paragraphs with the same tag or with the same Above and Below settings, leave the Inter-Paragraph value zero.

If you understand interline (leading) spacing, space above, space below, and interparagraph spacing, you have a good grasp of how Ventura controls vertical space.

5.49 Tip

For best alignment in multiple-column documents, use multiples of the body text interline spacing value for other tags.

If you have several tags with widely varying leading, only luck will make anything line up correctly across columns. In other words, lines of text in column 1 may be slightly above or below lines of text in column 2 as you read across the page. This may not seem serious because the difference in most cases is slight and not noticeable. To achieve professional appearances and proper alignment, however, use whole-number multiples (1, 2, 3 and not 1.3, 2.1, 3.6) of the Body Text leading when specifying leading in other tags.

If the leading (Inter-Line value) for the Body Text tag is 12 points for 10-point type, for example, and a heading is 20 points, set the leading for the heading to 24 points—exactly twice that of the Body Text leading. (If you use the Inter-Paragraph setting, give it the same value as the leading.)

The same rule applies to Above and Below values. Be sure that you include additional space caused by ruling lines above or below the paragraph. If the overall height of the ruling line above is 6, for example, set Above to 18, making the total amount of space 24—twice the space of the leading for the Body Text tag.

These calculations are not complicated; you just need to do some planning. The payoff is a more aesthetically pleasing document.

5.50 Tip

Learn how to create indented paragraphs (not to be confused with an indented line).

With word processors, you can usually create two types of indented paragraphs: indented from the left margin and indented from both the left and right margins. Ventura allows a third type: indented from the right.

The SPACING dialog box has In From Left and In From Right options. You can give values to either or both of these options.

Indented paragraphs are often used for emphasis and blocks of quotations. You may even want to change the font of an indented paragraph for additional emphasis.

Don't use the In From Left and In From Right options if you just want to indent a single line. These options indent the entire paragraph. To indent a single line, use the In/Outdent option on the ALIGNMENT dialog box.

The Relative Indent option can be set to On or Off. If set to On, the first line of the paragraph is indented the amount of the first line of the preceding paragraph. You can use this feature with line breaks to create lead-in paragraphs. See Tip 5.52 for more information.

Inserting Page, Column, and Line Breaks

Ventura allows you a great deal of control over where text breaks to begin a new page, column, or line. The tips in this section provide helpful information when you need to break text at specific points.

5.51 Tip **Learn the three kinds of breaks that Ventura allows.**

Just like word processors, Ventura allows you to force a page and column break. In addition, Ventura allows you to specify a line break, making possible some great special effects. Break settings are applied from the BREAKS dialog box, which you access by clicking Breaks from the Paragraph menu. The three types of breaks available on the BREAKS menu are explained next:

- ❑ Page Break. You can force a paragraph to begin on a new page or on the next left or right page, or you can force the next paragraph in sequence to the top of a new page. You also can force a paragraph to finish on the page on which it starts. Table 5.2 lists the various settings available for the Page Break option and the effects these settings have on the text to which the settings are applied.

- ❑ Column Break. You can force the current paragraph to begin at the top of the next column (Before) or force the next paragraph to begin at the top of the next column (After). You also can force a paragraph in a column by itself by breaking columns before and after the paragraph.

Table 5.2
Page Break Settings

Setting	*Effect*
No	Normal setting, no effect
Before	Forces the current paragraph to the top of the next page
After	Forces the next paragraph to the top of the new page
Before & After	Forces the current paragraph to appear by itself on the new page
Before/Until Left	Forces the current paragraph to the next left page; if the next page is a right page, a blank page is inserted
Before/Until Right	Forces the current paragraph to the next right page; if the next page is a left page, a blank page is inserted

- `Line Break`. This feature would cause less confusion if it were called ''Paragraph without Leading between Paragraphs Break'' because `Line Break` controls whether the first or last line of a paragraph has any space (leading) between it and the preceding or subsequent paragraph. By setting a line break, you force a new paragraph to begin without the normal interline spacing. The `Line Break` option is a wonderful way to create the special effects described in Tip 5.52.

5.52 Tip **Use the Line Break option for special effects.**

If you set `Line Break: Before` for a paragraph, or if the preceding paragraph has `Line Break: After` set, normal interline and interparagraph spacing rules are followed.

If `Line Break: No` is set between paragraphs, the two paragraphs overlap (because the second paragraph starts at the same place as the first paragraph). The paragraphs do not overlap if you change the vertical spacing by using the `Next Y Position` option (from the BREAKS dialog box) or if you change the horizontal spacing for both paragraphs by using the `In From Left` or `In From Right` options from the SPACING dialog box.

Y position refers to the vertical space a paragraph occupies. Next Y Position has two options. If set to Normal, and if Page Break: No, Column Break: No, and Line Break: No settings are chosen, then the normal Y position is for the paragraph to begin at the same place as the first line of the preceding paragraph, creating overlapping paragraphs. If Next Y Position is set to Beside Last Line of Prev. Para, the paragraph will overlap the preceding paragraph, but at the last line.

To keep the overlap from occurring, if Next Y Position is set to Normal, control the horizontal space by changing the In From Left and In From Right settings on the SPACING dialog box. If Next Y Position is set to Beside Last Line of Prev. Para, control horizontal space by setting Relative Indent to On from the ALIGNMENT dialog box.

Table 5.3 lists the various settings available for the Line Break option and the effects the settings have on the text to which the settings are applied.

Table 5.3
Line Break Settings

Setting	*Effect*
No	No line break occurs before or after the paragraph. The space between this paragraph and preceding and following paragraphs is controlled by Next Y Position. Use this setting for special effects such as vertical tabs.
Before	No line break occurs after the paragraph unless the next paragraph has Line Break set to Before or Before & After. If the next paragraph has Line Break set to No or After, vertical space is controlled by Next Y Position. Before is the default setting for the Body Text tag.
Before & After	This option forces line breaks before and after the tagged paragraph, regardless of how the line breaks for the preceding or subsequent paragraphs are set.
After	No line break occurs before this paragraph unless the preceding paragraph has Line Break set to Before or After. If the preceding paragraph has Line Break set to No or Before, vertical space is controlled by Next Y Position.

Figure 5.29 shows several examples of special text effects created with line breaks. Notice how text is kept from overlapping with the use of the In From Left, In From Right, and Relative Indent options from the SPACING dialog box. Notice also how the use of line breaks can create tables of tabular data (vertical tabs).

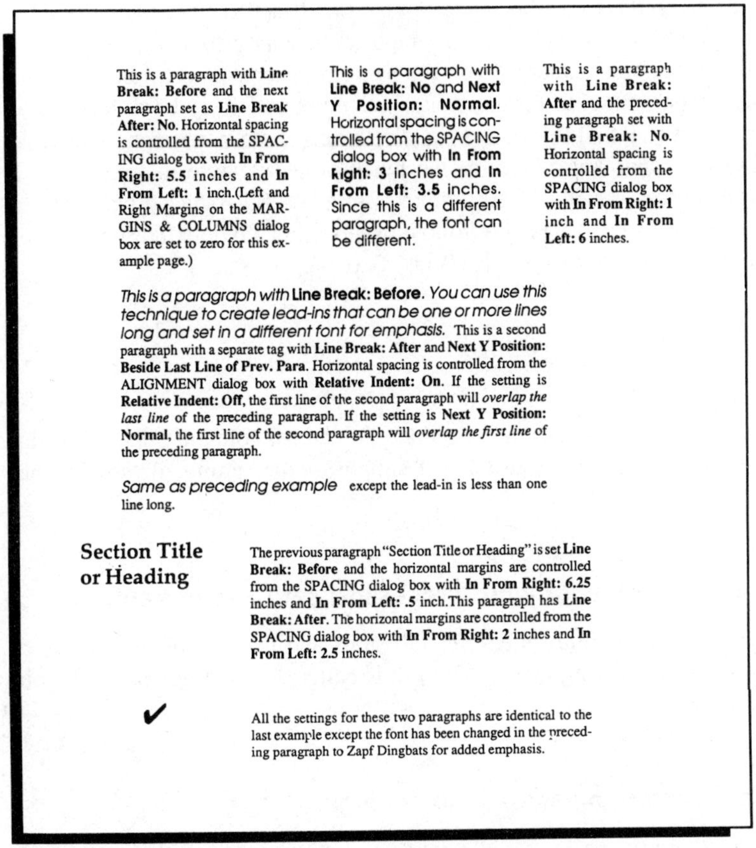

This is a paragraph with **Line Break: Before** and the next paragraph set as **Line Break After: No.** Horizontal spacing is controlled from the SPACING dialog box with **In From Right: 5.5** inches and **In From Left: 1** inch.(Left and Right Margins on the MARGINS & COLUMNS dialog box are set to zero for this example page.)

This is a paragraph with **Line Break: No** and **Next Y Position: Normal.** Horizontal spacing is controlled from the SPACING dialog box with **In From Right: 3** inches and **In From Left: 3.5** inches. Since this is a different paragraph, the font can be different.

This is a paragraph with **Line Break: After** and the preceding paragraph set with **Line Break: No.** Horizontal spacing is controlled from the SPACING dialog box with **In From Right: 1** inch and **In From Left: 6** inches.

This is a paragraph with **Line Break: Before.** *You can use this technique to create lead-ins that can be one or more lines long and set in a different font for emphasis.* This is a second paragraph with a separate tag with **Line Break: After** and **Next Y Position: Beside Last Line of Prev. Para.** Horizontal spacing is controlled from the ALIGNMENT dialog box with **Relative Indent: On.** If the setting is **Relative Indent: Off,** the first line of the second paragraph will *overlap the last line* of the preceding paragraph. If the setting is **Next Y Position: Normal,** the first line of the second paragraph will *overlap the first line* of the preceding paragraph.

Same as preceding example except the lead-in is less than one line long.

Section Title or Heading

The previous paragraph "Section Title or Heading" is set **Line Break: Before** and the horizontal margins are controlled from the SPACING dialog box with **In From Right: 6.25** inches and **In From Left: .5** inch.This paragraph has **Line Break: After.** The horizontal margins are controlled from the SPACING dialog box with **In From Right: 2** inches and **In From Left: 2.5** inches.

✔

All the settings for these two paragraphs are identical to the last example except the font has been changed in the preceding paragraph to Zapf Dingbats for added emphasis.

Fig. 5.29.

Examples of line breaks.

5.53 Tip

Use the Allow Within and Keep With Next options to keep paragraphs intact or properly grouped.

On the BREAKS dialog box are two additional settings for controlling paragraphs. These options don't directly force breaks; they keep the selected paragraphs together:

- Allow Within can be set to Yes or No. If set to No, the paragraph is never broken over page or column breaks. If the entire paragraph cannot fit on a page or in a column, the entire paragraph is placed on the next page or column. Think of Allow Within as word wrap for a paragraph. This option is normally set to Yes, meaning that the paragraph is allowed to break.
- Keep With Next can be set to Yes or No. If set to Yes, the current paragraph moves with the paragraph immediately following it. If both paragraphs cannot fit on the same page or column, both paragraphs move to the next page or column. If Keep With Next is set to Yes, set Allow Within to No to keep both paragraphs intact. Think of Keep With Next as the block protect feature in some word processors. Keep With Next is most useful for headings that you want to keep with the following text. For obvious reasons, don't set this to Yes for the Body Text tag.

Setting Tabs

Ventura allows you to specify tabs so that you can set columnar data. The tips in this section provide information that simplifies the setting of tabs in your documents.

5.54 Trap

Don't set tabs with your word processor; set them in Ventura.

Because of the way Ventura measures tab stops and because of the variety of font sizes available, setting tabs in Ventura is better than setting tabs with your word processor.

5.55 Tip

Learn how Ventura measures tab settings.

Tab stops in Ventura are measured from the margins, not from the edge of the page. If you have more than one column on a page, the tab stop is measured from the left margin of the column.

5.56 Tip

Learn how to use each of the four types of tabs in Ventura—left, right, center, and decimal.

Ventura offers four types of tabs:

- Left tabs are flush left with the tab location measurement.

- Right tabs are flush right with the tab location measurement.
- Center tabs are centered on the tab location measurement.
- Decimal tabs have the decimal character centered on the tab location measurement.

5.57 Trap **Tabs do not work in paragraphs that are justified.**

If tabs are to function properly, set the paragraph alignment in the ALIGNMENT dialog box to left-aligned.

5.58 Tip **Any tab can have a leader. The leader can be any character.**

In the TAB SETTINGS dialog box, which you access from the Paragraph menu, you can allow a tab to have an autoleader. An *autoleader* is a repeating character, such as a period, that leads from the end of any text in the tab to the beginning of the next tab.

To allow an autoleader, set `Auto-Leader: On`. At the `Leader Char` option, type the ASCII decimal value of the leader character of your choice (see Appendix A for decimal values of the Roman character set). The default character is ASCII value 46, a period. You also can set the `Leader Spacing` (the number of spaces between each leader character) to a number between 0 and 8.

Using Special Effects

The Special Effects command on the Paragraph menu allows you to specify bullets and big first letters. Because these effects are really font effects, they are discussed in detail in Chapter 9.

Understanding Ruling Lines

You can use ruling lines to accent your text. Ventura allows you to draw *rules* (typesetter terminology for *lines*) above, below, or around a selected paragraph or group of paragraphs. The tips in this section provide helpful information about rules.

5.59 Tip

Learn about ruling lines and ruling boxes.

The Paragraph menu lists three commands for rules. These commands are briefly described in the following list:

- Ruling Line Above draws lines above a paragraph.
- Ruling Line Below draws lines below a paragraph.
- Ruling Box Around draws lines that go all the way around a paragraph—like a box.

When you select any of these commands, a RULING LINES dialog box appears. You specify the same information in all the dialog boxes; depending on the command selected, the rules appear in different locations around the paragraph. You can specify as many as three rules in each dialog box (that is, you can have three rules boxing a paragraph). When specifying rules, you can set the following options:

- `Width`. Set this option to `None` (no rule at all), `Text` (as wide as the first line of the paragraph), `Margin` (as wide as the margins allow), `Column` (the entire column width regardless of margins), `Frame` (the width of the entire page or frame regardless of margins), or `Custom` (and then set your own width and indent values; indent values can be preceded by + or − to specify an indent or outdent).
- `Color`. Set this option to `Black`, `White`, or any of six other colors.
- `Pattern`. This option controls the ink density. You can set this option to any value in the range 1 to 7 or `Solid`. To see how these values look on your printer, print a series of text rules with different patterns.
- `Dashes`. You can turn this option `On` or `Off`. If the option is `On`, you can customize the dash width and dash spacing in the associated RULING LINES dialog box.
- `Space Above Rule 1` and `Space Below Rule 3`. These options govern the distance between rules and between the rules and text. The `Overall Height` of the rules, including any added space, is added to the `Space Above` measurement and automatically calculated by Ventura to control the vertical space between paragraphs.
- `Height of Rule`. This option also can be called the thickness of the line. As you create your rules, a representation of the thickness of the rule is displayed in the dialog box.

- ❑ Space Below Rule 3. This option allows you to shift the rules up or down without moving the paragraph text (see Tip 5.60).

5.60 Tip **Use a negative value for the space below rule 3 on the RULING LINES ABOVE dialog box to create a white-on-black effect.**

You can set the Space Below Rule 3 option to a negative number in the RULING LINES ABOVE dialog box to create a rule that overlaps text. If the font for the text is set to the color white, a reverse white text on black is created (see fig. 5.30).

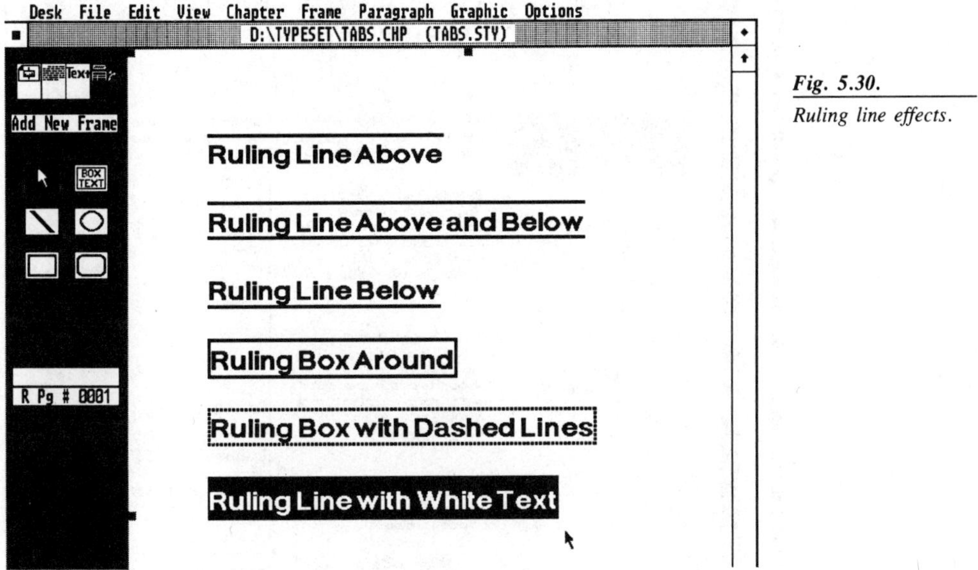

Fig. 5.30.
Ruling line effects.

To create the white text on black effect shown in figure 5.30, do the following:

1. In Paragraph mode, select the desired line of text.
2. Select Ruling Lines Above from the Paragraph menu.
3. Set the Width option on the RULING LINES ABOVE dialog box to Text; set the Color option to Black.
4. Set Height of Rule 1 to a value greater than the point size of the text in the selected paragraph. You will need to experiment to get the desired look.
5. Set Space Below Rule 3 to one half the sum of the point size of the text and the height of rule 1. If, for example, the text point

size is 14 and the height of rule 1 is 18, the `Space Below Rule 3` value is 16.

6. Make the value for `Space Below Rule 3` negative by clicking on the – button.

Note: Some printers do not print white text on a black background. Print the CAPABILI.CHP found in the TYPESET directory to see whether your printer can print reverse text (see fig. 5.31).

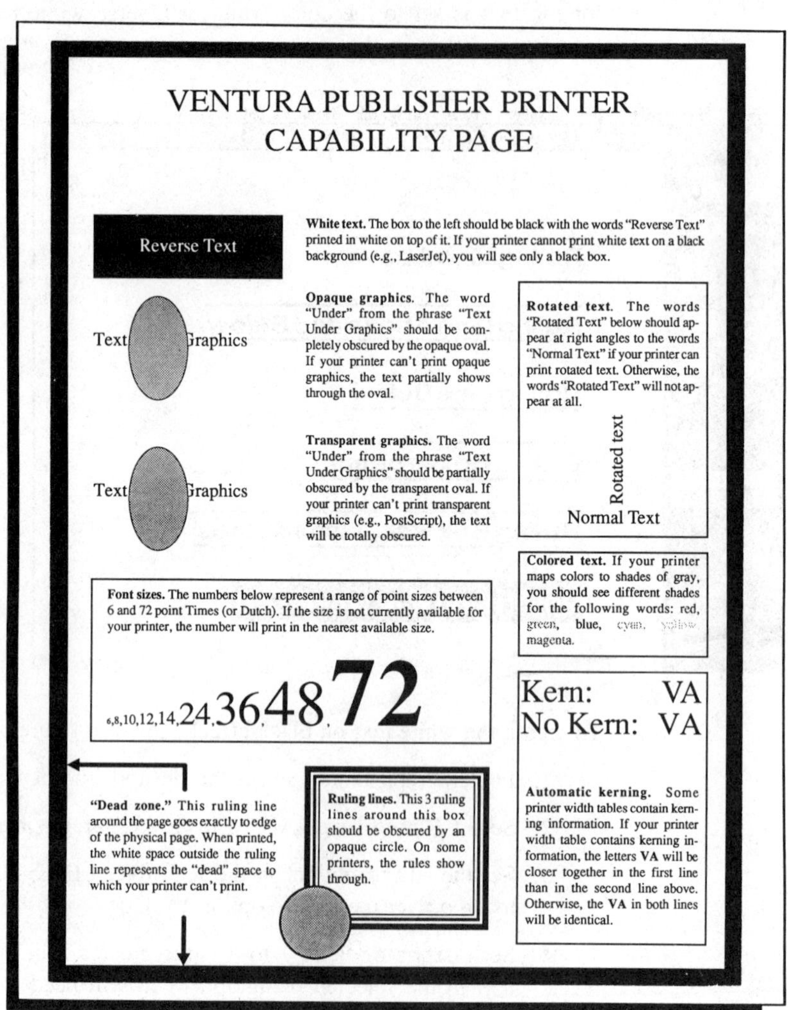

Fig. 5.31.
CAPABILI.CHP printed on PostScript printer.

5.61 Tip **Use dashed lines with a ruling box around the paragraph to create coupon boxes.**

An easy way to create a clip-out coupon box is to set `Dashes: On` in the RULING BOX AROUND dialog box (see fig. 5.30).

Chapter Summary

In this chapter, you learned about the capabilities and power of tags and style sheets. You learned about tags—how to create them and how to apply them. You learned how to apply tags to paragraphs both from within Ventura and in a text file using your word processor.

You learned how to create, modify, name, rename, save, and retrieve style sheets, and you learned about the elements of a style sheet. In addition to tags, style sheets keep track of printer width tables, columns, and margins.

This chapter discussed text attributes—how to change font characteristics to override the tag settings. You learned about the attributes of underline, overscore, strike-through, bold, italic, superscript, subscript, and small. You learned how to kern individual letters or words and how to change point size from a dialog box.

You saw how much power tags exert over the look of a paragraph, and you learned how tags control alignment, hyphenation, line breaks, tabs, and ruling lines.

Now that you have a grasp of tags and style sheets, you will learn how to place text on the page using frames, the topic of the next chapter.

Chapter

6

Understanding Frames

Every program has a basic building block. Most word processors use the page, spreadsheet software uses the cell, and database programs use the record.

In Ventura, the basic building block of a document is the *frame*. The concept of the frame is simple, but new users of Ventura often become confused. The confusion may stem from the terminology chosen by Ventura's developers. Here are some key concepts that will help you understand frames:

- Frames are either rectangular or square.
- Frames are like boxes that contain or hold things. In the case of Ventura, the frame holds text or graphics.
- A page without frames is sometimes called the *underlying frame*. The term underlying frame is confusing because it implies that a frame is on the page when one really isn't. As long as you understand that the underlying frame is really just a page without any frames on top of it, you will not be confused.
- You have a choice: you can place graphics or text directly onto the page (the underlying frame), or you can create a frame and put the graphics or text into the frame.
- Just as you can place frames on top of pages, you also can put frames on top of each other.

- ❑ Frames can be empty as well as contain text or graphics. An empty frame can be used as a "place holder" (where text or graphics will be placed later) or to keep text or graphics from going into certain areas—blocking out areas of another frame or page.

If you have used PageMaker before using Ventura, the concept of frames will be puzzling at first and may even seem restricting or unnecessary. Once you begin using frames, however, you will find that you can do many tasks easier in Ventura than you could in PageMaker, and you will be able to do some tasks in Ventura that weren't even possible in PageMaker.

The rest of this chapter examines the underlying frame, page layout, and how to add and delete frames and pages. You will learn how to set the columns and margins in a frame and how to load text and graphics into frames. You also will create templates by using dummy text and frames as place holders. You will set up vertical rules and anchor frames so they will not move or so they will follow certain text. In addition, you will learn how to set up rules above, around, or below frames; how to set different frame backgrounds; and how to make type appear in inverse video. You also will examine some special effects you can achieve with frames.

Examining the Underlying Frame

You control the underlying frame or page from the Chapter and Frame menus.

6.1 Tip

When you begin designing a chapter, first set up the underlying frame or page by using the PAGE LAYOUT dialog box.

When you begin a new chapter, you need to let Ventura know the basic layout of the underlying page. Choose the Page Size & Layout command from the Chapter menu to access the PAGE LAYOUT dialog box. Table 6.1 explains the choices in the PAGE LAYOUT dialog box.

Table 6.1
The PAGE LAYOUT Dialog Box

Option	*Explanation of Choices*
Orientation	
Portrait	The page is vertical and taller than it is wide (see fig. 6.1).

Table 6.1—*Continued*

Option	*Explanation of Choices*
Landscape	The page is horizontal and wider than it is tall (see fig. 6.2).
Paper Size & Dimension	
Half	This size is 5.5 by 8.5 inches, which is half as long as the standard 8.5-by-11-inch size.
Letter	This size is 8.5 by 11 inches, the normal letter size.
Legal	This size is 8.5 by 14 inches, the normal legal size.
Double	This size is 11 by 17 inches, twice as wide as the regular letter size. When folded in half the long way, this choice is 8.5 by 11 inches.
B5	This size is 17.6 by 25 centimeters, a European size.
A4	This size is 21 by 29.7 centimeters, a European size.
Broad Sheet	This size is 18 by 25 inches. Select this choice if you are outputting newspaper size pages to a typesetting machine.
Sides	
Single	Select this choice if you plan to print only on one side of a page. This choice is useful for fliers or reports.
Double	Select this choice if you plan to print on both sides or facing pages. Select this option if you want to view your document in Facing Pages View or if you have different headers, footers, margins, and other space-specific elements applied differently on left and right pages.
Start On	Your choices are left or right. With these options, you tell Ventura whether the first page is a left-hand or right-hand page.

Fig. 6.1.

Portrait orientation.

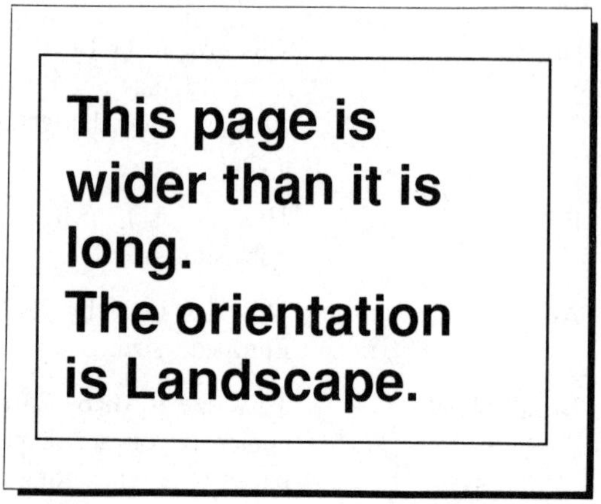

This page is taller than it is wide.
The orienta-tion is Portrait.

Fig. 6.2.

Landscape orientation.

This page is wider than it is long.
The orientation is Landscape.

6.2 Tip

Once you have set the basic layout and orientation, control the page margins and columns from the MARGINS & COLUMNS dialog box.

Once you have chosen the chapter's page layout, you can set the underlying frame or page margins and columns. Click the Margins & Columns command from the Frame menu (see fig. 6.3). Table 6.2 explains the choices in the MARGINS & COLUMNS dialog box.

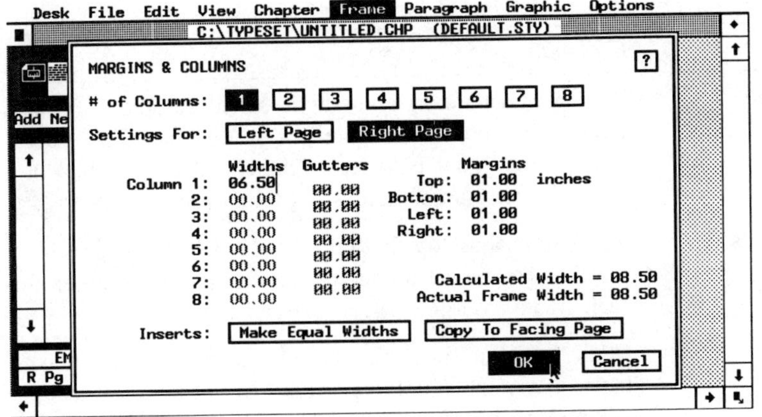

Fig. 6.3.

The MARGINS & COLUMNS dialog box.

Table 6.2
The MARGINS & COLUMNS Dialog Box Settings

Option	*Explanation of Choices*
# of Columns	Choose from one to eight columns. (If you need more than eight columns on a page, see Tip 6.5.) As you select the number of columns you want, the `Widths` number changes. Ventura calculates the default width of the column by dividing the `Actual Frame Width` number by the number of columns you choose.
Settings For	`Left Page` or `Right Page`. If you have chosen a double-sided page layout, you can have different margin and column settings for the left and right page. Choose the page you want for your settings. If you previously chose a single-sided page layout, only the settings for the start-on page are used, even if you set up separate settings for the left and right page.
Widths	Each column can have a custom width. Edit the `Widths` table to your satisfaction. Watch the `Calculated Width` and `Actual Frame Width` numbers. If a single column or the total width of several columns causes the calculated width to exceed the actual frame width, you may generate an error message telling you that the widths you have set exceed the capacity of the frame. The error message is not always generated, however; in such cases, the columns may not all fit on the page or in the frame.

Table 6.2—*Continued*

Option	*Explanation of Choices*
Gutters	The space separating columns is called the *gutter*. You can set the gutter to any number you choose. The space used by the gutter is added to the calculated width. You have different gutter figures between each column.
Margins	You can change top, bottom, left, and right margins. Margins can be set for the underlying page as well as for each frame. Margins affect text and graphics.
Inserts	Click `Make Equal Widths` and any custom settings you have made for the column widths are recalculated to make all widths equal. Click `Copy To Facing Page` to make the settings the same for both left and right pages—except for the right and left margins being reversed. Existing pages are not affected; only newly created pages reflect the new settings. Frames other than the underlying frame are unaffected by the `Copy To Facing Page` option.

6.3 Trap

Existing pages are not affected by the Copy To Facing Page option of the MARGINS & COLUMNS dialog box.

Once you have created a page, you can change the settings for each individual underlying frame by using the MARGINS & COLUMNS dialog box, but you cannot globally affect already created pages by clicking `Copy To Facing Page`. Only pages created after you modify the margins and columns will be affected. If you need to change the margins or columns of existing pages, you will need to make the change one page at a time.

6.4 Trap

You would think that you set the underlying page margins and columns from the Chapter menu, but you actually set them from the MARGINS & COLUMNS dialog box.

A source of confusion to Ventura users is which menu to use to set up the margins and columns for the underlying page. You logically would think that the settings should be on the Chapter menu because the settings for the underlying page affect the entire chapter. But Ventura treats the underlying page as a frame. Therefore, the MARGINS & COLUMNS dialog box (accessed from the Frame menu) is where you make margin and column settings for the underlying page, as well as any other frame.

Remember, all frame margins and columns are set from the Frame menu, even if the frame selected is the underlying page.

6.5 Trick

Use multiple frames to have more than eight columns on a page.

If your document requires more than eight columns, add a frame and set it for eight columns; then add another frame and set it for additional columns.

You also can use this technique to create frames with different column settings in order to have, for example, a frame with two columns on the bottom half of the page and another frame with three columns on the top half of the page (see Tip 6.6 for a way to accomplish this effect another way).

6.6 Tip

Think of the underlying page as the default setting and additional frames as ways of overriding the defaults.

Set up the underlying page to reflect most of your chapter's design. Use added frames to override the underlying page defaults or to place specific text or graphics exactly where you want.

Suppose, for example, that you have an overall design of three columns and you want one page to have two columns. The default design is three columns and should be reflected in the settings you choose for the underlying page. For the page with two columns, create a new frame on top of the underlying page and set the frame to have only two columns. Figure 6.4 shows an example of both three and two columns on the same page.

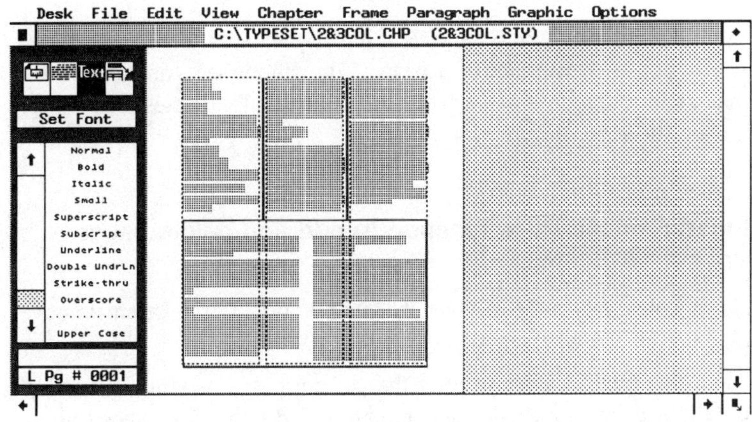

Fig. 6.4.

A page mixing three columns and two columns.

Adding and Deleting Pages

You can add pages in one of two ways:

- ❏ Load a text file into an underlying page. As many pages as needed to hold the file will be created.
- ❏ Use the Insert/Remove Page selection from the Chapter menu.

6.7 Tip

As many pages as are required to hold a text file are created automatically if you load the file into an underlying frame or type text directly into an underlying frame.

To have Ventura automatically create enough pages to hold your article, do the following:

1. Select an empty underlying page by clicking on it while in the Frame mode.
2. Load a text file by using the Load Text/Picture command from the File menu.

Ventura will flow the article, automatically creating pages as needed. You are limited in Ventura to about 2 megabytes of text per chapter. If you need additional capacity and have enough EMS memory, the Professional Extension to Ventura can handle up to 32 megabytes of text!

If you are typing text directly into an underlying frame, your text cursor disappears when you get to the bottom of a page. You cannot see your text cursor because it has gone to the next page. Ventura automatically creates a new page to accommodate the text you are typing.

6.8 Tip

Use the Insert/Remove Page function to add and delete pages selectively.

You can add or delete any page in your chapter by clicking the Insert/Remove Page command from the Chapter menu (see fig. 6.5).

You can insert new pages before or after the current page, or you can remove (delete) the current page. Some rules about adding and removing pages follow:

- ❏ Automatically created pages cannot be removed unless you first remove the text from the underlying page or the assignment list.
- ❏ Automatically created pages are removed automatically if the text file you loaded onto the underlying page is shortened.

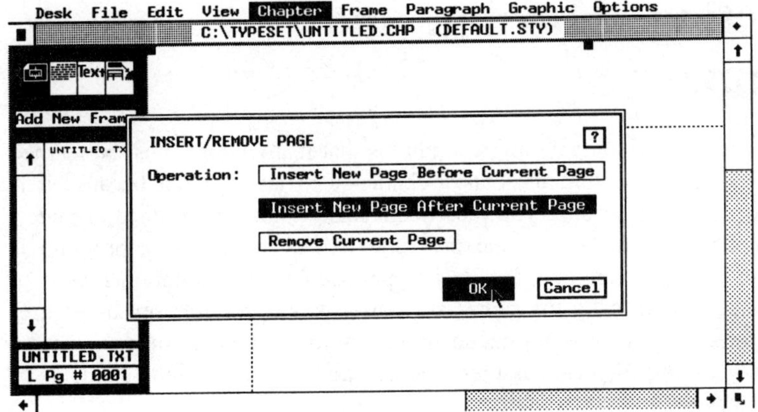

Fig. 6.5.
The INSERT/REMOVE PAGE dialog box.

- ❑ When you remove pages with frames on them, the created frames are deleted also. Frames deleted when you use the INSERT/REMOVE PAGE dialog box are not placed on the Frame Clipboard. You cannot recover the deleted frames.

- ❑ If you have loaded a document onto an underlying page and several pages were created automatically to accommodate the text, you can add pages before, after, or in the middle of the chapter. If you add pages in the middle of the previously loaded text, the new page will be blank; the text will skip and not reflow to the inserted page.

- ❑ If you have loaded a document onto an underlying page and the only pages in the document are those that were created automatically, you cannot delete any pages by using the INSERT/REMOVE PAGE dialog box. If you want fewer pages, delete the text from the last page, go to the next-to-last page, and delete text until the end-of-file marker appears. Because the pages were generated automatically, the pages are also ungenerated automatically.

- ❑ If you have loaded a document onto an underlying page to create pages automatically, if you change the point size, Ventura may increase or decrease the number of pages as needed to contain the text.

Adding, Deleting, Moving, and Resizing Frames

One obstacle to learning anything complex is that many things must be learned at the same time. Ventura presents a challenge to learning not because it is overly difficult, but because you must learn many things all at once to understand the basic philosophy of the program. When people say a program is "intuitive," they mean that the design philosophy—the program's way of doing things—is basically the same as the user would have chosen if the user had designed the program. No matter how "intuitive" a program is, however, design choices must be made and terminology must be given to the elements of those choices.

Ventura has been criticized for the complexity of the "frame" system of managing text and graphics. Most of the confusion comes from not understanding the basic design of Ventura. In this section, concepts are introduced that will help you understand and become comfortable with the frame system.

6.9 Tip

Learn the difference between *automatic* and *semiautomatic* text flow.

Ventura doesn't use the terms *automatic* and *semiautomatic* text flow, but these terms are applied here to explain the two ways Ventura handles text. If you understand these concepts, you will more easily understand the way frames work when compared with the way pages work.

If you load text directly onto an underlying page, Ventura automatically flows the text, creating pages as needed until the end of the text file. With automatic text flow, Ventura assumes that you want the entire article flowed and accommodates that desire by creating the space for the text.

If you load text into a frame, Ventura stops flowing text when the frame is full. To flow more text, you need to create the space by adding a frame and tell Ventura that you want to continue flowing text into the new frame. With semiautomatic text flow, Ventura assumes that you only want a particular frame filled with text and will not continue the flow of text until you tell the program where you want the text flowed.

6.10 Tip

Learn how to add a single frame.

Creating a frame with Ventura is simple. To create a frame, follow these steps:

1. Change to Frame mode by clicking the Frame mode button or using the keyboard shortcut Ctrl-U.

2. Click the Add New Frame button or use the keyboard shortcut Ctrl-2.
3. Position the add new frame cursor on the page where you want one corner of the frame.
4. Press and hold down the left mouse button. The cursor changes to the resize frame pointing finger.
5. Drag the mouse until the frame is the size you want.
6. Release the mouse button. You will see a frame outlined on the page with all eight resizing handles visible (see fig. 6.6).

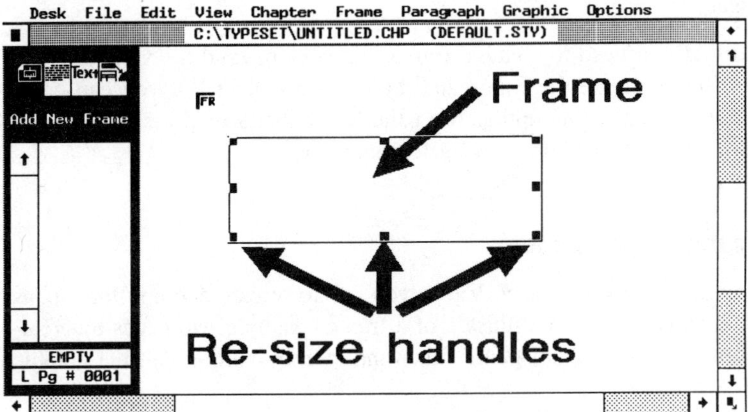

Fig. 6.6.
A frame with resizing handles visible.

6.11 Tip **Create multiple frames by holding down the Shift key.**

Once you have clicked the addition button, you can add more than one frame by holding down the Shift key. The add new frame cursor remains visible, and you can continue adding frames.

Just prior to adding the last frame, release the Shift key. After you create one more frame, the cursor changes to the Frame mode cross.

If you forget to release the Shift key and don't want to add any more frames, you can do one of two things:

- ❑ Click the page (creating a small frame) and immediately press the Del key. The last frame created remains the selected frame, and pressing the Del key deletes the selected frame.
- ❑ Click another mode button, which cancels the Add New Frame button.

6.12 Trap

The screen will not scroll automatically if you try to create a frame larger than the work area.

One idiosyncrasy of Ventura is that it is incapable of scrolling automatically when you move the cursor to the edges of the visible work space. If you are used to PageMaker or desktop publishing programs on the Macintosh, this inability to scroll automatically will be irritating and will take some getting used to.

The screen utility called the Soft Kicker (from AristoCad, Incorporated) adds the automatic scrolling capability to Ventura when you're using an EGA or VGA video card and monitor. If you have a full-page monitor, usually the entire page in the work area is displayed so the automatic scrolling problem isn't an issue.

If you find that you need to create a frame that goes beyond the visible screen area, you still can create the frame and then resize it later. Or you can go to Reduced View (choose this option from the View menu or press Ctrl-R) and add or resize the frame while viewing the entire page.

6.13 Trap

Frames cannot span pages.

Even if you are in Facing Pages View, you cannot create a frame that spans two pages. You can create the illusion of a frame spanning two pages by creating two frames that butt against each other and then by putting half the graphic or text in each frame.

Examine figure 6.7 to see how two frames are butted at the page border. Half the graphic was placed in the left page, and half the graphic was placed in the right page, creating the illusion of a single frame spanning two pages.

If your printer cannot print all the way to the edge of the page, a bit of a white margin will be on both pages. This white margin should not be a problem if the pages are going to be bound in a folder or book.

6.14 Tip

Use the Del key to cut frames. Use the Shift-Del key combination to copy frames.

You can cut (delete) or copy a single frame by switching to Frame mode, clicking the frame you want to delete or copy, and then either pressing Del (or choosing Cut from the Edit menu) or pressing Shift-Del (or choosing Copy from the Edit menu). The frame is now on the Frame Clipboard, and you can recover it or duplicate it by pressing the Ins key (or choosing Paste from the Edit menu).

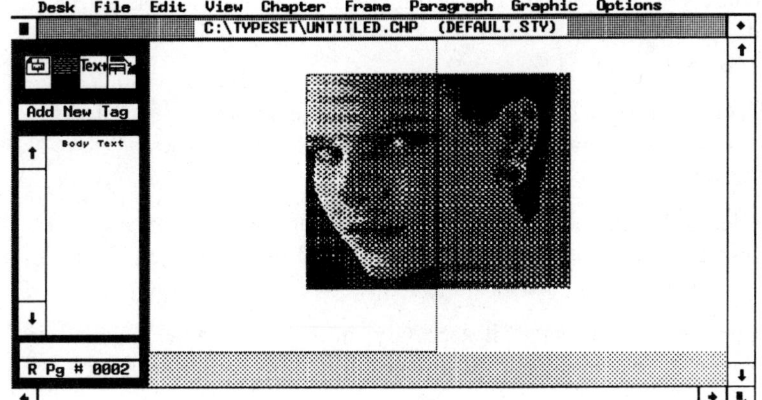

Fig. 6.7.
Two frames on adjacent pages creating the illusion of one large frame spanning two pages.

You can cut or copy more than one frame on a single page by holding down the Shift key and clicking several frames. Press Del or Shift-Del, and all the selected frames will be cut or copied. All the frames just cut or copied are now on the Frame Clipboard, and you can recover or duplicate them by pressing the Ins key (or Paste from the Edit menu).

6.15 Tip

Use Cut and Paste or Copy and Paste to move frames from one page or one chapter to another.

Because cutting or copying a frame moves that frame to the Frame Clipboard, you can move to another page or even another chapter and press Ins (or choose Paste from the Edit menu) to paste the frame or frames onto the new page.

Remember, only the last frames you cut or copied are on the Frame Clipboard. Each time you use the cut or copy frame function, only the last cut or copy is saved to the Clipboard.

6.16 Trick

Use the Cut and Paste or Copy and Paste function to move a number of frames to a blank page. You then can copy all the frames on the page to move to another chapter.

If you have a number of frames scattered throughout a chapter and you want to move or copy those frames en masse to another chapter, do the following:

1. Insert a blank page at the end of the chapter.
2. Move through the chapter a page at a time. Cut or copy frames from each page and paste the frames onto the blank page you created in step 1.

3. When you have pasted all the frames you want to transfer, select all the frames on the page you created in step 1 and cut or copy them.

4. Open or create a new chapter. While in Frame mode, press Ins or choose Paste from the Edit menu. All the frames are now transferred to the new chapter.

5. Selectively cut and paste the frames to their correct positions throughout the chapter (unless you want all the transferred frames on a single page).

6. Remove the extra page, if necessary, in the new chapter. Also, remember to remove the extra page from the preceding chapter.

If the frames you transfer contain either graphics or text, the graphics or text are loaded automatically into the new chapter. Verify the transfer by looking at the assignment list while in the Frame mode. The assignment list doesn't immediately update; you need to change to another mode and then back to Frame mode before the assignment list update verifies what you have transferred. Also, if text was transferred, the tags assigned to it may not exist in the new chapter if the new chapter uses a different style sheet. Remember to double-check that the tags on the imported text are set how you want them.

6.17 Tip

Use the resizing handles on the frame to resize frames.

One benefit of the WYSIWYG (what you see is what you get) capabilities of Ventura is that you can visually resize frames and immediately see the result of the resizing on the design of the page.

To resize a frame, do the following:

1. Switch to Frame mode.

2. Click the frame you want to resize.

3. Position the cursor over one of the eight resizing handles. Click and hold down the mouse button. Wait for the cursor to change to the resize frame pointing finger cursor.

   If you're not exactly on the resize button, the cursor shape may change to the move frame shape. So wait until you're sure that the cursor has changed to the pointing finger before you try to resize.

   If you select one of the corner handles, you can resize the frame vertically and horizontally. If you select one of the middle handles, you can resize either vertically or horizontally, but not both.

If either or both Column Snap and Line Snap are set to On at the Options menu, the frame will resize accordingly (see Tip 6.20).

4. While continuing to hold down the mouse button, drag the resizing box. You will see an outline of the frame as it changes size. Once the frame is the size you want, release the mouse button (see fig. 6.8).

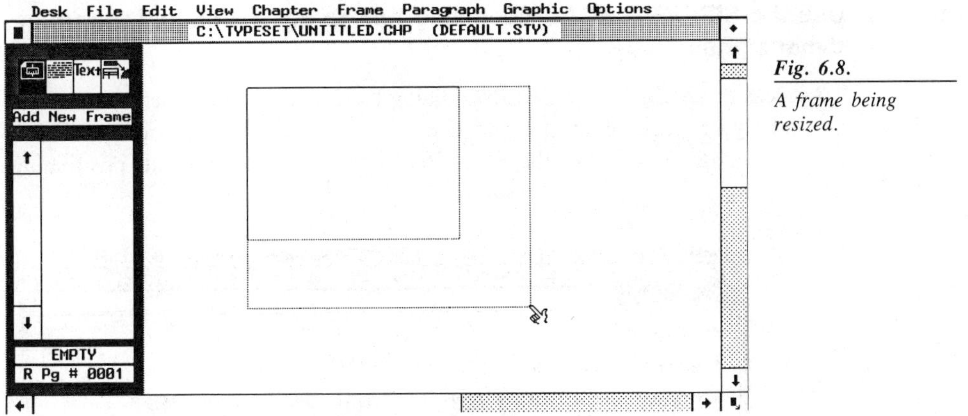

Fig. 6.8.

A frame being resized.

6.18 Trap

Be sure to have only one frame selected when you resize.

If you have more than one frame selected, all selected frames change size when you resize one.

6.19 Tip

If the ruler is visible, you will be able to resize the frame more accurately.

From the Options menu, click Show Rulers. With the ruler displayed, you can more easily set frame dimensions as you resize the frame.

6.20 Tip

Select both Column Snap On and Line Snap On when creating or resizing frames.

An invisible grid is created for every Ventura page and frame. The grid is governed by the margins and columns and the interline spacing of the body text.

If you select Column Snap On and Line Snap On from the Options menu, whenever you create or resize a frame, the frame boundary snaps to the invisible grid. The grid ensures that the frame will be aligned properly with respect to the margins, columns, and text.

If you want free-form frames or need to resize a frame to a dimension that causes a frame boundary to be between two grid lines, select Column Snap Off and/or Line Snap Off.

6.21 Tip

Use the SIZING & SCALING dialog box to set absolutely the frame dimensions.

To access the SIZING & SCALING dialog box, change to Frame mode, select an underlying page or frame, and choose Sizing & Scaling from the Frame menu (see fig. 6.9). After the `Flow Text Around` option are four positioning options.

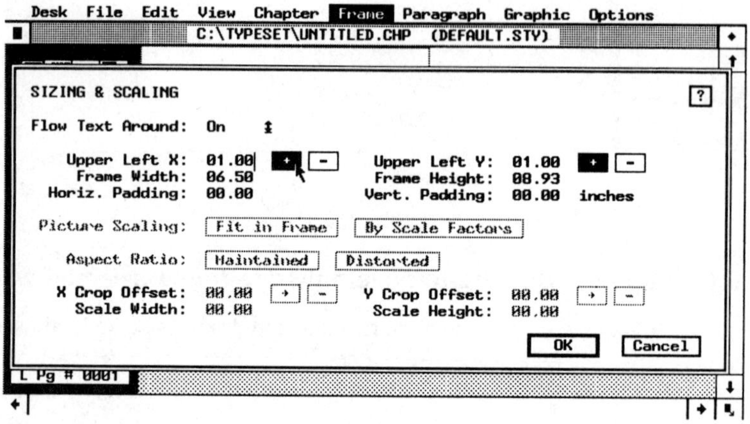

Fig. 6.9.

The SIZING & SCALING dialog box.

Desk File Edit View Chapter Frame Paragraph Graphic Options
C:\TYPESET\UNTITLED.CHP (DEFAULT.STY)
SIZING & SCALING
Flow Text Around: On
Upper Left X: 01.00 Upper Left Y: 01.00
Frame Width: 06.50 Frame Height: 08.93
Horiz. Padding: 00.00 Vert. Padding: 00.00 inches
Picture Scaling: Fit in Frame By Scale Factors
Aspect Ratio: Maintained Distorted
X Crop Offset: 00.00 Y Crop Offset: 00.00
Scale Width: 00.00 Scale Height: 00.00
OK Cancel
L Pg # 0001

You will examine the positioning options shortly. First, consider this brief explanation about X and Y coordinates: The designers of Ventura used jargon rather than English for setting coordinates. X coordinates are side to side; Y coordinates are up and down—regardless of whether the page is wider than it is tall or taller than it is wide. Don't be intimidated by Xs and Ys—just remember side to side and up and down.

Table 6.3 provides an explanation of the positioning options.

Changing the upper left X and Y coordinates affects the *position* of the frame on the page. Changing the frame width and height affects the *size* of the frame.

Table 6.3
Sizing & Scaling Positioning Options

Option	*Explanation*
Upper Left X	The upper left corner of the frame measured from the left edge (not the margin) of the page
Upper Left Y	The upper left corner of the frame measured from the top (not the margin) of the page
Frame Width	The width of the frame
Frame Height	The height of the frame

Figure 6.10 gives a visual representation of the Upper Left X, Upper Left Y, Frame Width, and Frame Height options.

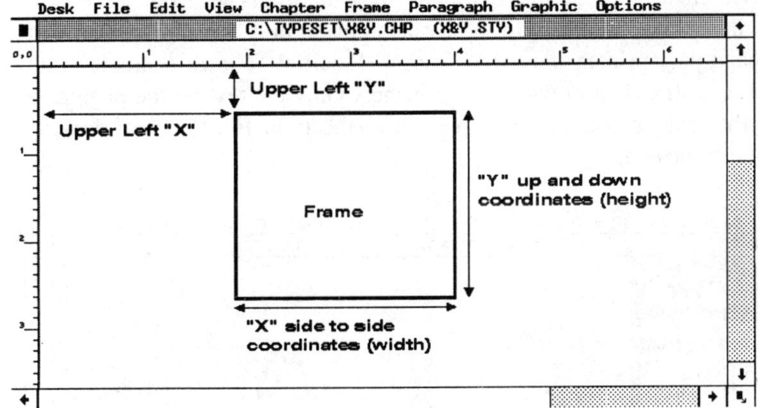

Fig. 6.10.
Visual representation of the Upper Left X, Upper Left Y, Frame Width, *and* Frame Height *options.*

Changing the upper left X and Y coordinates affects the *position* of the frame on the page. Changing the frame width and height affects the *size* of the frame.

6.22 Tip

Create custom page sizes by using the SIZING & SCALING dialog box.

If you don't find a page size you like by using the PAGE LAYOUT dialog box (accessed from the Chapter menu), you can create custom page sizes by using the SIZING & SCALING dialog box (accessed from the Frame menu).

While in the Frame mode, click the underlying page and then select the Sizing & Scaling option from the Frame menu. (Here is another example of a Chapter function being on the Frame menu.) Once in the SIZING & SCALING dialog box, you can change the size of the page by decreasing the frame width and height.

Keep the new width and height within the boundaries of the Paper Type & Dimension settings on the PAGE LAYOUT dialog box. You can set custom page sizes, and if you want, you even can center the new page size by altering the Upper Left X and Upper Left Y values; otherwise, the custom page will begin in the upper left corner.

Unless your document has a number of pages, a simpler procedure for you may be to create a frame the size you want instead of creating a custom page size, because the visual effect is the same.

6.23 Trap **Ventura will not properly print custom pages that exceed the boundaries of the Page Type & Dimension settings.**

Ventura will not properly print custom pages that are larger than the size you selected from the PAGE LAYOUT dialog box. And Ventura will not warn you that you have created a custom page larger than the limits set from the PAGE LAYOUT dialog box. If you try to print such a page, only the amount that will fit on the page your printer is using will print. Figure 6.11 is an example of an 8.5-inch page with a custom width of 15 inches. Only the text on the page area will print; the text on the too wide portion to the right (on the gray desktop area) will be truncated.

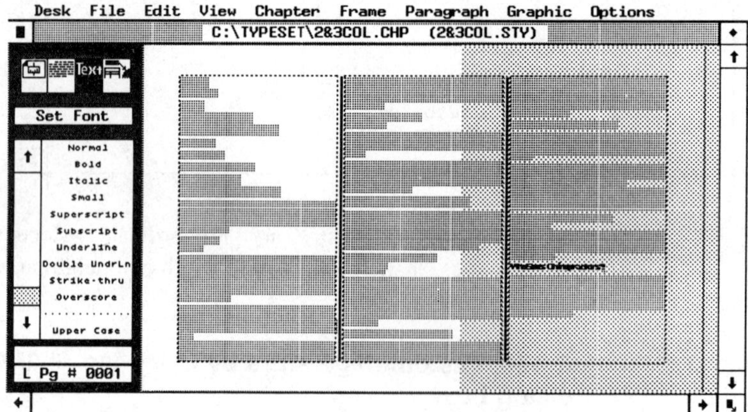

Fig. 6.11.

A custom page setting that is too wide.

Working with Frame Contents

Once you have created a frame, you can leave it empty or fill it with either graphics or text (graphics are discussed in Chapter 7). One of the great strengths of Ventura is the semiautomatic flowing of text through text frames.

6.24 Tip

Create frames to control the semiautomatic flow of text.

You need to remember only two rules about semiautomatic text flow through frames:

- ❑ Text can flow only forward through a chapter.
- ❑ Text can flow into a frame only if you have told Ventura that you want text to flow into a frame.

6.25 Tip

Text can flow only forward through a chapter.

The four frames on facing pages in figure 6.12 each contain part of a text file (in the example, the file contains only the numbers 1 through 4 set in 128-point [2-inch] Helvetica type). The following steps were performed so that the text was forced to flow through the four frames:

1. Change to Frame mode and create two frames each on two pages.
2. Use the Load Text/Picture command from the File menu to load your text file.
3. Click the first frame to select it and then click the name of the file that appears in the assignment list. The first part of the text file will flow into the selected frame.
4. Repeat step 3 with the second, third, and fourth frame.

If you follow these steps, your example will look like figure 6.12, but instead of large numbers, you will see text.

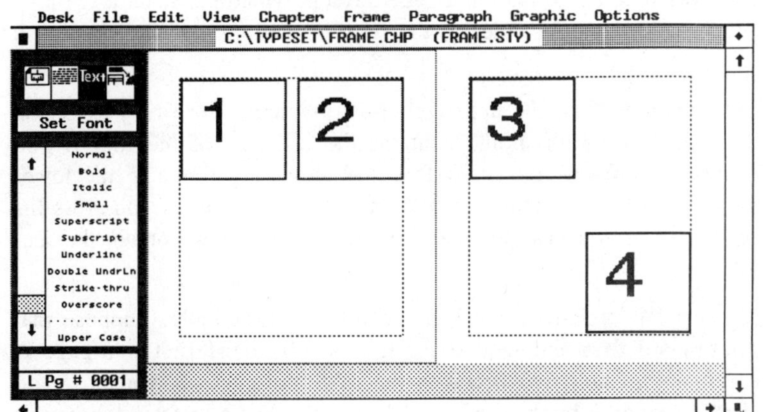

Fig. 6.12.
Examples of text flow through multiple frames.

6.26 Tip

Text will not flow backward through a chapter although blocks of text can flow backward on a page.

You can make text flow in any order through a series of frames on a given page (see fig. 6.13). Depending on the order in which you select the frames and click the file name in the assignment list, you can force the text to flow through frames in any order on the page. You cannot, however, force blocks of text to flow backward (in reverse order) from page 6 to page 1. If you try to force text to flow backward, Ventura just makes it flow forward.

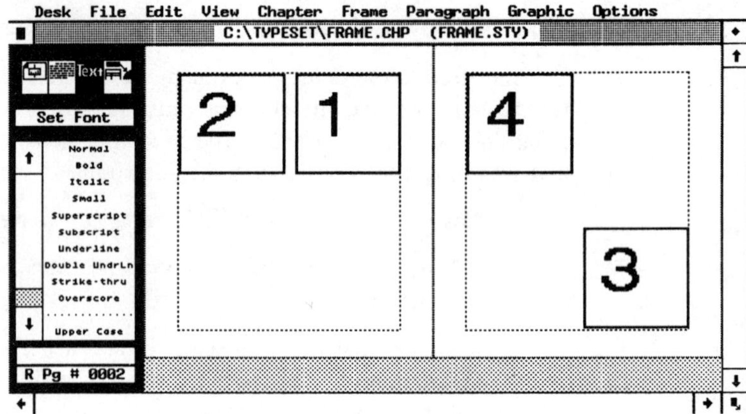

Fig. 6.13.
Text flow through multiple frames.

6.27 Trick

Change the text flow order on a given page by using the Cut and Paste commands.

If you have more than one frame on a page through which the same text file is flowing, you can change the order of the flow by cutting and then pasting a frame.

Suppose, for example, that the upper left frame contains the first part of the text file and the lower right frame contains the last part of the file. If you select the upper left frame and press Del, the remaining frame in the lower right of the page will now contain the first part of the text file. If you press Ins to paste in the frame you just cut, the pasted frame will now contain the second part of the text.

If you are financially minded, consider the following example. Suppose that the two frames are first and second mortgages. Once the first mortgage is gone, the remaining mortgage becomes the first mortgage. If you now add back the first mortgage, because of precedence, the latest mortgage becomes the second mortgage regardless of whether it used to be the first mortgage.

6.28 Trick **Break up your text files to allow backward flow of text through a chapter.**

If you are creating a mailing flier, you may want the layout to be similar to the example shown in figure 6.14.

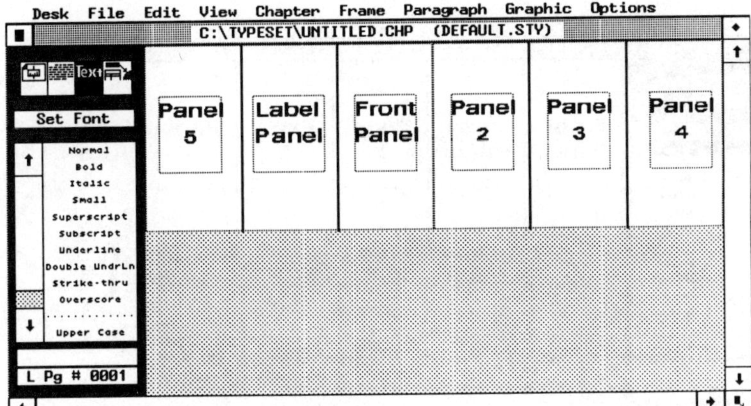

Fig. 6.14.
An example of a six-panel brochure.

The six-panel brochure is a common type of layout. The brochure is set up in a landscape orientation with text printed in six panels. After the brochure has been folded, the right panel of page 1 is the front panel, and the middle panel of page 1 contains the mailing information. Text flows from the front panel through panels 2, 3, 4, and back to panel 5, which is the leftmost panel on page 1. Because Ventura only flows text *forward* through a chapter, how can you get the last bit of text to flow *backward* to panel 5? You can't. But you can do the following:

1. Set up a three-column brochure format beginning on the left page. Create a separate frame for each panel of the brochure.

2. Flow the text semiautomatically from the fifth panel to panels 1 through 4. The text you want in panel 5 is now in panel 4, and the front-panel text is now in panel 5 (see fig. 6.15).

3. While in Text mode, select all the text in panel 4 (the text you ultimately want in panel 5) and press Del. The text that was in panel 4 is now on the Text Clipboard.

4. Switch to Frame mode and click the panel 5 frame. Select Remove Text/File from the Edit menu and choose `Frame` from the `Remove from` option. Click OK or press Enter. Now the panel 5 frame is empty, and the front panel and panels 2 through 4 are in their proper places.

5. Change to Text mode and place the text cursor in panel 5. Press Ins to copy the previously deleted text from the Clipboard into the panel 5 frame.

Now all the panels are in their proper places, and panel 5 with the concluding text appears to flow "backward" through the chapter.

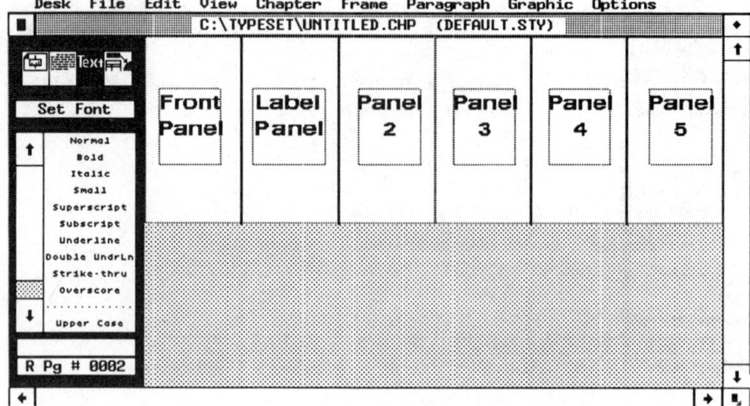

Fig. 6.15.

The six-panel brochure after completing step 2.

6.29 Trap

Ventura will not automatically create additional frames to hold overflow text from either a previously created file or text you are entering in Ventura.

If you load or create text in a frame that is on top of a page, Ventura will fill the frame but not place the overflow text anywhere automatically. You need to create additional frames and then tell Ventura to place the overflow text in the new frame.

6.30 Tip

When creating a document template, you can use empty frames as place holders.

The example chapters supplied with Ventura and the various books that contain chapter and style sheet samples are useful as templates. A *template* is a framework for you to use for your own document. If you want to create a newsletter, you may want to begin with the newsletter sample available in your TYPESET directory or from an outside source. Once you remove the text and pictures, the empty design of frames and underlying pages is the template into which you can pour your own text and pictures. A template saves you time and effort.

If you decide to create your own templates from scratch, use frames as text and picture place holders. Then, when you create your final document, you will have an idea of where you want to place your text and pictures for the best effect. You easily can modify the template to your needs, but at least you have a starting point.

Templates are especially useful if you find that you're regularly creating similar documents such as letters or regular company newsletters. Instead of creating style sheets and setting up frames for each new document, rely on templates to save time. Remember, *frame layout* plus *style sheet* equals *template*, which translates to efficiency in designing.

6.31 Tip

Use the Remove Text/File command to remove either graphic or text files from the frame or assignment list.

When you are in Frame mode and click a frame or underlying page, if anything is in the frame or on the page, the name of the file is shown in the current selection box. You can remove from the frame or assignment list the file that is listed in the current selection box. Do the following:

1. Choose Remove Text/File from the Edit menu.
2. The name of the file you want to remove is listed in the REMOVE FILE dialog box. Choose whether to remove from the list of files (assignment list) or the frame. Selecting `Frame` leaves the file on the assignment list for later use. If you will not be using the file later, choose `List of Files`.
3. Click OK or press Enter.

Using Anchors

In this section, you will receive detailed information about how to use anchors in Ventura Publisher.

6.32 Tip

Use Ventura's capacity to anchor frames to keep together text, pictures, or other material in frames.

One frustrating aspect of page layout is getting all your text and graphics "just so" and then having to make a last minute change that forces you to move frames and text around so everything is in the right place again. Whether you have experienced this situation with scissors and paste or electronically doesn't matter; the frustration is deeply felt.

Ventura has a frame anchor capability that allows you to "tie" text and frames together. How is this capability useful? As an example, if you have a bar graph referenced by some specific text, you want the graph and the text right next to each other; if the text moves, you want the graph to move. You don't want the text to move three columns over and have the graph stay put.

Anchoring frames is a two-step process. You need to assign an *anchor name* to a frame, and you need to insert an *anchor point* in your text. Think of this process like buttoning a button: you need both a button and a button hole. The anchor name is like the button, and the anchor point is like the button hole.

To anchor frames, follow these steps:

1. To create an anchor name, select a frame while in Frame mode.
2. Choose Anchors & Captions from the Frame menu.
3. In the ANCHORS & CAPTIONS dialog box, type an anchor name on the line beside the `Anchor` option and then click OK or press Enter.
4. To create an anchor point, switch to Text mode and insert the text cursor at the point where you want to anchor the frame.
5. Choose Ins Special Item from the Edit menu or press the keyboard shortcut Ctrl-C.
6. A dialog box with several choices appears; either click Frame Anchor or press F5.
7. In the INSERT/EDIT ANCHOR dialog box, type *exactly* the same anchor name you typed in the ANCHORS & CAPTIONS dialog box. (If you do these steps in order, the frame's anchor name will be entered automatically as it was keyed in step 3.)
8. Click one of the four choices of the `Frame's New Location` option.
9. Click OK or press Enter.

If you try to insert a nonexistent anchor name, you see an error message asking whether you want to ignore, rename, or delete the anchor insertion. For this reason, creating the anchor name before creating the anchor point is best.

Choosing Ignore creates the anchor insert, but you later will have to create the anchor name. Choosing Rename puts you back in the INSERT/EDIT ANCHOR dialog box for another try at typing in the frame's anchor name. Choosing Delete cancels the Insert/Edit Anchor command.

Two clues tell you that the anchor is in place. Next to the text cursor you see a degree sign indicating the position of the anchor. And in the current selection box, `Frame Anchor` is displayed.

You can delete the frame anchor by positioning the text cursor just in front of the frame anchor degree symbol and pressing Del or by placing the text cursor just after the degree symbol and pressing Backspace.

6.33 Tip

Select relative positioning of the frame from the INSERT/EDIT ANCHOR dialog box.

You have four choices for positioning:

Positioning Choice	*Effect*
Fixed, On Same Page As Anchor	The frame will follow the text anchor, but the frame will stay fixed in the original position regardless of the page the frame ends up on.
Relative, Below Anchor Line	The frame will go below or after the line of text that contains the anchor.
Relative, Above Anchor Line	The frame will go above or before the line of text that contains the anchor.
Relative, Automatically At Anchor	The frame follows the anchor automatically and acts as another character in the line of text. You do not need to issue the Re-Anchor Frames command to reposition this type of frame. Also, if you cut or copy the anchor, the frame also will be cut or copied.

Figure 6.16 shows an example of the four types of anchor insert points.

6.34 Trap

The Relative, Above Anchor Line positioning choice does not function correctly.

In the initial release of Ventura 2.0, the `Relative, Above Anchor Line` positioning choice does not work correctly. Avoid using this option until the bug is corrected. Currently, the option places the anchored frame before or after—but not above—the anchor point.

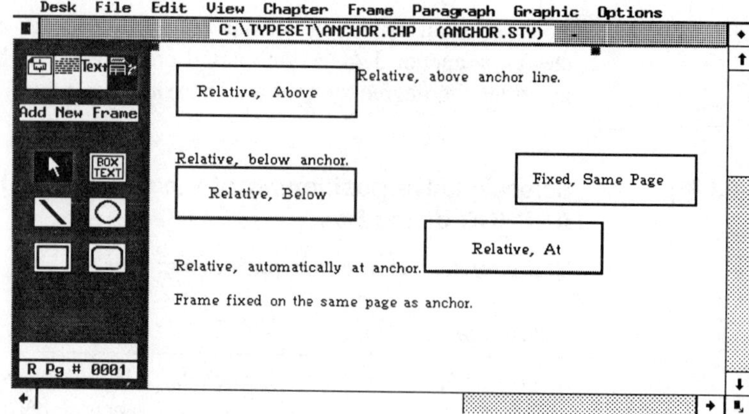

Fig. 6.16.
Anchor examples.

6.35 Tip

To edit the anchor, position the cursor so the current selection reads Frame Anchor.

If you need to change the name or positioning of the text frame anchor, place the text cursor just before the small degree symbol (visible only if tabs and returns are showing). Choose Edit Special Item from the Edit menu or press the keyboard shortcut Ctrl-D. You then can make changes from the EDIT/INSERT ANCHOR dialog box.

6.36 Trap

Deleting a Relative, Automatically At Anchor anchor insert also deletes the anchored frame.

If you delete the anchor insert point for a `Relative, Automatically At Anchor` frame, the anchored frame also is deleted. This frame deletion is undocumented. If you delete anchor insert points for the other locations, only the insert point is deleted and the anchored frame is unaffected.

To work around this problem, you need to edit the anchor insertion, changing the location to something other than `Relative, Automatically At Anchor`.

6.37 Tip

Develop a system for remembering anchors.

Ventura doesn't give you much help in naming anchors. Wouldn't it be nice if a way was available to list the anchors in some kind of assignment list? Unfortunately, the only way to remember anchor names is to write them down.

An easy way to remember anchor names is to make up a three-column chart on paper. Column 1 is the name of the anchor for the frame, column 2 is a brief description of what is in the frame, and column 3 is checked off once the anchor is placed in the text.

6.38 Tip **Use the Re-Anchor Frames command to rearrange anchored frames.**

After making changes in your chapter, you will need to reanchor the frames. Select Re-Anchor Frames from the Chapter menu and click `This Page` to anchor only the current page or click `All Pages` to reanchor frames in the entire chapter.

If you have unassigned anchor names, you will be prompted to ignore, rename, or delete the anchor frame name.

Using Rules with Frames

Rules are narrow lines that fit in the gutter between columns to help visually separate columns, making the page easier to read. You can place vertical rules elsewhere on the page as well to separate sections or to serve as a design element of the page.

6.39 Tip **Use the Vertical Rules command to create vertical rules between columns in frames.**

Ventura offers sophisticated and complete control over intercolumn rules. You have a rule of any width between columns.

To create intercolumn vertical rules, do the following:

1. If you want intercolumn rules, while in Frame mode, create columns by using the MARGINS & COLUMNS dialog box, which you access from the Frame menu. Specify a gutter width, or the intercolumn vertical rule will not show or print.
2. If the vertical rule isn't visible, choose Vertical Rules from the Frame menu.
3. From the VERTICAL RULES dialog box (see fig. 6.17), select `Inter-Col. Rules: On`.
4. The `Width` setting has a default of 0.007 inches (0.48 points). You can modify the width if you want.
5. Click OK or press Enter.

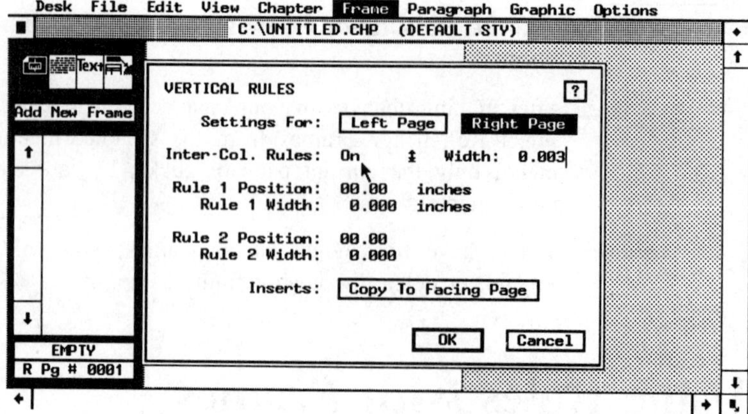

Fig. 6.17.
The VERTICAL RULES dialog box.

6.40 Tip

Use the Vertical Rules command to create up to two vertical rules anywhere in a frame.

In addition to the intercolumn rules, you can create up to two vertical rules per frame by using the VERTICAL RULES dialog box. Such rules can be used at the edge of a column, frame, or page (see fig. 6.18).

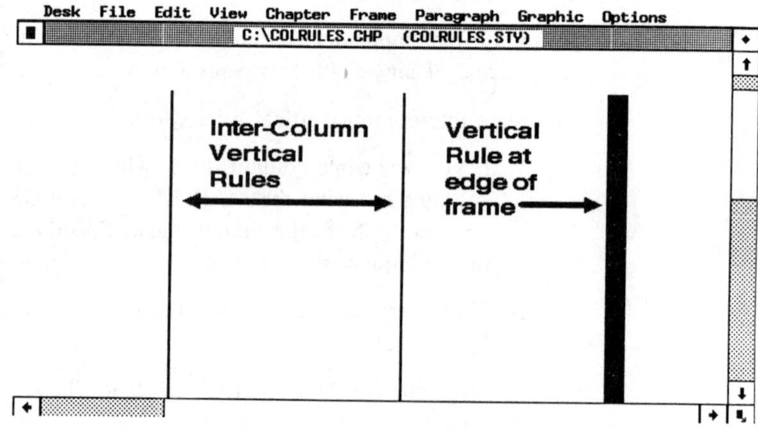

Fig. 6.18.
Examples of intercolumn rules and rule at the edge of a frame.

To create vertical rules at the edge of a column, frame, or page, do the following:

1. If you want intercolumn rules, while in Frame mode, create columns by using the MARGINS & COLUMNS dialog box, which you access from the Frame menu.
2. Choose Vertical Rules from the Frame menu.

3. From the VERTICAL RULES dialog box, you can create one or two vertical rules. The `Rule 1 Position` or `Rule 2 Position` setting is measured from the left margin of the page (not frame). Set the position so the rule will line up with the edge of a column, frame, or page.
4. Set the `Rule 1 Width` or `Rule 2 Width` settings.
5. Click OK or press Enter.

Rule 1 and rule 2 should be at the edge of a column, frame, or margin. You may have to change the `In From Left` or `In From Right` settings in the SPACING dialog box (which you access from the Paragraph menu) to keep the rule from covering text. If you set `Overall Width` to `Frame-Wide` in the ALIGNMENT dialog box (also accessed from the Paragraph menu), paragraphs with the frame-wide tag will interrupt the vertical rules (see fig. 6.19).

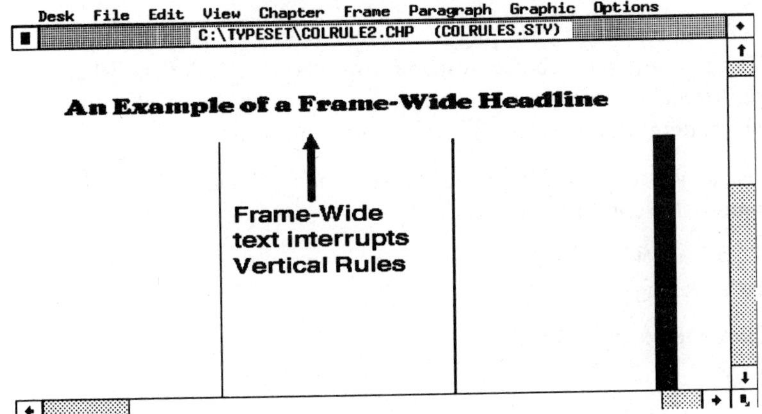

Fig. 6.19.
Vertical rules interrupted by frame-wide text.

6.41 Tip **Use the Graphic mode line function to create a vertical or horizontal rule.**

If you need specialized vertical rules for tables or special intercolumn rules requiring more than one rule, you can create rules by using the line function in Graphic mode.

See Chapter 8 for details about creating graphics lines.

6.42 Tip

You can add rules to frames by using the Ruling Line Above, Ruling Line Below, and Ruling Box Around commands from the Frame menu.

Just as you can add rules above, below, and around paragraphs by using the Paragraph menu (see Chapter 5), you can add rules above, below, and around frames by using the appropriate command from the Frame menu.

To add rules above, below, or around frames, do the following:

1. Switch to Frame mode and click a frame to select it.
2. From the Frame menu, choose Ruling Line Above, Ruling Line Below, or Ruling Box Around.

   Depending on your choice, you will see either the RULING LINES ABOVE, RULING LINES BELOW, or RULING BOX AROUND dialog box.
3. Define the rules by selecting the `Frame` choice of the `Width` options (`Frame` is the only choice available from the `Width` options when you're adding rules to a frame); then select your choice of color and pattern and whether you want dashes on or off.
4. Just as you did for paragraphs, set the `Space Above` and `Height` options for one to three rules.
5. If you selected `Dashes: On`, you can set custom dash width and dash spacing.
6. Click OK or press Enter.

6.43 Tip

You can put a ruling line above, ruling line below, or ruling box around the underlying page.

Remember, Ventura treats the underlying page as a frame, so you can add rules to the frame by using the Frame menu's Rule options. From the Frame menu, click the underlying page to select it; then follow steps 1 through 6 in the preceding tip.

6.44 Trick

Use the Dashes: On option to create coupon clip-out boxes.

If you want to create a coupon, choose Ruling Box Around from the Frame menu. Set the `Width` option to `Frame` and set `Dashes` to `On`. Set the `Height of Rule 1` and change `Dash Width` and `Dash Spacing` to suit your tastes (see fig. 6.20).

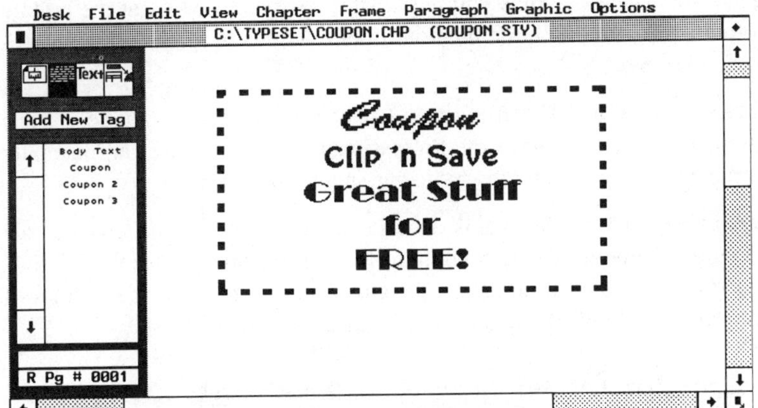

Fig. 6.20.

Coupon box created with a ruling box around and with dashes on.

Creating Special Effects with Frames

You can use frames to create certain kinds of special effects. Frames can contain as well as restrain text or graphics. Frames also can be set with various background shades. The shading effect can have an impact on text contained in the frame (if your printer supports such effects).

6.45 Tip **When working with multiple frames or frames that are on top of each other, use the Shift key with the mouse to select more than one frame; use the Ctrl key with the mouse to select frames that are behind other frames.**

If you have more than one frame on a page, you can select more than one of the frames by holding down the Shift key while clicking each frame you want selected. Many commands, such as Ruling Box Around or Frame Background, affect only the first frame selected. Deleting or copying en masse is best for selecting multiple frames.

If you have more than one frame on a page and the frames overlap one another, you can step through the layers of frames by holding down the Ctrl key while clicking the frame(s). Each click moves you one layer deeper in the stacked frame layer.

6.46 Trick **Use empty frames to help vertically justify columns.**

When you have documents with multiple columns—and the columns contain frames with graphics, or you have some paragraphs tagged for headings and subheadings—adjacent columns will not always have text line up at the bottom of the columns. This lining up at the bottom of columns is called *vertical justification* of columns.

The Ventura Professional Extension (see Chapter 12) offers automatic vertical justification. If you do not have the Professional Extension, you can manually create vertically justified columns by using small empty frames.

Create a small empty frame that is as wide as the width of the column and place the empty frame in the short column. Manually adjust or use the SIZING & SCALING dialog box to adjust the height of the frame until the bottom of the column lines up with the adjacent columns (see fig. 6.21).

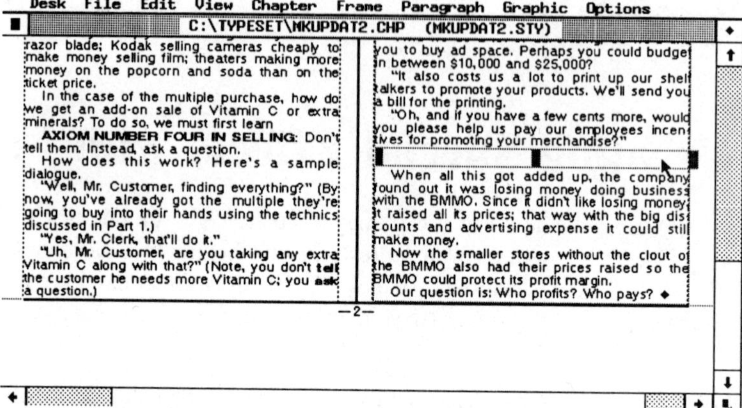

Fig. 6.21.

Example of an empty frame being used to vertically justify adjacent columns.

6.47 Tip

Use the Frame Background command from the Frame menu to set frame shading.

Ventura has nine shade patterns (if you count the `Hollow` option as a shade) of backgrounds for frames. To set the frame background, do the following:

1. While in Frame mode, click the frame for which you want to set the background.
2. Choose the Frame Background command from the Frame menu to access the FRAME BACKGROUND dialog box.
3. Select one of the eight colors for the frame background.
4. Select one of the nine patterns, ranging from hollow to solid.
5. Click OK or press Enter.

Figure 6.22 shows an example of the nine patterns printed with a PostScript printer (not all printers are capable of printing white letters). Notice that the numbers become increasingly difficult to read as the pattern becomes denser (the shading gets darker).

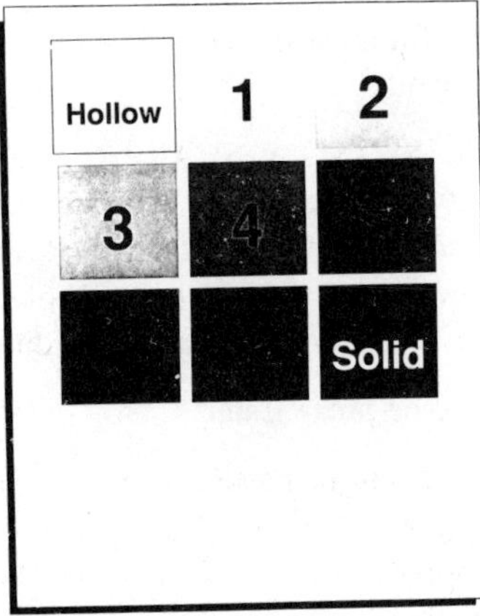

Fig. 6.22.
Examples of the nine patterns available for the frame background.

Unless you are using the frame background for spot color or are using large, bold fonts, I recommend that you don't use a pattern higher than option 2.

You may have noticed that the nine patterns are the same as those available for a ruling line above, ruling line below, and ruling box around.

6.48 Tip

Set the frame background to Solid to create text blocks with white text on a black background.

If you have a printer capable of printing white text on a black background, you can set the frame background to `Solid`; any text in the frame or added to the frame later will turn to white automatically. You don't need to change the font color by using the Font menu.

6.49 Trick

Use three frames to create a drop shadow effect.

A drop shadow frame can have a strong visual impact if used sparingly. If your printer will support it, you can create a drop shadow effect in Ventura by using three frames. To create a drop shadow frame, do the following:

1. Add a frame that is the size you want to use for the text or graphic.
2. While in Frame mode, select the frame and press Del. The frame is now on the Frame Clipboard.

3. Press Ins to paste the frame back onto your work area.
4. Select the frame, choose Frame Background from the Frame menu, and set the background to `Black` and `Solid`.
5. Click OK or press Enter.
6. With the frame still selected, choose Sizing & Scaling from the Frame menu.
7. From the SIZING & SCALING dialog box, add 0.2 inches to the `Upper Left X` and `Upper Left Y` figures. Increasing the X and Y figures causes the frame to shift down and to the right 0.2 inches. (If you want the shadow to be above or to the left, you can decrease the X or Y figures accordingly.)
8. Click OK or press Enter.
9. Press Ins again to paste a frame on top of the black frame. Notice that the new frame is offset up and to the left of the black frame. The reason is that you shifted the black frame down and to the right in step 7.
10. With the newly pasted frame selected, choose Frame Background from the Frame menu. Set the frame background to `White` and `Solid`.

    The white frame is necessary to keep the black frame from bleeding through and blocking the graphic or text that will be placed in the top frame.
11. Click OK or press Enter.
12. Press Ins a third time to paste a frame on top of the white frame.
13. You now can place either text or a graphic into the top frame (see fig. 6.23). If you want, you can put a ruling box around the top frame.

6.50 Trap

When an added frame doesn't quite reach the underlying frame's border, single characters of the text will be squeezed into the resulting space.

Examine figure 6.24 to see the effect of overlapping frames on text contained in the underneath frame. If the overlapping frame extends across the entire frame, the text in the underneath frame moves below (or above) the overlapping frame (see top example in fig. 6.24). If the overlapping frame does not extend to the edges of the underneath frame, the text of the underneath frame is squeezed into the remaining space.

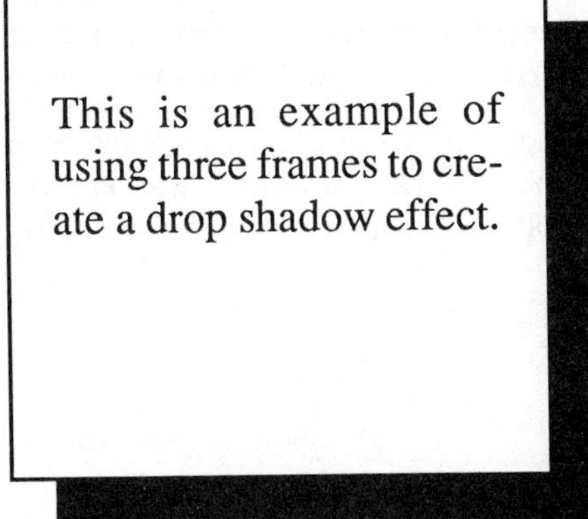

Fig. 6.23.

A drop shadow effect with three frames.

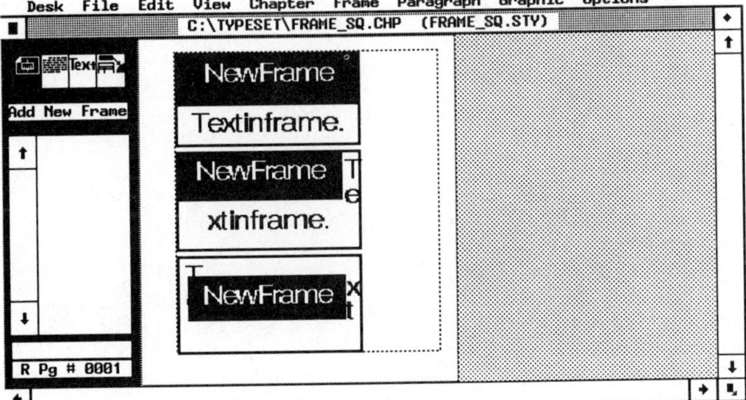

Fig. 6.24.

Examples of text in underneath frame affected by positioning of overlapping frame.

Chapter Summary

In many ways, learning about frames is both the simplest and the most complex aspect of Ventura. After reading this chapter, you should have a good grasp of what frames are and how to work with them.

In this chapter, you learned about the underlying page and about placing frames on the underlying page. You know how to add and delete pages as well as how to add, delete, move, and resize frames. And you learned how to make text flow automatically and semiautomatically.

You examined the contents of frames and how to use anchors to keep frames where you want them, tied to a specific point or paragraph. You learned about vertical rules between columns and at the edge of a page, column, or frame. And you learned about special effects and tricks using frames to create vertically justified columns and drop shadow frames.

The next chapter covers graphic images and deals less with Ventura itself than with the graphics world that feeds images and pictures to Ventura. This chapter should be both interesting and fun to read.

Part

III

Working with Graphics

Includes

Importing and Changing Graphics

Using Ventura's Graphics Tools

Chapter

7

Importing and Changing Graphics

One of the most exciting aspects of desktop publishing is its capability of putting graphics images on the same page as text—without the use of scissors and a pot of paste.

When the Macintosh became available in 1984, graphics in the DOS world were primitive. With the introduction of the Macintosh, people began to see that personal computers could offer sophisticated graphics capabilities.

The PC world did not stay idle. Although the Macintosh still has an edge in graphics production for graphics designers, new graphics software for PC systems (usually running in a Windows or GEM environment) has recently eaten away most of the Macintosh's competitive advantage. New graphics software available for PCs rivals and, in some cases, exceeds the capabilities of similar programs developed for the Macintosh.

This chapter focuses on not just how to bring graphics into a Ventura document, but also where to get those graphics in the first place. By the time you finish this chapter, you will have not only a good idea of sources for graphics but also a solid overview of the capabilities of graphics software currently available for the PC. This chapter also provides you with many examples of graphics that you can create yourself or use from commercially available sources of clip art.

Loading Pictures

Loading a picture into Ventura is just like loading text. The same options to load single or multiple files and load into a frame or onto the assignment list are available.

7.1 Tip

To load a picture, use Load Text/Picture from the File menu.

To load a picture into Ventura, do the following steps:

1. From the File menu, choose Load Text/Picture.
2. From the LOAD/TEXT PICTURE dialog box, you can choose between two kinds of pictures: `Line-Art` or `Image`.

   If you click `Line-Art`, you are presented with 10 format choices (see fig. 7.1). If you click `Image`, you have a choice of 4 formats (see fig. 7.2). Click the correct format for the figure you want to load (if you want to load more than one file of the same format, click `Several` on `# of Files`). Click OK or press Enter.
3. The ITEM SELECTOR dialog box appears with the file filter for the type of file you are trying to load. Either click the graphics file name of your choice or type the file name on the `Selection` line. Click OK or press Enter.

   If you selected an empty frame before loading a picture, the picture is loaded into that frame. Otherwise, the name of the picture appears in the assignment list.

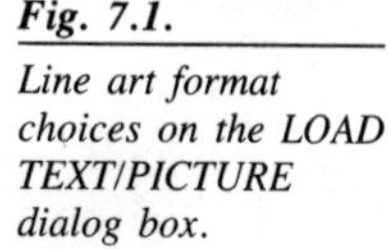

Fig. 7.1.

Line art format choices on the LOAD TEXT/PICTURE dialog box.

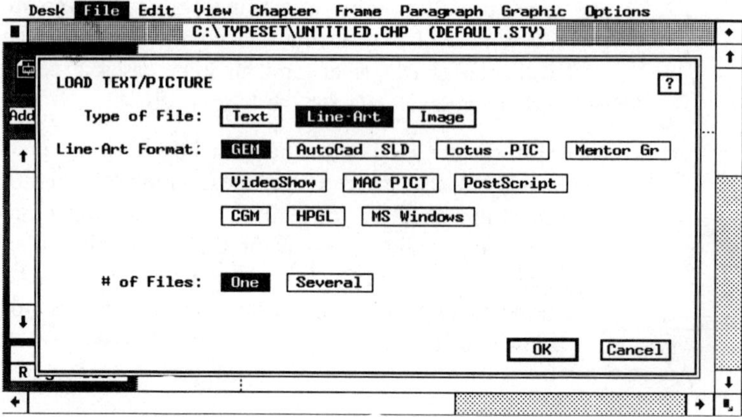

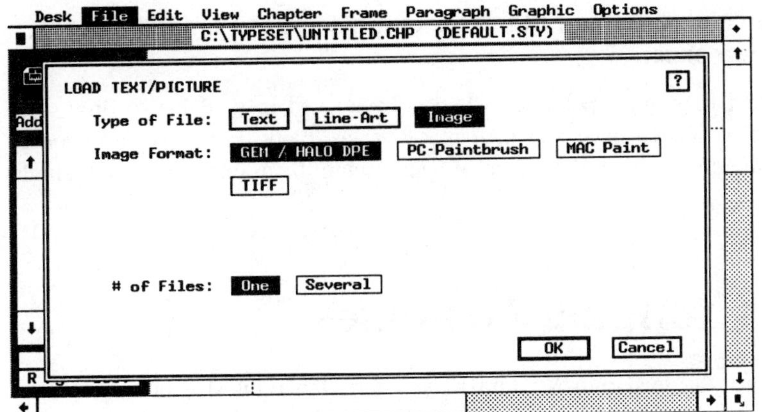

Fig. 7.2.
Image format choices on the LOAD TEXT/ PICTURE dialog box.

To load a picture from the assignment list into a frame, make sure that you are in Frame mode, select a frame, and click the name of the desired graphic in the assignment list. The graphic is loaded into the selected frame.

7.2 Tip **If you select the incorrect file format for the type of graphic you try to load, Ventura warns you.**

Ventura will not let you load a file unless the file type and the converter are the same. If you try to load an IMG file using the TIFF converter, for example, Ventura warns you that the wrong converter is being used.

If you use the /A switch on the command line to load Ventura, you may not have enough memory to convert certain types of graphics files. Ventura warns you that too little memory is available and suggests that the /A switch may be the culprit. The solution is to reduce the /A switch memory allocation or, if possible, eliminate the /A switch. See Chapter 1 for additional information about the /A switch.

7.3 Trap **If the picture is to be converted automatically to either a GEM or an IMG file by Ventura, be sure that the file names you provide are distinctive; otherwise, Ventura does not know which file to use, and the program may crash back to the DOS prompt.**

If you have several graphics files with the same name but different extensions, change the names to be unique. Ventura can convert many files to IMG or GEM files that are directly handled by the GEM environment. If you have two files with the same name in two different formats—for example, GRAPH.PCX and GRAPH.CGM—Ventura converts both images to GRAPH.IMG. The name conflict can cause Ventura to crash back to the DOS prompt.

7.4 Trick **You don't need to load the same graphic several times to use it more than once.**

Unlike text files that "run out" when no more text is available to flow, pictures can be loaded once and then placed in as many frames as you choose. Don't, therefore, load the same graphic more than once into any single chapter.

Scaling and Cropping Graphics

The image you load into Ventura may not be the right size or may not be cropped exactly the way you want. You don't need to go back to the "drawing board" to re-create the graphic in the correct size; instead, you can scale and crop graphics in Ventura.

7.5 Tip **Use the SIZING & SCALING dialog box to size and scale pictures.**

Once you load a picture into a frame, you can control several aspects of how the image is displayed. Although Ventura does not allow you to edit, rotate, invert, or flip the image, you can control scaling and cropping. To scale an image in Frame mode, select the frame in which the picture is loaded and choose Sizing & Scaling from the Frame menu (see fig. 7.3).

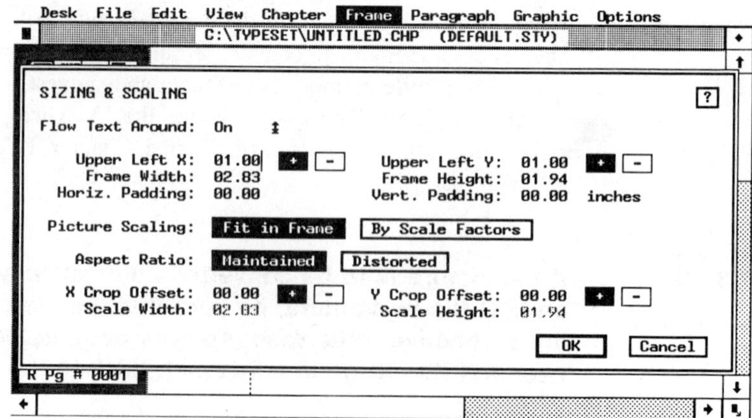

Fig. 7.3. *The SIZING & SCALING dialog box.*

The bottom half of the SIZING & SCALING dialog box controls scaling and cropping. Although it may seem that the designers of Ventura think they're dealing with a bunch of math whizzes, don't be discouraged. Sizing and scaling images is not as complicated as it first appears. Remember that changing

X Crop Offset makes the picture go left or right; changing Y Crop Offset makes the picture go up or down. If you look at the figures in this tip, you should gain a good understanding of terms like "aspect ratio" and "scale factors." The following information may help you understand how each option affects a picture.

Picture Scaling with Aspect Ratio: Maintained

The setting Fit in Frame ensures that if you change the size of the frame, the picture retains the same relative size and fit within the frame. Figure 7.4 shows that the logo retains its symmetry and fits in the frame regardless of frame size. The setting By Scale Factors means that size of the graphic remains constant regardless of the size of the frame. Because the graphic may be larger than the frame, not all the graphic necessarily fits. In figure 7.5, notice that the logo is the same size in all frames—even if it will not completely fit. If Aspect Ratio: Maintained is set, the Scale Width can be changed; if Aspect Ratio: Distorted is set, both the scale width and the scale height can be changed.

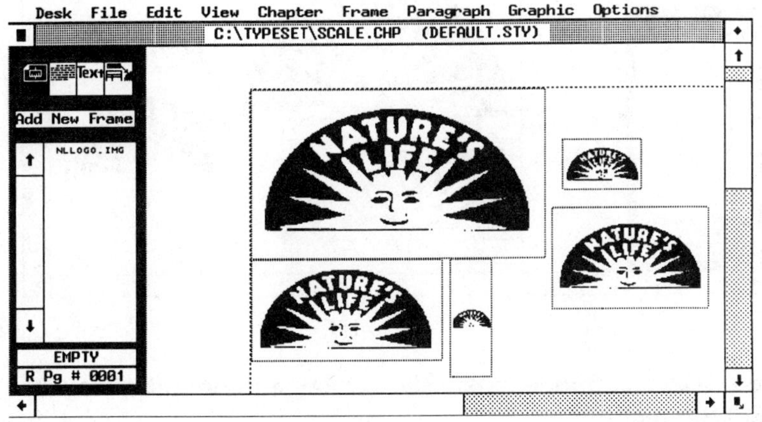

Fig. 7.4.

Five different frame sizes set to Fit in Frame.

Picture Scaling with Aspect Ratio: Distorted

The setting Fit in Frame ensures that if you change the size of the frame, the graphic distorts along both X and Y axes to fill the frame (see fig. 7.6). The setting By Scale Factors means that the size of the graphic remains constant regardless of the size of the frame (see fig. 7.5). When you set Aspect Ratio: Distorted, both the Scale Width and the Scale Height can be changed.

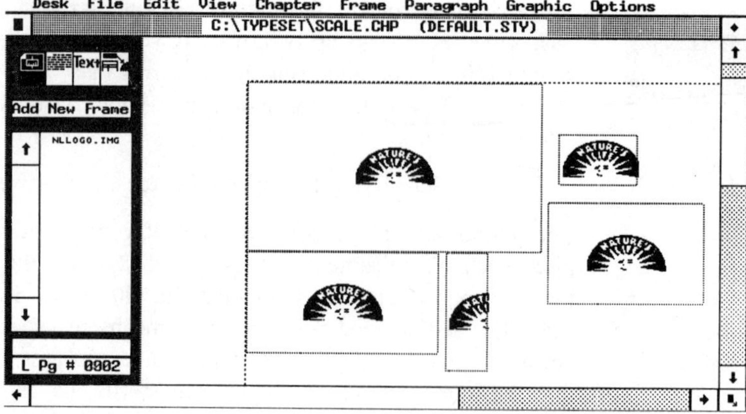

Fig. 7.5.

Five different frame sizes set to fit `By Scale Factors`.

Fig. 7.6.

Five different frame sizes set with `Aspect Ratio: Distorted`.

7.6 Tip

In Frame or Graphic mode, press the Alt key and hold the mouse button to crop pictures.

Ventura allows visual *cropping* of pictures. Whenever you move a picture around in a frame to make a part of the picture visible (or make a picture bigger so that only a part of the whole figure is visible), you have cropped the picture.

In Ventura, you can see how you crop a picture. Hold the Alt key and press the mouse button in Frame or Graphic mode. The cursor turns into a little hand with which you can push the picture left, right, up, or down in the frame (see figs. 7.7 and 7.8). To enlarge or shrink a picture, you must use the SIZING & SCALING dialog box. You must switch back between the screen and dialog box to see the effect of resizing (see Tip 7.5).

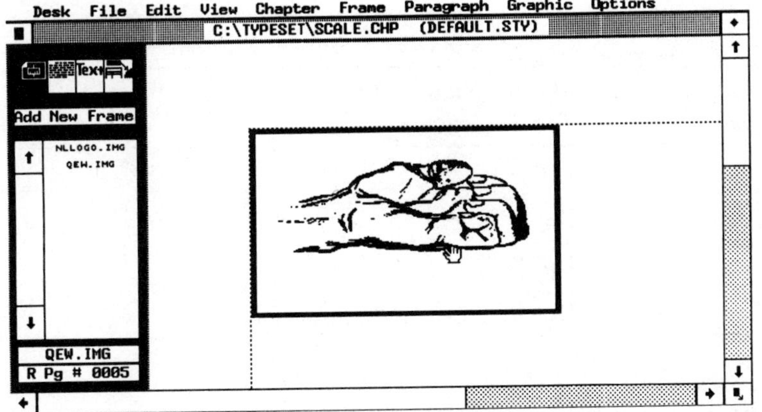

Fig. 7.7.

The move graphic cursor preparing to crop a graphic.

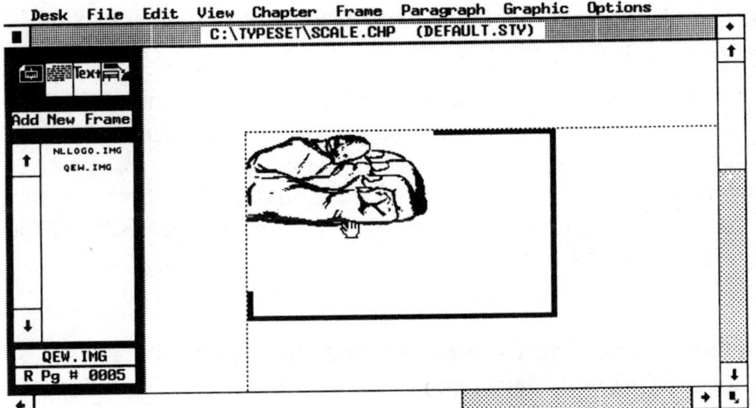

Fig. 7.8.

A cropped graphic.

7.7 Tip

Use the SIZING & SCALING dialog box to crop pictures.

When you visually crop a picture, you change the `X` and `Y Crop Offset` values in the SIZING & SCALING dialog box. To verify this, crop a picture visually and then look at the values in the `Crop Offset` fields. The offsets are measured in the measurement units set in the dialog box in relationship to the margins of the frame. See table 7.1 for the effect each offset has on a picture.

As an example, if you push the picture up and to the left, both the `X` and `Y Crop Offset` values should be positive. If you insert numbers greater than the frame dimensions, the picture will not be visible.

Table 7.1
Crop Offsets

Coordinate	*Moves Picture This Direction*
X +	Left
X −	Right
Y +	Up
Y −	Down

7.8 Trap

The frame retains settings from the SIZING & SCALING dialog box. If you replace a picture in a frame, the new picture may not look right until you modify the SIZING & SCALING dialog box settings.

If you use a frame that has been modified with settings from the SIZING & SCALING dialog box and remove the picture from the frame, the SIZING & SCALING dialog box settings are not reset. If you put a new picture in such a frame, therefore, the SIZING & SCALING dialog box settings from the previous picture may distort the new picture. You must modify these settings for each picture placed in the frame.

7.9 Tip

Control whether text flows around or through a frame by using the SIZING & SCALING dialog box.

Generally, when you create a frame, you want the frame to occupy space and not allow text surrounding the frame to flow through the frame.

For a special effect, however, you may want text to flow through the frame. Some examples are text runarounds (see Tip 7.11) or when text is to appear against the background of a graphic. Usually, box text is a better way to place text within a frame that contains a picture. Control text flow by setting `Flow Text Around` to `On` or `Off` on the SIZING & SCALING dialog box (see Chapter 8 for information on box text).

7.10 Tip

Control the distance between frames that contain graphics or text and surrounding text with horizontal and vertical padding on the SIZING & SCALING dialog box.

Padding refers to the white space between a graphic and text. For some reason, Ventura designers didn't refer to the horizontal and vertical padding options as X and Y padding. In figure 7.9, no padding is provided around the graphic frame, and text runs right into the ruling box around the frame. (If you create frames while Turn Line Snap On is selected, the tops and bottoms of the frames usually have some natural padding because they line up with the body text interline spacing.)

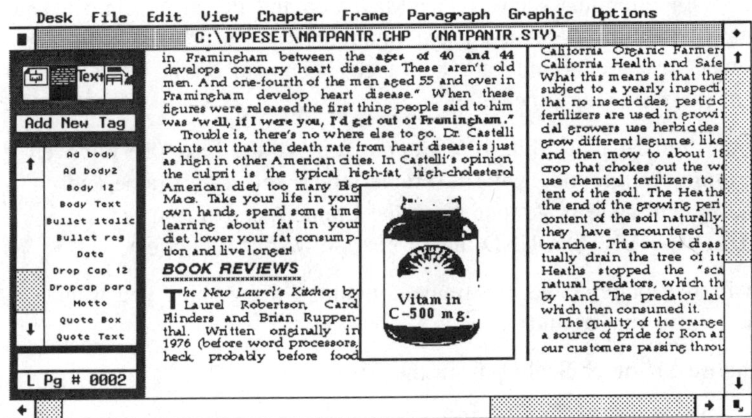

Fig. 7.9.

Frame with no horizontal or vertical padding.

To set padding, make sure that you are in Frame or Graphic mode and select the desired frame. Choose Sizing & Scaling from the Frame menu. Set the `Horiz. Padding` and `Vert. Padding` values to one-half of the value for the interline spacing of the body text. (To find the interline spacing, while in Paragraph mode, select a paragraph that is tagged as body text and look at the SPACING dialog box, which you access from the Paragraph menu.) Click OK or press Enter (see fig. 7.10).

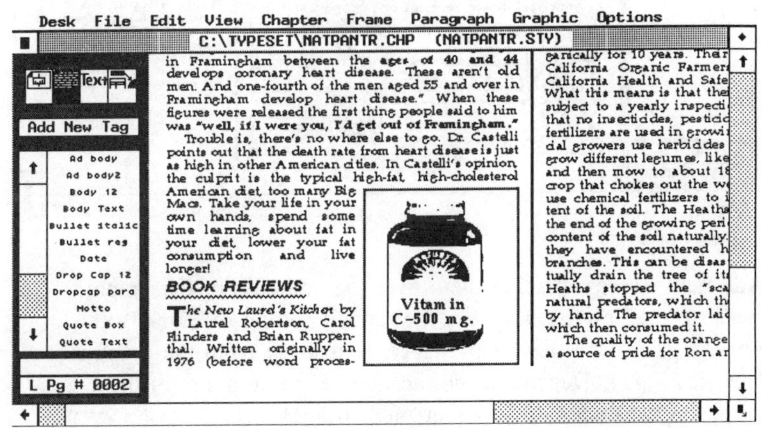

Fig. 7.10.

Frame with horizontal and vertical padding values set to one-half the interline spacing of body text.

7.11 Tip

You can create text that runs around graphics by using empty frames.

A *text runaround* is where text follows the contours of a graphic. Many traditional designers may argue that text runaround is not good design. This belief is quickly dying in the wake of desktop publishing programs that allow text runaround. With programs such as PageMaker on the PC or Macintosh and Ready, Set, Go! on the Macintosh, text runarounds are a breeze. With Ventura, however, text runarounds are a drudge. You can do it, however, as described in the following procedure:

1. If the frame has a ruling box around, remove the box. (To remove a ruling box around, while in Frame mode, select the frame and choose Ruling Box Around from the Frame menu. From the RULING BOX AROUND dialog box, set `Width` to `None`.)

2. In Frame mode, select the frame containing the graphic you want the text to run around.

3. Choose Sizing & Scaling from the Frame menu.

4. Set `Flow Text Around` to `Off`. Click OK or press Enter.

5. Notice that your text now flows under the graphic frame instead of around it (see fig. 7.11).

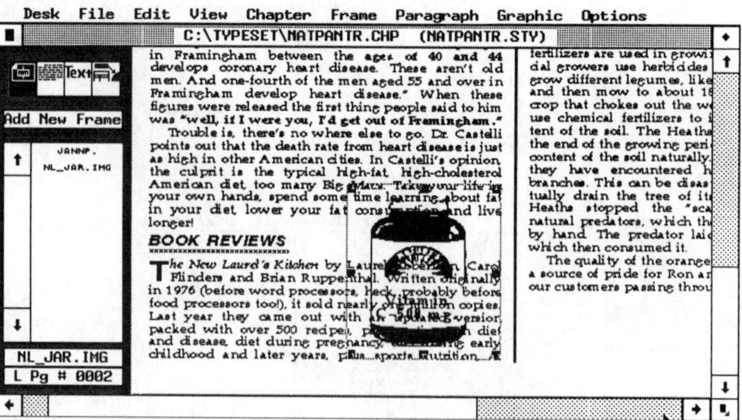

Fig. 7.11.
Frame with `Flow Text Around: Off`.

6. Add new frames, placing them over the contours of the graphic. Because the new frames have the default setting of `Flow Text Around: On`, each new frame forces text away from the graphic (see fig. 7.12). Depending on the number of contours in the graphic, you must add fewer or more frames.

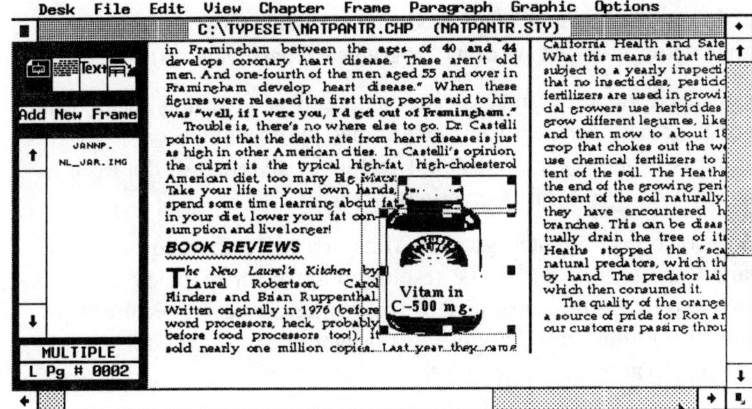

Fig. 7.12.

Frame with added frames to create a text runaround.

Understanding Graphics Formats

As you know, text files come in a variety of formats such as WordPerfect, Microsoft Word, DisplayWrite, and ASCII. The same lack of a common format exists in the world of computer graphics.

One of the challenges a designer of desktop publishing software has in this era of format variety is trying to be compatible with as many formats as possible. Just as with text files, the various graphics formats were developed to complement the type of data being stored. In addition, some Macintosh graphics formats are different from graphics formats used by PC programs. This section examines what the different graphics formats try to accomplish.

7.12 Tip

Learn the difference between bit-mapped and vector graphics file formats.

Despite the variety of graphics file formats, all the formats fall into one of two categories: bit-mapped or vector. Ventura calls bit-mapped graphics ''images''; vector drawings are called ''line art.''

Resolution of graphics is measured by the number of dots or pixels (picture elements) that can be placed in a square inch. A dot-matrix printer can have resolution as high as 180 dpi, and a laser printer (either Hewlett-Packard or PostScript compatible) can produce 300-dpi output. (However, low-resolution bit-mapped graphics do not become high-resolution graphics just because a better printer is used.)

In general, bit-mapped graphics are produced by paint programs or scanners; vector graphics are produced by draw programs. What is the difference?

- Bit-mapped graphics (images) are composed of little dots. The number of dots per inch (dpi) determines the resolution or sharpness of an image. A 180-dpi picture is always 180 dpi even if printed on a 300-dpi laser printer.
- Vector or object-oriented graphics (line art) are composed of straight and curved lines. The resolution of vector graphics depends only on the capability of the printer. A vector picture prints at 300 dpi on a 300-dpi laser printer and at 1,200 dpi on a 1,200-dpi typesetter.

7.13 Trap

Bit-mapped graphics can get the "jaggies" if enlarged. Vector graphics retain their resolution when scaled.

Because bit-mapped graphics are collections of dots or pixels, their resolution is limited by the software and hardware that created them. If, for example, you create a picture by using a bit-mapped graphics program on a low-resolution monitor, the final picture does not have higher resolution than the screen resolution. (Some bit-mapped graphics programs can save files at 300 dpi, which allows for higher resolution when printed on laser printers.)

If you enlarge bit-mapped graphics, what appeared as curves when the picture was small now appear as jagged lines and little steps. Because "jaggies" are usually not acceptable, try to avoid enlarging bit-mapped pictures. When you create bit-mapped graphics, create the picture at the size you ultimately use.

Vector graphics can be scaled without any loss of resolution. You can create vector graphic pictures and enlarge them without worrying about the "jaggies." If you plan to print your final document on a high-resolution device such as a typesetter, use vector graphics unless you are willing to sacrifice resolution.

See figure 7.13 for a comparison of vector and bit-mapped images.

7.14 Trick

Keep the original proportions when scaling bit-mapped art.

If you change the size of bit-mapped graphics, you can minimize the "jaggies" by keeping the original proportions intact (see Tip 7.5 for information on scaling graphics).

Fig. 7.13.
Vector and bit-mapped graphics.

7.15 Tip

When using scanned art, try to scan the picture at the dimensions used in the final document.

Scanned art is stored as bit-mapped pictures. Because of the problems with distortion and the ''jaggies,'' scanned art is best used at the size you originally scan. Most scanning software allows you to enlarge or shrink the art during the scanning process. If you find you need to resize the picture, do so in whole-figure multiples. Rather than increase a picture by 27 percent, for example, increase it by 100 percent or 200 percent. Do the same when shrinking the picture: don't shrink by 18 percent, shrink by 100 percent (1/2) or 200 percent (1/4).

7.16 Tip

Learn about the various graphics file formats.

Ventura supports a variety of graphics file formats. Examine table 7.2 to see which Ventura-supported file format is produced by which software packages. The file formats are on the LOAD TEXT/PICTURE dialog box. Which formats are available as button choices depends on whether you have selected `Line-Art` or `Image`. The extensions on the file name are usually the same as those listed in the table, but check your software documentation to be certain.

Table 7.2
Graphics File Formats

File Format	*Software Package*
Line-Art	
GEM	Draw programs like GEM Artline using the Digital Research GEM environment produce graphics in the GEM format. Some formats are indirectly supported as GEM files, first requiring conversion. For example, convert DXF files using the DXF to GEM (DXFTOGEM.EXE) conversion utility found on the Ventura Utilities disk.
AutoCad.SLD	AutoCAD files can be converted to either SLD or HPGL files for use in Ventura. The Ventura manual advises that the HPGL format produces images of higher resolution.
Lotus.PIC	Business programs like 1-2-3 can create graphs and charts that can be read into Ventura.
Mentor Gr	Output from Mentor Graphics can be read by Ventura.
VideoShow	General Parametric's VideoShow format is supported. Some business graphics programs produce output in VideoShow-compatible format.
MAC PICT	PICT is the format most widely supported by draw types of programs on the Macintosh. Not all PICT formats are exactly the same (some programs make modifications to the PICT standard), so you must experiment to see whether the particular PICT file you want is usable.
PostScript	Many Macintosh applications and a growing number of PC applications produce PostScript files. Ventura can import two types of PostScript files: EPS (Encapsulated PostScript) and images of Ventura pages (not true EPS files). You must have a PostScript printer to print EPS images. If a bit-mapped image is

Table 7.2—*Continued*

File Format	*Software Package*
	included with the EPS file (sometimes included so a visual representation of the picture can be seen within Ventura), the bit-mapped image can be printed by non-PostScript printers.
CGM	Computer Graphic Metafiles are produced by a variety of business software such as Draw Applause, Freelance Plus, and Harvard Graphics. The WordPerfect graphics format (WPG) is usually compatible with CGM files. You may be able to import WPG files into Ventura as CGM files.
HPGL	An HPGL file is a file printed to disk with the use of a Hewlett-Packard Graphics Language (HPGL) driver. Programs supporting the HP 7470 and HP 7475 implementations of HPGL can be imported into Ventura. You must experiment with other HPGL variants.
MS Windows	Microsoft Windows programs producing Window Metafiles (WMF) can be imported directly. If the Windows application cannot create WMF files, you can convert Clipboard files to WMF files using the CLIP2VP program.
Image	
GEM / HALO DPE	IMG files created by GEM paint and scan applications can be read by Ventura.
PC-Paintbrush	The PCX and PCC formats popularized by the ZSoft family of paint products including PC Paintbrush™, PC Paintbrush for Windows, and Publisher's Paintbrush can be read by Ventura. Many other PC paint programs support the PCX format.
MAC Paint	Macintosh applications supporting the MacPaint file format can be transferred to the PC and imported into Ventura. MacPaint files transfer as full pages, so unless the original graphic

Table 7.2—*Continued*

File Format	*Software Package*
	filled the page, you may need to enlarge the image considerably for it to be visible in a Ventura frame.
TIFF	The Tagged Image File Format (TIFF) is used by many scanners. TIFF files are not identical, and some TIFF files cannot be loaded into Ventura. You will need to use trial and error to see whether your TIFF file can be read by Ventura. For example, many TIFF files created on the Macintosh cannot be used by Ventura. TIFF files can be large and consume a great deal of disk space because they may also contain gray-scale information. However, compressed TIFF formats are available as an option (when you're using the HP ScanJet™ and Scanning Gallery software, for example) and, although undocumented, seem to work with Ventura. Compressed TIFF files may use only 10 percent of the space occupied by an uncompressed TIFF file.

7.17 Tip

Use the CLIP2VP.EXE program supplied with Ventura to create a Windows Metafile (WMF) from a Windows Clipboard image.

Some Windows programs cannot export their files in a format that can be read by Ventura. Usually, Windows graphics programs can create a Windows Metafile (WMF) that is directly supported by Ventura. If your Windows program doesn't create a Ventura-compatible file, you can try the following:

1. Copy the CLIP2VP.EXE file from disk 5 (if you're using 5 1/4-inch disks) or disk 3 (if you're using 3 1/2-inch disks) to your WINDOWS directory by using the DOS COPY command.

2. Run Windows. Double-click the CLIP2VP.EXE file name in the Windows Executive window to load the graphics converter. Once it is loaded, shrink the program to an icon (consult your Windows documentation if you don't know how to do this step).

3. Load your graphics program and create your graphic in the Windows program.

4. Select the graphic and cut or copy it to the Clipboard. (If the Clipboard for the software you are running offers you the choice, select Windows Metafile for the Clipboard format.)
5. Double-click the icon that says CLIP->GEM to invoke the CLIP2VP.EXE program you ran earlier.
6. Type the file name of your choice and click Save. The WMF extension is automatically added.

Now you can load the Windows graphics that have been converted into Ventura by using the LOAD TEXT/PICTURE dialog box, selecting Line-Art, and choosing MS Windows.

7.18 Trap

Not all PostScript graphics (EPS) files have screen images.

PostScript is a rich graphics description language. Because a PostScript image is really a text file with instructions to a PostScript printer about how to print the image, PostScript images aren't displayed on the screen. Instead of the image, a large X appears. Some Encapsulated PostScript (EPS) graphics files include a screen image in either TIFF or Windows Metafile (WMF) format. If an EPS file displays, you are really seeing the TIFF or WMF image (see figs. 7.14 and 7.15). The lack of a visual display for some EPS graphics makes positioning, scaling, and text wrap-around effects tedious and difficult.

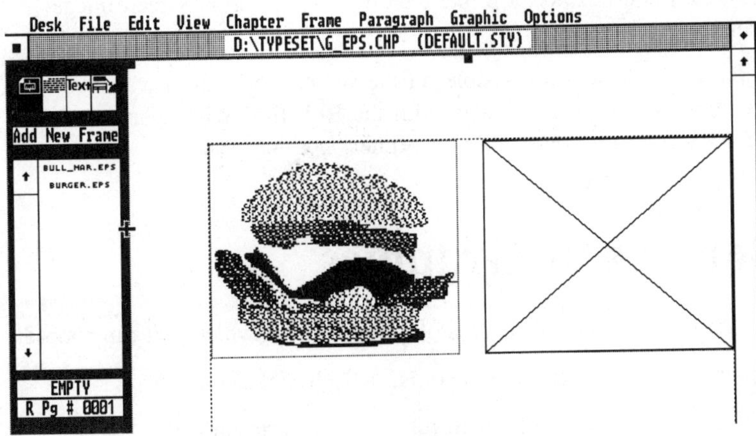

Fig. 7.14.

Two EPS graphics, one with a screen image and one showing only an X.

Fig. 7.15.

Printout of the on-screen EPS graphics shown in figure 7.14.

7.19 Trap **Not all printers are capable of printing Encapsulated PostScript files.**

PostScript printers translate the PostScript programming language into text and pictures. If you import EPS files and try to print them, one of two things happens:

- ❑ If you saw an image on-screen, what displayed was a lower resolution screen image included with the EPS file. When you print to a non-PostScript printer, the lower resolution screen image prints.
- ❑ If the EPS file was not visible on the screen, the reason was that no screen image was included with the EPS file. When you print the EPS file to a non-PostScript printer, nothing prints.

Examining Sources of Graphics

Following are the four general sources of graphics from which you can choose:

- ❑ Scanned art from drawings, photos, and clip-art books
- ❑ Digital or electronic clip art in ready-to-use form on disk
- ❑ Graphics you create yourself with either a paint or draw program
- ❑ Charts and graphs generated by programs from data

The following sections explain each of these sources more fully.

Using Scanned Art

The tips in this section explain how you can use art from books, drawings, and photos in your own publications by scanning the image and importing the scanned image into Ventura.

7.20 Tip

Inexpensive clip-art libraries of illustrations are available in book form.

Clip-art libraries are ready-made images that you can incorporate into your document without any additional work.

Clip-art books are sold in book and art stores. One of the best series currently available is the Dover Clip-Art Series, which includes the following volumes: *Food and Drink*, *Old-Fashioned Animal Cuts*, *Accents and Attention-Getters*, *Art Deco Small Frames and Borders*, *Old-Fashioned Transportation Cuts*, *Decorative Letters*, and *Victorian Spot Illustrations, Alphabets & Ornaments*. Each volume contains hundreds of illustrations that you can use in your documents without paying royalties (see fig. 7.16). Other publishers produce similar clip-art books. To use clip art from books, you must either "cut and paste" them or use an electronic scanner to convert the clip art into a digital image that can be used directly by Ventura.

7.21 Tip

Use a scanner or scanning service to digitize drawings, pictures, or clips.

Think of scanning devices as copy machines for your computer. Unlike a regular copier that produces an identical paper copy, scanners produce an electronic (digital) copy that can be stored in your computer's memory. Although you can make digital copies of text that your word processor can understand, reasonably priced text or character recognition technology has not yet been fully realized.

Scanning graphics is another story. Images can be scanned at high resolution with relatively inexpensive equipment. Numerous scanners (the hardware) and scanning control programs (the software) are available. Scanners are usually one of three types: hand-held models suitable for rough scanning of small images, drum types that require feeding a single-sheet document into a slot, and flat-bed models that can accept single sheets as well as books.

The collection of illustrations in figure 7.16 is an example. The page was scanned by a Hewlett-Packard ScanJet (a flat-bed scanner capable of scanning pages from open books). The control software for the ScanJet is Scanning Gallery and runs under Windows. If you study figure 7.17, you can see that the

Fig. 7.16.

A page from Food and Drink Spot Illustrations *(Mineola, NY: Dover Publications, Inc., 1982).*

page from the Dover book was scanned. Scanning Gallery allows you to select a portion of the page to save as a graphic image. The bowls, eggs, sugar, and flour picture was selected with the mouse and converted to a GEM IMG file.

Figure 7.18 shows how the IMG file can be imported into a Ventura file and then printed out in the example as an illustration for a directory.

Scanners save files in a bit-mapped format. Most scanners allow you to save files in the PCX format; more sophisticated scanners allow the TIFF format; some even let you store in Microsoft Paint format for use in Windows.

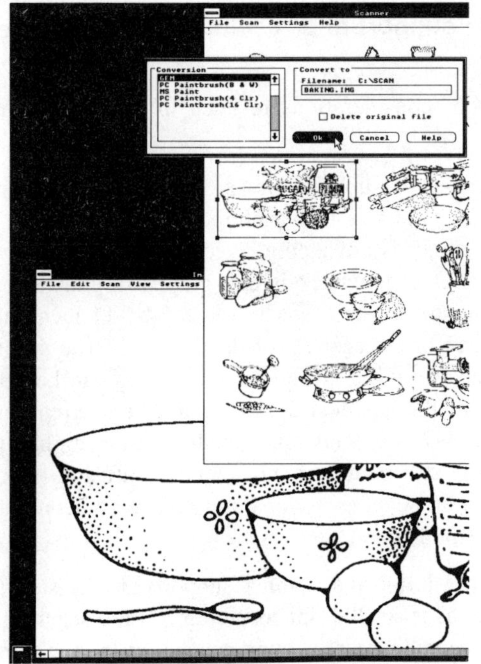

Fig. 7.17.

Hewlett-Packard Scanning Gallery control software running Windows, showing scanned page and selected graphic being converted to GEM IMG format.

Fig. 7.18.

A scanned image incorporated into a Ventura document.

7.22 Tip

Consider gray-scale support and resolution when purchasing a scanner.

Following are two major considerations to keep in mind when purchasing a scanner:

- The level of gray-scale support. Newer scanners can capture levels of gray by varying the size of a picture element (pixel) on a fixed grid. This technology is advancing rapidly, but two major drawbacks exist. One drawback is that gray-scale images can take up enormous amounts of disk space—an 8.5-by-11-inch page can take up more than one megabyte of disk storage. The second drawback is that resolution is not yet as good as can be obtained with traditional methods. Most desktop publishers agree that to have gray-scale photos of maximum quality, using traditional half-toning methods is still better. If this sounds confusing, talk to your dealer about current scanner options and talk to someone at your print shop about half-tones.
- The maximum resolution the scanner supports. Make sure that the scanner supports at least 300-dpi resolution. Some scanners (like the Hewlett-Packard ScanJet) support resolution higher than 300 dpi (the maximum output of most laser printers). If you purchase a scanner not capable of 300 dpi, understand that the images it scans cannot be reproduced on laser printers at higher resolutions than originally scanned.

7.23 Tip

Use scanners for line art.

Because of the issues surrounding gray-scale images, the infant stage of scanner technology, and the amount of disk space required for gray-scale images, scanners produce the best results with line art and black-and-white images.

7.24 Tip

Use a paint program like Publisher's Paintbrush to touch up scanned images.

Publisher's Paintbrush from ZSoft Corporation can serve not only as the software for many scanners, but as a capable bit-map editor as well. Refer to figure 7.19 for a perspective of the scanned image taken from figure 7.16. Figure 7.19 enlarges the word *FLOUR* on the flour sack so that each letter is composed of a series of dots. Using Publisher's Paintbrush, you can turn each dot on or off to clean up or enhance an image. From a regular editing screen, you can add, erase, invert, rotate, flip, or otherwise change the image as you choose.

Fig. 7.19.
Publisher's Paintbrush used to edit a scanned image.

Using Electronic Clip Art

Clip art on disks is already in digital format and can be used directly by Ventura. As mentioned earlier, many graphics formats are available in both the PC and Macintosh worlds. Ventura can accept most graphics formats. This flexibility makes available to you almost all the electronic clip art now available in the marketplace.

Electronic clip art is of mixed quality and value. The reason for the unevenness of the market is because, until recently, most electronic clip art was recycled public-domain images. Newer volumes of clip art, especially the EPS and CGM types, are much higher quality.

Another major consideration with electronic clip art is its usefulness. Many of the images in a collection will not be of any use to you. Either the images you find aren't exactly what you are looking for or are inappropriate for your publication.

Finally, with electronic clip art, you often mix styles of graphics. You may not mind having one picture as a cartoon, another as an art deco, and a third as an 18th-century wood-cut; but then again, you may want all the graphics in your publication to be similar in style. A single clip-art disk may not offer that consistency.

On the positive side, many electronic clip-art packages offer terrific value because you get so many images for your money.

7.25 Tip

Use electronic clip-art volumes.

Electronic clip art is available in collections that provide either varied or specific groupings of art. Following is a representative (not a comprehensive) list of some electronic clip-art packages compatible with Ventura. Comments about the packages are provided to give you a feel for the kind of art provided on the disk. The examples shown in this tip were printed with Ventura and a PostScript printer.

- *T/Maker Click-Art (EPS) Illustrations*. This is a compilation of high-resolution click-art illustrations in EPS format. The package contains 180 images, all of excellent quality, and includes TIF headers so that the illustrations can be viewed in Ventura (see fig. 7.20).

Fig. 7.20.
EPS clip art from T/Maker.

- *T/Maker Click-Art*. This inexpensive version of *Click-Art* provides medium-resolution click art images in PCX, GEM, and IMG formats. Five collections are available: *Business*, *Personal*, *Publications*, *Holidays*, and *Christian Images*. Because these graphics are in PCX format, you can edit them with bit-mapped graphics editors like Publisher's Paintbrush. Each package contains up to 1,000 excellent-quality images. The assortment is so extensive, you certainly will find something useful (see fig. 7.21).

Fig. 7.21.
Low-resolution, bit-mapped clip art from T/Maker.

- *Metro Imagebase Electronic Art*. This package offers high-resolution (300 dpi) bit-mapped images in PCX or TIFF format. The package is one of the more expensive with only 100 images per collection, but the images are well grouped and interesting. Numerous choices (14 packages in all) are offered, including *Weekend Sports*, *Report Maker*, *Business Graphics*, *Art Deco*, and *Newsletter Maker* (see fig. 7.22). Metro has supplied graphics images to major news services for more than 75 years. Because of the high resolution of the images, the files can be quite large and require a great deal of disk space. Fortunately, the files are well indexed, and you easily can transfer just the image you want from the floppy disk. The files come onto your hard disk.

Fig. 7.22.
High-resolution, bit-mapped clip art from Metro.

- *Marketing Graphics Incorporated (MGI) Publisher's PicturePak.* The MGI package offers graphics in high-resolution WPG/CGM, PCX, EPS, PNT, and PICT formats. Figure 7.23 shows the difference in output resolution between vector and bit-mapped formats. Each moderately priced collection has between 178 and 209 images; collections include *Executive & Management*, *Finance & Administration*, and *Sales & Marketing*. Although the images are not sophisticated, they are clean and useful.

- *3G Graphics Images with Impact.* This package offers high-resolution graphics in EPS format that currently come with TIFF headers so the images can be viewed in Ventura. Many modern-looking images are in each collection: *Graphics & Symbols 1* (72 images) or *Business 1* (176 images). Many images are composites of multiple images that can be cropped in Ventura or edited with draw programs capable of importing EPS files. Originally available only for the Macintosh, 3G has recently ported the images to the PC world (see fig. 7.24).

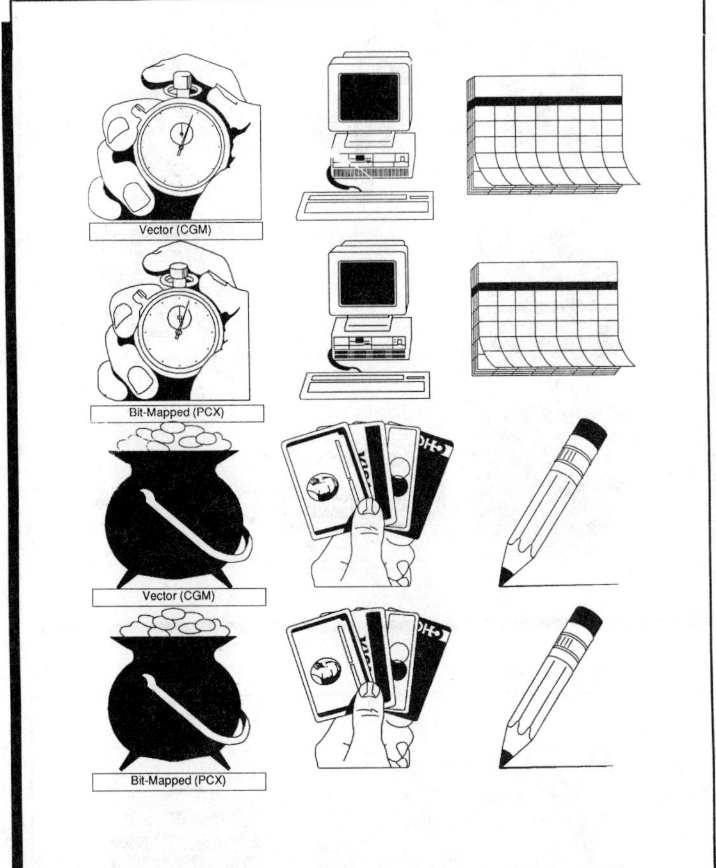

Fig. 7.23.
MGI Publisher's PicturePak graphics.

- *Image Club Digit Art*. This package provides high-resolution images in EPS format that do not currently come with TIFF or WMF headers. The images, therefore, cannot be viewed in Ventura. This is another modern-looking collection of original art from a Macintosh vendor. Images are available in several volumes of general-category images (see fig. 7.25).

- *Micrografx Clip Art Library*. This library of images is in proprietary draw and picture file formats that can be converted to Windows Metafile (WMF) format with the Portfolio software included with the library (see fig. 7.26). Figure 7.27 gives an example of a graphic used in a form. To convert a Micrografx graphic to Encapsulated PostScript (EPS), use Micrografx

Fig. 7.24.
EPS clip art from 3G.

Fig. 7.25.
EPS clip art from Image Club.

Designer, Draw Plus, or Graph Plus. All three programs run in the Windows environment and are among the most sophisticated drawing programs found in either the Macintosh or the PC world. In addition to the applications software, Micrografx offers more than 20 clip-art libraries varying in price and complexity (see fig. 7.28). Micrografx offers special editions of clip art for professionals who require libraries of extensive map or anatomical drawings.

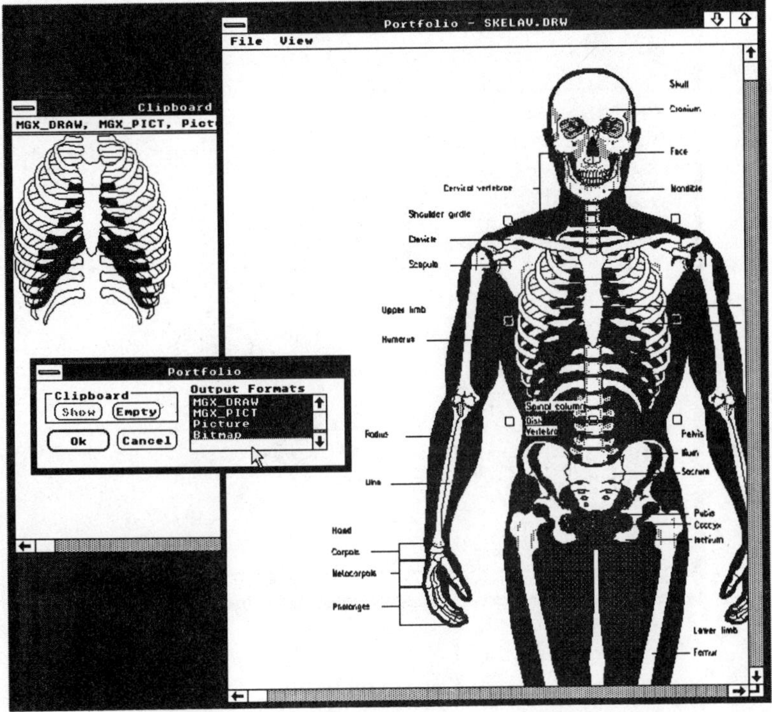

Fig. 7.26.

The Micrografx Portfolio program transferring a portion of clip art with the Windows Clipboard.

Notice that some of the most original and clever electronic clip art has been ported from the Macintosh after being created in PostScript draw programs like Adobe Illustrator™, Aldus Freehand, and Cricket Draw. If you plan to take advantage of this exceptional clip art, you should have access to a PostScript printer. Other clip-art vendors, especially those using public domain or more traditional art, provide their pictures in lower resolution formats that can be printed on a variety of printers, including Hewlett-Packard LaserJets (and compatibles) and certain dot-matrix printers.

Fig. 7.27.

An office form with graphics imported from Micrografx clip art using the Portfolio program.

COMPLAINT AND SPINAL EXAMINATION

Patient Name: ____________ **Date of Examination:** ________

Complaint: ____________

First Occurrence: ____________

Distribution Of Pain: ____________

Extent Of Pain: ____________

Frequency of pain: ____________

Aggravated By: ____________

Work Affects: ____________

Alleviated By: ____________

Other Symptoms: ____________

Medication: ____________

Other Treatments: ____________

Mark subluxation levels as determined by instrumentation, motion and static palpation. Mark areas of pain determined by patient complaint.

Mark any area of rib tenderness.

Bull Run Chiropractic Clinic. Sandy, OR. Examination, Page 1.

7.26 Tip

Ventura can use much of the excellent Macintosh clip art available in EPS, MacPaint, and PICT formats.

Although software on the Macintosh is not compatible with software on the PC, you can use much of the data produced by the Macintosh. This data includes word processing files, spreadsheets, and graphics.

Graphics on the Macintosh are usually in one of three formats: MacPaint, PICT, or EPS. Unfortunately, individual software companies do not always implement these standards exactly the same. You may, therefore, find that some MacPaint, PICT, and EPS files will not work in Ventura. PICT files are the most fussy in loading and in looking how you expect when they load.

Fig. 7.28.
High-resolution vector clip art from Micrografx.

If you have graphics in Macintosh format, you can use several strategies to transfer files from the Macintosh to the PC where Ventura can use them. Following is a brief—not meant to be totally explanatory—list of strategies.

- Modem. A modem (or null-modem cable) can connect the Macintosh and the PC; transfer the files by using a program like MacLink+ or xFer.
- Extra drive. Certain external disk drives for the Macintosh can read and write PC-formatted 5 1/4-inch disks.
- Option Board. The PC Option Board from Central Point Software fits into a slot in your PC and allows the 3 1/2-inch disk drive to read and write Macintosh formatted disks.
- Macintosh IIx or SE/30 drive. Newer Macintosh systems have drives that can read and write PC-formatted disks.
- Network. If you use a network connecting PC and Macintosh computers, you can directly transfer files between the two systems.

Remember, only data files such as spreadsheets, text, and graphics can be transferred successfully. You cannot, for example, transfer a program like MacDraw and run it on a PC.

7.27 Tip

Use a program like The Curator on the Macintosh to convert files to formats usable by the PC.

The Curator, a Macintosh program, can catalog your graphics images and convert between TIFF, PICT, and MacPaint files. You also can convert a Macintosh EPS file to a PC EPS file that installs a TIFF header to make the image visible in Ventura. You also can convert a Macintosh EPS (or PC EPS) file to a MacPaint or PICT file for use in Ventura if you don't have access to a PostScript printer.

7.28 Tip

Use a program like Hijaak on the PC to convert files from one graphics format to another.

For formats not directly or indirectly supported by Ventura, you may be able to use the PC program Hijaak to convert the file into something Ventura can use (see fig. 7.29). Hijaak currently supports 16 PC and Macintosh formats (more are added all the time).

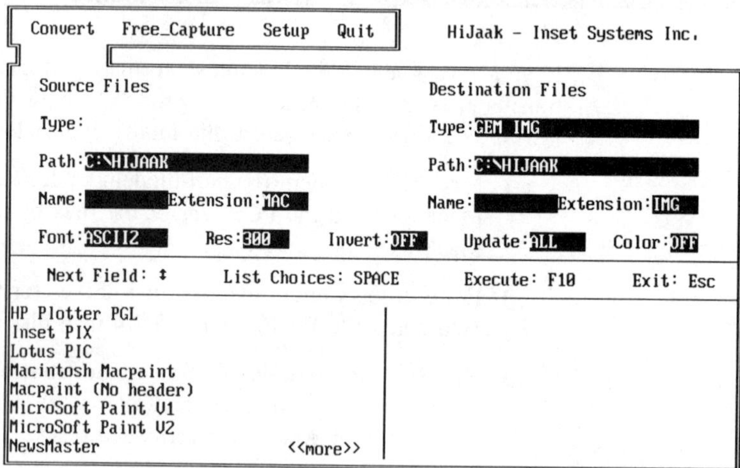

Fig. 7.29.

Hijaak converting a Macintosh MacPaint file to a GEM IMG file.

Creating Your Own Graphics

More and more, you can create your own electronic art. Be aware, however, that if you cannot use a regular pencil to draw, the likelihood of your being able to draw with an electronic pencil isn't very strong. In short, if you are not a graphic artist, don't expect these programs to make you one.

That said, even nonartists can be heartened by the capabilities of the next generation of PC drawing programs like Adobe Illustrator, Corel Draw, and Micrografx Designer. With features such as those for tracing scanned images automatically, even the rest of us may become "artists."

Other capabilities, like manipulating and creating text effects, are features that most people can master without artistic skills. The creation of incredible headlines and logos is within anyone's reach. The font-manipulation capabilities of these programs are discussed in Chapter 9.

Finally, some programs like Micrografx Designer, Draw Plus, Adobe Illustrator, GEM Artline, and especially Arts & Letters™ provide built-in art symbols that you can manipulate to create sophisticated graphics even if you cannot draw with a pencil.

7.29 Tip Think about the capabilities you want and need in a paint or draw program.

Each paint and draw program has its strong points. When deciding on a paint or draw program, consider the following:

- ❑ Freehand drawing capabilities. Draw programs offer you the ability to draw with freehand tools, creating lines and curves.
- ❑ Font control. Almost all paint and draw programs offer a degree of font control. Some programs offer superb control for terrific headline or logo effects (see Chapter 9 for more information on fonts).
- ❑ Editing control. Look for the ease with which you can edit bit-mapped images (to clean up scanned images or modify files) and objects (created by vector graphics programs). Some editing capabilities include moving, stretching, scaling, rotating, mirroring, and skewing.
- ❑ Importing and exporting various formats. Some programs have proprietary formats and cannot easily import or export file formats used by other programs like Ventura.
- ❑ Color control. Some programs have the capacity to support a full range of industry-standard colors (like the Pantone color standard) or cyan, yellow, magenta, and black color separations. Others offer only monochrome-image control. Even if the program supports color images, Ventura does not as of yet. To incorporate a color image into Ventura, you will need to paste the color image manually—not electronically.

- ❑ Complexity. If you use a paint or draw program regularly, the complexity of the software is not as much an issue as if you are only an occasional user.
- ❑ Clip art included. Some packages offer clip art with the program; with others, clip art is either a separate purchase or is not available at all.

7.30 Tip

Pick a paint or draw program that meets your needs.

The following lists summarize the capabilities of several paint and draw programs now available for PCs.

Draw Programs

Corel Draw (runs under Windows; see fig. 7.30)

Freehand drawing capabilities: Excellent. Includes autotrace and calligraphic pen shapes.

Font control: Excellent. Fonts can be made into objects and manipulated. Includes a variety of fill patterns and special effects. Many fonts included at no extra cost.

Editing control: Allows editing of objects and bit-mapped images through autotracing. Can group and ungroup objects.

Importing and exporting various formats: Imports TIFF and PCX formats that cannot be edited unless they are traced first. Tracing bit-mapped images is necessary for you to convert the graphic to vector form. Also imports PIC, GDF, CGM, and Adobe Illustrator PostScript formats. Exports PCX, TIFF, EPS, and WMF formats.

Color control: Pantone and cyan, yellow, magenta, and black.

Complexity: Simplified and intuitive menu structure makes this program sophisticated yet uncomplicated.

Clip art included: Yes.

Adobe Illustrator (runs under Windows; see fig. 7.31)

Note: Requires a minimum of 1 megabyte of memory. An 80386 system is also recommended. This program will run too slowly to be useful on an 80286 system.

Freehand drawing capabilities: Excellent. This company invented freehand drawing.

Font control: Adequate. Special effects are complex to create.

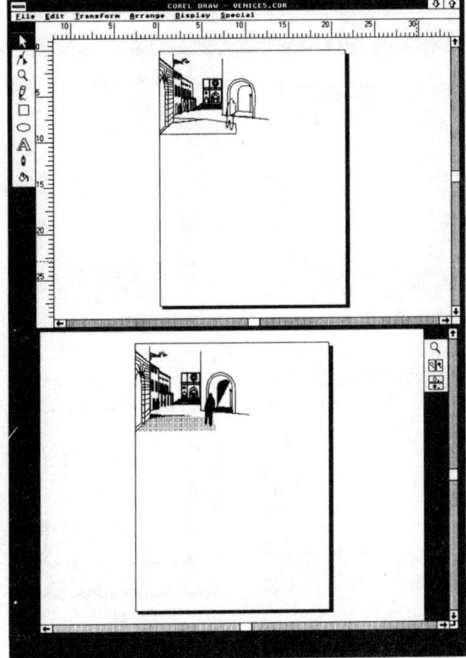

Fig. 7.30.
Corel Draw with two windows—one for editing and one for previewing.

Editing control: Allows editing of objects and bit-mapped images through autotracing. Can group and ungroup objects.

Importing and exporting various formats: Can import MacPaint, TIFF, and PCX files for use as tracing templates. Exports only EPS and Adobe Illustrator format, which means that images cannot be printed by any printer other than a PostScript printer.

Color control: Cyan, yellow, magenta, and black only. Program does not show colors on-screen and files must be ported to a Macintosh where the Adobe Separator (a separate cost program) can create separations.

Complexity: Good menu structure, clear commands, good manuals, and introductory videotape lessen learning curve.

Clip art included: Includes Adobe Collector's Edition of symbols, borders, and letter forms—300 elements in all.

Micrografx Draw Plus (runs under Windows)

Freehand drawing capabilities: Excellent. Includes tracing and also draws circles, ellipses, rectangles, rounded rectangles, squares, polylines, polygons, and arcs.

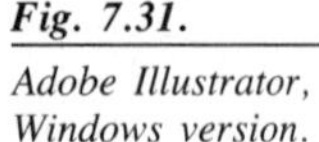

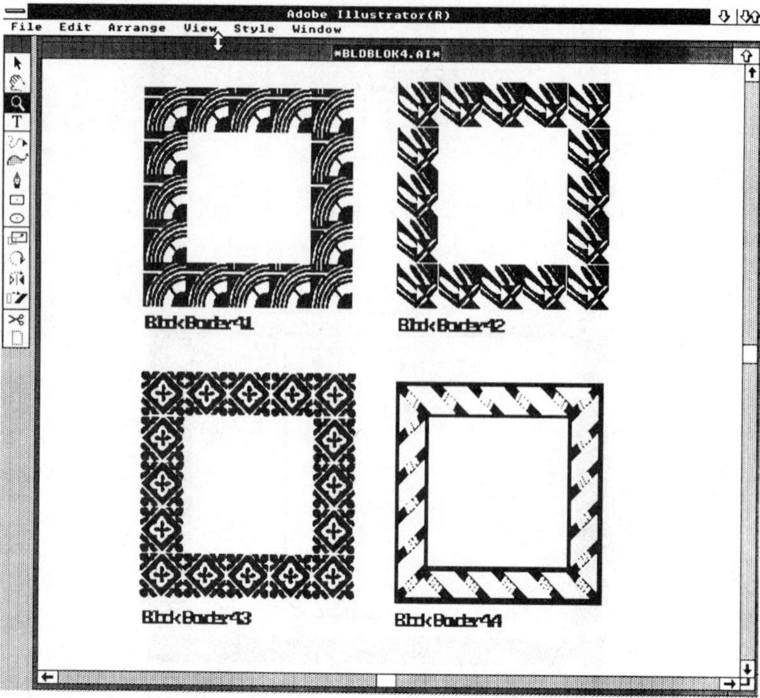

Fig. 7.31.

Adobe Illustrator, Windows version.

Font control: Elementary. Minimal effects possible.

Editing control: Excellent editing control over objects, including alignment options. Bit-mapped images must be manually traced before editing. Line styles also show lengths of objects.

Importing and exporting various formats: Imports formats supported by Windows Clipboard, text, and PIC. Bit-mapped images can be imported only through the Clipboard; you need another program (like Windows Paint) to place the file initially on the Clipboard. Exports PIC, DRW (proprietary Micrografx format), and WMF formats. You can print EPS to disk.

Color control: Color and pattern control are good, but the colors are not standard Pantone.

Complexity: Micrografx programs are rich but complex.

Clip art included: Yes. Some of the best clip art around is available from Micrografx. Specialty headline fonts are also available as clip art.

Micrografx Designer (runs under Windows; see fig. 7.32)

Freehand drawing capabilities: Superb. Probably the most sophisticated drawing program available on the PC.

Font control: Adequate. Fonts cannot be manipulated for many special effects, but specialty headline fonts are available at extra cost from Micrografx.

Editing control: Excellent. Allows superb line control and precise control of objects, including reshaping. You can set widths within 1/1000 of an inch and rotation within 1/10 of a degree. Bit-mapped images can be traced.

Importing and exporting various formats: Imports formats supported by Windows Clipboard, text, and PIC. Bit-mapped images can be imported only through the Clipboard; you need another program (like Windows Paint) to place the file initially on the Clipboard. Exports PIC, DRW (proprietary Micrografx format), and WMF formats. You can print EPS to disk. Also included is a conversion program to convert from Micrografx PIC to AutoCAD DXF formats and back again.

Color control: Allows custom or standard Pantone palettes of up to 16 million colors. Permits up to 64 layers for sophisticated color separation.

Complexity: Very complex. Steep but rewarding learning curve for graphics designers.

Clip art included: Yes. Samples are included as is a coupon for your choice of a package of general clip art from Micrografx.

GEM Artline (runs under GEM; see fig. 7.33)

Freehand drawing capabilities: Provides good freehand drawing tools.

Font control: Excellent font control with a built-in font collection as well as access to the Bitstream Fontware collection. Can make the font into an object for special effects.

Editing control: Good object control. Edits bit-mapped images only if the images are first in IMG format and then traced.

Importing and exporting various formats: Imports IMG, GEM, PCX, and some TIF formats for tracing. Exports as GEM and PostScript printer files.

Color control: Up to 16 colors.

Complexity: Easy-to-learn interface. Familiar GEM surroundings for Ventura users.

Clip art included: Yes. Nice library of clip-art symbols included.

Fig. 7.32.
Micrografx Designer.

Fig. 7.33.
GEM Artline.

Arts & Letters Composer (runs under Windows; see fig. 7.34)

Freehand drawing capabilities: None. Includes some graphics primitives (more capability is available in Arts & Letters Graphics Editor program). This program is perfect for nonartists because a library of more than 3,500 symbols is included that you can mix and edit to create your own unique art.

Font control: Excellent font control with 15 typefaces included and 18 additional available at extra cost.

Editing control: Good editing control of symbols including rotating, slanting, and aligning.

Importing and exporting various formats: Imports from TIF, WMF, PIC, ASCII, and DIA (Diagraph proprietary) formats. Exports as EPS (with or without screen images), CGM, and WMF.

Color control: Good color control with choices of RGB (red, green, blue), CMY (cyan, magenta, yellow), or hues.

Complexity: Very easy to use.

Clip art included: Yes. Includes more than 3,500 symbols to make the most extensive collection of any PC program.

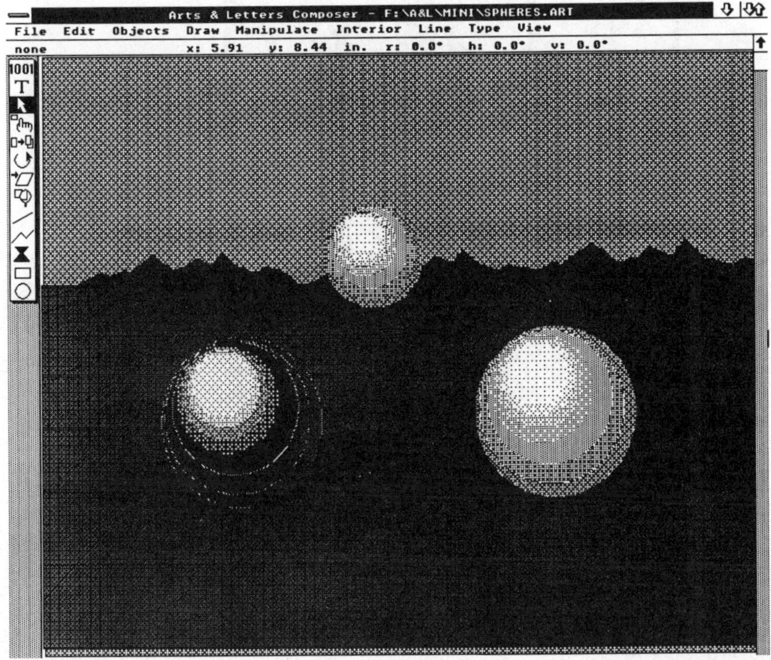

Fig. 7.34.
Arts & Letters with a sample file of combined symbols.

Paint Programs

Publisher's Paintbrush (runs in own environment; see fig. 7.35) and *PC Paintbrush Plus for Windows* (runs under Windows)

Freehand drawing capabilities: Good. Provides control of line, curve, and graphic primitives.

Font control: Adequate font control; special effects are difficult.

Editing control: Excellent editing of PCX bit-mapped files in zoom or normal views.

Importing and exporting various formats: Imports PCX. Can serve as control software for many scanners, saving files as PCX. Exports as PCX.

Color control: Good color and pattern control.

Complexity: One of the easiest programs to use.

Clip art included: Yes. Only a few samples are included.

Fig. 7.35.
Publisher's Paintbrush.

Figure 7.36 shows examples of Ventura's output of pictures from GEM Artline, Corel Draw, Arts & Letters, Micrografx Designer, Publisher's Paintbrush, and Adobe Illustrator.

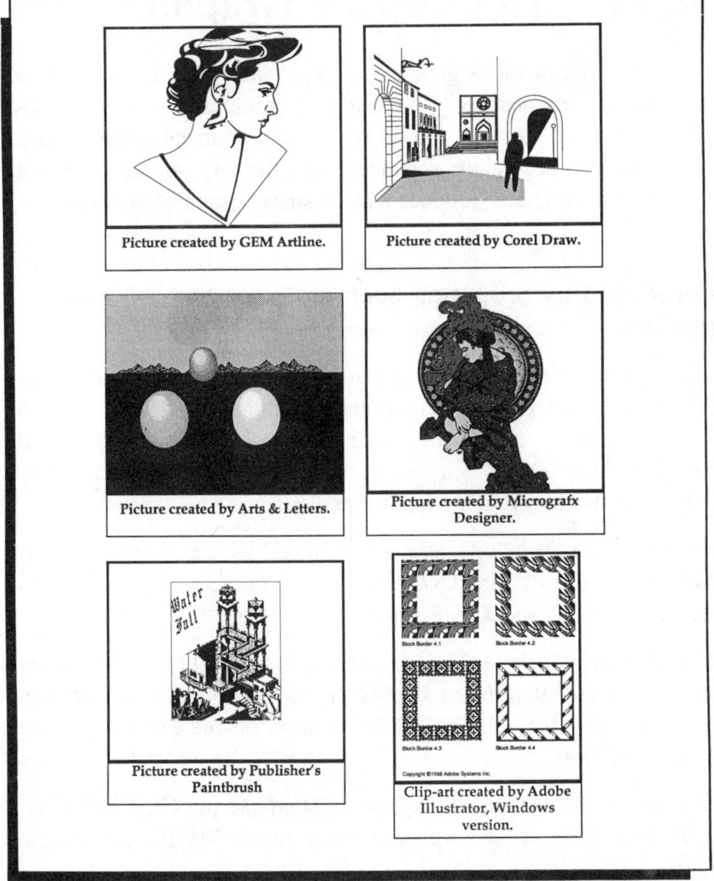

Fig. 7.36.
Examples of several draw and paint programs printed by Ventura.

7.31 Tip

Use T/Maker's Scrapbook Plus if you do much graphics work in Windows.

Scrapbook Plus is an excellent organizational tool for working in Windows. Unlike the scrapbook provided with Windows, Scrapbook Plus allows you to keep multiple images stored with thumbnail images (small versions of the graphics) or text descriptions of each graphic. You can mix text, rich text (with formatting retained), bit-mapped images, TIFF, EPS, and WMF formats all in the same scrapbook.

If you use Windows much, you need Scrapbook Plus to catalog, organize, display, and transfer graphic images within the Windows environment.

Using Business Software To Generate Graphics

Some business software applications generate graphics that you can incorporate into Ventura documents. Spreadsheet, ''presentation graphics,'' and other programs providing images that you may like to weave into your publications may be usable. Documents can be greatly enhanced with the appropriate inclusion of sophisticated graphs and charts produced by business graphics software.

7.32 Tip

Use graphs produced by programs such as Excel or 1-2-3 as a source of graphics.

Many business programs allow you to output data in a visual form. Lotus 1-2-3 was probably the first personal computer program that created graphs. Often, spreadsheets such as SuperCalc® and Quattro® create sophisticated graphs. You can save these graphs in a Ventura-compatible format such as PIC or EPS, depending on the program's capabilities.

Microsoft Excel runs under Windows and is considered by many experts to be the best spreadsheet available for DOS systems. You can export Excel's sophisticated graphs in two ways for use in Ventura.

Choose the HP Plotter printer driver and set the output to OUTPUT.PRN (consult your Windows documentation for details on how to do this procedure). Print the Excel chart. The file OUTPUT.PRN is now on the HPGL file that can be loaded into Ventura.

Copy the Excel chart to the Windows Clipboard. Then use the CLIP2VP.EXE utility (see Tip 7.17) to convert the Clipboard image to a WMF file that can be loaded into Ventura.

Figure 7.37 gives an example of an Excel chart imported into Ventura and annotated with box text.

7.33 Tip

Use presentation software such as Harvard Graphics or Freelance Plus to create Ventura-compatible graphics.

The newest category of software is ''presentation graphics.'' Programs like Harvard Graphics or Freelance Plus allow the creation of sophisticated and attractive graphs complete with their own clip-art images for inclusion in overheads, slides, and reports produced by desktop publishing programs like Ventura.

Figure 7.38 shows the same chart created by Harvard Graphics exported as an EPS, HPGL, and CGM file. Notice that the 3-D effect is lost with the HPGL format; the gray coloring of the group of people is lost with the CGM format.

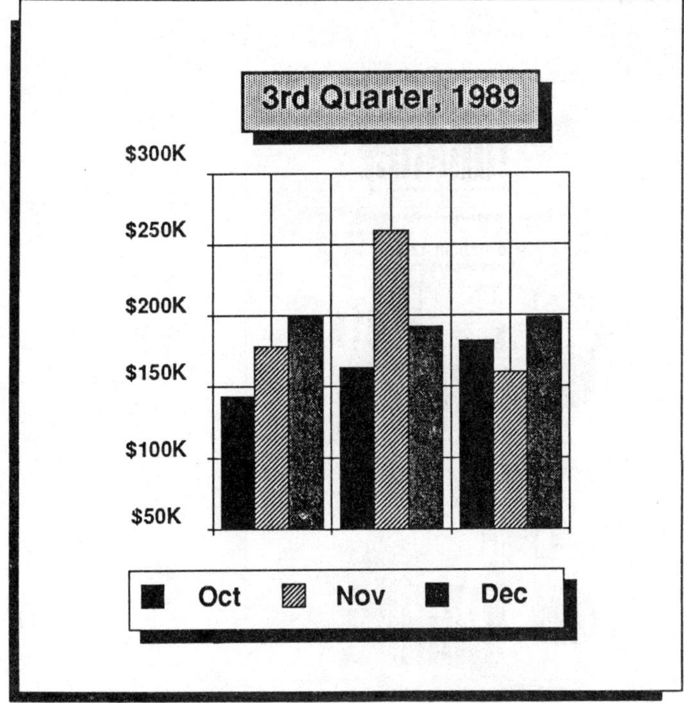

Fig. 3.37.
Excel chart imported into Ventura.

7.34 Tip **Use a screen-capture utility when you need to create screen shots of software.**

In the preparation of this book, I used the Capture utility from INSET Systems, Inc. to capture software screens. Not only can you capture screen shots from a variety of monitors, but you can edit the screen image later. I used the editing features of InSet to create screens where multiple cursors were shown as examples.

Other programs offering similar capabilities include the excellent Hot Shot Graphics from SymSoft Corporation and Collage Plus from Inner Media, Inc.

Controlling Gray Scale

The term *gray scale* is used to refer to the various shadings of black in graphic images. Different shades of gray can be applied to an image by the paint or draw program you use; you may even be able to use color. When you print a highly varied gray-scale image or an image with several colors on a black-and-

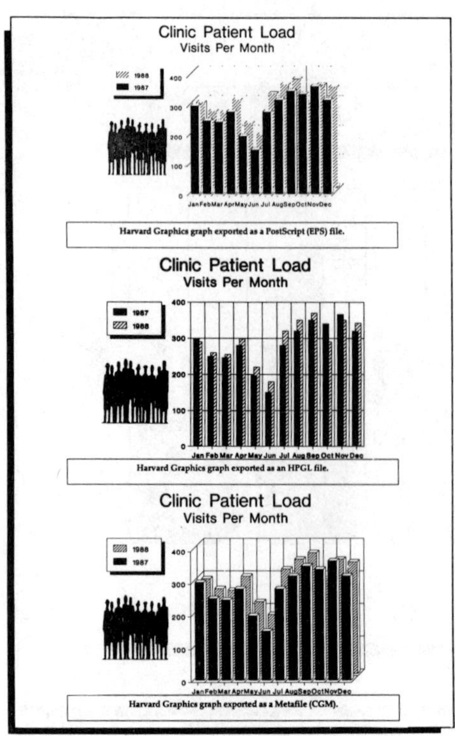

Fig. 7.38.
Three charts exported from Harvard Graphics in EPS, HPGL, and CGM formats and printed by Ventura.

white printer, the printer ''translates'' the grays or colors so that it can print them. Some printers are better than others at producing accurately shaded images. Ventura provides some ways that you can help control the shades that are printed.

Ventura supports the printing of gray-scale and halftone pictures. Both gray scale and halftones are ways you can print images that are not just tiny black and white dots.

Gray scale is really a ''deep bit-map.'' Pixels in an image can be black, white, or a shade of gray. Depending on the capabilities of the scanner used to obtain the image, the number of shades for a pixel varies from 16 to 256 (depending on whether you have a four-bit or eight-bit scanner).

Halftones are images using black dots in lighter or denser patterns to represent lighter or darker shades of gray.

7.35 Tip

Use the Frame menu's Image Settings command to control gray scale and halftones printed on PostScript printers.

Some scanners offer sophisticated controls over the scanning of gray scale. The pros and cons of different "dithering" techniques (as the controls are called) is beyond the scope of this tip. Note, however, that Ventura ignores dithering information and does not consider dithered images as true gray-scale images; therefore, such images cannot be altered with the Image Settings command.

Gray scale and halftones are available only as EPS or TIFF files, and only when those images actually contain gray tones. Regardless of whether EPS or TIFF files are used, the Image Settings command works only on PostScript printers.

To change the Image Settings in Frame mode, select the frame containing the EPS or TIFF file. Then choose Image Settings from the Frame menu to display the IMAGE SETTINGS dialog box (see fig. 7.39).

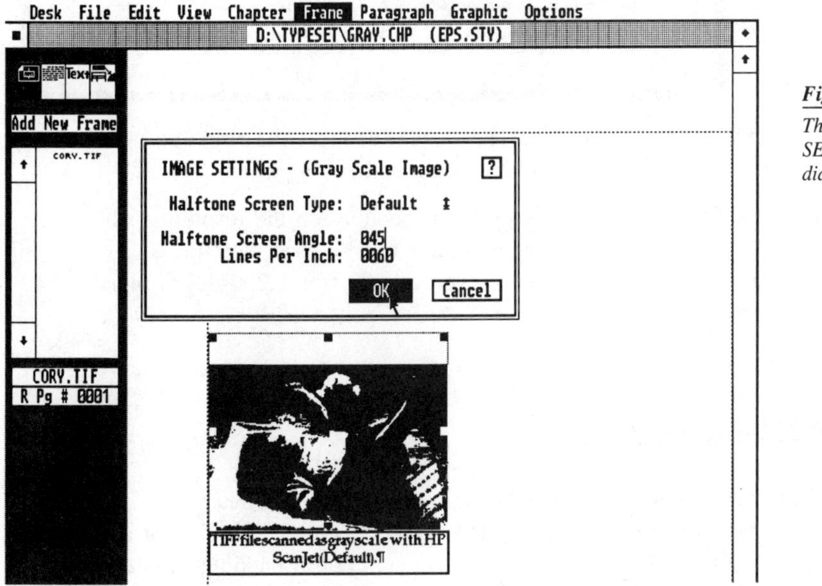

Figure 7.39.
The IMAGE SETTINGS dialog box.

Three settings can be changed in the IMAGE SETTINGS dialog box:

- `Halftone Screen Type`. This option can be set to `Default` (for most pictures), `Dot`, `Line`, `Ellipse`, or `Custom`. You can create effects by printing the screen in dots, lines, or ellipses. You can also set a custom effect by modifying the PS2.PRE file (see Chapter 10). You cannot set different screen types for various frames; only one setting per chapter is allowed (see fig. 7.40).

Fig. 7.40.

Examples of halftone screen types and their effects on a picture.

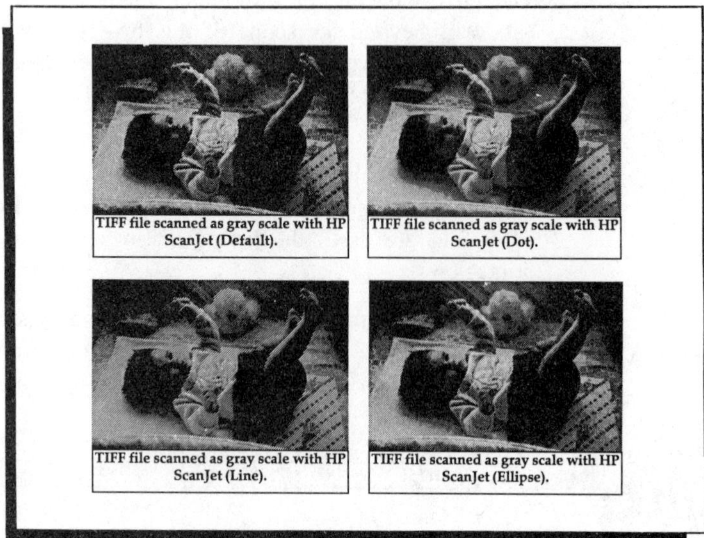

- `Halftone Screen Angle`. This option controls the angle at which the screen is rotated. The recommended setting is 45 degrees.
- `Lines Per Inch`. Set this option depending on the resolution of your printer. Although other figures can be used, Ventura recommends 60 (for 300-dpi printers), 90 (for 1,200-dpi printers), or 150 (for 2,540-dpi printers).

Chapter Summary

This chapter covered a great deal of information. You learned how to load pictures into Ventura and how to determine the correct file format acceptable to Ventura. Ways to scale and crop pictures, control padding, and create text runarounds of odd-shaped graphics were described. You learned about different graphics formats including the types broadly categorized as bit-mapped and vector. You also learned about scanned artwork.

Samples of the various types of clip art, from scanned to electronic to graphics, produced by paint, draw, and business programs, were described. Finally, you took a brief look at gray scale.

The next chapter looks at Ventura's own graphic-drawing tools.

Chapter

8

Using Ventura's Graphics Tools

Ventura is not a draw or a paint program, but it does have three useful graphics primitives. *Graphics primitives* are basic shapes that you can use to build more complex shapes. Ventura's primitives include lines, ellipses, and boxes. The lines can only be straight (they cannot be curved), and the boxes can have either square or rounded corners.

You cannot create great art with these primitives, but you can produce useful graphics. In this chapter, the term *graphics* refers to the primitives you create while you are in Graphic mode and not to pictures or other images.

Using Graphics Tools

Ventura has a special mode for using the graphics tools. When you click the Graphic mode icon (or use the keyboard shortcut Ctrl-P), the assignment list is replaced by six icons. These six icons represent the options Pointer, Box Text, Line, Ellipse, Square Corner Box, and Rounded Corner Box.

- ❑ Pointer. After you use any of the other graphics tools, Ventura reverts to the pointer. You use the pointer to select previously drawn graphics and frames.
- ❑ Box Text. Box text is like a regular frame, but it is only a single column. You use box text like a Post-it™ note to place text to overlap or augment pictures, graphics, or other text.

- Line. You can draw straight lines with the Line option. You can change the endings, thickness, and color of the line in the LINE ATTRIBUTES dialog box from the Graphic menu.
- Ellipse. With this option, you can draw circles and ovals. You can change the fill pattern by using the FILL ATTRIBUTES dialog box and the line used to draw the graphic with the LINE ATTRIBUTES dialog box; both dialog boxes are available from the Graphic menu.
- Square Corner Box. With this option, you can draw squares and rectangles. You change the fill pattern and the line used to draw the box the same way you change them for an ellipse.
- Rounded Corner Box. This option is the same as the Square Corner Box option but with rounded corners.

8.1 Tip

Learn the effects of the Pointer.

When you select Graphic mode, the pointer is active, and the Pointer icon is highlighted in the Graphic toolbox area. The cursor is shaped like a pointer.

You use the pointer to select previously drawn graphics, which can be edited, cut, or copied. You also can use the pointer to create, select, and resize frames.

If you click the Add New Frame button or press Ctrl-2, for example, the add new frame cursor appears and you can add a regular frame. You can move and resize the frame, and you can access the Frame menu to modify it. (The frame resizing handles are shown in gray rather than black when you are in Graphic mode.)

You cannot delete, copy, or paste a regular frame while you are in Graphic mode, but you can load text or pictures into the frame. Once you complete the loading process, Ventura automatically puts you in Frame mode.

Creating and Editing Graphics

Creating and editing a graphic is easy. Select a graphic tool, place the cursor where you want the graphic to begin, click, and draw. To edit your graphic, click it with the pointer and then use the resizing handles to resize the graphic, or move it the same way you would move a frame.

8.2 Tip

Create a graphic by selecting the appropriate graphic tool.

You can create graphics with the Line, Ellipse, Square Corner Box, or Rounded Corner Box options by first clicking the appropriate graphic tool and then clicking and dragging the mouse cursor around the work area.

Table 8.1 shows the shapes of the various cursors used in Graphic mode.

Table 8.1
Graphic Mode Cursor Shapes

Pointer		Box Text	
Line		Ellipse	⊕
Square Corner Box		Rounded Corner Box	

8.3 Tip

Hold down the Shift key to keep a graphics tool available.

If you hold down the Shift key while you select a graphics tool, that tool remains active and you can draw more than one line, ellipse, or box without having to reselect the tool. Once you release the Shift key, you can draw one more graphic before the graphic tool is deselected. If you accidentally keep a tool active, switch back and forth between modes to deactivate the tool.

8.4 Tip

To edit a graphic, first select it with the pointer.

You use the pointer to select a graphic for editing. You can select more than one graphic by holding down the Shift key and continuing to select graphics. Unlike regular frames, you can apply line and fill attributes to multiple frames.

Once you have selected a graphic, you can move, resize, cut, and copy single or multiple graphics the same way you would perform those operations on a regular frame.

If you cannot select a graphic after clicking it, the graphic may be tied to an unselected frame. See Trap 8.9 to learn how to select these graphics.

Constraining Graphics

You can create circles and squares and horizontal, vertical, or 45-degree lines by using Ventura's constrain feature.

8.5 Tip

Constrain the graphics tool by holding down the Alt key while clicking and dragging the mouse cursor.

Holding down the Alt key while creating or editing a graphic constrains the graphic, which creates the following effects:

- ❑ Lines become either perfectly vertical, horizontal, or slant at 45 degrees.
- ❑ Ellipses become circles.
- ❑ Boxes (whether with square corners, rounded corners, or box text) become squares.

8.6 Tip

Further constrain graphics with Grid Snap.

Using the Grid Snap feature in Graphic mode is similar to using Line and Column Snap in Frame mode. (Line Snap forces frames to conform to the interline spacing of body text, and Column Snap forces frames to conform to page and frame margins or column settings.) Grid Snap allows you to force graphics to align along an invisible grid.

To set the `Grid Snap` option to `On`, follow these steps:

1. Create a graphic or select a graphic with the pointer.
2. Choose Grid Settings from the Graphic menu.
4. In the GRID SETTINGS dialog box, set `Grid Snap` to `On`.
5. Change the `Horizontal Spacing` and `Vertical Spacing` options to suit your preference (see fig. 8.1).
6. Click OK or press Enter.

You must bear in mind several things when using the Grid Snap feature. Each frame can have its own unique grid setting, and grid settings affect all graphics in the frame. If you change the grid setting and then try to edit or position graphics, the graphics resize or move according to the new grid settings. Grid settings are unaffected by margins and columns; you measure grid settings from the edge of the page. You cannot make the grid visible.

Tying Graphics

You can link graphics and frames. This section describes how to accomplish this task.

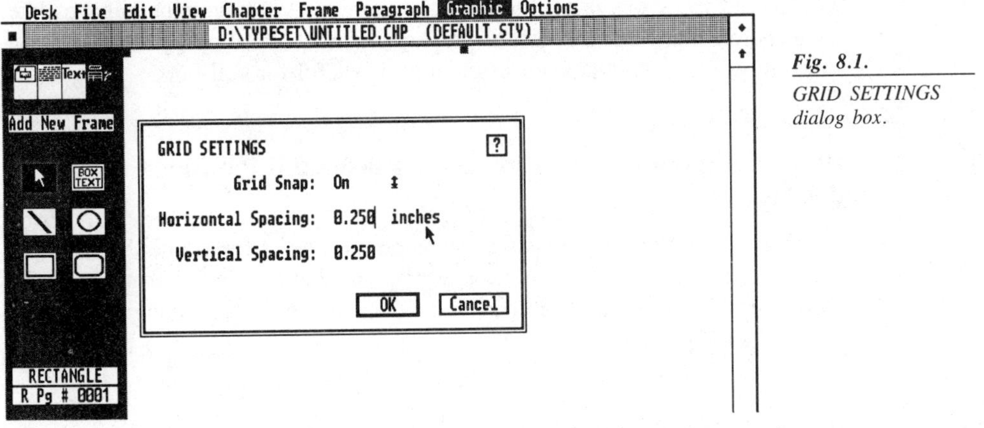

Fig. 8.1.
GRID SETTINGS dialog box.

8.7 Tip

Graphics can be tied to either the underlying page or a frame.

Whenever you create a graphic, that graphic is tied to either the underlying page or a frame. This tying feature is one of the most confusing things about graphics. Reading this section carefully will help you avoid frustration when you use the graphics tools.

Whichever frame is selected at the time you create the graphic is the frame the graphic is tied to or associated with.

When a graphic is tied to a frame, certain things you do to the frame affect the graphic. (Altering the graphic, however, does not have an effect on the frame.) When you move, cut, copy, or paste a frame that has tied graphics, the graphics are also moved, cut, copied, or pasted with the frame. Resizing the frame, however, does not affect the graphic.

Becoming confused is easy because often you don't realize that you have tied a graphic to a frame. When you switch from Frame, Paragraph, or Text mode, Ventura selects the last frame you were working with. So, if you were creating, pasting, or resizing a frame, tagging a paragraph in a frame, or typing text into a frame, the frame you were working on is selected automatically when you switch to Graphic mode. If you then create graphics without first selecting the underlying page, you have tied the newly created graphics to whichever frame was selected for you by Ventura.

Because an underlying page cannot be moved, cut, copied, or pasted, you are less likely to affect your graphic inadvertently if you tie it to the underlying page. To be safe, develop the habit of always selecting the underlying page before you create a graphic unless you have a specific reason (like using box text as a call out) for tying a graphic to a frame (see Tip 8.17 for more information on call outs).

You should think of tying in terms of anchoring. A tied graphic behaves like an anchored frame except that the graphic retains its positioning relative to the frame's position. This kind of association is useful for call outs.

8.8 Trap **Graphics that are tied to frames are deleted if the frame is deleted.**

Remember, the fate of graphics depends on the fate of the frame they are tied to. If the frame is deleted, so are any graphics that are tied to that frame. To eliminate this potential problem, remember to select the underlying page before creating any graphics.

8.9 Trap **You cannot simultaneously select different graphics that are tied to different frames.**

If you have two or more frames on a page that have graphics tied to them, you can select only graphics tied to the same frame; if you select graphics associated with another frame, the graphics associated with the first frame are automatically deselected.

Choosing Select All from the Graphic menu (or pressing the keyboard shortcut Ctrl-Q) selects all the graphics tied to the selected frame (see fig. 8.2). If you have two or more frames on a page that have graphics tied to them, the Select All command selects only those graphics tied to the currently selected frame. If the selected frame does not have any graphics tied to it, the Select All command has no effect even though graphics are on the page.

To find out which graphic is tied to which frame, select the graphic, and the frame it's tied to is displayed as selected.

Repeating Graphics

Ventura allows you to create a graphic once and have it repeat on every page in the chapter. This section describes how to accomplish this task.

8.10 Tip **Choose the Show On All Pages option from the Graphic menu to make a graphic repeat on all pages; choose the Show On This Page option to make the graphic nonrepeating.**

If you want a graphic to repeat on all pages, select the graphic and then choose Show On All Pages from the Graphic menu.

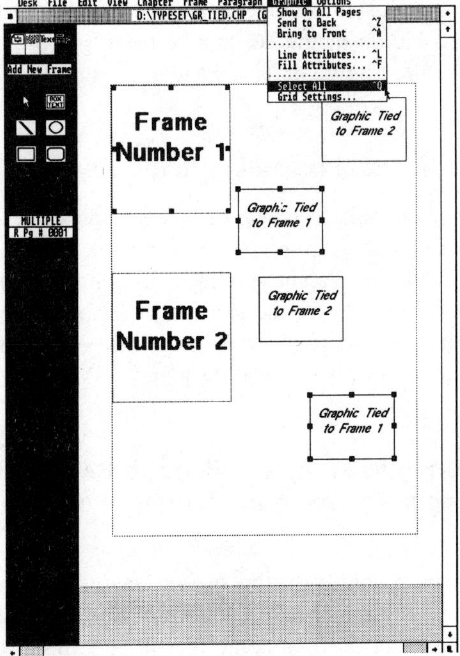

Fig. 8.2.

The Select All command affecting graphics tied to a specific frame.

To reverse the process, select the graphic and choose Show On This Page from the Graphic menu. Regardless of what page the graphic was created on, if you select the graphic and click Show On This Page, the graphic disappears from all other pages.

8.11 Trap

Show On All Pages and Show On This Page only work as expected with pages Ventura automatically generates.

The Show On All Pages and Show On This Page commands both work as expected with pages Ventura automatically generates (pages created automatically by Ventura to accommodate the flow of a text file).

If, however, you set a graphic to show on all pages before you create pages with the Insert/Remove Page command, that graphic appears on all newly created pages but not on previously created pages.

Likewise, if you set a graphic to show on this page with pages that you created with the Insert/Remove Page command, the Show On This Page command has no effect.

If you want a graphic to repeat on all pages that you manually insert, first create the graphic, set the graphic to Show On All Pages, and create new pages with the Insert/Remove Page command. All newly created pages will have the graphic on them. To remove these graphics, you need to delete them individually; the Show On This Page command does not work.

8.12 Trick **A graphic tied to a repeating frame also repeats.**

If you want a graphic to repeat on every page associated with a frame, tie the graphic to a repeating frame (see Chapter 6). If you have set up your chapter as double-sided, the graphic is offset differently on left and right pages. If you want the graphic to be in the same spot on both left and right pages, set one frame to repeat on left pages; then go to the next page and create another frame with the graphic to repeat on right pages.

8.13 Tip **Use the Bring to Front and Send to Back options from the Graphic menu to create the proper relationship between stacked graphics.**

You can stack graphics on top of one another. Each new graphic you create overlays previous graphics. If you want to change that relationship, you can select, cut, and paste the graphic that is underneath to move it to the top. Or you can select the graphic you want to move to the top or bottom and choose Send to Back (or press Ctrl-Z) or Bring to Front (or press Ctrl-A).

If you have multiple layers, moving graphics to the front or back bypasses all the intermediate layers. Figure 8.3 shows an example of multiple-layer stacking. (Note that some printers may not be able to achieve this effect.) In the example, Layer 1 is on top and Layer 4 is on the bottom.

Using Line Attributes

Ventura allows you to choose the thickness, color, and end style for lines. This section presents tips associated with line attributes.

8.14 Tip **Select Line Attributes from the Graphic menu to change the attributes of the line used to draw a line, box text, ellipse, square corner box, and rounded corner box.**

After you create a line, box text, ellipse, square corner box, or rounded corner box, you can change the attributes of the line used to draw it. To set line attributes, while you are in Graphic mode, select the graphic you want and choose Line Attributes from the Graphic menu (or use the keyboard shortcut Ctrl-L).

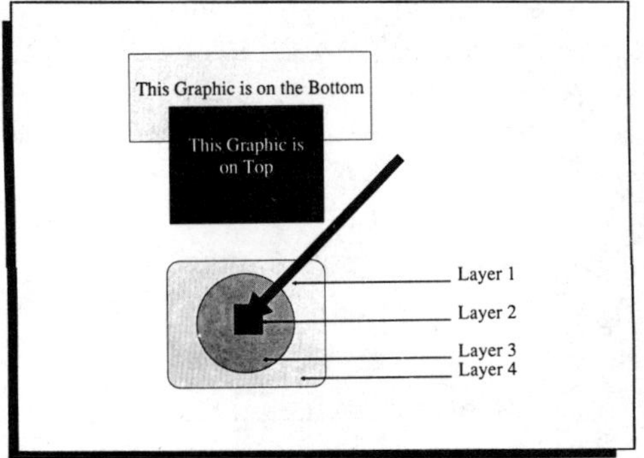

Fig. 8.3.
Stacking graphics.

You see the LINE ATTRIBUTES dialog box for the type of graphic object you selected. Although the LINE ATTRIBUTES dialog boxes all look the same, separate ones are available for each of the Line, Box Text, Ellipse, Square Corner Box, and Rounded Corner Box options.

From the dialog box, you can set Thickness and Color for box text, ellipses, square corner boxes, and rounded corner boxes, and you can set End Styles for lines.

You can set Thickness to any of the following settings:

None
Thin (0.001 inch, 0.06 point)
2 (0.018 inch, 1.26 points)
3 (0.051 inch, 3.66 points)
4 (0.125 inch, 9 points)
Thick (0.250 inch, 18 points)
Custom

If you choose the Custom option, you can change the inches to any thickness you want. But if you set the figure too high, Ventura may not display properly.

You can set the Color to White, Black, Red, Green, Blue, Cyan, Yellow, or Magenta. If you have a color printer or if you want to make color separations, you can set the color for the lines used to draw lines, box text, ellipses, square corner boxes, and rounded corner boxes.

You can set the End Styles for lines to blunt, rounded, or arrow ends in the LINE ATTRIBUTES dialog box (see fig. 8.4).

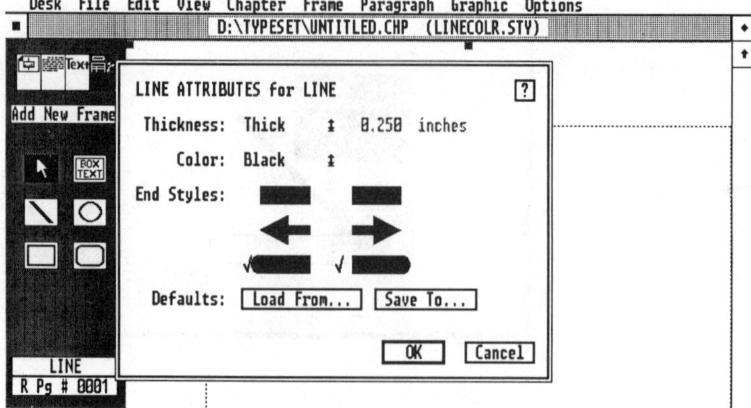

Fig. 8.4.
The LINE ATTRIBUTES dialog box.

The three styles on the left affect the beginning of the line, and the three styles on the right affect the end of the line. The beginning and end of the line are determined by where you start and stop drawing a line. If you want the left end of the line to be an arrow, select the arrow for the left end of your line and begin drawing the line from this arrow end (see fig. 8.5).

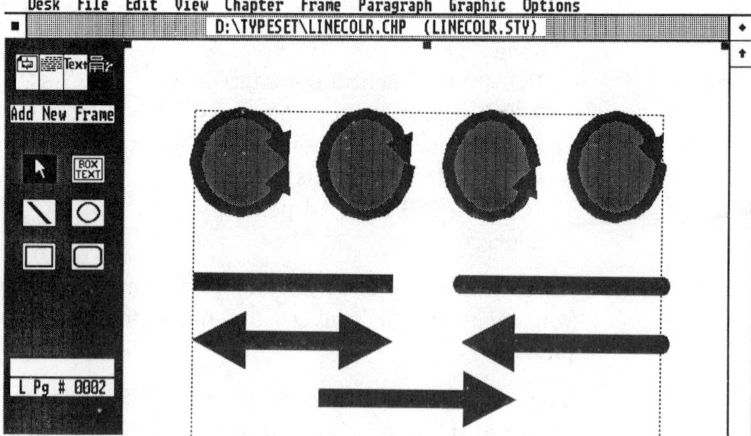

Fig. 8.5.
End style examples for lines and ellipses.

If you set the End Styles for box text, square corner boxes, or rounded corner boxes to other than the blunt end, no change occurs. However, an undocumented feature allows an arrow at one or both ends to show for ellipses; the arrows show on only the right side (see fig. 8.5). Arrows appear in circles only if supported by your printer. The example in figure 8.5 was printed on a PostScript printer.

Using Fill Attributes

Just as frames can have fill attributes, so can graphics.

8.15 Tip **Select Fill Attributes from the Graphic menu to change the fill pattern for box text, ellipses, square corner boxes, or rounded corner boxes.**

After you create box text, ellipses, square corner boxes, or rounded corner boxes, you can change the fill pattern. The *fill pattern* is the background color or pattern of the graphic primitive (see fig. 8.6).

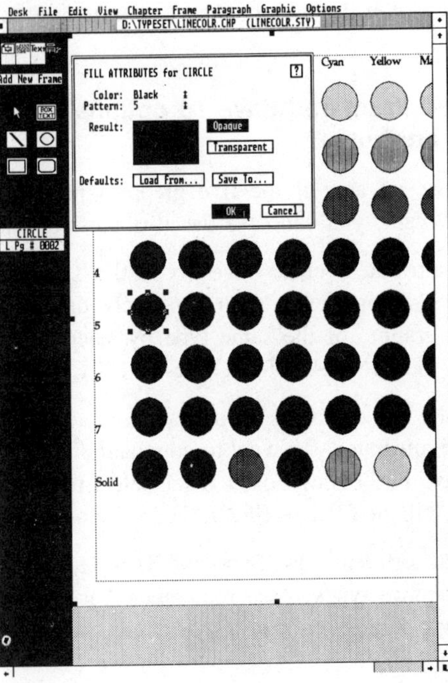

Fig. 8.6.
The FILL ATTRIBUTES dialog box.

To set fill attributes, select the graphic and choose Fill Attributes from the Graphic menu (or use the keyboard shortcut Ctrl-F).

You see the FILL ATTRIBUTES dialog box for the type of graphic object you selected. Although the FILL ATTRIBUTES dialog boxes look the same, separate ones are available for the Box Text, Ellipse, Square Corner Box, and Rounded Corner Box options. From the FILL ATTRIBUTES dialog box, you can change the color or pattern.

Select the Color option to set the color to White, Black, Red, Green, Blue, Cyan, Yellow, or Magenta. If you have a color printer or if you plan to make color separations, you can set the color for the fill.

You can set the amount of Pattern from Hollow to Solid with 7 intermediary steps (1 to 7). Colors don't show much differentiation on noncolor printers. There are 57 combinations available with color output (7 colors multiplied by 8 patterns—white and hollow make the last combination).

Saving Your Preferences

You can create defaults for both line and fill attributes to be used by subsequent graphics when they are created or previous graphics.

8.16 Tip **Use the Load From and Save To options to save preferences for line and fill attributes.**

Once you have set any of the five graphics primitives with the line or fill attributes you want, you can save the attributes for each graphic primitive.

To save the attributes, click Save To in the LINE ATTRIBUTES or FILL ATTRIBUTES dialog boxes. You can apply the saved attributes to a previously created graphic of the same type by selecting the graphic and clicking Load From in the LINE ATTRIBUTES or FILL ATTRIBUTES dialog boxes.

You can apply the attributes from one graphic to another by selecting the graphic whose attributes you want to copy and clicking Save To in the LINE or FILL ATTRIBUTES dialog boxes. Then select the new graphic and click Load From in the LINE or FILL ATTRIBUTES dialog boxes.

Remember that different Load From and Save To options are available for each of the five graphics types. Also remember that the line and fill attributes are kept as Ventura defaults, not just style sheet changes.

Using Box Text

Box text is Ventura's answer to the Post-it note. You can electronically "stick" box text anywhere on the page, and it is useful for creating forms.

If you want to place your text inside a box, you must use the Box Text option. Although the Square Corner Box, Rounded Corner Box, and Box Text options each have their own tool, they are only variations of the same primitive.

One confusing aspect of Ventura is knowing when to use the Box Text option and when to use a regular frame and frame text. If your text acts like a Post-it note, use the Box Text option. If your text acts like a sidebar or text block, use a regular frame and frame text.

8.17 Tip

Use box text to place text inside a frame with a picture.

To call attention to a certain aspect of a picture, for example, you can create a call out. *Call outs* are small blocks of text appended to pictures. You may even want to attach an arrow to point from the call out to the part of the picture you are commenting on.

Figure 8.7 shows a picture with two call outs and arrows pointing from the call outs to the graphic.

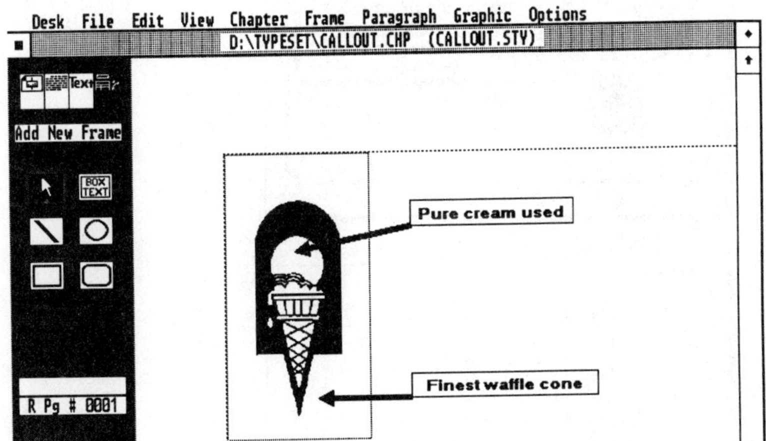

Fig. 8.7.

Picture with call outs and arrows.

To keep the call outs and arrows with the graphic even if you move the picture, remember to tie the graphics to the picture by selecting the frame the picture is in before you create the graphics.

8.18 Tip

Use box text to create forms or tables.

The Professional Extension (see Chapter 12) has the capability of making and editing tables. Although the basic version of Ventura lacks automatic table generation, you can create forms and tables by using the graphics tools.

You easily can create a calendar like the one shown in figure 8.8 by using box text with a 1-inch grid.

With a narrower grid, you can create a form like the one shown in figure 8.9. You also can use graphic lines to create fill-in blanks for forms.

Fig. 8.8.

A calendar created using the Box Text option.

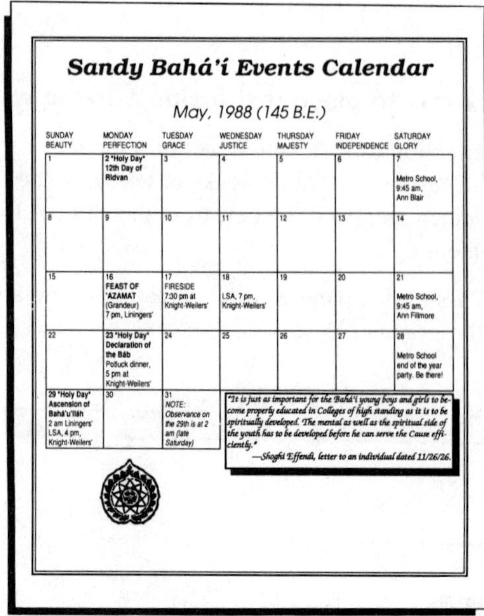

Sandy Bahá'í Events Calendar

May, 1988 (145 B.E.)

SUNDAY BEAUTY	MONDAY PERFECTION	TUESDAY GRACE	WEDNESDAY JUSTICE	THURSDAY MAJESTY	FRIDAY INDEPENDENCE	SATURDAY GLORY
1	2 **"Holy Day" 12th Day of Ridvan**	3	4	5	6	7 Metro School, 9:45 am, Ann Blair
8	9	10	11	12	13	14
15	16 **FEAST OF 'AZAMAT** (Grandeur) 7 pm, Liningers'	17 FIRESIDE 7:30 pm at Knight-Weilers'	18 LSA, 7 pm, Knight-Weilers'	19	20	21 Metro School, 9:45 am, Ann Fillmore
22	23 **"Holy Day" Declaration of the Báb** Potluck dinner, 5 pm at Knight-Weilers'	24	25	26	27	28 Metro School end of the year party. Be there!
29 **"Holy Day" Ascension of Bahá'u'lláh** 2 am Liningers' LSA, 4 pm, Knight-Weilers'	30	31 *NOTE: Observance on the 29th is at 2 am (late Saturday)*				

"It is just as important for the Bahá'í young boys and girls to become properly educated in Colleges of high standing as it is to be spiritually developed. The mental as well as the spiritual side of the youth has to be developed before he can serve the Cause efficiently."

—Shoghi Effendi, letter to an individual dated 11/26/26.

Fig. 8.9.

A form created using the Box Text option.

Bull Run Chiropractic Clinic
38916 Proctor, PO Box 97
Sandy, OR 97055
503/668–3530

ATLAS	
AXIS	
3C	
4C	
5C	
6C	
7C	
1T	
2T	
3T	
4T	
5T	
6T	
7T	
8T	
9T	
10T	
11T	
12T	
1L	
2L	
3L	
4L	
5L	
6L	
SACRUM	
RT ILIUM	
LT ILIUM	
COCCYX	

Chiropractic Emergency Card

Patient ______________________

8.19 Tip Use the Box Text option to create a calendar.

To create a useful calendar, follow these steps:

1. In a new chapter, choose Margins & Columns from the Frame menu and set the right margin to 0.50 inch. On a 1-column page, the column is 7 inches wide and the left margin aligns at 1 inch.
2. Change to Graphic mode and select the Box Text option. Draw a box on the page.
3. Select the box and set the `Grid Snap` to `On` with 1-inch `Horizontal Spacing` and 1-inch `Vertical Spacing`. (These settings force box text to be 1 inch by 1 inch.)
4. Click the four resizing handles on the box to force it into the 1-inch-by-1-inch grid.
5. Move the box to the left margin of the page. Because the page has a 1-inch left margin, you can align the box exactly on the margin.
6. With the box still selected, choose Copy Graphic from the Edit menu or press Shift-Del.
7. Move the box to the right. Because the grid is set for 1 inch, the box jumps 1 inch at a time to the right.
8. Choose Paste Graphic from the Edit menu or press Ins.
9. Repeat steps 5 through 7 but select both boxes by holding down the Shift key while you select or choose Select All from the Graphic menu (or press Ctrl-Q).
10. Repeat step 9 but select three boxes. You should now have seven boxes in a row—enough for one week. Notice that the boxes align with the left and right margins.
11. Select all seven boxes, choose Copy Graphic, move the entire row down 1 inch, and choose Paste Graphic (see fig. 8.10).
12. Select all 14 boxes and repeat step 10 but remember to move the boxes down 2 inches before you choose Paste Graphic.

Continue this process until you have created enough boxes for your calendar. When you are finished, you can select all the boxes and move them as a group to the proper position on the page.

Enter text by changing to Text mode and clicking in a box. The end-of-file marker in each box is where the text cursor is positioned for typing. The Z_BOXTEXT tag can be changed just like any other tag, or you can apply another tag to the text in the box. The Z_BOXTEXT tag is copied from the

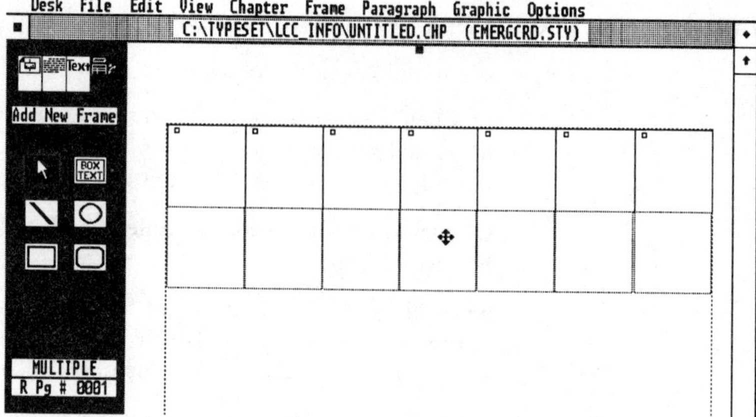

Fig. 8.10.

Using the Box Text, Copy, and Paste options to rapidly create multiple rows of boxes for a calendar.

body text tag and reflects those settings. You cannot set margins for box text, but you can achieve a left and right margin effect by using In From Left and In From Right on the SPACING dialog box, which is available from the Paragraph menu.

You use the same method to create other forms with multiple boxes. Remember to use the Box Text option and not the Square Corner Box or Rounded Corner Box options if you want to place text inside the box.

If you want to shade a box, select the one you want shaded and choose Fill Attributes from the Graphic menu. You also can shade multiple boxes (see fig. 8.11).

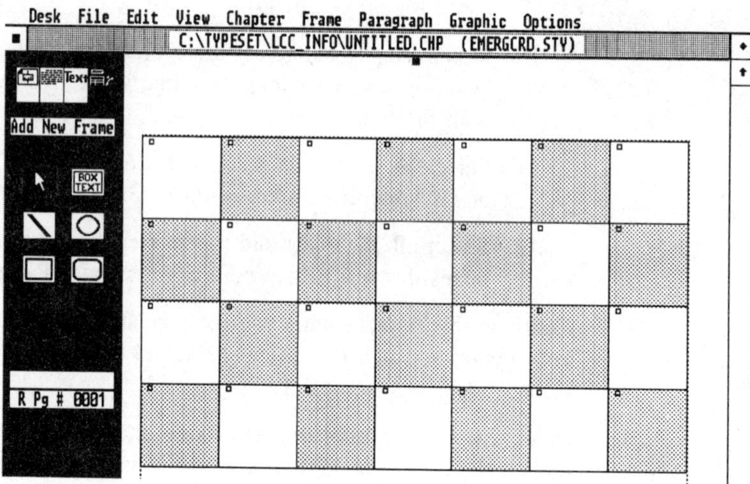

Fig. 8.11.

Shading alternating text boxes.

8.20 Tip

To avoid receiving an error message when your text doesn't fit, either remove the text from the frame or change the font size.

If you create a box with the Box Text option and it is too small to hold the text placed in it, you receive an error message. Unfortunately, this sometimes also happens with empty boxes because the box text tool inserts an end-of-file marker in each box as it is created.

The error message appears every time you move to or past the page on which a problem occurs. You can eliminate this irritating message by making the box bigger, or by tagging the paragraph and making the font size smaller so that the end-of-file marker (or text) fits in the box.

Special Effects

You can perform special effects and techniques such as anchoring a graphic and using transparent graphics by using the graphics tools.

8.21 Tip

Use graphic lines to create fill-in lines for forms.

If you want to create a form with fill-in lines, you can use a graphic line rather than the underline character. The underline character doesn't always yield a solid line.

8.22 Trick

Use a small, hollow frame as an anchor for graphics.

You can create a small frame and tie a graphic to it. If you create an anchor name and insert point for the frame, the graphic also becomes anchored. To anchor a graphic to a specific point in the text like in the example shown in figure 8.12, follow these steps:

1. On a blank page, switch to Text mode and type

   Here is a sentence with an arrow (   ) anchored.

   (Insert several spaces in between the parentheses; this is where the graphic goes.)

2. Switch to Frame mode and click the Add New Frame button or press Ctrl-2.

3. Position the add new frame cursor anywhere on the work area and click the mouse button once to create a small frame.

4. Choose Anchors & Captions from the Frame menu (see Chapter 6 for more information about frame anchors).
5. In the ANCHORS & CAPTIONS dialog box, type *Arrow* at the Anchor option. Click OK or press Enter.
6. Change to Text mode and place the cursor just after the opening parenthesis in the sentence you typed in step 1.
7. Choose Ins Special Item from the Edit menu or press Ctrl-C.
8. Click Frame Anchor or press F5.
9. In the INSERT/EDIT ANCHOR dialog box, type *Arrow* at the Frame's Anchor Name option.
10. Choose Relative, Automatically At Anchor. Click OK or press Enter.
11. Make sure that the frame you created in step 3 is still selected and switch to Graphic mode.
12. Choose the line tool and, while holding down the Alt key, draw a horizontal line that fits inside the parentheses.
13. Choose Line Attributes from the Graphic menu or press Ctrl-L.
14. Change Thickness to 3 and choose an arrow point for the right End Styles. Click OK or press Enter.

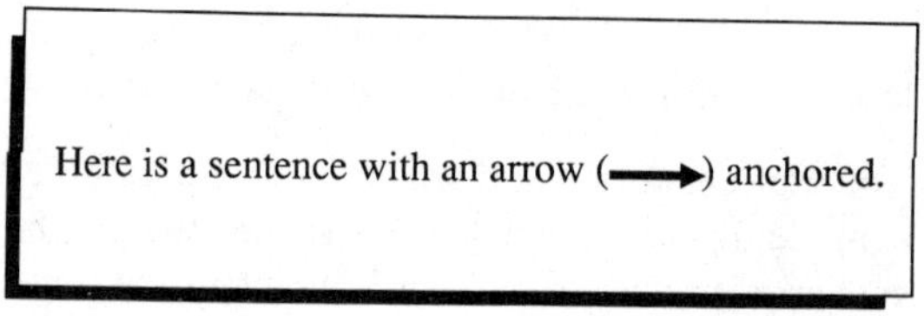

Fig. 8.12.

Using frame anchors to tie a graphic to text.

Here is a sentence with an arrow (⟶) anchored.

8.23 Tip

Use the Opaque and Transparent fill attributes to allow graphics to show through one another.

You can create interesting special effects with fill attributes. To have one graphic show through another, for example, select the top graphic and click Transparent in the FILL ATTRIBUTES dialog box. To block the underlying graphic or text, click Opaque in the FILL ATTRIBUTES dialog box.

Some printers, including some PostScript printers, cannot print transparent graphics and treat them the same as opaque (see figs. 8.13 and 8.14).

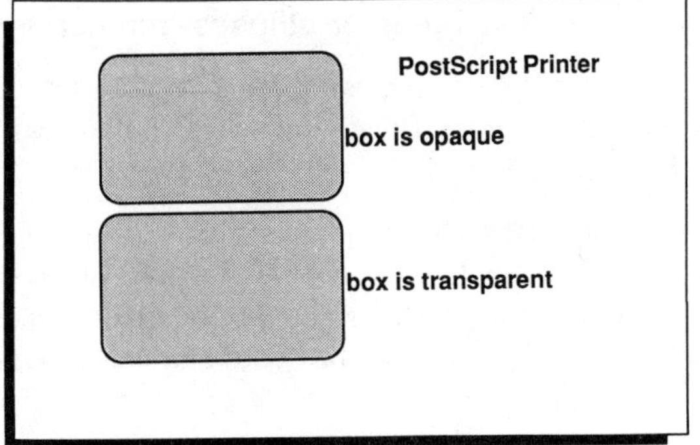

Fig. 8.13.

Opaque and transparent graphics on a PostScript printer.

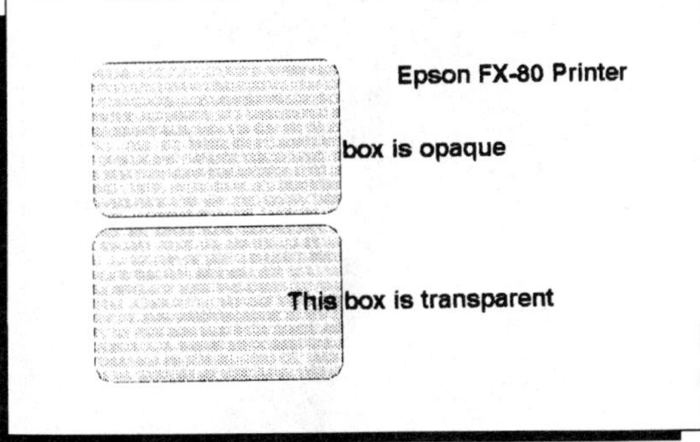

Fig. 8.14.

Opaque and transparent graphics on an Epson FX-80 dot-matrix printer.

If you try to join graphics (placing two lines at right angles, for example) make sure that they join exactly by changing to Enlarged View (choose Enlarged View from the View menu or press Ctrl-E).

8.24 Tip **If your printer supports opaque graphics, you can use an opaque white rectangle as electronic "white-out."**

If you have imported a picture and you want part of it blocked out, create an opaque, solid white rectangle (or use box text with `Thickness` set to `None` in the LINE ATTRIBUTES dialog box).

Place the rectangle over the portion of the graphic you want blocked. This technique is not possible on all printers.

8.25 Trick

Use box text on rectangles or ellipses that serve as mortises.

A *mortise* is a blank shape that can serve as a place to put text. Many clip-art packages provide mortises that look like billboards, signs, frames, or blackboards.

You can create mortises with the graphics tools and then add box text to them. Figure 8.15 is an example of a mortise created with the use of the Rounded Corner Box option to make the sign, a thick line to create the signpost, and thin lines to draw the grass. The box text area holds the message.

Fig. 8.15.
Using the Rounded Corner Box option to create a sign mortise.

8.26 Trick

You can create shadow effects with graphics.

Not all printers support shadow printing, but if your printer does support this feature, you can create interesting shadow effects with the graphics primitives. Figure 8.16 shows an ellipse set to solid white, blocking most of a circle set to solid black. The box text area holds the message.

8.27 Trick

Use the line tool to allow the HP LaserJets and compatibles to create a shadow effect even though they cannot print overlaying graphics.

HP LaserJet printers cannot create drop shadows using frames (see Chapter 6). You can, however, achieve this effect by using the following procedure:

Fig. 8.16.
Using the graphics primitives to create shadow effects.

1. Create a frame with a ruling line around.
2. Enter your text in the frame.
3. Switch to Graphic mode by clicking the Graphic icon or pressing Ctrl-P. Click the line tool.
4. Hold down the Shift and Alt keys as you use the mouse to draw lines along the right and bottom sides of the frame. These lines give the impression of a shadow (see fig. 8.17).
5. Change to the pointer and hold down the Shift key while you select the two lines you just drew. Select Line Attributes from the Graphic menu (or press Ctrl-L) and, in the LINE ATTRIBUTES dialog box, set `Thickness` to `4`. Click OK or press Enter.
6. Position the lines against the frame to create a shadow effect (see fig. 8.18).

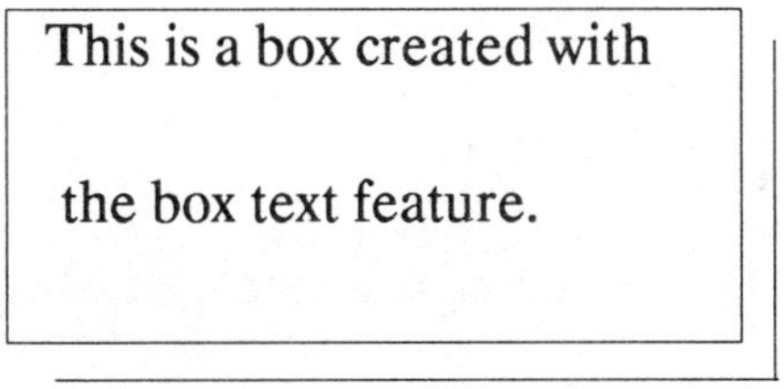

Fig. 8.17.
Using lines to create shadow effects on an HP LaserJet.

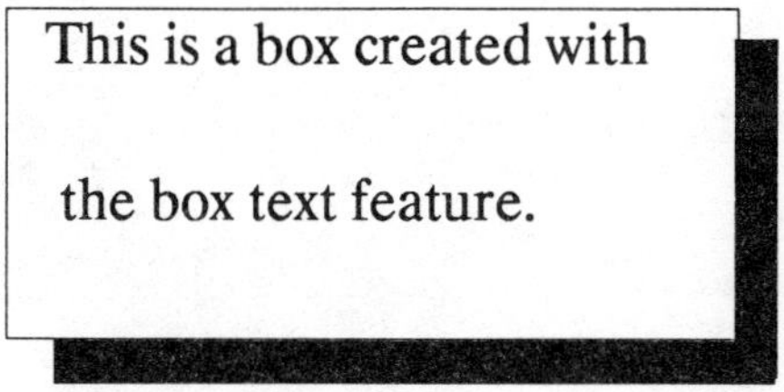

This is a box created with

the box text feature.

Fig. 8.18.
Fatter lines making the shadow more pronounced.

This is a box created with

the box text feature.

Chapter Summary

In this chapter, you learned about the basic graphics tools provided by Ventura. You learned how to create, edit, and constrain both single and multiple graphics. You also learned how graphics are tied to frames and how that can be both useful and hazardous.

You learned how to make repeating graphics and about the limitations of the repeating feature on manually inserted pages. You learned how to set line and fill attributes for all types of graphics. You learned about the versatility of the Box Text option and how to use it as a tool to create forms. Finally, you learned some effects with graphic anchors and transparent graphic attributes.

In the next chapter, you will learn how to make what you have written look good in print with the wide variety of fonts available, and you will examine graphics programs that create special effects with fonts.

Part IV

Printing Ventura Documents

Includes

Chapter

9

Using Fonts

During the design of your document, you need to consider your text and the quantity and placement of your graphics. You also need to consider what fonts you will use.

This chapter gives you good working definitions for the new terminology of computer typesetting. You learn how to change fonts in tags and for individual characters, words, or parts of paragraphs.

You learn to tell Ventura what printer you are using and what fonts are available for use. You learn how to add, delete, and merge font choices.

You learn the font capabilities of dot-matrix, PostScript, and other laser printers, including how to use built-in and downloadable fonts. This chapter discusses screen fonts and the WYSIWYG aspects of Ventura. You have an opportunity to look over extensive font selections and gain an appreciation of which font to use for which application. You learn how to save money by purchasing font collections rather than individual fonts.

Finally, this chapter presents special effects such as rotated text, drop caps, bullets, and headline effects available from sophisticated graphics programs.

Understanding Font Basics

Before you can begin to use fonts, you must understand something about the words used to describe fonts, how to define the fonts to be used in your document, and the concept of a width table. This section provides tips, tricks, and traps with useful information about these aspects of fonts.

9.1 Tip **Learn the terminology of fonts.**

Like any new area of expertise, the terminology used with fonts is not only new, but sometimes confusing. Some helpful definitions follow:

- ❑ *Typeface* (Face in Ventura) refers to the design of a letter. Typefaces can be divided into three broad categories: *serif*, *sans serif*, and *decorative* or *display*. Serif fonts have little finishing strokes on the tops or bottoms of the characters (like Times); sans serif fonts have only main strokes (like Helvetica); decorative or display fonts can be either serif or sans serif and are used for impact, not for long stretches of body text (see fig. 9.1).
- ❑ *Style* refers to whether the letter is regular or italic. In Ventura, style refers to the combination of style and weight—the terms are not differentiated.
- ❑ *Weight* refers to the thickness of each letter—regular, light, bold, black, and so on.
- ❑ *Size* (Size or Custom Size in Ventura) refers to the vertical height of a letter, usually measured in points (72 points equal 1 inch).
- ❑ *Font* is the combination of the typeface, style, weight, and size elements. For example, *12-point Times Bold Italic* is a font. In common usage, the terms *font* and *typeface* are often used interchangeably. In this chapter, the term *font* not only refers to the combination of elements just described, but also refers to the Font choice on the Paragraph menu used in Paragraph mode and the Set Font button used for selected text in Text mode.

Fig. 9.1.

Examples of serif, sans serif, and decorative typefaces.

Times is a serif font. Notice the small strokes that finish off the main strokes on each letter.

Helvetica is a sans-serif font. Notice there are no finishing strokes on the letters.

Windsor is a serif decorative font.
Hobo is a sans-serif decorative font.

9.2 Tip

Change fonts in one of two ways: from the FONT dialog box or from the FONT SETTING FOR SELECTED TEXT dialog box.

In Ventura, you can change font settings in two ways:

- If you want to set or change a tag's font settings, change to Paragraph mode, select a paragraph tagged with the tag you want to modify, and choose Font from the Paragraph menu to access the FONT dialog box (see fig. 9.2). Remember, all paragraphs tagged with the same tag are affected by a font change to that tag.

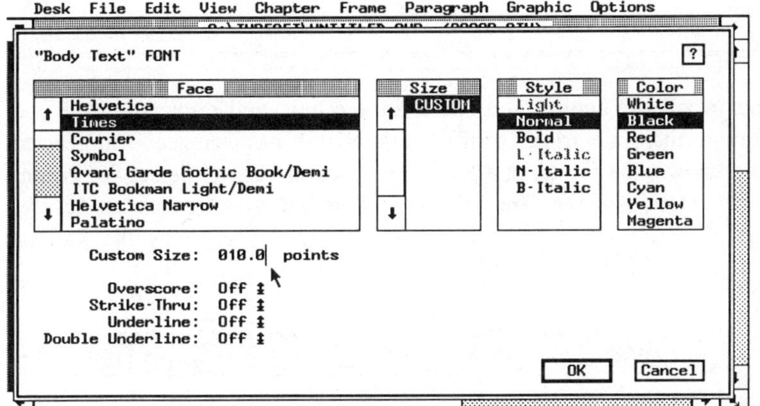

Fig. 9.2.
The FONT dialog box.

- If you want to change the font for only a letter, word, or portion of a paragraph, change to Text mode, select the desired text, and click the Set Font button or press the keyboard shortcut, Ctrl-2, to access the FONT SETTING FOR SELECTED TEXT dialog box (see fig. 9.3).

Minor differences exist between the two dialog boxes: with the FONT SETTING FOR SELECTED TEXT dialog box you can `Shift` text `Up` or `Down` and `Kern` text `Tighter` or `Looser`. Kerning for tags is handled through the TYPOGRAPHY SETTINGS dialog box (which you access by using the Paragraph Typography command from the Paragraph menu). Shifting text up or down does not apply to paragraphs.

9.3 Tip

Specify printer and font information in the SET PRINTER INFO dialog box.

As part of general "housekeeping" chores, let Ventura know what printer you are using and to which port the printer is connected. More on this topic (and installing new printers) is included in Chapter 10.

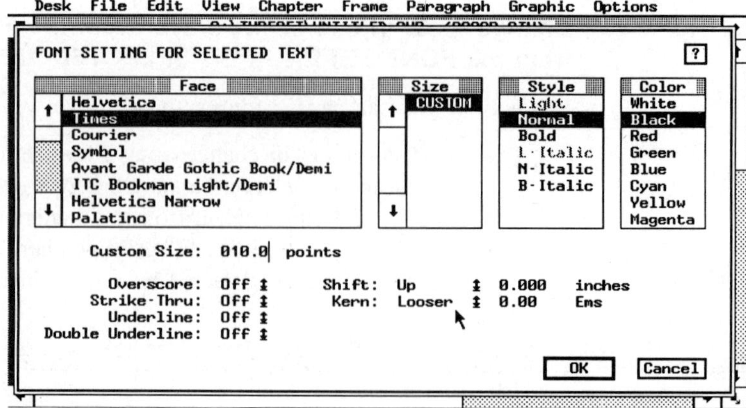

Fig. 9.3.

The FONT SETTING FOR SELECTED TEXT dialog box.

When you installed Ventura, you specified a printer and printer port. If you specified more than one printer or if the printer port has changed, you need to let Ventura know what printer and printer port you are using. Select Set Printer Info from the Options menu. The SET PRINTER INFO dialog box has several parameters that can be set (see fig. 9.4). Table 9.1 explains the various options.

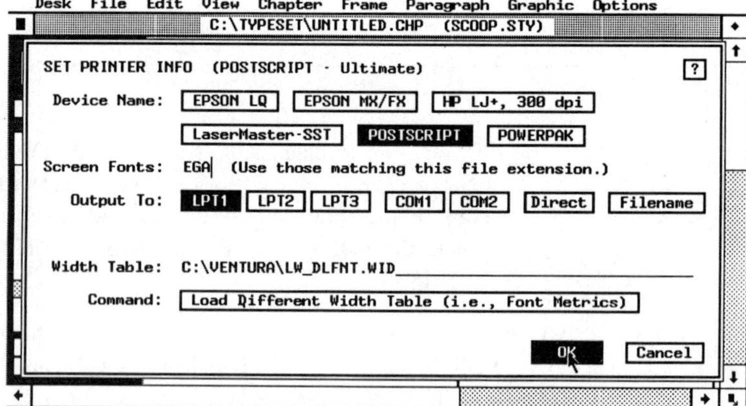

Fig. 9.4.

The SET PRINTER INFO dialog box.

Table 9.1
SET PRINTER INFO Dialog Box Options

Device Name	This option lists all printer drivers installed with Ventura or with Ventura add-on products such as LaserMaster or Publisher's Powerpak. Click the device name you want to use to print the publication. In the VENTURA directory, printer drivers have the prefix *PD_*. You can add additional printer drivers by reinstalling Ventura.

Table 9.1—*Continued*

Screen Fonts	Type the extension used for screen fonts. Normally this extension is not changed because Ventura installed the correct screen fonts for your monitor type during installation. Typical extensions are EGA (Enhanced Graphics Adapter), VGA (Virtual Graphics Adapter), and PSF (PostScript Fonts). For more about screen fonts, refer to "Using and Understanding Screen Fonts" later in this chapter.
Output To	This setting isn't normally changed from what was specified during installation. If you change printers or ports, or decide to output to a file, choose the correct output port. If you select `Filename`, you are asked to supply the name of the file when you begin printing. Some printer boards, such as the JLaser™, and some printers, such as Interpress or Cordata, use cards with direct printer cable connections. For these types of printers, choose `Direct`.
Width Table	Information about the width, shape, and height of each character for a specific font is maintained in a width table. Using width-table information, Ventura spaces printed text and adjusts screen font positioning. Select the width table containing fonts corresponding to the `Device Name` (printer) option. If you choose a width table that does not correspond to your printer (a PostScript width table for an EPSON® dot-matrix printer, for example), the word at the top of the SET PRINTER INFO dialog box switches from `Ultimate` to `Draft`. This change reminds you that a mismatch between width tables and devices exists. Print in `Draft` on a dot-matrix printer to proof text that is to be output later to a laser printer. You can create new or merged width tables by using the Add/Remove Fonts command from the Options menu. Only one width table can be active at one time.
Command	Click `Command` to load the ITEM SELECTOR dialog box that allows you to change width tables. Click the new width table from the list presented and then click OK or press Enter.

9.4 Tip **Use the Add/Remove Fonts command from the Options menu to change width tables by merging or renaming them, or by adding and removing individual fonts, sizes, or styles.**

You access the ADD/REMOVE FONTS dialog box by choosing Add/Remove Fonts from the Options menu (see fig. 9.5).

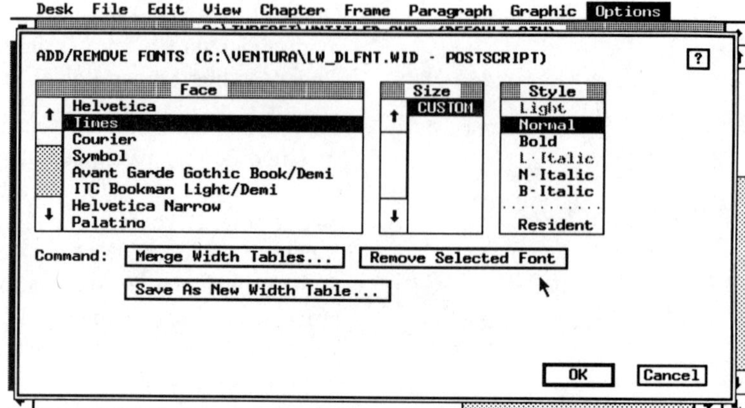

Fig. 9.5.
The ADD/REMOVE FONTS dialog box.

The ADD/REMOVE FONTS dialog box offers three major options:

- `Merge Width Tables` calls up the ITEM SELECTOR dialog box that allows you to specify another width table to merge with the currently selected width table.
- `Save As New Width Table` allows you to rename the currently selected width table. If you select this option, the newly named width table becomes the current width table just as if you had selected it from the SET PRINTER INFO dialog box.
- `Remove Selected Font` deletes the specific font face, size, and style from the width table. If you want to delete a font with three sizes in each style, you must delete each size in each style separately. PostScript fonts don't have individual sizes because they can be scaled to custom-size (more on font scaling later in this chapter).

When you use the ADD/REMOVE FONTS dialog box to add fonts, you aren't really adding fonts to the existing width table so much as you are merging two width tables. Merging width tables adds the fonts in the selected width table to the current width table as designated in the SET PRINTER INFO dialog box. If you want to keep your current width table intact, rename it before merging it with other width tables.

Once all the fonts are included in your width table, you can see what styles are available for each face by clicking the desired font in the `Face` selection box. Available styles appear in bold; unavailable styles appear in gray. You should also verify that the font is accurately listed as either resident (built into the printer) or downloadable (not built in, requiring Ventura to send the font information to the printer at print time). Click the word `Download` or `Resident` in the `Style` selection box to switch back and forth. If you use a downloadable font and it doesn't print properly, verify that you have designated `Download` correctly.

9.5 Trap — Fonts are not alphabetized in the Face list.

For some unknown reason, Ventura chose not to alphabetize font names in the `Face` selection box. Instead, face names are added in the order you merge width tables. Be aware of this when looking for a font. If it's not where you expect it to be in alphabetical order, look through the rest of the font selections. Although this is not a problem with a few fonts, if you have many fonts (some width tables for large font collections contain more than 50 fonts) it is a major inconvenience to scroll though all the fonts, hunting for a particular one.

9.6 Trick — Create separate width tables for special jobs.

Width tables take up room in memory. Consider creating special width tables with only the fonts used for a particular job.

9.7 Tip — If you have more than one width table, develop a system for managing the tables.

If you enjoy using different fonts and have a need (and the budget) for a font collection, consider grouping fonts together in special width tables. You may, for example, have a group of fonts used for newsletters, another for posters, and a third for brochures.

Remember that fonts take up disk space, and a large collection can quickly fill a disk—especially for printers that require a font file for each point size, such as the Hewlett-Packard LaserJet. Either archive and delete unused fonts, or delete unused fonts and sizes to free disk space.

Another strategy is to keep fonts from specific collections or manufacturers together in their own width tables.

If you keep relatively small numbers of fonts in each width table, you can create larger width tables for specific jobs by merging width tables and then removing any extraneous fonts.

If you use several printers, you may want to name the width tables (as Ventura does) for the printer. If, however, you use only a few fonts and only one or two printers, you may never need to use the Add/Remove Font command and can manage nicely with the Ventura-supplied width tables for your printer.

As in many areas, Ventura provides you with the flexibility to customize width tables to your own preferences and needs.

9.8 Trap

Width-table information is stored with style sheets.

Each style sheet contains information about the width table to be used. If the width table you specified when you saved the chapter is not available, a width table called *Output* is used as a default. If the formatting doesn't look correct on-screen, or if the printed output doesn't look right, verify that you are using the correct width table.

9.9 Tip

If you have an unsupported dot-matrix or other printer or want more capability with your supported printer, use the Publisher's Powerpak utility from Atech Software.

The Publisher's Powerpak from Atech Software is an impressive Ventura add-on utility. Publisher's Powerpak provides Ventura printer drivers for more than 200 dot-matrix and other previously unsupported printers. Some of the printers that Publisher's Powerpak allows you to use are most models of Alps, Apple ImageWriter®, Brother, C. Itoh, Canon Bubble Jet, Citizen®, Data Technology, DataSouth, Diablo®, EPSON, Fujitsu, Genicom, Hewlett-Packard (DeskJet™, LaserJet, Quiet Jet+, and ThinkJet™), IBM, Kyocera, Mannesmann Tally, NEC®, Okidata®, Olympia, Panasonic, Siekosha, Smith Corona, Star Micronics, Tandy®, Texas Instruments, Toshiba, and Xerox.

If Publisher's Powerpak only let you use your dot-matrix printer with Ventura, that would be an accomplishment. But Publisher's Powerpak also gives you three typefaces, with four more available at reasonable cost. Each typeface comes in basic form as well as Thin, Condensed, Wide, Expanded, Hollow, Hollow Thin, Hollow Condensed, Hollow Wide, and Hollow Expanded. Each of the 10 faces can be made normal, bold, or italic for a total of 30 combinations. The utility does not limit you to just a few point sizes; you can scale the fonts from 6 to 250 points—just like PostScript. The resolution of the output is also impressive: 240 by 216 dpi on 9-pin printers, 360 by 360 dpi on 24-pin printers, and 300 by 300 dpi on inkjet and bubblejet printers.

Figure 9.6 shows a sampling of the versatility of Publisher's Powerpak. If you use a dot-matrix or other supported printer for your final output, Publisher's Powerpak expands your capabilities immensely. If you use a dot-matrix printer only to proof your final output, this printer driver is not as useful.

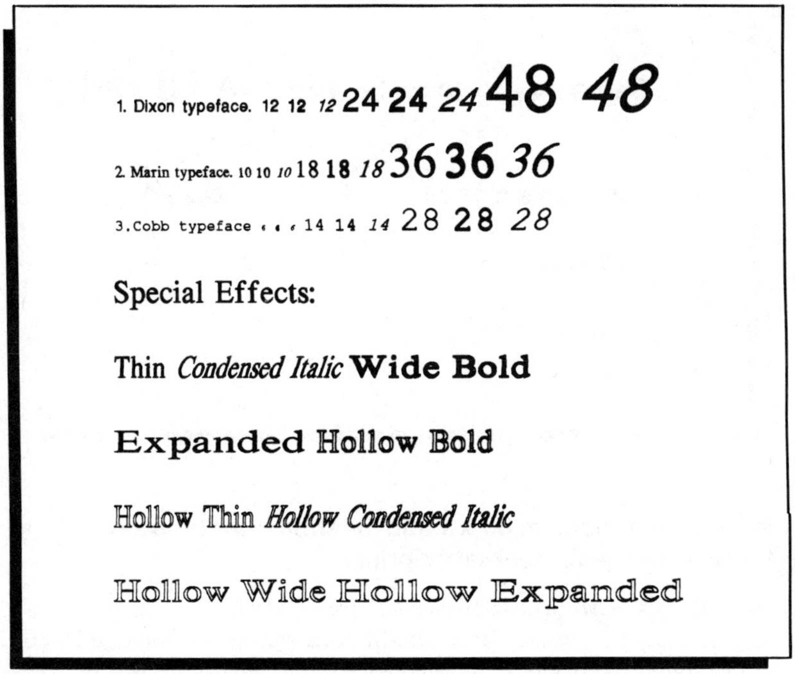

1. Dixon typeface. 12 12 *12* 24 24 *24* 48 *48*

2. Marin typeface. 10 10 *10* 18 18 *18* 36 36 *36*

3. Cobb typeface . . . 14 14 *14* 28 28 *28*

Special Effects:

Thin *Condensed Italic* **Wide Bold**

Expanded Hollow Bold

Hollow Thin *Hollow Condensed Italic*

Hollow Wide Hollow Expanded

Fig. 9.6.
Sample output on an Epson LQ-850 dot-matrix printer using the Publisher's Powerpak printer driver.

Using Fonts with Dot-Matrix Printers

Ventura supplies some fonts for use with supported dot-matrix printers. You can add impressive regular and decorative fonts from vendors, such as Bitstream™ and Atech. Dot-matrix printers can print between 120 by 140 dots per inch (9-pin printers) and 180 by 180 dots per inch (24-pin printers).

9.10 Tip

Create a test page to view the dot-matrix fonts supplied by Ventura.

Ventura directly supports the Epson MX-80, FX-80, RX-80, and LQ-1500 printers; the IBM ProPrinter; and Toshiba dot-matrix printers. If your printer can emulate any of the supported 9-pin or 24-pin printers, choose the printer driver that your printer manual suggests. The Epson LQ-850 printer, for example, emulates the LQ-1500, so the Epson LQ driver also drives the LQ-850 (see fig. 9.7).

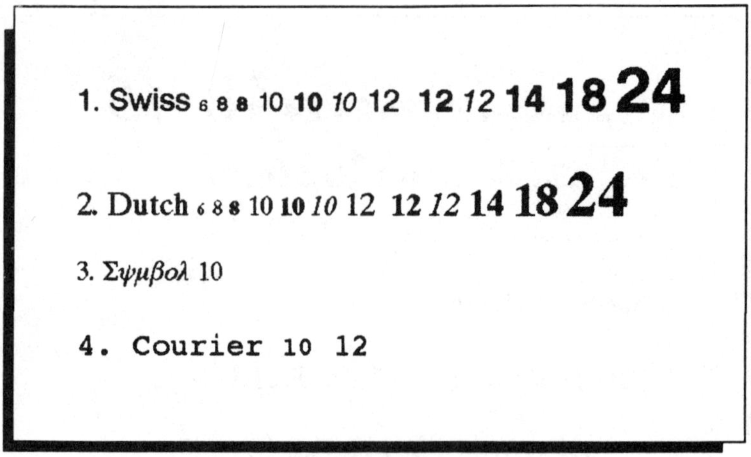

Fig. 9.7.

Test page showing Epson LQ fonts included with Ventura.

1. Swiss 6 8 8 10 10 10 12 12 12 14 18 24

2. Dutch 6 8 8 10 10 10 12 12 12 14 18 24

3. Σψμβολ 10

4. Courier 10 12

9.11 Tip

Use the Fontware installation kit and Bitstream fonts to create fonts for use with your dot-matrix printer.

Although more expensive than Publisher's Powerpak fonts, the Bitstream font library is much more extensive. Bitstream offers a selection of more than 160 typeface and style combinations. As a bonus, if you purchase Bitstream fonts for your dot-matrix printer and later purchase either a Hewlett-Packard LaserJet or PostScript-compatible printer, you can use all your Bitstream fonts on the new printer. (You must reinstall the fonts for the new printer, but you don't need to buy new fonts.)

See Appendix A for information on how to use the Fontware installation kit, provided with Ventura, to install Bitstream fonts.

Figure 9.8 shows examples of decorative Bitstream fonts printed on an Epson LQ-850 printer.

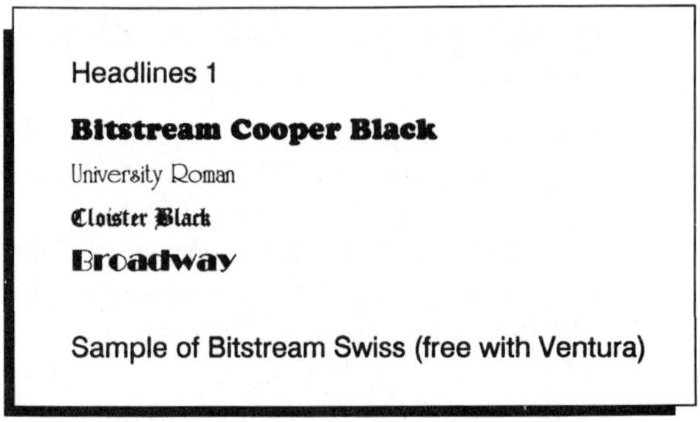

Fig. 9.8.

Bitstream fonts printed on an Epson LQ-850 dot-matrix printer.

Headlines 1

Bitstream Cooper Black

University Roman

Cloister Black

Broadway

Sample of Bitstream Swiss (free with Ventura)

9.12 Trick

When the toner cartridge in a laser printer runs low, a "low toner" message or light appears even though you can still print more pages. Keep printing until pages begin printing incompletely.

You can usually print from 20 to 100 more pages after the message appears, but this printer feature warns you far enough in advance so that you can locate a new cartridge.

Fading or streaking on a page is also a warning of lack of toner, although it does not mean that the toner is exhausted. You can squeeze several more pages from a cartridge by removing it from the printer and rocking it 45 degrees away and toward you several times to distribute the remaining toner. If you ever experience fading or streaking when the "low toner" message is not present, rocking the toner cartridge usually clears up the problems by settling the toner particles.

9.13 Tip

If you plan to use many fonts on a single page, or a graphic image larger than one-quarter the size of a sheet of paper, you may want to invest in a memory-expansion board for the LaserJet printer.

One of the unique features of the new HP LaserJet II series is that you can add more printer memory by plugging expansion boards into the printer. The HP LaserJet II has an optional memory slot into which you can insert memory boards from Hewlett-Packard to expand memory by 1, 2, or 4 megabytes.

Expanding the printer's memory allows the printer to print full-page graphics and multiple fonts downloaded to the printer. If you do not use graphic design as part of your desktop publishing, or if your office prints mostly text, memory-expansion boards are not needed.

Using Fonts with PostScript Printers

PostScript was developed by Adobe Systems for use with the Apple Laser Writer and the Macintosh computer to produce typeset-quality output on laser printers.

Unlike most printers at the time PostScript was released, the LaserWriter included an on-board microprocessor. A page processed for PostScript is actually converted into a computer program, like a program written in BASIC or FORTRAN. The PostScript program is a description of the page that is then transmitted to the microprocessor in the laser printer where the program is interpreted. Page Description Languages (PDLs) have become popular since then, and several are now available. Some PDLs are ''clones'' of PostScript; others are alternatives.

Five characteristics distinguish PostScript:

- ❑ PostScript turns a page into a graphic. This means all elements, whether pictures or fonts, are interpreted as graphics. By interpreting each element as a graphic, PostScript can be very versatile. This versatility explains why PostScript doesn't care about the size of the font or whether the font is in landscape, portrait, or at an odd angle. Because PostScript creates a program, the program can be sent to any device that can interpret PostScript—allowing the same output to be sent to a laser printer or a typesetting machine like Linotronic.
- ❑ PostScript fonts can be custom-scaled. With PostScript fonts, you can choose any point size from 0.5 to 254 points in 0.5 increments.
- ❑ Support of PostScript is extensive. Clearly, PostScript enjoys a competitive advantage that cannot be overtaken soon, if ever. Support for PostScript has manifested itself in several ways: the widest variety of the highest quality fonts are available for PostScript, the highest quality and most sophisticated clip art and graphics software are either in PostScript or produce output in PostScript, and the potential of PostScript still has not been exhausted—more sophisticated applications will be available soon..
- ❑ PostScript can be slow. Because PostScript is an interpreted language that must be processed by the printer's on-board microprocessor, nothing is printed until the computing is complete. A complicated page rich in pictures and multiple fonts of varying size can take a long time to print. On the other hand, a simple page using on-board fonts can be printed quickly.
- ❑ PostScript is expensive. PostScript is more expensive than other solutions because royalties for the interpreter must be paid to Adobe Systems. PostScript capability can add an additional $2,000 to the cost of a laser printer. Add-on boards providing PostScript capabilities to non-PostScript printers cost almost as much.

In summary, PostScript is the most versatile printing solution in the marketplace today for applications like Ventura. You must pay a price for that versatility in speed as well as dollars.

9.14 Tip — Learn about the built-in PostScript fonts.

Almost all PostScript printers on the market offer a basic 35-font set. Unlike other printers, when PostScript devices specify a number of fonts, point sizes are not included in the count. Therefore, the 35 fonts built into a printer include the sum of only face and style combinations.

The fonts supplied with the Apple LaserWriter Plus established the original standard of built-in fonts; most vendors of PostScript printers or add-on boards use the same font set. Table 9.2 and figure 9.9 show the standard Apple LaserWriter Plus PostScript font set.

Table 9.2
The Basic PostScript Font Set

Avant Garde	N, B, I, BI*	Sans serif
Courier	N, B, I, BI	Monospaced serif
Helvetica	N, B, I, BI	Sans serif
Helvetica Narrow	N, B, I, BI	Sans serif
ITC Bookman	N, B, I, BI	Serif
ITC Zapf Chancery	I	Decorative serif
ITC Zapf Dingbats	N/A	Specialty symbols
New Century Schoolbook	N, B, I, BI	Serif
Palatino	N, B, I, BI	Serif
Symbol	N	Greek letters and mathematical symbols
Times	N, B, I, BI	Serif

*Normal, Bold, Italic, Bold Italic

9.15 Tip — Expand your font library with fonts you can download.

One of the most exciting things about desktop publishing is the immediacy of the response you get when you make changes. You can print a document, completely alter its look, and print it again. Within minutes you can evaluate your new design and either return to your original or make additional changes. This instant feedback gives you a real sense of control over the way your documents look. You don't have to wait for days for proofs to come back from the printer for evaluation; you can make changes on the spot.

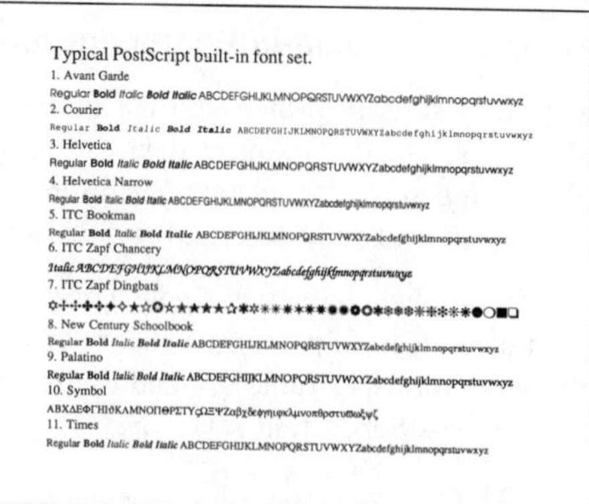

Fig. 9.9.

Sample of the basic PostScript font set resident in an Apple LaserWriter Plus.

It follows, then, that the level of experimentation increases when you have more tools with which to work. A wide variety of typefaces lets you experiment freely with the look of your document. Once you exhaust the possibilities of your printer's built-in fonts, you can begin to explore the fascinating world of downloadable fonts.

A package of PostScript fonts that works with Ventura contains disks with the information your PostScript printer needs to create scalable fonts. Also included is a program to install the printer, screen fonts, and printer width table to let Ventura know how to place the fonts on the page and on the screen. (Before you purchase fonts, be sure to ask whether the fonts are compatible with Ventura.) Once you install the fonts on your hard disk, add the new fonts by merging the new width table with your regular width table. From then on, whenever you use one of your new fonts, Ventura automatically downloads the font information to your printer.

Until Ventura was developed for the PC, there was not much demand for PostScript fonts in the PC world; most people who had laser printers used Hewlett-Packard LaserJet-compatible printers. Because of the lack of demand for PostScript in the PC world, most of the early font vendors concentrated on providing fonts for the Macintosh.

In the past few years, however, Adobe Systems and Bitstream have both developed extensive font libraries for use with many PC applications, including Ventura. In addition, some of the companies, such as Casady & Greene, that formerly supplied fonts only for the Macintosh have begun offering fonts for the PC and specifically for Ventura.

You should be aware of three things concerning downloadable PostScript fonts:

- Fonts take up disk space. PostScript fonts in general, however, require much less disk space than Hewlett-Packard LaserJet-compatible fonts because only an outline file rather than files for each point size is required.
- Fonts take time to download: the more downloadable fonts on a page, the longer the page takes to print.
- PostScript fonts are expensive: typical font sets consisting of a single typeface with four weights (regular, bold, italic, and bold italic) sell for about $200 from Adobe and Bitstream. Casady & Greene's fonts are less expensive.

The trade-off in disk space, printing time, and expense is increased versatility in how your document looks.

9.16 Tip

Store downloadable PostScript printer fonts in the PSFONTS directory.

The Adobe fonts-installation package insists that you place PostScript printer fonts in a directory called PSFONTS. When you install Ventura, a file called POSTSCPT.CNF is copied to the VENTURA directory telling Ventura to look for downloadable PostScript printer fonts in the C:\PSFONTS directory. If you put PostScript fonts in another directory or if the PSFONTS directory is on a drive other than C, you *must* edit the POSTSCPT.CNF file with an ASCII text editor and modify the C:\PSFONTS line to reflect the proper drive and directory.

If you modify the POSTSCPT.CNF file and later reinstall Ventura, check to ensure that the modified POSTSCPT.CNF wasn't overwritten. If it was, you must modify the C:\PSFONTS line again.

9.17 Tip

Save money and quickly expand your font library by purchasing bundled packages of Bitstream fonts.

Bitstream provides an extensive library of regular and decorative fonts. One benefit of Bitstream fonts is that they can be used on either PostScript or non-PostScript printers. A great way to buy fonts from Bitstream is to purchase either the Headlines Typefaces or Fundamentals Typeface Series. Each package has several typefaces grouped by experts for a specific use. The Headlines packages, for example, have groups of four decorative typefaces (remember, decorative typefaces are used for impact or display). Currently, Bitstream has five Headline sets (see fig. 9.10).

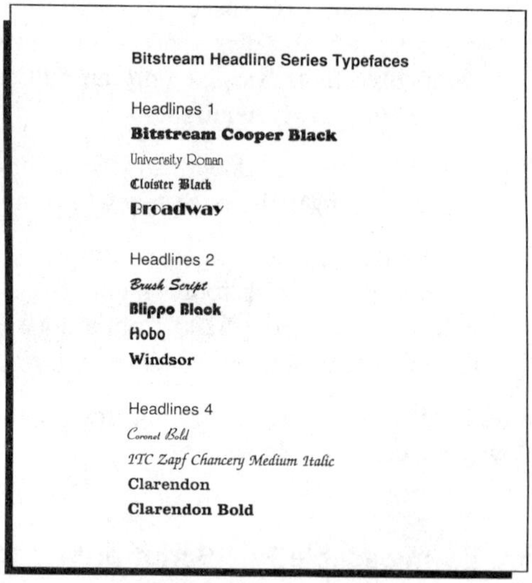

Fig. 9.10.

Samples from three of the Bitstream Headline packages.

Bitstream Headline Series Typefaces

Headlines 1

Bitstream Cooper Black

University Roman

Cloister Black

Broadway

Headlines 2

Brush Script

Blippo Black

Hobo

Windsor

Headlines 4

Coronet Bold

ITC Zapf Chancery Medium Italic

Clarendon

Clarendon Bold

Bitstream offers three different Fundamentals Typeface Series sets of fonts. Each has 12 face and style combinations. The Books & Manuals set, for example, contains Baskerville, Goudy Old Style, and Zapf Calligraphic (also called Palatino) in regular, bold, italic, and bold italic (see fig. 9.11). As another example, the Flyers set contains Futura (four weights) and Headlines sets 2 and 4. Headlines 2 contains Brush Script, Blippo Black, Hobo, and Windsor; Headlines 4 contains ITC Zapf Chancery Medium Italic (already built into many PostScript printers), Coronet Bold, Clarendon, and Clarendon Bold. Separately, these fonts cost about $600; as a Fundamentals set, they cost about $400—a savings of 33 percent.

Fig. 9.11.

Fonts from Bitstream's Books & Manuals collection.

Bitstream Fundamentals Typeface Series

Books & Manuals

1. Baskerville
Normal *Italic* **Bold** ***Bold Italic***
ABCDEFGHIJKLMNOPQRSTUVWXYZabcdefghijklmnopqrstuvwxyz
2. Goudy Old Style
Normal *Italic* **Bold** **Extra Bold**
ABCDEFGHIJKLMNOPQRSTUVWXYZabcdefghijklmnopqrstuvwxyz
3. Zapf Calligraphic
Normal *Italic* **Bold** ***Bold Italic***
ABCDEFGHIJKLMNOPQRSTUVWXYZabcdefghijklmnopqrstuvwxyz

9.18 Trap

Although fonts cannot be copyrighted, their names can be. Different suppliers of fonts may supply the same font under different names.

Table 9.3 lists some fonts that are known by different names from Adobe and Bitstream. When purchasing fonts, make sure that you are not buying the same font under a different name. The practice of renaming fonts is industry-wide and is not limited to Adobe and Bitstream.

Table 9.3
Same Fonts, Different Names

Adobe	*Bitstream*
Times Roman	Dutch
Helvetica	Swiss
Palatino	Zapf Calligraphic
Optima	Zapf Humanist
Melior	Zapf Elliptical
Univers	Zurich

Even if the font is supposed to be the same, subtle differences may exist (see fig. 9.12).

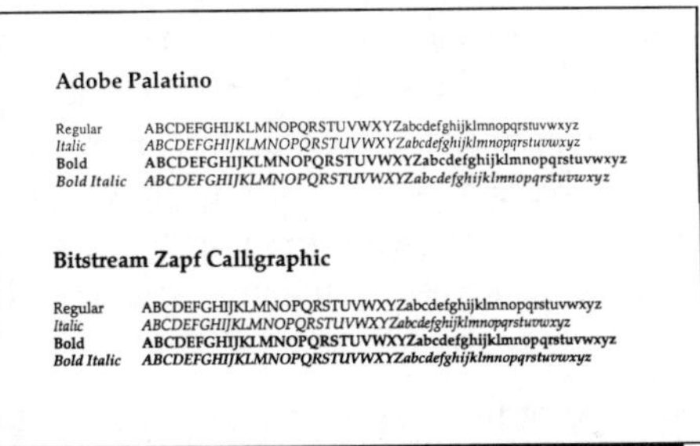

Fig. 9.12.
Adobe Palatino and Bitstream Zapf Calligraphic (both the same font).

9.19 Trap

Many vendors sell Bitstream fonts, but not all Bitstream font packages are created equal.

Font packs purchased directly from Bitstream or sold under the Bitstream label by regular software outlets contain font-outline information. This information creates bit-mapped fonts (used by Hewlett-Packard LaserJet-compatible and other non-PostScript printers) and PostScript fonts. Some suppliers of programs that enhance bit-mapped fonts sell Bitstream fonts but omit the PostScript information. This omission may not cause you problems, but if you ever change to a PostScript printer, you must repurchase the fonts. To protect your options, purchase only Bitstream fonts containing PostScript information (contained in the files with a BEZ extension).

If you look at the directories of the free sample fonts supplied with the Bitstream installation kit, you see only files with BCO and TDF extensions. Because no BEZ files are present, these free fonts cannot be used to make PostScript fonts.

9.20 Trap

Creating a significant number of Bitstream fonts can take a long time.

The time estimates given in the Bitstream installation kit when you create fonts are just that—estimates. If you have a large number of printer and screen fonts, your computer make take several hours to generate the required fonts. You may want to start the creation project in the late afternoon and let your system do the work overnight.

9.21 Trap

Bitstream fonts created for one software package don't necessarily work with another package. You may have to go through another installation procedure.

Because Bitstream fonts take so long to generate, one major inconvenience is having to create them again for another software package. Bitstream fonts work with Ventura as well as with PageMaker (and many other Microsoft Windows-based applications), Lotus Manuscript, Microsoft Word, GEM applications, and WordPerfect. Unfortunately, you cannot use Bitstream fonts generated for Ventura with these other applications unless you install the fonts again with a Fontware installation package designed specially for the other application.

The way each of these programs connects with Bitstream fonts is a little different. Table 9.4 shows some names of Bitstream font files generated from the BCO.TDF and BEZ outline files and which applications they will work with. If you have several Bitstream-supported applications and place all the printer fonts in the same directory, you may need to know which fonts belong to which application. If you decide to delete some fonts to free disk space or because you don't use them anymore, table 9.4 helps you identify the fonts.

Table 9.4
Bitstream File Name Extensions

Software	*Bitstream Font Files by Printer Type*
Windows	PFM (PostScript), HPF (Hewlett-Packard LaserJet compatible), FON (screen font)
Manuscript	PSO (PostScript), HPF (Hewlett-Packard LaserJet compatible)
Word	PSO (PostScript), HPF (Hewlett-Packard LaserJet compatible)
GEM/Ventura	PFA (PostScript), SFP (Hewlett-Packard LaserJet compatible—portrait), SFL (Hewlett-Packard LaserJet compatible—landscape), B30 (JLaser, Cordata), EPS (9-pin dot-matrix), 180 (24-pin dot-matrix), W30 (AST TurboLaser®), EGA/VGA (screen fonts)
WordPerfect	PSO (PostScript), HPF (Hewlett-Packard LaserJet compatible)

9.22 Tip

Use Adobe fonts for the widest variety of PostScript fonts.

Adobe invented the PostScript language and produces a terrific selection of more than 40 font packages. Like Bitstream, Adobe offers cost-saving font collections. Among others in the Adobe Publishing Pack series are packs for newsletters and forms and schedules.

In the Newsletters Publishing Pack, Adobe bundles Century Old Style (3 weights), ITC Franklin Gothic (6 weights), and ITC Galliard (4 weights) for a total of 13 font and style combinations. In the Forms & Schedules Publishing Pack, Adobe bundles Lucida (4 weights), News Gothic (4 weights), and Univers (8 weights) for a total of 16 font and style combinations (see fig. 9.13).

Fig. 9.13.
Typefaces from the Adobe Newsletters and Forms & Schedules Publishing Packs.

When buying fonts, consider that Adobe provides a great deal of information for novice or intermediate desktop publishers. In addition to the great calendar posters Adobe provides on request at no charge, a *Form & Function* catalog is available and shows examples of Adobe fonts, illustrates correct usage, and offers numerous tips on layout. Even if you don't use Adobe fonts, you should ask for the fantastic catalog.

The publishing packs contain fonts selected by experts; the experts provide information about why the particular fonts were selected and give some examples of how to use the fonts. This information is a terrific bonus that is both interesting and useful.

Adobe fonts are priced comparably to Bitstream fonts, ranging from under $100 (for single-font packages) to $275 (for 6-font sets). Adobe fonts can be distinguished from Bitstream fonts in the following ways:

- ❑ Because Adobe invented PostScript, the company kept some key knowledge about how to print small point sizes optimally. These "hints" are not known to other vendors, so fonts from other vendors don't look as good as Adobe fonts at small sizes. The advantage is lost at larger point sizes, however, and other vendors' fonts look just as good as Adobe fonts to most people.
- ❑ Adobe fonts can be used *only* on PostScript printers. You do not have the option of creating fonts for Hewlett-Packard LaserJet-compatible or dot-matrix printers with Adobe font outlines. On the other hand, all applications on the PC that are compatible with Adobe fonts use the same font outlines. You may have to install separate screen fonts for the various applications, but the printer fonts only need to be installed once for WordPerfect, Microsoft Windows applications (including PageMaker), and GEM-based programs like Ventura.
- ❑ Because Adobe fonts are dedicated to PostScript systems, the installation process is much less time-consuming than Bitstream's installation process. The Adobe installation process is so simple and automated that a detailed explanation of how to install Adobe fonts isn't required in this book.

9.23 Tip

Consider either Adobe Stone or Bitstream Charter fonts for high quality at 300 dpi.

Realizing that most traditional fonts were never intended to print at the relatively low resolution provided by 300-dpi laser printers, Adobe and Bitstream created fonts that attempt to accurately render their letter forms at 300 dpi as well as they do on high-resolution typesetters.

The Bitstream Charter font was designed by Matthew Carter. Charter is an elegantly modern serif font with a chiseled look that comes in four weights and is sold as a font family (see fig. 9.14).

1. **Normal**
ABCDEFGHIJKLMNOPQRSTUVWXYZabcdefghijklmnopqrstuvwxyz
2. **Italic**
ABCDEFGHIJKLMNOPQRSTUVWXYZabcdefghijklmnopqrstuvwxyz
3. **Bold**
ABCDEFGHIJKLMNOPQRSTUVWXYZabcdefghijklmnopqrstuvwxyz
4. **Bold Italic**
ABCDEFGHIJKLMNOPQRSTUVWXYZabcdefghijklmnopqrstuvwxyz

Fig. 9.14.

The Bitstream Charter font.

Even more ambitious is Sumner Stone's collection of 18 combinations of typefaces and styles. Available in serif, sans serif, and an informal serif, each Stone typeface comes in six styles—normal, italic, semibold, semibold italic, bold, and bold italic. The benefit of such a fine collection for novices and those not completely comfortable with their abilities to select fonts that work well together is that any of the 18 fonts can be used interchangeably in a document without creating disharmony. From the elegant serif and sans serif to the playful informal, Stone has a collection worthy of the most discriminating designer (see fig 9.15).

1. Serif Normal
ABCDEFGHIJKLMNOPQRSTUVWXYZabcdefghijklmnopqrstuvwxyz
2. Serif Italic
ABCDEFGHIJKLMNOPQRSTUVWXYZabcdefghijklmnopqrstuvwxyz
3. Serif Bold
ABCDEFGHIJKLMNOPQRSTUVWXYZabcdefghijklmnopqrstuv
4. Serif Bold Italic
ABCDEFGHIJKLMNOPQRSTUVWXYZabcdefghijklmnopqrstuvw
5. Serif Semibold
ABCDEFGHIJKLMNOPQRSTUVWXYZabcdefghijklmnopqrstuvwxyz
6. Serif Semibold Italic
ABCDEFGHIJKLMNOPQRSTUVWXYZabcdefghijklmnopqrstuvwxyz
1. Sans Serif Normal
ABCDEFGHIJKLMNOPQRSTUVWXYZabcdefghijklmnopqrstuvwxyz
2. Sans Serif Italic
ABCDEFGHIJKLMNOPQRSTUVWXYZabcdefghijklmnopqrstuvwxyz
3. Sans Serif Bold
ABCDEFGHIJKLMNOPQRSTUVWXYZabcdefghijklmnopqrstuvwxyz
4. Sans Serif Bold Italic
ABCDEFGHIJKLMNOPQRSTUVWXYZabcdefghijklmnopqrstuvwxyz
5. Sans Serif Semibold
ABCDEFGHIJKLMNOPQRSTUVWXYZabcdefghijklmnopqrstuvwxyz
6. Sans Serif Semibold Italic
ABCDEFGHIJKLMNOPQRSTUVWXYZabcdefghijklmnopqrstuvwxyz
1. Informal Normal
ABCDEFGHIJKLMNOPQRSTUVWXYZabcdefghijklmnopqrstuvwxyz
2. Informal Italic
ABCDEFGHIJKLMNOPQRSTUVWXYZabcdefghijklmnopqrstuvwxyz
3. Informal Bold
ABCDEFGHIJKLMNOPQRSTUVWXYZabcdefghijklmnopqrstu
4. Informal Bold Italic
ABCDEFGHIJKLMNOPQRSTUVWXYZabcdefghijklmnopqrstuvwxyz
5. Informal Semibold
ABCDEFGHIJKLMNOPQRSTUVWXYZabcdefghijklmnopqrstuvwxyz
6. Informal Semibold Italic
ABCDEFGHIJKLMNOPQRSTUVWXYZabcdefghijklmnopqrstuvwxyz

Fig. 9.15.

Adobe Stone Serif, Stone Sans Serif, and Bitstream Charter.

9.24 Tip

For high-quality, imaginative fonts that are a less expensive alternative to Adobe or Bitstream fonts, consider Fluent Laser Fonts™.

Casady & Greene has long been a supplier of bit-mapped and PostScript fonts for the Macintosh. Only recently have some of the exclusive Macintosh laser fonts become available for Ventura. Casady & Greene's Fluent Laser Fonts consist of 22 volumes of fonts that can be used for body text but are intended primarily as decorative or display fonts (see fig. 9.16). Each set of fonts installs easily and includes screen fonts and a printer width table. These fonts also can be used by Windows applications such as PageMaker.

1. Bodoni **Bold** *Italic* ***Bold Italic***
3. Ritz Italic Condensed Right Bank
4. Monterey Italic Medium Bold Bold Italic
5. Regency Script Calligraphy
6. Prelude Script Bold Bold Italic Light Slant
7. Coventry Script Zephyr Script
8. Gregorian Dorovar Italic
13. Gatsby Italic Demi Bold Demi Bold Italic
19. Jott Casual Italic Light Light Italic
20. Gazelle Kells Meath
22. Collegiate Black Outline

Fig. 9.16.
Samples from volumes 1 through 7 of Casady & Greene's Fluent Laser Fonts.

Each volume has from two to six font or style variations. Not only are the fonts useful and beautiful, but they are bargain priced at less than $90 per volume. Casady & Greene also offers combination sets for additional savings. If your documents require decorative fonts, Fluent Laser Fonts are hard to resist.

9.25 Tip

For special fonts that you can easily create, use Corel Newfont.

Corel Newfont is a program that allows you to create your own downloadable fonts for use with PostScript printers. Newfont is somewhat complex to use, but 82 example fonts are provided, so you should be able to create a font with the look you want.

Although the creation process is not WYSIWYG, the interactive screen is self-explanatory and the manual is straightforward. Once the fonts are created, you can print test pages of your fonts before using them with Ventura. Among the PostScript features supported by Newfont is the capacity to change the baseline slope of the font, character skew, character fill, front and back character outline density and fill, and shadow creation, offset, outline, and fill density.

Included with Newfont are numerous sample fonts identified with a number ready for use in Ventura (see fig. 9.17).

Corel also has a Draw program (see Tip 9.44) that allows you to interactively modify fonts on-screen for special headline effects. Corel Draw is a Windows program, and its output can be saved as a file that can be printed by any printer Ventura supports.

139 Bold *Italic* **Bold** ***Italic***
140 Bold *Italic* **Bold** ***Italic***
141 Bold *Italic* **Bold** ***Italic***
144 Bold *Italic* **Bold** ***Italic***
146 Bold *Italic* **Bold** ***Italic***
155 Bold *Italic* **Bold** ***Italic***

Fig. 9.17.

Sample fonts from Corel Newfont.

9.26 Tip

You can save time during printing by sending the PERMVP.PS file to your printer before starting Ventura.

The *preamble* is a file, required by PostScript printers, which is sent to the printer either once before loading a Ventura print session or as each chapter is printed.

If you want to avoid waiting every time you invoke the print command (see Chapter 10) for Ventura to send the printer preamble, you can use the DOS COPY command to load the preamble "permanently."

Insert the Utility disk into your drive and change to the POSTSCPT subdirectory. Use the DOS COPY command to copy the PERMVP.PS file to your VENTURA directory. Change to the VENTURA directory and delete the PS2.PRE file. If you don't delete the PS2.PRE file, Ventura sends a preamble each time you print, even if you load the PERMVP.PS file.

From the DOS command line, before loading Ventura, type *copy\ventura\permvp.ps prn* and press Enter. After a moment, DOS tells you the file has been copied, and your printer has the preamble "permanently" loaded —permanently until you turn off the printer. You may want to add the COPY command to your VP.BAT file.

If you delete the PS2.PRE file and forget to load the PERMVP.PS file into your printer, your printer will not print.

9.27 Tip **Ventura supplies a few special PostScript font effects when you use the PS2.EFF or PERMVP.EFF printer preamble.**

PostScript offers a variety of built-in special text effects. Ventura takes advantage of few of these effects when compared with powerhouses like GEM Artline or Corel Draw but does offer some consolation with six basic effects.

To gain access to the PostScript effects, you must change the printer preamble (see Chapter 10 for more information on printer preambles). Insert the Utility disk into your drive and change to the POSTSCPT subdirectory. Two files are of interest. If you use the PERMVP.PS preamble, copy the PERMVP.EFF file to your VENTURA directory; if you use PS2.PRE, copy the PS2.EFF file to your VENTURA directory.

Return to the VENTURA directory. Delete the old preamble file (PERMVP.PS or PS2.PRE) and rename the new preamble file (PERMVP.EFF or PS2.EFF) with the name of the old preamble file. This replaces the PS or PRE file with an EFF file that contains the instructions for the PostScript special effects.

Figure 9.18 shows the effects available in PostScript. As you can see, the effects are basic: some shading variations and 90-degree or 270-degree rotation. If you have a color monitor, the tagged text will appear in different colors, but the rotation does not show on-screen. If you are a PostScript programmer, you can edit the EFF files for different effects.

To apply the effects to text, set the paragraph's tag to one of the six colors other than white or black. You also can select text and apply color as an attribute to a portion of a paragraph. On a color monitor, the text appears in the selected color. When printed, however, the text is in the effect associated with the color. That's all there is to it.

Using Fonts with Hewlett-Packard LaserJet-Compatible Printers

More Hewlett-Packard LaserJets and compatibles (referred to as HPs) exist than any other kind of laser printer. HPs were introduced into the laser-printer market early on; these non-PostScript printers dominate the PC world of computing but have made no forays into the PostScript world of the Macintosh. When the printers were introduced, the business world was primarily text oriented. The early HPs had very limited graphics capability; they just didn't have the memory available to process images effectively.

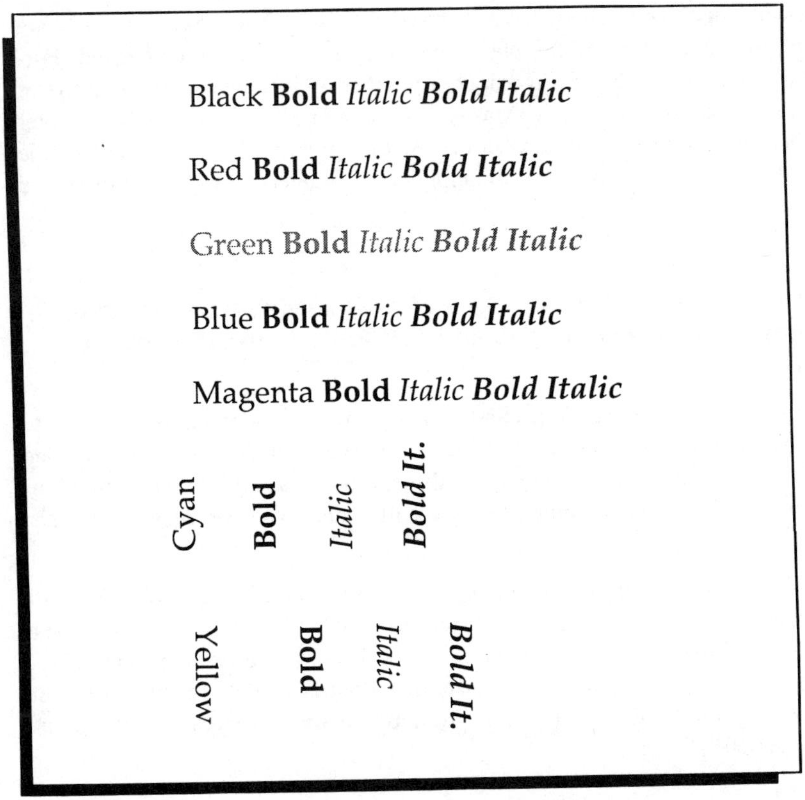

Black **Bold** *Italic* ***Bold Italic***

Red **Bold** *Italic* ***Bold Italic***

Green **Bold** *Italic* ***Bold Italic***

Blue **Bold** *Italic* ***Bold Italic***

Magenta **Bold** *Italic* ***Bold Italic***

Cyan **Bold** *Italic* ***Bold It.***

Yellow **Bold** *Italic* ***Bold It.***

Fig. 9.18.

Special PostScript effects using the EFF files. Paragraphs are set to different font "colors."

The HP comes with 512K of memory and can print Times, Helvetica, Courier, and Symbol fonts when used by Ventura Publisher. Font cartridges and soft fonts are available from HP and other vendors to expand the number of fonts produced by the printer. Up to two font cartridges can be used at one time. Downloadable fonts are available from Bitstream and other manufacturers.

The LaserJet printer is most effectively used in situations that emphasize communication over design, such as law offices, insurance companies, and corporations. In these types of environments, graphics are not used much, and communication depends on well-written documents presented in a clean and concise style. In contrast, a business that produces fliers, newsletters, advertisements, and other documents emphasizing graphic design and variety need a PostScript printer or an HP with a PostScript or LaserMaster LC2 add-on card.

The PC communicates with HP printers using Page Control Language (PCL). Fonts are generated differently for HPs than for PostScript printers. Each font size and weight must be available if it is to be used. No dynamic font scaling exists. If you need a 20-point font and none is in the cartridge or available to be downloaded, you cannot have a 20-point font. As text printers, HPs are superb; as printers for desktop publishing, they leave much to be desired. Fortunately, the aftermarket has provided a number of excellent solutions—one of which is a board from the LaserMaster Corporation that is discussed in Chapter 10. Please read through the tips in the PostScript section because most of the tips concerning Bitstream fonts can apply to HP printers as well. Just disregard any PostScript-specific information.

9.28 Tip

HP printers use either cartridges or downloadable soft fonts to generate text. Use cartridges and soft fonts to expand your font library.

Many vendors supply cartridges and soft fonts for HP printers. Some of those available are briefly described here. Cartridge vendors are not included because of the number and variety of these vendors as well as the limitations of most cartridges when compared with soft fonts (your HP dealer can assist you).

One of the most notable soft-font suppliers is Bitstream. Your copy of Ventura came with a Bitstream Fontware Installation kit and font outlines for Swiss (Helvetica), Dutch (Times), Symbol, and one weight of Bitstream Charter (see Appendix A for information about installing Bitstream fonts for the HP). You can use any of the font outline kits from Bitstream to generate fonts for use with your HP printer.

9.29 Tip

Use the Font Solution Pack from SoftCraft, Inc., to create special fonts and effects.

SoftCraft has a terrific value in the Font Solution Pack. Included are SpinFont and Font Effects, used to create special effects for headlines and logos. Also included is the SoftCraft Fontware program, with one Bitstream typeface package of your choice, that is capable of generating fonts in any size from 3 to 120 points. The package also comes with a program called WYSIFonts that can automatically create screen fonts and width tables for SoftCraft and other vendors' fonts for use with Ventura. Finally, the SoftCraft Font Editor is included, capable of editing fonts you already have or creating entirely new ones from scratch or from images scanned in PCX format. Besides being able to use Bitstream fonts, SoftCraft offers a varied library of more than 80 sets of inexpensive laser fonts of its own.

9.30 Tip

Use Digi-duit to create inexpensive fonts for the HP.

Another vendor worth mentioning is Digi-Fonts. Digi-Fonts offers a large library of inexpensive laser fonts for under $30 per font family. The basic set of eight fonts and font-generating program is called Digi-duit and sells for less than $70. With the entire collection of 33 font families (264 typefaces) available for under $350, Digi-Fonts offers a great value in fonts. Fonts can be generated in sizes from 3 to 720 points. You can specify the width, slant, and rotation of fonts and can create flipped and reversed fonts.

9.31 Trap

Software fonts for the HP use a great deal of hard disk space and RAM space on the printer.

A large collection of soft fonts in various sizes can take up much disk space, and when downloaded to the printer, these fonts use up much of the printer's memory. Depending on the amount of memory your printer has, multiple soft fonts coupled with graphics can either slow printing or generate an error message requiring you to simplify the page before it can be printed.

9.32 Trap

Different font manufacturers count their fonts differently.

When you purchase fonts, read carefully to see how the manufacturer counts the fonts. Some suppliers count all the point sizes and advertise that you get "16 fonts" when you really get only 1 font in regular and bold but in 8 point sizes. Such calculations make it sound like you're getting a great deal; when you end up with only 1 font in 2 weights you may be disappointed.

A more accurate method is for font suppliers to count fonts and not point sizes and weights when advertising. The preceding example would be more truthfully labeled "one font in regular and bold in a choice of eight point sizes."

This problem is more acute with nonscalable fonts. In the PostScript world, point sizes aren't an issue because each font can be scaled within the limits of Ventura.

Using and Understanding Screen Fonts

With the interactive nature of Ventura, you can make a change and instantly verify and assess the change on the display monitor, without having to wait for a printout. Screen fonts corresponding to the printer fonts are crucial to true WYSIWYG, interactive creation of typeset-like pages.

9.33 Tip Learn about the screen fonts provided by Ventura.

When you install Ventura, screen fonts for a serif (Times), sans serif (Helvetica), monospaced (Courier), and Symbol font are created to specifically match your display monitor. The screen-font file names begin with the letters IBME, SWIS, DUTC, COUR, or SYMB; the remaining letters of the file name designate the screen font type and point size. The file extension is EGA, VGA, and so forth, depending on your monitor type. Examples of screen font names are SWISV36N.VGA and IBMEH08I.EGA.

If you don't have fonts other than the ones provided with Ventura, you don't need additional screen fonts. If you have printer fonts from other vendors or if your printer has built-in fonts (as do PostScript printers), you may want additional screen fonts to correspond with the additional printer fonts.

Normally, the vendor of the printer font, such as Bitstream, Adobe, or Casady & Greene, either provides the screen fonts or makes it possible for you to create your own (see fig. 9.19).

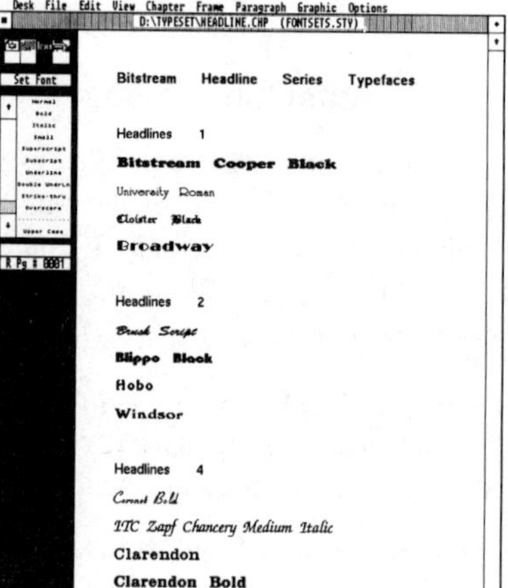

Fig. 9.19.

Screen fonts for Bitstream fonts.

If no screen fonts correspond to the selected printer fonts, Ventura substitutes generic serif or sans serif screen fonts. If you use the serif font Palatino, for example, but don't have the corresponding screen font, Ventura uses the serif Times screen font for display purposes. The correct printer font still prints, and the display is positionally accurate because the width table information for Palatino is used even though the screen font is not Palatino. Here are some reasons that you may not have screen fonts for additional printer fonts:

- ❑ The vendor didn't provide screen fonts with the printer fonts.
- ❑ You may not want to devote disk space to additional screen fonts.
- ❑ You may not want to slow down Ventura's screen redraw. The more screen fonts available, the slower Ventura loads and runs.

9.34 Tip

Put screen fonts in the VENTURA directory or the VPFONTS subdirectory.

Place screen fonts in the VENTURA directory. Alternatively, create a VENTURA subdirectory called VPFONTS and place the screen fonts there.

As you get additional fonts, you can accumulate a large collection of screen fonts. Too many screen fonts clutter the VENTURA directory and make it hard to find files. To assist with this problem, Ventura allows you to move screen fonts to a subdirectory of the VENTURA directory called VPFONTS. The VPFONTS subdirectory isn't automatically created by Ventura, so you must create the VPFONTS subdirectory with the DOS MDIR command or with a disk-management utility.

Copy all the screen fonts to the new subdirectory (don't forget to copy the Ventura-supplied generic screen fonts as well). After you are done, be sure to delete *all* the screen fonts from the VENTURA directory. Don't leave screen fonts in two directories or Ventura can become confused. Be careful not to delete the screen driver with the same extension as the screen fonts but with the prefix SD_, or else Ventura will not load. Remember, all screen fonts have the extension VGA, EGA, CGA, or something similar.

9.35 Tip

If you use a particular font only in large or small point sizes, don't install screen fonts for unused sizes.

Ventura allows you to have up to 700 screen fonts, and the maximum size allowed for any one font is 35K. If it takes a long time to load Ventura with screen fonts, change the BUFFERS statement in the CONFIG.SYS file to BUFFERS=30. Loading is also speeded up if you have more than 640K of RAM and install a disk cache (see Chapter 1).

If you use a font like Cooper Black as a display font in point sizes above 24, delete any screen-font files for point sizes less than 24. If you don't use them, why force Ventura to load them?

9.36 Tip

For best screen-font management, install screen fonts for distinctive fonts only when the screen display of those fonts will be helpful.

Many serif and sans serif fonts used for body text look similar on the screen even when different screen fonts are installed. If the difference isn't discernible on the screen, you may want to delete the extra screen fonts to free disk space and speed Ventura's loading time.

Figure 9.20 shows samples of seven screen fonts—four serif and three sans serif. If you think the screen fonts are so distinctive that you can easily distinguish between the serif fonts Palatino, Times, New Century Schoolbook, and Bookman, keep all four screen fonts on your disk. Personally, I think they look pretty much the same, except for some distinctive letters, and am willing to sacrifice absolute WYSIWYG in order to have fewer files on my hard disk and a more rapid response from Ventura.

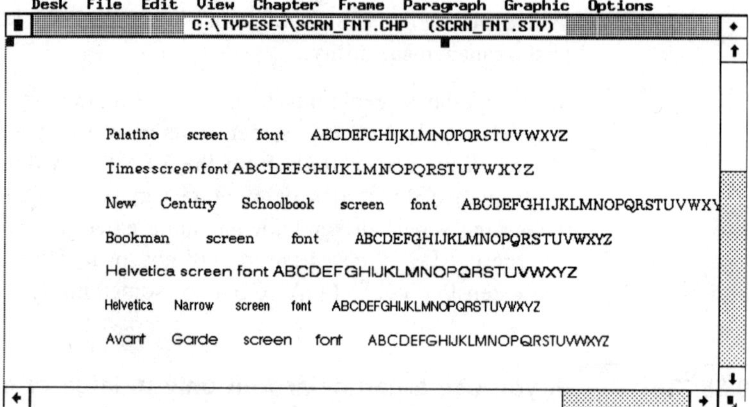

Fig. 9.20.
Seven different screen-display fonts.

The sans serif fonts in figure 9.20 are a different matter. Helvetica, Helvetica Narrow, and Avant Garde are varied enough that I want to see the differences using screen fonts.

If you wonder where to get screen fonts for the built-in Adobe fonts found on most PostScript printers, contact Ventura Publisher Users' Group (VPUG) Central at the following address:

VPUG Central
7502 Aaron Place
San Jose, CA 95139
(408) 227-5030

VPUG publishes a terrific magazine called *Ventura Professional!*, full of useful "tips, tricks, and traps." VPUG also sells a complete set of screen fonts for the built-in printer fonts of most PostScript printers for $25. Especially useful are the screen fonts for Zapf Dingbats. If you're a serious Ventura user, joining VPUG is a good idea.

9.37 Tip **Although Adobe screen fonts have the extension PSF, you can change this extension to match the extension used by your other screen fonts.**

If your screen fonts use the extension VGA, for example, and you install Adobe screen fonts with the extension PSF, change the Adobe screen fonts' extensions to match the rest of your screen fonts.

If you have screen fonts from other vendors that use lower resolution extensions—the screen font is an EGA font and you have a VGA monitor, for example—rename the font file with the VGA extension used by the rest of your screen-font files. The resolution will be lower, but the screen fonts will work just fine. Only one screen-font extension at a time is recognized by Ventura, so one way to control screen-font memory use is to have screen-font file name extensions that correspond to various printer width tables. Screen fonts with extensions other than that currently used by Ventura are not used, and generic screen fonts are substituted.

9.38 Tip **Make sure that the screen-font file name extension for new fonts matches the file name extension of existing screen fonts and the Screen Fonts field of the SET PRINTER INFO dialog box.**

If you have several printers installed, each with different sets of screen fonts, be sure that the file name extensions of any new files you add match the extensions of existing screen fonts for that particular printer. When you change from a printer using one file name extension to a printer using another file name extension, change the `Screen Fonts` field on the SET PRINTER INFO dialog box (which you access from the Options menu).

9.39 Trap **If you use the VPFONTS subdirectory, be sure to transfer the Ventura-installed screen fonts from the VENTURA directory.**

Ventura looks in only one directory for screen fonts. If you have screen fonts in both the VENTURA and VPFONTS directories, Ventura can become confused and use incorrect screen fonts.

9.40 Trick **If weird problems crop up with Ventura, delete the INF files and see whether that fixes the problem.**

When Ventura encounters screen fonts, it either checks or builds a screen-font information file. These files have INF extensions. (The VP.INF file in the VENTURA directory contains information about current style sheet, printer preference, and other settings that you change when using Ventura.) If you have a problem with display fonts, try deleting the INF files. Don't worry, the INF files are automatically rebuilt the next time Ventura is loaded. If other unusual problems crop up, try deleting the VP.INF file. Many times errors creep into this file; forcing Ventura to re-create the VP.INF file often fixes the problem you are encountering.

Deleting the INF files is the electronic equivalent of kicking or hitting something that is broken in an effort to fix it. You don't know why you do it, but it just seems to work often enough to make the effort worthwhile. Besides, it feels good just to do *something*.

9.41 Trap **If the VPFONTS subdirectory exists, some dot-matrix printers do not print text.**

For some reason, if you have a VPFONTS subdirectory, some dot-matrix printers do not print text. Graphics print fine, but text is missing. If you experience this problem, move all screen fonts to the VENTURA directory and remove the VPFONTS subdirectory.

If you create a VPFONTS directory and don't move the generic screen fonts provided by Ventura into the VPFONTS directory, you may not see correct screen display of some fonts.

Creating Special Font Effects

Ventura offers great flexibility for special font effects. If you cannot create the effect you want in Ventura, chances are that a compatible software program can allow you to do what you want. This section lists a variety of special font effects that you can achieve with Ventura and other graphics applications. One caveat: not all printers support all effects.

9.42 Tip

Use the SPECIAL EFFECTS dialog box from the Paragraph menu, the Set Font button in Text mode, or graphics to create big first characters and drop caps.

A lead paragraph in a book chapter or the lead paragraph of an article or section often has more impact with a drop cap. *Drop caps* (called *big first characters* by Ventura) are large initial letters of a paragraph that cut into the paragraph.

To create a big first character or drop cap in Ventura, do the following:

1. In Paragraph mode, tag the paragraph you want to have a drop cap. Click the Add New Tag button and create a tag called *Drop Cap*.
2. Choose Special Effects from the Paragraph menu to access the SPECIAL EFFECTS dialog box (see fig. 9.21).
3. Click `Big First Char` on the `Special Effect` line. After you click, the `Set Font Properties` and `Space for Big First` options become available for selection.
4. Click `Set Font Properties` to access the FONT SETTING FOR BIG FIRST CHARACTER dialog box. This dialog box is similar to the FONT SETTING FOR SELECTED TEXT dialog box except that there is no provision for kerning.
5. Change the font, size, style, and color to be assigned to the big first character to suit your preferences. The idea is to create a font size two or three lines tall. You can use a different font (or a dingbat or symbol) for the drop cap. Click OK or press Enter to return to the SPECIAL EFFECTS dialog box.
6. On the `Space for Big First` line is a figure that tells you how many lines the drop cap will occupy. If you don't have the luxury of many font-size choices, you can force the number of lines by clicking the `Custom` button. If, for example, you set custom to 3, the drop cap will settle on the baseline of the third line in the paragraph. If the drop-cap point size is too small for the number of custom lines you specify, the drop cap may look like a letter that fell into a pit instead of a dramatic lead-in to an important paragraph.
7. Click OK or press Enter. You may have to repeat steps 5 and 6 until you are completely satisfied.

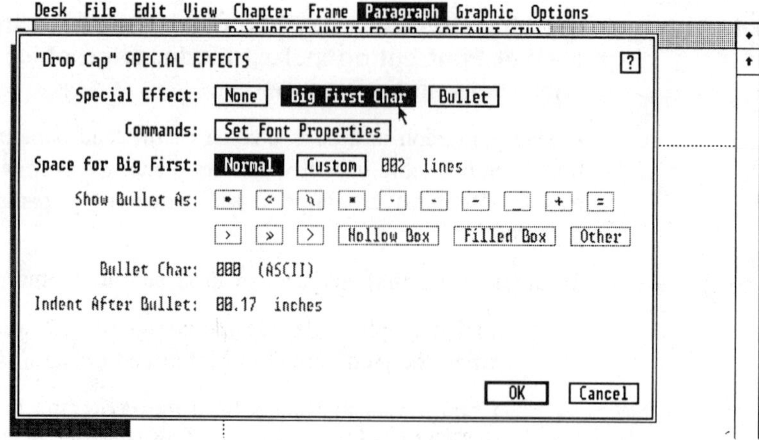

Fig. 9.21.
SPECIAL EFFECTS dialog box for big first character.

Another simple and quick way to create a large first character is to select the character in Text mode and click the Set Font button to change the point size of the first letter. If you prefer, you can hold down the Shift key and press the up-arrow key to increase the size of the selected letter in Text mode. Several presses are necessary for you to move between sizes (14 to 18, for example) when PostScript or intermediate point sizes are not available. This technique is a good way to alter the point size of more than one letter (important when the paragraph begins with a quotation mark).

If you don't have the font resources to create the sort of drop-cap paragraph you want or if you want to use exotic fonts for the big first character without purchasing an expensive font set, you can always create a frame and drop a graphic image of a letter into the frame. You can obtain exotic letter sets in PCX files from ProGraf. If you use this technique, you may want to anchor the frame to keep it from being left behind if the text moves (see Chapter 6).

Figure 9.22 shows samples of different ways you can create drop caps and the effect of different settings on the appearance of the paragraph.

9.43 Trick

Create special headline effects by using graphic lines on top of text.

Create text with white lines through it by doing the following:

1. Type a headline in a large point size (the example in fig. 9.23 was done in 48-point Adobe Stone Sans Bold).

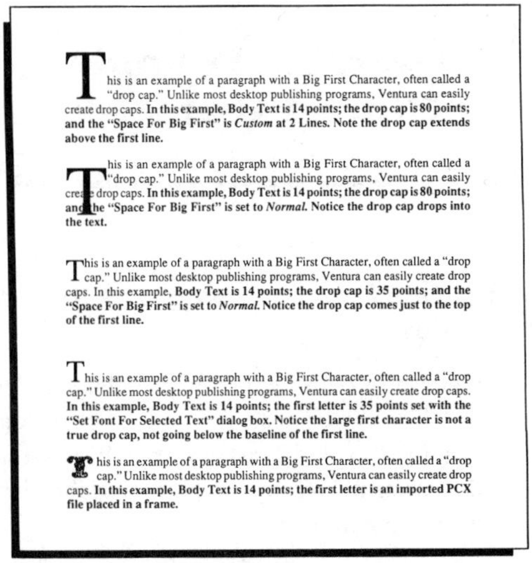

This is an example of a paragraph with a Big First Character, often called a "drop cap." Unlike most desktop publishing programs, Ventura can easily create drop caps. **In this example, Body Text is 14 points; the drop cap is 80 points; and the "Space For Big First" is *Custom* at 2 Lines. Note the drop cap extends above the first line.**

This is an example of a paragraph with a Big First Character, often called a "drop cap." Unlike most desktop publishing programs, Ventura can easily create drop caps. **In this example, Body Text is 14 points; the drop cap is 80 points; and the "Space For Big First" is set to *Normal.* Notice the drop cap drops into the text.**

This is an example of a paragraph with a Big First Character, often called a "drop cap." Unlike most desktop publishing programs, Ventura can easily create drop caps. In this example, **Body Text is 14 points; the drop cap is 35 points; and the "Space For Big First" is set to *Normal.* Notice the drop cap comes just to the top of the first line.**

This is an example of a paragraph with a Big First Character, often called a "drop cap." Unlike most desktop publishing programs, Ventura can easily create drop caps. **In this example, Body Text is 14 points; the first letter is 35 points set with the "Set Font For Selected Text" dialog box. Notice the large first character is not a true drop cap, not going below the baseline of the first line.**

This is an example of a paragraph with a Big First Character, often called a "drop cap." Unlike most desktop publishing programs, Ventura can easily create drop caps. **In this example, Body Text is 14 points; the first letter is an imported PCX file placed in a frame.**

Fig. 9.22.

Drop cap samples.

2. Change to Graphic mode and choose Grid Settings (from the Graphic menu). From the GRID SETTINGS dialog box, set `Grid Snap` to `On` and `Vertical Spacing` to 4 points.

3. Draw a line through all or part of the headline text. To do so, hold down the Alt key and drag the mouse to keep the line perfectly horizontal.

4. Continue drawing horizontal lines until lines appear every four points along the vertical height of the headline.

5. Select all the lines by choosing Select All from the Graphic menu. Alternatively, use the keyboard shortcut Ctrl-Q.

6. Choose Line Attributes from the Graphic menu (or use the keyboard shortcut Ctrl-L).

7. From the LINE ATTRIBUTES dialog box, set `Thickness` to `Custom` and to 2 points, and set `Color` to `White`. Click OK or press Enter.

8. On the screen, white lines appear through the text. Print the page to see the white lines through the text, creating an imaginative special effect. Try variations of this trick with thicker or thinner lines, fewer or more lines, vertical lines, or lines that don't go all the way through a letter (see fig. 9.23).

Fig. 9.23.
White graphic lines drawn through text for special effect.

Headline Example
Clipped Text

9.44 Tip **Use sophisticated graphics programs to create special headline fonts and logos.**

Several graphics programs described in Chapter 7 can do more than draw a pretty picture. If you ever need to create special logos, distinctive mastheads, or creative headlines, you can use either GEM Artline or Corel Draw (see fig. 9.24). Besides offering strong graphics capabilities, these programs provide sophisticated text handling.

Fig. 9.24.
Text samples from Corel Draw (top three) and GEM Artline (bottom two) produced in minutes by an amateur graphics designer (the author).

GEM Artline runs under GEM and can export files in either GEM vector (not IMG) or EPS (PostScript) format. Corel Draw runs under Windows and can export files in EPS, WMF, PCX, or TIFF format. Both programs provide graphics in formats compatible with Ventura and can be used with any printer Ventura supports.

Both programs allow you to treat text as a graphic. This capability means that you can manipulate the text in ways not possible otherwise. Table 9.5 provides a summary and comparison of the features of these two programs.

Table 9.5
Comparison of GEM Artline and Corel Draw

Feature: Fonts

GEM Artline:	Serif (4 styles), sans serif (4 styles), and Bitstream Charter (regular weight only). Allows use of any Bitstream font.
Corel Draw:	Comes with analogues of all the usual built-in PostScript fonts as well as several decorative fonts for a total of 24 typefaces in various styles.

Feature: Tracing

GEM Artline:	Allows manual tracing of IMG, PCX, and some TIFF files.
Corel Draw:	Allows autotracing of PCX and TIFF files.

Feature: Outline and Fills

GEM Artline:	Provides 16 colors and fills from 1 to 100 percent in cyan, magenta, yellow, and black. Can adjust object outline thickness and color. Provides choice of line endings (similar to Ventura).
Corel Draw:	Sophisticated halftone capability (PostScript only). Uses Pantone or cyan, magenta, yellow, and black color standards. Allows you to adjust screen angle and frequency in dots or lines (PostScript only) for various patterns. Fills from 0 to 100 percent in eight increments; fountain fills (linear or radial) with control of radial center, fountain angle, and range of color. Provides choice of 43 preset or user-customized textures (PostScript only).

Feature: Text Handling

GEM Artline:	Allows you to copy, rotate, scale, flip, mirror, skew, and shape individual letters or text blocks.
Corel Draw:	Allows you to stretch, scale, mirror, skew, shape, and rotate individual letters. Allows interactive kerning and can cause a line of text to follow a shape.

Table 9.5—*Continued*

Feature: Text Editing

GEM Artline:	Allows you to edit text that has not been changed to graphic image. Provides you with the ability to change kerning, point size, and type selection.
Corel Draw:	Allows you to edit text that has not been changed to graphic image. Provides you with the ability to change kerning, point size, and type selection. Allows you to set left, right, or center alignment.

Feature: Symbol Library

GEM Artline:	Excellent selection of symbols that can be edited or included in output.
Corel Draw:	None.

Feature: Font Changes

GEM Artline:	Provides imprecise control of outline thickness. Fill choices are limited.
Corel Draw:	Allows you to set the outline shape to appear as if drawn by calligraphic pen. Provides you with the ability to set outline type and thickness and control letter fill.

Although you can do the job well with GEM Artline, Corel Draw is a feature-laden program that isn't bogged down with a complicated user interface. Corel Draw is the program of choice. If you have access to a PostScript printer, Corel Draw is currently *the* PC program to get the most out of PostScript, but its extensive file export capability allows any Ventura-supported printer to produce stunning effects.

Another program that produces special text effects for PostScript printers is Corel Headline. With the advent of Corel Draw, however, the functions of Headline are superseded. Corel Headline is a good program and is less expensive than Corel Draw, but Headline provides no WYSIWYG display and has a less friendly feeling than Draw.

Programs that produce special text effects tailored to Hewlett-Packard LaserJets and compatibles include Spinfont and Font Effects from SoftCraft. Spinfont produces output in PCX or TIFF files and can thus be printed by any Ventura-supported printer (see fig. 9.25).

Fig. 9.25.
Using special effects.

9.45 Tip **Use Arts & Letters if you want special font effects and a clip-art library.**

The Arts & Letters Graphic Editor is a sophisticated drawing program with an extensive typeface library and clip-art collection.

With little experience, I created figure 9.26 using Arts & Letters' built-in fonts and images. This program is terrific.

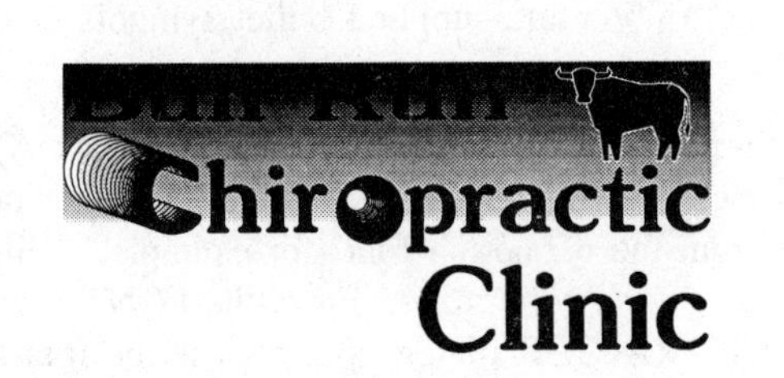

Fig. 9.26.
A logo created with the Arts & Letters Graphic Editor.

9.46 Tip

Use the SPECIAL EFFECTS dialog box from the Paragraph menu to create bullets.

A *bullet* is a small circle appearing to the left of a paragraph that sets the paragraph apart from surrounding text. With Ventura, creating bullets is easy—and you are not restricted to small circles. You can use any of the 15 Ventura-supplied characters or any character from the fonts you have available as a bullet. To create a bullet, do the following:

1. In paragraph mode, select the paragraph you want to have a bullet. Click the Add New Tag button and give the tag a name like *Bullet*.

2. Choose the Special Effects command from the Paragraph menu. On the SPECIAL EFFECTS dialog box, click `Bullet` (see fig. 9.27).

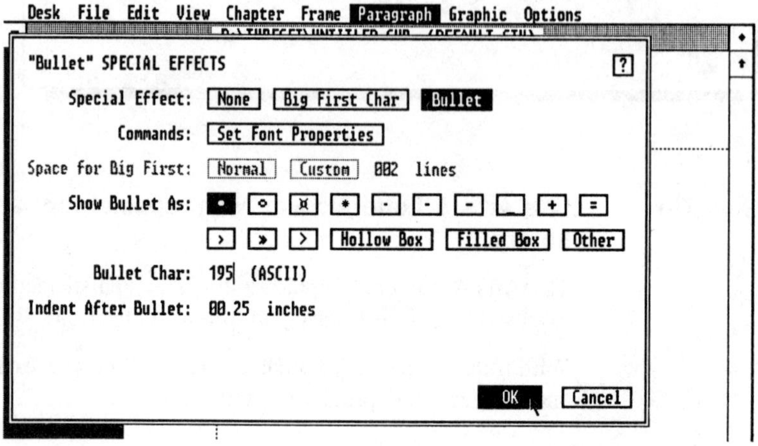

Fig. 9.27.
The SPECIAL EFFECTS dialog box for bullets.

3. Choose one of the 15 Ventura-supplied bullet symbols or click `Other`.

   If you select `Other`, type the ASCII code (see Appendix A) for the character of your choice. If you want the bullet character in a font that is different from the paragraph font (for example, a dingbat or symbol), click `Set Font Properties`. From the FONT SETTING FOR BULLET CHARACTER dialog box, choose the font and change the point size, style, and color. Click OK or press Enter.

4. The `Indent After Bullet` value specifies how much the paragraph (not just the first line) is indented from the bullet. If you make the bullet character much larger than the point size of the paragraph font, you may have to increase the indent. Click OK or press Enter.

Figure 9.28 shows some examples of different bullet ideas.

☐ Hollow box used as a bullet.

☞ Dingbat used as a bullet.

⇒ Symbol used as a bullet.

• Bullet used as a bullet.

Fig. 9.28.

Examples of different bullets.

9.47 Tip **If your printer supports rotated text, use the Text Rotation feature on the ALIGNMENT dialog box from the Paragraph menu.**

The `Text Rotation` option in Ventura is on the ALIGNMENT dialog box, which you access from the Paragraph menu. This means that text rotation affects an entire paragraph. A special paragraph tag, therefore, must be created to rotate text. You can rotate text in 90-degree increments, so text cannot be sloped at just any angle. Finally, some printers cannot print in both landscape and portrait orientation at the same time, and text rotation doesn't work at all.

Text rotation is good for use in tables, when annotating charts, and so forth. You can go crazy trying to figure out where rotated text appears on the page unless you first create a frame and then put the text in the frame. Keeping the text in a frame allows you to move the frame to position the rotated text correctly. You also can anchor the frame to keep it where you want it. To implement text rotation, do the following:

1. Create a paragraph tag for the paragraph you want to rotate.
2. Choose Alignment from the Paragraph menu.
3. From the ALIGNMENT dialog box, select the degree of `Text Rotation`. The choices are `None`, `90`, `180`, and `270` (see fig. 9.29). Click OK or press Enter.
4. If the text is in a frame, you can now resize the frame to accommodate the new shape of the rotated text. If you leave the rotated text on the underlying page, you may need to change the `Maximum Rotated Height` value in the ALIGNMENT dialog box to clear space for the rotated text.

Creating Special Characters in Ventura

You can use special characters to add interest to your publication. Ventura lets you specify special characters in several ways, which are described in this section.

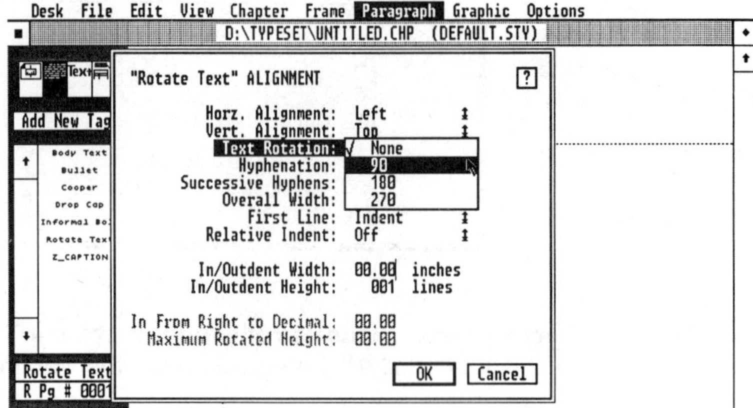

Fig. 9.29.
The ALIGNMENT dialog box with rotated text options.

9.48 Tip

Use the Alt key and the numeric keypad to create special characters.

The Ventura character set is richer than just the letters you see on your keyboard. Appendix A gives a chart with all the characters available in Ventura. To produce these special characters, find the desired character in the *Roman* column and make a note of the number in the *Decimal* column. In your document at the place you want to insert the special character, hold down the Alt key and type the decimal-column number on the numeric keypad. Don't use the numbers on the top of the keyboard; they will not work.

9.49 Tip

If you use Text mode to enter foreign characters frequently, consider a utility like IK.COM from Corel.

One of the programs in the Corel Ventura Utilities package is IK.COM. Insert the Corel Utilities disk and type *ik* on the DOS command line to run IK.COM just before loading Ventura; IK then waits in the background to help you enter foreign characters.

If you want to enter the character í with IK loaded, for example, just type *'i*. IK creates the letter *i* with an acute accent. Similar convenience is added for letters with grave accents, umlauts, ligatures, tildes, and so forth.

Of course, all these characters are accessible with the Alt key and numeric keypad, but if you enter many foreign characters, IK saves you time.

9.50 Tip

Use the Alt key and the numeric keypad to access either the Symbol or the Zapf Dingbat character sets.

In Appendix A, notice that are two special character sets are available; one is the Symbol character set, and the other is the Zapf Dingbat character set. The Symbol font is available for all printers; the Zapf Dingbat set is only available for PostScript printers (the font must be built in or purchased for downloading).

You can use the Symbol or Zapf Dingbat character set in one of three ways:

- ❑ While in Text mode, type the letter (if it is available on the keyboard) or the decimal number (using the Alt key and the numeric keypad). Once the character is entered, select the character and click the Set Font button. From the FONT SETTING FOR SELECTED TEXT dialog box, change the font to either Symbol or Zapf Dingbat. (If you select a Zapf Dingbat and have the Zapf Dingbat screen font, the character on the screen changes appropriately. If you don't have the screen font, the character on the screen looks the same as it did before you changed the font but prints correctly.)
- ❑ If an entire paragraph consists of Symbol or Zapf Dingbat characters (as it may if you use the character as a lead-in and combine it with appropriate breaks), you can change the font for the paragraph tag to Symbol or Zapf Dingbat.
- ❑ You also can use Symbols or Zapf Dingbats as bullets.

9.51 Tip

Use the Fraction function to create fractions.

You can create true fractions in Ventura. To create fractions, do the following steps:

1. In Text mode, insert the cursor where you want the fraction to appear.
2. Choose Ins Special Item from the Edit menu or press the keyboard shortcut Ctrl-C.
3. On the INSERT SPECIAL ITEM dialog box, click `Fraction` or press F4 (see fig. 9.30).
4. A special fraction-editing screen appears. Select Choose Fraction Text from the Edit menu or use the Ctrl-C keyboard shortcut.

5. A small dialog box appears with the option of two types of fractions—those with diagonal bars (F1) or those with horizontal bars (F2). Make your choice by clicking your preference or pressing F1 or F2.

6. On the editing screen, you see either `1/2` or ½. Edit the numbers to create the desired fraction; after a few seconds, the correct fraction appears below the double line.

   Alternatively, without using the F1 or F2 template (as you did in step 5), you can type the desired fraction in the format *1/2* or *9/16*; the fraction appears below the double line with a diagonal bar. If you want fractions with a horizontal bar, type the desired fraction in the format *1 over 2* or *9 over 16*; after a few seconds, the fraction appears below the double line with a horizontal bar. Be sure that you remember to put spaces on either side of the word *over*.

7. Choose Exit Fraction Editing from the Edit menu or press the keyboard shortcut Ctrl-D.

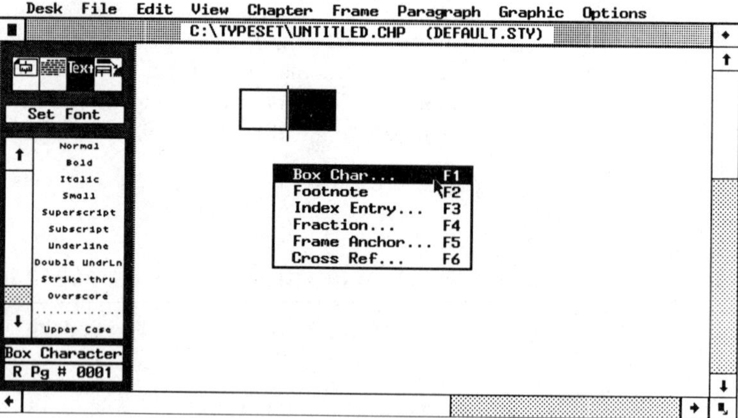

Fig. 9.30.

The INSERT SPECIAL ITEM dialog box with Box Character showing on-screen.

To delete the fraction, move the cursor until you see the word `Fraction` in the current selection box and then press the Del key.

If you require more sophisticated mathematical equation editing, consider purchasing the Professional Extension (see Chapter 12). The Professional Extension offers extensive formatting options for scientific equations that work much like the fraction-editing option just presented.

9.52 Tip **Use the Box Character function to create hollow or filled boxes.**

Some font sets like Zapf Dingbats have boxes available as special characters (see Appendix A). Zapf Dingbat boxes are either solid black squares or have a shadow behind them. Ventura provides hollow and solid boxes called *box characters*. To create a box character, do the following:

1. In Text mode, position the cursor where you want the box character to be inserted.
2. Choose Ins Special Item from the Edit menu or use the keyboard shortcut Ctrl-C to access the INSERT SPECIAL ITEM dialog box (see fig. 9.30).
3. Click `Box Char` or press F1.
4. Choose either `Hollow` or `Filled` from the dialog box that appears.

A hollow or filled box in the current point size appears on the screen. The boxes do not have shadows and can be used as dingbats or as check-off or ballot boxes. You can change the size of the box by selecting the box and using the Set Font function. To delete the box character, position the cursor until the words `Box Character` appear in the current selection box and press Del.

Note that either fractions or box characters can be selected in Text mode and have text attributes (including point size) applied.

Chapter Summary

This chapter covered a great deal of material. You learned about the three major classes of fonts: dot-matrix, PostScript laser, and Hewlett-Packard LaserJet-compatible laser. In each of those categories, you saw samples of fonts from many different font manufacturers.

You learned about printer fonts and screen fonts, how to install them, and how to manage them. This chapter also covered special font effects that you can use to enhance the look of your document. The last section covered the use and creation of special characters.

Chapter 10 explains how to print the document you have worked on for the last nine chapters.

Chapter

10

Proofing and Printing Your Chapter

Printing is what desktop publishing is all about. After all, the end product of all your efforts and the concrete evidence of your labor, your writing and editing, your graphics ability, and your design skills ends up on the sheet of paper kicked out by your printer after you click OK on the PRINT INFORMATION dialog box.

Because Ventura is a WYSIWYG system, you already have a good idea what your printed document will look like, but "seeing is believing" and holding the printed result of your efforts is both fun and rewarding.

This chapter concentrates on the options associated with printing and proofing your work.

Printing Your Work

Before you print your document, you should know a little about the types of printers that are available for use with Ventura. You also should become familiar with the PRINT INFORMATION dialog box from which you give Ventura all the information needed to print your document. The tips in this section provide this information.

10.1 Tip

Learn which printers Ventura supports and the capabilities and limitations of your printer.

Ventura directly supports a number of printers and compatibles. Third-party vendors support hundreds more. If you cannot find support for your printer directly from Ventura, contact the manufacturer of your printer to see whether he or she has developed drivers to enable your printer to work with Ventura. Another option is to contact Atech (see the entry in table 10.1 for unsupported printers).

Table 10.1 provides information about printers, their capabilities, and their limitations.

Table 10.1
Printer Capabilities and Limitations

Epson MX-80, FX-80, RX-80, LQ-1500; IBM ProPrinter; Toshiba; and compatibles

120-by-144-dpi (9-pin) to 180-by-180-dpi (24-pin) resolution. Can print text and graphic lines only in black, not gray.

Hewlett-Packard LaserJet and compatibles

300-dpi text and 75-dpi graphics resolution. Cannot use Ventura's included downloadable fonts; can use only the HP 92286F cartridge.

Hewlett-Packard LaserJet Plus, LaserJet II, LaserJet 2000, and compatibles

300-dpi text and either 150-dpi or 300-dpi graphics resolution, depending on driver installed. May run out of memory and not print properly if too many fonts are used, if the fonts are too large, or if too many graphics are used. Cannot print landscape and portrait in same pass. Cannot print reverse text. Cannot print larger than 36-point fonts. Cannot print pictures that cover underlying text. Can only print text and graphic lines in black, not gray.

Interpress

Cannot print reverse text. Can print text and graphic lines only in black, not gray. Cannot print pictures that cover underlying text or picture. May run out of memory if the page is too complex. Resolution depends on the Interpress device.

Table 10.1—*Continued*

JLaser

300-dpi resolution. Cannot print larger than 30-point fonts. Cannot print to file. Can only print text and graphic lines in black, not gray.

PostScript

300-dpi to 2,540-dpi resolution depending on output device (laser printer or typesetter). If pictures overlap, picture on the bottom is blocked. Cannot print ruling box around an image.

Xerox 4045 Laser

300-dpi resolution. Does not print pictures containing rotated text. Does not print reverse text. Can only print text or graphic lines in black, not gray. Approximately 40 points maximum size for fonts. May run out of memory and not print if too many fonts, too large a font, or too many graphics appear on single page.

Xerox 4020 Color Ink Jet

120-dpi resolution. Can print up to 8 colors. Cannot mix colors by overlapping. Can only print text or graphic lines in 100 percent color, not gray or shades.

Unsupported printers

Publisher's Powerpak from Atech (see Chapter 9) offers support for more than 200 printers not directly supported by Ventura. In addition, Publisher's Powerpak adds font-scaling capability to many supported printers that do not normally offer that feature.

10.2 Tip **To print all or part of a chapter, choose To Print from the File menu.**

To protect your work, before printing, *always* save your chapter by choosing Save or Save As from the File menu (for Save, you can use the keyboard shortcut Ctrl-S). If your chapter hasn't been named, you are prompted to name the chapter.

When you are ready to print all or part of a chapter, choose To Print from the File menu to access the PRINT INFORMATION dialog box (see fig. 10.1). Examine table 10.2 for information about each of the items in the dialog box.

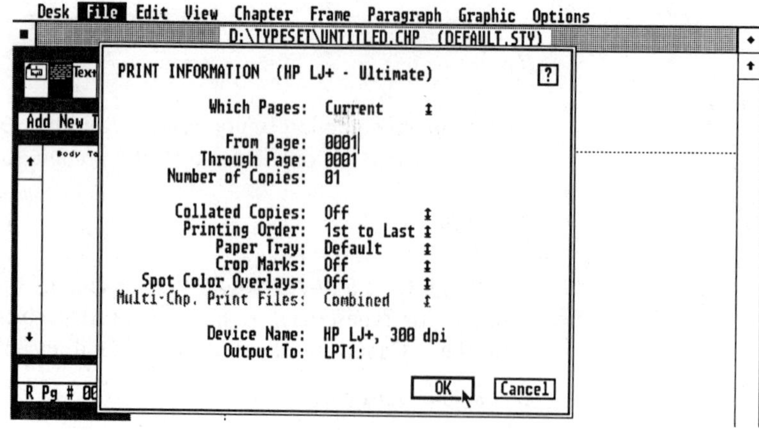

Fig. 10.1.

The PRINT INFORMATION dialog box.

Table 10.2
PRINT INFORMATION Dialog Box Settings

Item	*Options*
Print Information	This option lists the selected printer driver chosen from the SET PRINTER INFO dialog box. If the printer and the width table correspond, the word `Ultimate` appears after the printer name at the top of the box. If the width table doesn't match the printer, the word is `Draft`. You cannot change the printer or width table from this dialog box.
Which Pages	Options are `All` (prints all pages), `Selected` (prints the specified pages), `Left` or `Right` (prints only the left or right pages if the PAGE LAYOUT dialog box has `Sides` set to `Double`), or `Current` (prints the page currently on-screen).
From Page and Through Page	Enter the range of pages to be printed from first to last.
Number of Copies	Specify a number from 1 to 9,999. If the number is not 1, multiple copies are printed. The copies are not collated unless `Collated Copies` is set to `On`.

Table 10.2—*Continued*

Item	*Options*
Collated Copies	Options are `Off` or `On`. If collating is set to `On` and more than one copy is to be printed, one complete copy of selected pages is printed before the next copy is started. Collating this way can take more time, especially on laser printers where printing a page can take quite awhile. If `Collated Copies` is set to `Off`, each page is printed the specified number of times before the next page is started; printing is as fast as the printer is capable.
Printing Order	Choices are `1st to Last` or `Last to 1st`. If your printer stacks printed pages in order face up, set `Printing Order` to `Last to 1st`. That way, the pages are in correct order when the printing is finished. If your printer stacks printed pages so that they are automatically stacked in correct order, set `Printing Order` to `1st to Last`.
Paper Tray	Options are `Default`, `Alt #1`, `Alt #2`, or `Manual`. For printers without multiple paper bins, leave the setting at `Default`. If you have multiple bins, depending on your printer, you may be able to choose `Alt #1` or `Alt #2` to access the bins. If your printer has a manual-feed slot or if you want to feed the paper one page at a time, choose `Manual`.
Crop Marks	Options are `On` or `Off`. Crop marks are used by typesetters to line up pages for printing large quantities. If you set the page size smaller than your paper, crop marks are printed.
Spot Color Overlays	Options are `Off` or `On`. If you have defined and applied colors to graphics or text, set `Spot Color Overlays` to `On`. Ventura prints a separate page for each of the eight colors. The color name is listed at the top of the page. Your print shop can use these pages to create multiple colors during printing. Be warned that

Table 10.2—*Continued*

Item	*Options*
	Ventura prints all eight pages even if you have defined only two colors. Once chosen, Ventura offers you a last chance to print only one page or cancel printing altogether.
Multi-Chp. Print Files	Choose `Combined` or `Separate`. This option is available only if you set `Output: Filename` in the SET PRINTER INFO dialog box and are printing a publication from the MULTI-CHAPTER OPERATIONS dialog box. When you select Print, you access the PRINT INFORMATION dialog box to set printing preferences. Choose `Combined` if you want the entire publication to be placed in one file; if you want each chapter in its own file, choose `Separate`. See Chapter 11 for more information on printing publications.
Device Name and Output To	Both device and output are specified in the SET PRINTER INFO dialog box and cannot be changed from this dialog box. If either are incorrect, change them by using the SET PRINTER INFO dialog box. If `Output To` is set to `Filename`, you are prompted to enter a file name when you click OK to begin printing.

Using Laser Printers

Although Ventura can print to dot-matrix printers, best results are obtained from laser printers. Because laser printers are so flexible, they also can be more complicated to control. The tips, tricks, and traps in this section help you manage your laser printer.

10.3 Tip

If you use a Hewlett-Packard LaserJet or compatible or PostScript printer, verify that the CNF file contains the correct information.

Both HP and PostScript printers use a configuration (CNF) file that provides information such as where downloadable fonts are located. For HP printers, the file is HPLJPLUS.CNF; for PostScript printers, the file is POSTSCPT.CNF. The CNF file is in ASCII format (so you can edit it) and is located in the VENTURA directory.

The HPLJPLUS.CNF file has as its first four lines

```
downpath(C:\SOFTFONT\)
permfont(1 EXAMPLE1.SFP)
permfont(2 EXAMPLE2.SFP)
fontspec(HELVTINY,2,2,0,0)
```

The `downpath` line contains the path of the directory in which you plan to store any downloadable soft fonts. You can have only one soft-font directory, so be sure that all soft fonts are stored in the same directory and that the CNF file lists the correct path for the directory. The `permfont` line contains the name of any soft font you want permanently downloaded. The number you supply specifies the order of the downloading. You can have multiple `permfont` lines depending on your printer's memory capacity.

If you have at least 1M of memory available on your printer, you can use the HPDOWN utility supplied by Ventura to download soft fonts to your printer before you run Ventura.

After you specify the `permfont` in the HPLJPLUS.CNF file, you can copy the HPDOWN utility from the Ventura utility disk into your VENTURA directory. While your printer is on but before loading Ventura, type *hpdown*, and the fonts specified in the HPLJPLUS.CNF file are downloaded to LPT1. If you want them sent to another port, specify it (for example, LPT2).

If you are downloading fonts, remember to change the width table from the ADD/REMOVE FONTS dialog box (accessed from the Options menu) so the downloaded fonts are specified as resident.

The `fontspec` line contains the name of any font to be used as a draft substitute for fonts used on the ultimate typesetting device. Each `fontspec` must have its own line. ***Note:*** the words "downpath" and "permfont" must be all lowercase to work properly. On the `permfont` line, you must include a space after the font ID number. For example, use

permfont(2 EXAMPLE2.SFP)

rather than

permfont(2EXAMPLE2.SFP)

If you ultimately use a PostScript printer, for example, but proof your document on an HP LaserJet, set the width table to POSTSCPT and the printer to HP LJ+ in the SET PRINTER INFO dialog box. If you want to print your document in Palatino on the PostScript printer, you have two choices of typefaces used in the HP draft: if no `fontspec` is specified in the CNF file, the HP defaults to the serif font Dutch (Times); if you specify a substitute `fontspec`, the HP uses the substituted font.

The name of the substitute font (`fontspec`) is followed by four digits, each separated by commas (no spaces between commas). The digits represent, in order the following:

- The typeface ID number for the font you are trying to match (see your Ventura manual for a list of typeface font ID numbers). In most cases, especially if you use a PostScript printer for final output, the ID numbers should work.
- The point size
- Style attribute where 0=normal, 1=medium, 2=bold, 5=italic, 6=bold italic
- 0

The POSTSCPT.CNF file has the following information:

```
psfonts(c:\psfonts\)
eoftype(PC)     ; PC or Mac (choose one or the other)
imgtype(FAST)   ; FAST or COMPACT (choose one or the other)
coltype(COLOR) ; GRAY or COLOR (choose one or the other)
font(AvantGarde-Book,51,M,TEXT,RES)
etc.
```

The `psfonts` line tells Ventura in which directory to look for any downloadable PostScript fonts. Because Adobe requires that the directory be named PSFONTS, you may as well leave the name of the directory alone; just be sure to store all your printer fonts in whatever directory you specify on this line. Whenever you reinstall Ventura and reinstall a PostScript printer, this CNF file is overwritten. If this happens, be sure that the `psfonts` line specifies your actual font directory location and name.

If you print on an Apple network, set the `eoftype` line to `Mac`; otherwise, leave it at `PC`.

If you print to disk, you may want to have the resultant PostScript file as compact as possible. Because PostScript files can be large, especially if they contain images, changing the `imgtype` line to `COMPACT` reduces the size of the file but slows printing. Unless you are printing to file, leave the `imgtype` line set to `FAST`.

If you use a color printer, change the `coltype` line to `COLOR`; otherwise, leave it `GRAY`.

The `font` line involves font substitution as on the HP. Read the section in this tip on HP `fontspecs` for information about changing these settings. The format is as follows:

Fontname,ID,Style,Character,Location

No spaces separate the items. The following list briefly explains the items:

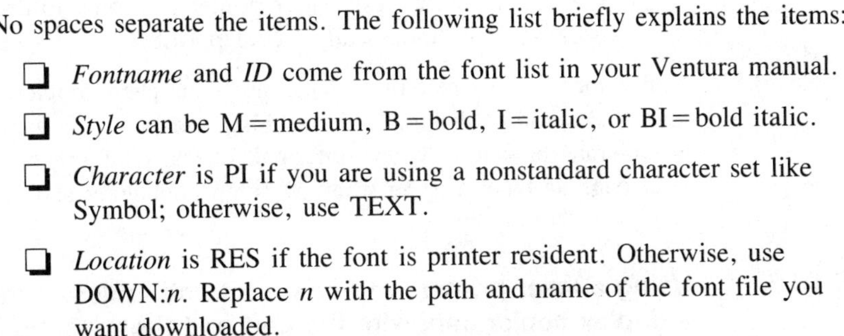

- ❑ *Fontname* and *ID* come from the font list in your Ventura manual.
- ❑ *Style* can be M = medium, B = bold, I = italic, or BI = bold italic.
- ❑ *Character* is PI if you are using a nonstandard character set like Symbol; otherwise, use TEXT.
- ❑ *Location* is RES if the font is printer resident. Otherwise, use DOWN:*n*. Replace *n* with the path and name of the font file you want downloaded.

This information about font substitution may not be used by most users. You should make sure, however, that all downloadable fonts are in the same directory and that the CNF file lists the correct path for that directory.

You can download PostScript fonts before starting Ventura. Use the utility that comes with your Adobe fonts or a program like Corel Loader to download the fonts. How many fonts you can download depends on your printer's memory capacity. Once the fonts are downloaded, start Ventura. The downloaded fonts will act like resident or built-in fonts (until you turn off your printer), so you need to access the ADD/REMOVE FONTS dialog box and change the affected fonts from `Download` to `Resident`.

10.4 Trap

Depending on the complexity of the page, laser printers can take time—often a great deal of time—to print.

Imagine my surprise. I just purchased a terrific laser printer that promised to print eight pages a minute. The first page I tried to print was one with graphics and several font changes. I waited and waited and waited. Finally, after 15 minutes, the page appeared from the printer. Beautiful, but slow.

Laser printers rated at eight or more pages per minute are common, but your printer achieves that rate of output only after the first of multiple copies (one reason not to use the `Collated Copies` feature). Pages with text using only built-in fonts print steadily and fairly close to the rated output per minute. Pages with multiple font changes—even with built-in fonts—are slower to print. Pages with multiple downloaded fonts requiring extensive memory swapping, or pages loaded with pictures, take a long time to print—sometimes as long as 20 or 30 minutes. During printing time, your computer is tied up.

You can improve this speed bottleneck in two ways:

- ❑ Use LaserTORQ or another print spooler to spool your files. Although printing still takes time, you can use your computer (see Tip 10.7).
- ❑ Use LaserMaster's LC2 laser printer controller to decrease the printing time dramatically (see Tip 10.8).

Notice that I don't recommend making your page simpler. One of the great joys of desktop publishing is doing things the way you want. Unless you cannot tolerate the wait or your printer balks because of a memory overload, make your page as fancy as you want. Desktop publishing should be fun, after all.

10.5 Trick

Using a laser printer, you can print both sides of the page, just as a duplex copier can, with the Left and Right pages feature.

You can print both sides of a page by setting `Sides` to `Double` in the PAGE LAYOUT dialog box and then setting `Which Pages` to `Left` (if the chapter begins on a right page) or `Which Pages` to `Right` (if the chapter begins on a left page) in the PRINT INFORMATION dialog box. Set `Printing Order` so that the pages come out in proper order.

After printing all of one side, ''fan'' the pages to reduce static buildup that could cause the pages to stick together; then turn the pages over and put them back in the printer's paper tray. Change the `Which Pages` setting to the opposite of what you initially set and print again.

Some printer manufacturers don't recommend putting paper with printing already on it back into the printer. Look over your printer manual to see whether your printer can tolerate duplex printing.

10.6 Tip

If you have a PostScript printer, use the appropriate PS2.PRE or PERMVP.PS files to send setup information to your printer.

PostScript printers require a *preamble* to know how to process a file. When you install a PostScript printer for Ventura, the PS2.PRE file is automatically copied to your VENTURA directory. Whenever you issue the To Print command, Ventura first sends the PS2.PRE file to your PostScript printer. The loading of PS2.PRE each time you print takes time. You can permanently load a PostScript preamble at the beginning of each Ventura session by doing the following steps (the assumption here is that you have a working knowledge of DOS commands):

1. Place the Ventura Utilities disk into your floppy drive. Change to the POSTSCPT subdirectory of the Ventura Utilities disk.

2. Copy the PERMVP.PS file on the Ventura Utilities disk to your VENTURA directory.

3. Go back to the VENTURA directory and delete the PS2.PRE file.

4. Add the following line to your VP.BAT file:

   COPY C:\VENTURA\PERMVP.PS PRN

   Alternatively, you can type in this command before loading Ventura. This command loads the PERMVP.PS preamble into your PostScript printer before you start Ventura. Once it is loaded, and without the PS2.PRE file in the VENTURA directory, printing goes faster because you no longer wait for the preamble to be loaded each time you print.

To take advantage of the PostScript special effects mentioned in Chapter 9, replace the PS2.PRE or the PERMVP.PS files with the PS2.EFF or the PERMVP.EFF files found on the Ventura Utilities disk. Once they're copied, rename PS2.EFF to PS2.PRE. You don't have to rename PERMVP.EFF, but if you use a line in the VP.BAT file to load the permanent preamble, modify the VP.BAT file with the correct PERMVP file name (match the correct extensions).

Warning: If you print pages or chapters to disk, you must have the PS2.PRE file in the VENTURA directory to insert the PostScript preamble properly at the beginning of each disk file. If the preamble isn't in the file (or downloaded prior to printing), the files do not print properly with the technique described in Tip 10.14.

10.7 Tip

Use LaserTORQ from LaserTools Corporation to speed printing and allow you to use your computer while your document is printing.

When you print a document, you normally lose the use of your computer. If you print a Ventura page that takes your printer 3 1/2 minutes to print, for example, you have to wait until the 3 1/2 minutes are up before you can begin your next Ventura project or use another program. You spend a great deal of that time waiting because the printer's memory is full and unable to accept any more data. While the printer processes data, your computer has to wait until more data can be fed to the printer.

Good news: You don't have to wait any more if you use the indispensable utility LaserTORQ from LaserTools Corporation. LaserTORQ uses part of your hard disk, RAM disk, or extended or expanded memory as a print buffer. When you print from Ventura (or any other application), instead of the document going directly to the printer, the document goes to the print buffer to be managed by LaserTORQ. It only takes seconds to send large files to the buffer. In a test, for example, it took about 15 seconds to print a 274K file to the buffer; it took more than 3 additional minutes before the document came out of an HP LaserJet II. But after the first 15 seconds, I had my computer back. LaserTORQ handled the printing of the document in the background.

PostScript printers offer similar time savings. Although LaserTORQ works with dot-matrix printers, you can use TORQ if you only print to dot-matrix printers. TORQ does everything LaserTORQ does except support laser printers. The time you save using either of these print spooler/accelerators quickly repays the expense of the program.

Trading Post is another utility offered by LaserTools for PostScript printers is Trading Post. Trading Post allows software that produces text to use your PostScript printer even if the program normally doesn't support PostScript. Trading Post is a real help for users of accounting programs or dBASE III Plus that don't normally allow the use of a PostScript printer. Trading Post also can change the speed at which a serial PostScript printer can accept data. An Apple LaserWriter Plus normally accepts data at 9,600 baud (a measurement of speed). With Trading Post, I was able to boost the throughput speed to 38,400 baud. Having laser printers hooked into your network also speeds up printing. Spoolers are a normal part of Novell and 3-Com.

10.8 Trick

To speed printing dramatically or add Page Description Language (PDL) capabilities to Hewlett-Packard LaserJet-compatible printers, consider using the LaserMaster LC2 card.

The problem with Printer Control Language (PCL) printers like the HP series and PostScript or Interpress (PDL) printers like the Apple LaserWriter series is that printing complex pages with mixed fonts and graphics can take a long time.

The LaserMaster Corporation has developed an alternative to the HP and PostScript system for laser printers called the LC2 LaserMaster Controller. Slipping into a slot on your PC, the LC2 card has 2 megabytes of memory dedicated to image and font processing. The LC2 uses Bitstream font outlines and comes with 13 or 35 fonts (depending on price) to emulate the reduced or enhanced font sets available with most PostScript printers. The fonts can be scaled just as with PostScript printers. In addition, you can add any fonts from the Bitstream Fontware library. The LaserMaster LC2 card can be used with most laser printers on the market today, including PostScript printers; if used with a PostScript printer, however, the PostScript capabilities are overridden when the LC2 card is used.

The two major advantages that the LC2 gives HP printers are speed and font scaling. If used with a PostScript printer, the LC2 provides additional speed. Look at table 10.3 for comparisons of the print times necessary to print the Scoop page provided with your Ventura package. As you can see, the LC2 is *much* faster. In printing, speed doesn't kill; speed saves time.

Table 10.3
Print Time Comparisons

Time To Print	*Printer Specifications*
35 seconds	Apple LaserWriter Plus with LaserMaster LC2 card
127 seconds	HP LaserJet II (parallel)
148 seconds	Apple LaserWriter Plus (serial at 38,400 baud)
310 seconds	Apple LaserWriter Plus (serial at 9,600 baud)

Additionally, the LC2 provides drivers for other GEM and Windows applications as well as HP emulation (for applications that don't directly support the LC2 card). With the LC2 card and Ventura, you can do special effects such as point sizes greater than 254 points and pattern-fill characters; you also can rotate, angle, stretch, or invert characters.

Before you run out and buy an LC2 card, think about several things: because most applications do not have printer drivers for the LC2, you must often fall back on HP emulation or a PostScript translator called LM-Page provided by LaserMaster. Also, because the LC2 is not PostScript compatible, EPS graphics and fonts from vendors other than Bitstream are not supported. You can print EPS files using the LM-Page translator, but many of the speed benefits of the LC2 are then sacrificed. A final caution: the LC2 is expensive. If you already own a PostScript printer, the cost of the LC2 is hard to justify for the speed benefits alone; PostScript already scales fonts and does font special effects, and it has a greater variety of fonts available, better compatibility, portability to high-resolution printers, and the capacity to print EPS graphics. If you don't own a PostScript printer, the choice is less easy, but you will probably conclude that, for desktop publishing, you should get either a PostScript emulator board or the LC2. (The cost of a Hewlett-Packard LaserJet-compatible printer plus the LC2 board is about the same as the cost of a PostScript printer.) Desktop publishing on a PCL printer is too frustrating to be endured for long.

If you use your computer primarily for desktop publishing, the appeal of speed is alluring. Unless or until PostScript responds with faster output than is currently available, the LaserMaster LC2 deserves serious consideration.

10.9 Tip

Use the large-page printing capabilities of Ventura for large pages or broadsheets. You also can shrink copy to increase resolution.

Ventura supports paper sizes larger than 8 1/2 inches by 11 inches or 8 1/2 inches by 14 inches. If you set a page size of 11 inches by 17 inches (a double 8 1/2-by-11-inch page) from the PAGE LAYOUT dialog box (accessed from the Chapter menu), before printing begins, you are prompted to choose from three options:

- *Shrink* to 8 1/2 inches by 11 inches from 11 inches by 17 inches if you have a PostScript printer.
- *Overlap* four 8 1/2-by-11-inch pages to form an 11-by-17-inch page by pasting the pages together.
- *Nothing* if your printer really *can* print 11-by-17-inch pages.

If you set a page size of 18 inches by 24 inches (`Broadsheet`) from the PAGE LAYOUT dialog box, before printing begins, you are prompted to choose from three options:

- *Shrink* to 8 1/2 inches by 11 inches from 18 inches by 24 inches if you have a PostScript printer.
- *Print in strips* (three 8-inch strips, four overlapping 11-by-17-inch pages, or nine overlapping 8 1/2-by-11-inch pages) if you print to a typesetting machine such as a Linotronic.
- *Nothing* if your system really *can* print 18-by-24-inch pages.

10.10 Tip

To increase resolution of your final document, you can have your print shop shrink the document.

The concept of shrinking can be applied in another way. If you want to create a business card, for example, you can increase the effective dpi. A business card typically measures 3 1/2 inches by 2 inches. In Ventura, create a frame 7 inches by 4 inches (twice the size of a business card). If you ultimately want 10-point type, double the type to 20 points; if you want 2-point rules, double the size to 4 points; and so on. Print the image on a 300-dpi device such as a laser printer and, when you have the card printed, ask the print shop to shrink the card by 50 percent. The 300-dpi print job now becomes effectively 600 dpi. I routinely use this technique to quickly create business cards that no one can detect originated from Ventura and not an expensive typesetting system.

Using a Dot-Matrix Printer To Proof Your Work

Ventura is a unique desktop publishing program because it allows you to mismatch your printer and printer width tables. Using the printer width table of the ultimate output device with a dot-matrix printer, you can get an accurate idea of line endings and positioning of various elements on the page. If you don't have a laser printer available at your work station, this feature can be a terrific cost and time saver.

10.11 Tip **Use a dot-matrix printer to proof your work.**

If you plan to take your chapter to a local service bureau to print it on a PostScript printer or Linotronic typesetter, you may want to know ahead of time if the text fits on the page and roughly how the final document will look. Figure 10.2 shows a printout from an Epson FX-80 used as a proof; the final document was produced by an HP LaserJet II and is shown in figure 10.3. Both printouts were produced with the HPLJPLUS.WID width table. As you can see, all horizontal and vertical space is the same in both samples: the dot-matrix printer provided an inexpensive ''preview'' of the final document. In fact, if you place one image on top of the other and hold them up to the light, they superimpose almost perfectly.

Betaine Hydrochloride

Medical researchers since the 1930's have been concerned with the consequences of too little stomach acid ("hypochlorhydria").

Many minerals require proper stomach acid to be absorbed optimally—some examples are calcium, magnesium, and zinc.

The older you are, the less likely you absorb minerals effectively. You are also much more prone to low levels of hydrochloric acid production in your stomach. There is probably a link between these two health facts of life.

Complete protein digestion depends on hydrochloric acid. Partially digested protein (PDP) can provide a "feast" for unfriendly intestinal bacteria. PDP can lead to protein malabsorption and set the stage for some allergic reactions. It may be linked to *candida albicans* infections.

Some researchers have also found that certain diseases are often accompanied by an inability to produce normal levels of stomach acid. (This does not mean the disease is necessarily caused by too little stomach acid.)

Some examples of this are rheumatoid and osteo-arthritis, pernicious anemia, asthma, diabetes, lupus erythematosus and thyroid disease.

Fig. 10.2. *Proof printed on Epson FX-80 using the HPLJPLUS.WID width table.*

Fig. 10.3.
Final copy printed on HP LaserJet II using the HPLJPLUS.WID width table.

Betaine Hydrochloride

Medical researchers since the 1930's have been concerned with the consequences of too little stomach acid ("hypochlorhydria").

Many minerals require proper stomach acid to be absorbed optimally—some examples are calcium, magnesium, and zinc.

The older you are, the less likely you absorb minerals effectively. You are also much more prone to low levels of hydrochloric acid production in your stomach. There is probably a link between these two health facts of life.

Complete protein digestion depends on hydrochloric acid. Partially digested protein (PDP) can provide a "feast" for unfriendly intestinal bacteria. PDP can lead to protein malabsorption and set the stage for some allergic reactions. It may be linked to *candida albicans* infections.

Some researchers have also found that certain diseases are often accompanied by an inability to produce normal levels of stomach acid. (This does not mean the disease is necessarily caused by too little stomach acid.)

Some examples of this are rheumatoid and osteo-arthritis, pernicious anemia, asthma, diabetes, lupus erythematosus and thyroid disease.

If you send chapters to a typesetter for ultimate printing on a PostScript device but have an HP in your office, use the HP to proof the document (using the POSTSCPT.WID width table) before sending the chapter out for final work.

PostScript versus Non-PostScript Printers

When choosing a laser printer, your choices include both PostScript and non-PostScript devices. Before you can decide between them, you should know more about the devices and the software that runs them. This section provides information on these topics.

10.12 Tip **Examine the differences between PostScript and non-PostScript printers.**

As discussed in Chapter 9, desktop publishing was invented on the Macintosh with the unveiling of the Apple LaserWriter—the world's first commercial PostScript printer. PostScript was designed to take advantage of the desire to combine graphics and text on a page that looked typeset.

PostScript offers significant advantages:

- Fonts can be scaled.
- Fonts can be treated as graphics to make use of many special effects.

- Fonts can be printed in portrait or landscape orientation—even on the same page.
- Printers usually have a built-in collection of at least 35 fonts.
- Printers can work with either PC or Macintosh systems.
- Printers can print EPS-formatted graphics.
- Documents can be printed on PostScript typesetters with much higher resolution than the usual 300 dpi of laser printers.
- The marketplace has recognized PostScript as the dominant page description language.

Drawbacks to PostScript include the following:

- PostScript requires a great deal of processing capability and time to create a complex page because PostScript is an interpreted language.
- Printers cannot print transparent graphics.
- The cost of a printer is increased by a minimum of $2,000.

Hewlett-Packard LaserJet models hold about 55 percent of the laser-printer market, and Apple LaserWriters own about 15 percent of the market. The other 30 percent of the market is fragmented among many companies offering HP-compatible and PostScript printers.

If PostScript printers have so many advantages yet HP holds the lion's share of the market, it should not be surprising that HPs have good features also:

- HP printers cost less than PostScript.
- HP printers can serve at the entry level and can be upgraded later to PostScript or other page description language; printers also can take advantage of special cards like the LaserMaster LC2.

Of course, HP printers also have some drawbacks:

- Fonts cannot be scaled, so each point size must be specially created, requiring enormous amounts of disk space for storage (because of memory limitations, maximum point size is usually limited).
- Numbers of built-in fonts are minimal.
- Printers cannot print EPS-formatted graphics.
- Separate fonts are required for portrait and landscape printing; they cannot print both landscape and portrait on the same page.

Because the printer you are most likely to have is an HP or compatible, but the printers best suited for desktop publishing are PostScript compatible, what are your options?

- ❑ Use the HP or compatible for proofing and print the final copy on a service bureau PostScript device.
- ❑ Retro-fit the HP with a PostScript or a LaserMaster LC2 board.
- ❑ Work within your limitations.

10.13 Trap **Software that emulates PostScript does not yet provide a satisfactory alternative to real PostScript.**

Several companies offer software emulators that allow you to print PostScript files to non-PostScript printers. These programs are not yet, and may never be, satisfactory alternatives to the LaserMaster LC2 card or a real PostScript device. Be sure to test such emulators thoroughly before committing to such a solution; they are often very slow and not compatible with all PostScript fonts—including Adobe's.

Printing to File

For several reasons, you may choose to print to a file on either your hard disk or a floppy disk instead of printing to a printer. This section explores some of the reasons and techniques.

10.14 Tip **To print a page or chapter to a disk file, set Output To to Filename on the SET PRINTER INFO dialog box before printing.**

You can print a page or chapter in Ventura to a disk file. Here are several reasons that you may want to print to a disk file:

- ❑ You want to print the page or chapter at another location—such as at the office where you keep the printer or at a service bureau that has a special printer—and you can more easily carry a disk with a file than the entire Ventura program.
- ❑ You want to use a page as an EPS graphic in your Ventura chapter. You can do this by choosing PostScript as the type of file, printing the page to disk, and importing the file as an EPS file (see Trick 10.15 for details about how to do this procedure).

To print a file to disk, do the following:

1. Choose Set Printer Info from the Options menu.
2. Choose the proper device name and width table of the printer you will ultimately use and set `Output To` to `Filename`. Click OK or press Enter.
3. Choose To Print from the File menu.
4. From the PRINT INFORMATION dialog box, specify the pages you want to print and click OK or press Enter.
5. From the ITEM SELECTOR dialog box, choose or type the directory in which you want to store the disk file; type a name for the file (the extension C00 is added automatically). Click OK or press Enter.
6. Wait for the page or range of pages to print.

If you plan to transport the disk file to another location for printing, be careful that you do not create a file so large that you cannot fit it all on one disk. If you have high-density drives, you can store 1.2M on a 5 1/4-inch disk or 1.44M on a 3 1/2-inch disk; double-density disks store less, depending on the version of DOS you use. The amount of space a Ventura page or chapter will take up on disk depends on the length and complexity of the portion printed. Graphics take up more space than text.

10.15 Trick

Print a page to disk to create a pseudo-EPS file; then you can load that file into a frame in Ventura.

If you use `PostScript` at the `Device Name` prompt and print a page to disk, the file can be loaded into Ventura as an EPS file and placed in a frame (see fig. 10.4). This technique allows you to place several Ventura pages on a single page.

The PostScript file you create is treated by Ventura as an EPS graphic but does not display on-screen; all you see is a large X, indicating that an EPS file is present. Because the file you printed to disk is not really an EPS file, other programs that process EPS files do not recognize the file as a true EPS file. You cannot load the pseudo-EPS file into other programs for editing or printing.

Finally, non-PostScript printers cannot print pseudo-EPS pictures.

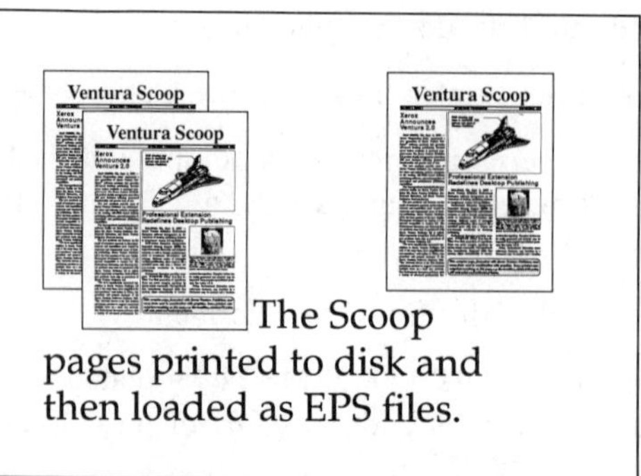

Fig. 10.4.

Page printed to disk and loaded into Ventura as a pseudo-EPS file.

10.16 Tip

Printing to a disk file lets you transfer the file to a Macintosh for printing on a PostScript printer, take the file to an offset printer to output on a Linotronic, or print the file from another computer using the DOS COPY command.

You can utilize a file that Ventura has printed to disk in three major ways:

- ❑ If you print the page or chapter to a file, you can transfer the file to a floppy disk and take the disk to an offset printer that can print the disk file on a Linotronic typesetter. (In some cases, the print shop may use Ventura and may prefer that you bring a copy of the entire chapter. See Chapter 3 for instructions on copying chapters to disk and Chapter 11 for how to copy a publication to disk.)

  Service bureaus or print shops often have access to a large number of PostScript fonts. Check with your printer to see whether you can use other Adobe fonts listed in the POSTSCPT.WID table. In such cases, you should supply the printer with the entire Ventura chapter.

  If you have Bitstream or Adobe downloadable fonts on your system, however, font information is copied to the disk file and prints even if your printer's system does not have those fonts. In such cases, supply only the disk file unless you know that your print shop's system has all the fonts available.

- ❑ You can transfer the file to a Macintosh and print to a PostScript printer by using the public-domain SENDPS program available from Adobe.

- You can print the file from any computer by using the DOS COPY command as long as the Ventura page or chapter was printed to disk with the appropriate printer driver. If, for example, you print a page to a file using an Epson LQ driver, you can take the file on floppy to another computer connected to an Epson LQ printer and type the following on a DOS command line:

  COPY <*filename*> PRN /B

  PRN is the default printer-device name for PCs. If your printer is connected to a serial (COM) port or if you have more than one printer connected to your PC, consult your DOS manual for the proper command to copy a file to a print device.

If you are using the DOS COPY command with a PostScript printer, you first need to insert your Ventura Utilities disk into drive A and type

COPY A:\POSTSCPT\DTR.TXT PRN

and press Enter.

Once the DTR.TXT file has been sent to your PostScript printer, you never need to resend it because it permanently alters information in the printer's memory.

The DTR.TXT file changes the way your computer talks to your printer so that files can be sent with the DOS COPY command. No other printer activity is affected by this action.

Chapter Summary

In this chapter, you reviewed the basics of printing. You learned the basic strengths and weaknesses of the various printers supported by Ventura and how to use those printers to print all or part of a chapter.

Because a laser printer is required to get the most out of Ventura, you learned the basics of using both Hewlett-Packard LaserJet-compatible and PostScript-compatible printer devices. You also learned how to print on both sides of a page. You learned about several options, such as the LaserMaster LC2 card, that increase the speed of laser printers and reviewed tips to minimize computer down time by using print spoolers such as LaserTORQ.

You learned how to use dot-matrix printers to proof documents before they are printed on the final output device. You learned how to print broadsheet pages and how to print your document larger than necessary to get the effect of higher resolution. Finally, you learned how and why to print a page or chapter to disk and how to print the disk file.

The next chapter goes over how to prepare large documents for publication and explains commands used for sophisticated document control.

Part

V

Using Advanced Ventura Applications

Includes

Using Sophisticated Document Controls and Creating Large Publications

Using the Professional Extension to Ventura Publisher

Chapter

11

Using Sophisticated Document Controls and Creating Large Publications

This chapter covers some of Ventura's more sophisticated capabilities. These capabilities include creating frame captions, numbering chapters and pages, and setting and updating counters. This chapter also discusses inserting headers, footers, footnotes, and cross-references; developing indexes and tables of contents for single-chapter or multichapter documents; and printing all your chapters as an assembled publication.

Using Sophisticated Document Controls

Desktop publishing experts generally agree that Ventura has the most sophisticated document controls available. Ventura's range of footnote, caption, header, and footer options is unmatched. Many of these features are just as useful to creators of small documents as they are to people who prepare longer ones.

11.1 Tip **Learn which items you can number from which menus.**

Ventura can number chapters, pages, tables, figures, and footnotes. The extensive number-tracking capabilities can be confusing because the commands are spread across many dialog boxes. Ventura refers to these numbering features as *counters*.

From the Chapter menu, you can set headers, footers, and automatic paragraph numbering, and you can control renumbering. From the Frame menu, you can track tables and figures inside frames. You can insert references to pages and chapters anywhere on the page by using the Edit menu. In addition, each counter has different formatting capabilities controlled by a specific dialog box.

Ventura counters are available from five dialog boxes: chapter and page numbers from HEADERS & FOOTERS; chapter, table, and figure numbers from ANCHORS & CAPTIONS; page and chapter numbers from CROSS REF; note numbers or user-defined strings from FOOTNOTE SETTINGS; and chapter and paragraph numbers (with five options) from AUTO-NUMBERING.

Table 11.1 summarizes the counters that Ventura automatically tracks.

Table 11.1
Numbering Features

Feature	*Dialog Box Access*
Chapter and page numbers	You insert these numbers into headers and footers from the HEADERS & FOOTERS dialog box. You also can insert chapter and page numbers into captions from the ANCHORS & CAPTIONS dialog box and anywhere on the page with CROSS REF (accessed from the Ins Special Item command on the Edit menu).
Table and figure numbers	You insert these numbers into captions from the ANCHORS & CAPTIONS dialog box (for items inside frames). You can track one set of frames as tables and another set as figures. Nothing is different about the two sets of frames, however.

Table 11.1—*Continued*

Footnotes	Footnotes are inserted into text only on the underlying page with the Footnote option (accessed from the Ins Special Item command on the Edit menu). Numbering style is controlled from the FOOTNOTE SETTINGS dialog box.
Paragraphs	You add inserts into paragraphs from the AUTO-NUMBERING dialog box.

11.2 Tip

Modify tags for generated text the same way you modify tags you have created. Text attributes for individual letters or words can be set only from the HEADERS & FOOTERS, ANCHORS & CAPTIONS, and AUTO-NUMBERING dialog boxes.

Text generated from the HEADERS & FOOTERS and ANCHORS & CAPTIONS dialog boxes produces tags prefixed with Z_, such as Z_HEADER, Z_FOOTER, Z_CAPTION, Z_LABEL FIG, and Z_LABEL TBL. You can modify these generated tags just like tags you have created yourself. Modifying tags affects the entire paragraph.

If you are in Edit mode, you cannot set text attributes for individual letters or words. To set text attributes for generated text, you must return to the dialog box where you created the header, footer, or caption.

You cannot set text attributes in these dialog boxes the way you normally do (by selecting the text and clicking a text attribute in the assignment list). To set text attributes from the dialog boxes, you must insert codes between angle brackets (<>). Chapter 4 explains how to embed formatting codes in text imported from your word processor. This procedure is complicated, but it is the only way to set text attributes in generated text. Table 11.2 lists a few of the codes you may need to use; for a more extensive list, refer to Chapter 4.

Table 11.2
Text Attribute Codes for Modifying Generated Text

Code	*Attribute*
<B>	Boldface
<U>	Underline
<^>	Superscript
<v>	Subscript
<X>	Strike-through
<M>	Medium-weight type
<I>	Italics
<=>	Double-underline
<O>	Overscore
<S>	Small type
<D>	Resume normal (inserted by Ventura when you click the Text Attribute button)
<P*n*>	Changes point size to *n*
<N>	Nonbreaking space (treats space as a character so words or names remain on the same line)
<R>	Line break; does not insert paragraph return but forces new line (useful in database applications)
<_>	Em space
<~>	En space
<+>	Figure space (less than a normal space)
<|>	Thin space
<F*n*>	Changes typeface to *n*, representing one of the font ID numbers recognized by Ventura
<C*n*>	Sets color to *n*, representing one of the eight colors available to Ventura (with PostScript printers, the colors may be set for special text effects rather than colors; see Chapter 9). Colors are white (0), black (1), red (2), green (3), blue (4), cyan (5), yellow (6), and magenta (7). Reset color to the tag default with 255.

Here is an example of how to use text attributes in a caption:

1. Change to Frame mode and click the Add New Frame button. Draw the frame any size you choose.

2. With the newly created frame selected, choose Anchors & Captions from the Frame menu.

3. From the ANCHORS & CAPTIONS dialog box, set `Caption` to `Below`.

4. The cursor is on the label line. Type

   Photo from the Portland Oregonian

5. Put the name of the newspaper in bold italic. You cannot position the cursor on the text line by clicking a new insertion point; instead, use the left-arrow key to back up until the cursor is just before the word *Portland*.

6. Click the Text Attribute button; the characters <D> are inserted. Use the left-arrow key to back up until the cursor is just before the D. Press Del to delete the D. Type *BI*. If you prefer, you can just type <*BI*>. The <D> is inserted to serve as a template for the attribute code. The label should now look like the following:

   Photo from the <BI>Portland Oregonian

7. Click OK or press Enter. The caption line under the frame should look like the following:

   Photo from the ***Portland Oregonian***

Creating Headers and Footers

Headers and footers are repeating text that Ventura automatically generates at the tops and bottoms of pages.

11.3 Tip

Set headers and footers from the HEADERS & FOOTERS dialog box.

Ventura offers you the option of headers or footers on every page, odd pages, even pages, and selected pages, or different headers on odd and even pages. Using the Cross-Reference and Repeating Frame features, you can create custom headers or footers. To create a header or footer, choose Headers & Footers from the Chapter menu. The HEADERS & FOOTERS dialog box (see fig. 11.1) offers you the features described in table 11.3.

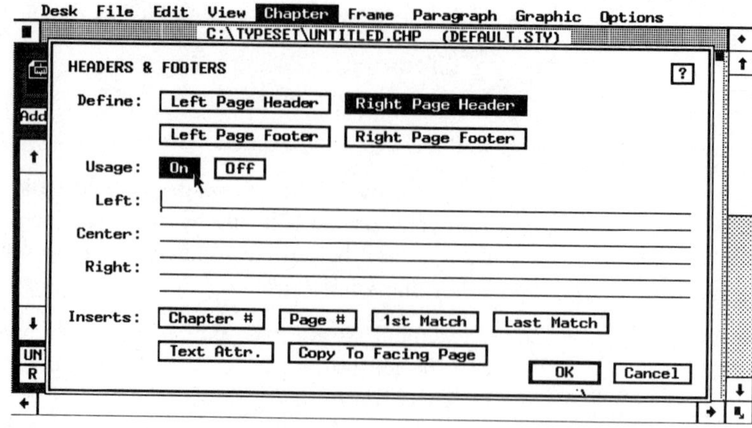

Fig. 11.1.
The HEADERS & FOOTERS dialog box.

Table 11.3
HEADERS & FOOTERS Dialog Box Options

Option	*Settings*
Define	You can choose Left Page Header, Right Page Header, Left Page Footer, or Right Page Footer. If you chose Sides: Double in the PAGE LAYOUT dialog box, you can have separate entries for left and right pages. You can use this dialog box to set all four entries by clicking each box in turn.
Usage	You can set this option to On or Off. After you define your header or footer, change to Usage: On. You can turn off all occurrences of a header or footer by changing to Usage: Off.
Left, Center, and Right	When Usage is set to On, you can enter and left-justify, right-justify, or center text. If you use more than one of these options, check after the header or footer is generated to make sure that none of the text overlaps. You can have either one-line or two-line headers or footers.
Inserts	You can insert chapter or page numbers by clicking the appropriate option. Copy to Facing Page repeats the selected header or footer on the opposite page. 1st Match and Last Match are discussed in Tip 11.4. Text Attr. is discussed in Tip 11.2.

11.4 Tip

Use 1st Match and Last Match to create automatic section, chapter, directory, or catalog headers or footers.

Ventura can automatically generate section, chapter, directory, and catalog headings.

Ventura allows you to copy the text from the first or last matching tag on a page. If you are creating a telephone directory listing, for example, you probably want the left-page header to list the first name on the page and the right-page header to list the last name on the page. To have the first and last occurrences of a tag appear in the header, do the following:

1. Choose Headers & Footers from the Chapter menu.
2. From the HEADERS & FOOTERS dialog box, choose `Define: Left Page Header` and `Usage: On`.
3. Using the arrow keys, move the cursor to the `Left` text line. Click `1st Match`. The correct syntax "[<tag name]" is inserted on the line.

   The brackets signify a command, and the open angle bracket indicates the first match. Replace the phrase *tag name* with the appropriate tag.
4. Use the left-arrow key to back up to the beginning of the words *tag name*. Now press the Del key until the words *tag name* are deleted. Type in the exact name of the tag you want matched.
5. Repeat steps 2 through 4, choosing `Define: Right Page Header` and entering the text on the `Right` line.
6. Click OK or press Enter.

Your directory should now have the first and last occurrences of whatever tag you typed in the HEADERS & FOOTERS dialog box in the left and right page headers.

The same technique can be used for creating section headings. If a tag doesn't exist on a certain page, Ventura uses the last occurrence of the tag, even if it was several pages earlier. This feature ensures that a long section can still have a correct header or footer.

You also can have more than one match at a time. You may want to have *Chapter 1, Section 1* in the header, for example. Create two tags, one for chapter and one for section. Define a left-page header and set `Usage: On`. On the `Left` line, type *Chapter [<Chapter], Section [<Section]*. If you have only numbers in the text of the tag, the header reads *Chapter 1, Section 1*. You can mix text attributes and text between the tags (not within the command brackets) to create a variety of effects to suit almost any need.

11.5 Tip

Use Ruling Line Below and Ruling Line Above to place lines under and over headers and footers.

You can have rules below or above headers or footers by changing to Paragraph mode and selecting the automatically generated header or footer paragraph. For footers, choose Ruling Line Above from the Paragraph menu; for headers, choose Ruling Line Below from the Paragraph menu. Set the ruling line as discussed in Chapter 6.

The width settings have some peculiar effects with respect to headers and footers. Because the header or footer is in its own frame, margin, column, and frame widths do not pertain to the underlying page but to the header or footer frame. Also, the text of the header or footer is considered to extend across the entire width of the frame, even if it is a single word. Choosing `Text` as the width of the line, therefore, doesn't work as expected. You can avoid this problem with a left-aligned header or footer by inserting the line-break character <*R*> as a text attribute. This procedure does not work with centered or right-aligned text.

You also can select the automatically generated header or footer frame and choose Ruling Line Above, Ruling Line Below, or Ruling Box Around from the Frame menu.

11.6 Tip

Change the vertical positioning of headers and footers by changing the tag's Space Above value in the SPACING dialog box.

You can move a header closer to the bottom of the header frame by selecting the header text in Paragraph mode and choosing Spacing from the Paragraph menu. From the SPACING dialog box, increase the `Above` figure.

You can move a footer closer to the top of the footer frame by selecting the footer text in Paragraph mode and choosing Spacing from the Paragraph menu. From the SPACING dialog box, decrease the `Above` figure.

Remember, you need to keep the total space above headers and below footers equal to or less than the top and bottom margins. If the space above headers and below footers exceeds the margins, the page may not print correctly.

11.7 Tip

Turn off the header or footer from the Chapter menu if you do not want a header or footer on a specific page.

You can disable a header or footer on any individual page by choosing Turn Header Off or Turn Footer Off from the Chapter menu. You may not want headers or footers on the first page of a chapter or the last page of a newsletter, for example.

You can reactivate the headers or footers by choosing Turn Header On or Turn Footer On from the Chapter menu.

Creating Repeating Frames and Using Cross-Reference

Ventura allows you to create frames that automatically repeat on either all pages or only left and right pages. Coupled with repeating frames, the cross-reference feature can be used to create thumb tabs or custom headers or footers.

11.8 Trick **Use a combination of the Repeating Frame and Cross-Reference features to position a header or footer anywhere you choose on a page or to create a header or footer that is larger, or positioned or shaped differently than is normally allowed by Ventura.**

If you want to place a frame that serves as a thumb tab or serves the same function as a header or footer, you can use a repeating frame. To create a repeating frame, do the following:

1. Change to Frame mode and click the Add New Frame button. Draw the frame to your specifications anywhere on the page.
2. With the new frame selected, choose Repeating Frame from the Frame menu to access the REPEATING FRAME dialog box (see fig. 11.2). Choose whether you want the frame to appear on all left, all right, or both left and right pages.
3. Click OK or press Enter.

If you selected `Sides: Double` on the PAGE LAYOUT dialog box, you can have a frame appear only on left pages, only on right pages, or on both left and right pages by selecting the appropriate option at the `For All Pages` prompt. If you choose `Left & Right`, the frame appears in mirrored positions on facing pages.

If you selected `Sides: Single` on the PAGE LAYOUT dialog box, whichever option you choose at `For All Pages` (except `Off`) causes the frame to repeat on all pages. The frame appears in the same place on each page.

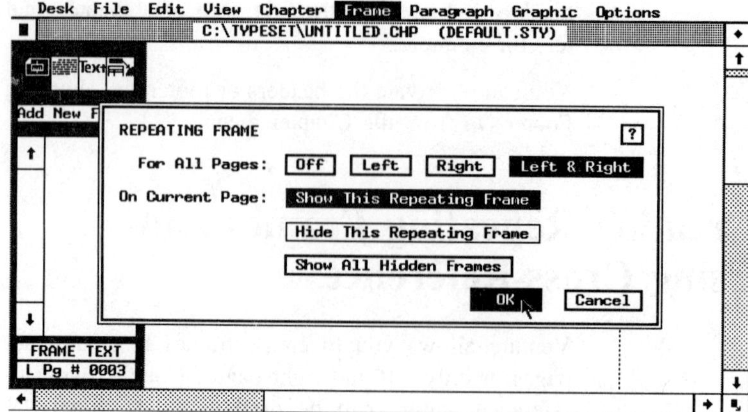

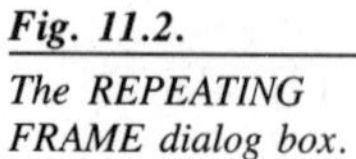

Fig. 11.2.

The REPEATING FRAME dialog box.

You can modify repeating frames just like any other frames by changing the settings for Frame Background, Ruling Line Above, Ruling Line Below, and Ruling Box Around.

The repeating frame can contain text or pictures. If the repeating frame contains text, you can have counters for chapter and page numbers by using the Cross-Reference feature and doing the following:

1. Change to Edit mode and position the cursor inside the repeating frame.
2. Type *Page*. Press the space bar to insert a space.
3. Next, either choose Ins Special Item from the Edit menu or press the keyboard shortcut Ctrl-C.
4. At the Ins Special Item menu, click Cross Ref or press F6.
5. At the CROSS REF dialog box, click Page #. (Notice that you also can insert Chapter # the same way.)

You can change the tag for the text in your frame to center the text and increase the point size.

These repeating frames can be used as thumbnail guides, logo holders, or custom headers and footers.

On pages where you don't want the repeating frame to appear, such as a title page, choose Repeating Frame from the Frame menu. From the REPEATING FRAME dialog box, you can select from the On Current Page options. Choosing Hide This Repeating Frame hides the frame on that page only; choosing Show This Repeating Frame reveals a previously hidden frame; choosing Show All Hidden Frames shows all the hidden repeating frames on the page, regardless of whether you have selected them.

You cannot copy or delete a repeating frame, you cannot have captions with repeating frames, and you cannot have more than six repeating frames in a chapter.

11.9 Trick **Use a repeating frame to create unusual columns or more columns than Ventura usually allows.**

If you first put text into a repeating frame, the same text repeats in all the repeating frames. If, however, you first put text onto the underlying page and then flow the text file into the repeating frame, the repeating frame acts like a regular frame with different text on every page.

As an example, create a text file on the underlying page. Create a frame and select it. Click the text file to force it to continue into the frame. Now make the frame a repeating frame. On all pages in the chapter that the repeating frame shows, the text flows on the underlying page and in the repeating frame. For this trick to work, at least some text must flow through the underlying page.

For a special effect, you can change the frame background to produce shading, or you can give the frame extra columns to overcome the limit of eight columns a page imposed by Ventura.

Creating Footnotes

Footnotes appear at the bottom of the page where they are referenced. This section presents tips for using footnotes.

11.10 Tip **Use the Ins Special Item command to create footnotes.**

Creating footnotes is a two-step process. First you have to mark the footnote reference in the text; then you have to define the position and style of the actual footnote.

To mark the text, while in Edit mode put the cursor where you want the footnote number to appear. Choose Ins Special Item from the Edit menu or press the keyboard shortcut Ctrl-C.

From the Ins Special Item menu, click Footnote or press F2.

If you have Show Tabs & Returns toggled on (or if you have pressed the keyboard shortcut Ctrl-T), you see a small degree symbol inserted just before the cursor. If you place the cursor before the degree symbol, the current selection box displays `Footnote`.

11.11 Tip **Use the FOOTNOTE SETTINGS dialog box to define the use and format of the actual footnote.**

Once you have inserted the footnote markers in the text, you can set how you want the footnotes to appear on the page. Choose Footnote Settings from the Chapter menu to access the FOOTNOTE SETTINGS dialog box (see fig. 11.3). Table 11.4 gives explanations of the various options in the FOOTNOTE SETTINGS dialog box.

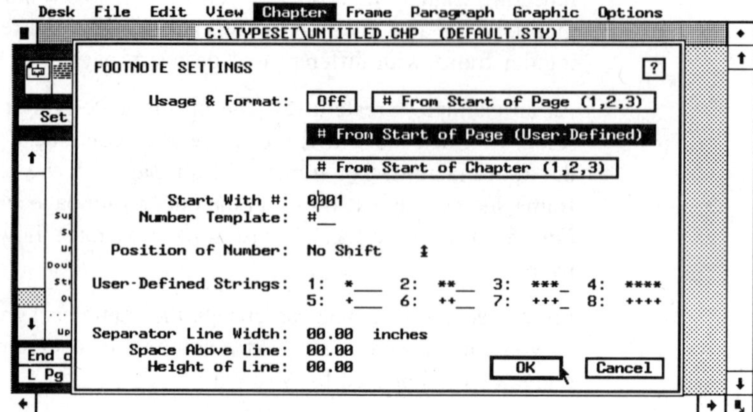

Fig. 11.3.
The FOOTNOTE SETTINGS dialog box.

Table 11.4
FOOTNOTE SETTINGS Dialog Box Options

Option	*Settings*
Usage & Format	You can choose from several settings. # From Start of Page (1,2,3) begins footnote numbers over on each page. Footnotes are numbered with arabic numerals. # From Start of Page (User-Defined) uses character strings you define (up to eight per page); this option begins numbering again on each page. # From Start of Chapter begins footnote numbers over at the beginning of each chapter. Footnotes are numbered with arabic numerals.
Start With #	The default is 1; your footnotes will begin with 1 unless you specify differently.

Table 11.4—*Continued*

Option	*Settings*
Number Template	The # represents the footnote number that appears at the bottom of the page. You can put the number between parentheses, place a period after it, or use up to three characters of any punctuation you choose. The number doesn't need to be in the string; Ventura knows it's there, but you should place all punctuation before the number. For example, you should type *(#)* to produce *(1)* for the first footnote number.
Position of Number	You can choose `No Shift`, `Superscript`, or `Subscript`.
User-Defined Strings	If you want to use symbols such as asterisks and plus signs instead of numbers in the text and footnotes, choose `Usage & Format: # From Start of Page (User-Defined)` and modify any of these strings to your preference. You can use up to eight strings per page before they begin repeating.
Separator Line Width	You can have a ruling line separate the footnotes from your text. Be sure to add in the left margin of the page when you calculate this figure. If you want a 3-inch line but have a 1-inch left margin, for example, you must set this option at 4 inches.
Space Above Line	This option lets you push the text up to give a cushion to your footnotes. Changing this figure may force the line into the footnotes, however, so you should control spacing by changing the generated footnote (Z_FNOT # and Z_FNOT ENTRY) tags.
Height of Line	Sets the height of the separator line.

11.12 Trap **You cannot set text attributes for the footnote number in the text.**

You can make only the following changes in the footnote number that appears in the text: set `Position of Number` to `No Shift`, `Superscript`, or `Subscript` in the FOOTNOTE SETTINGS dialog box. Selecting and changing text attributes has no effect on this generated number.

11.13 Tip **Modify the footnote frame by changing ruling line above, ruling line below, ruling box around, and frame background.**

In Frame mode, you can select the automatically generated footnote frame and change the ruling line above, ruling line below, ruling box around, and frame background. You cannot, however, change the size of the frame, which is determined automatically by the number of footnotes generated, nor can you create columns within the frame.

11.14 Tip **The footnote number and the footnote text each have separate paragraph tags that you can change.**

Ventura automatically generates two tags for footnotes: Z_FNOT # and Z_FNOT ENTRY. You must enter the text of the footnote the same way you insert any text. You must first delete the placeholding phrase *Text of Footnote* before entering your footnote text. The ENTRY tag is set `In From Left` automatically in the SPACING dialog box. This creates a paragraph with a hanging indent so the number stands alone to the left of the block of text. If you want more of an indent, you can change the `In From Left` figure for the tag.

The ENTRY tag is set to `Line Break After` in the BREAKS dialog box. This break setting keeps the footnote number and entry on the same line.

You can modify either tag. Note that unless you want all the footnote entries to appear double-spaced, you must set the space above and space below to zero for both the Z_FNOT # and Z_FNOT ENTRY tags.

Creating Frame Captions

Ventura can create captions for frames automatically. This section discusses how to use the caption feature.

11.15 Tip Use the ANCHORS & CAPTIONS dialog box to create captions.

You can create captions for any frame placed on the underlying page except for repeating frames.

To create a caption for a frame, select the frame in Frame mode and choose Anchors & Captions from the Frame menu. Once you see the ANCHORS & CAPTIONS dialog box, choose where you want the caption in relation to the frame: `Above`, `Below`, `Left`, or `Right` (see fig. 11.4).

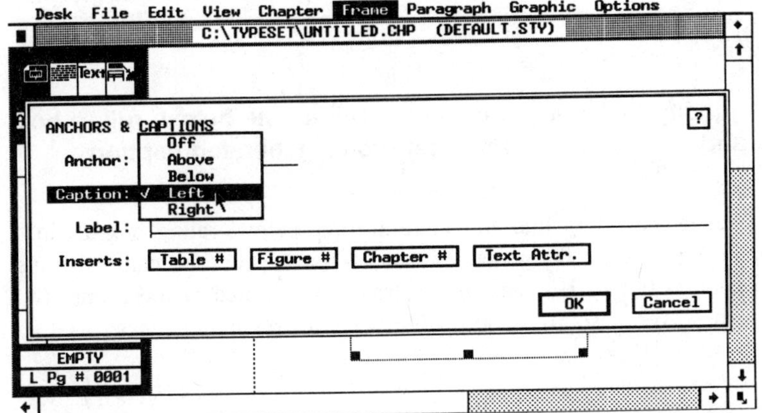

Fig. 11.4.
The ANCHORS & CAPTIONS dialog box.

At the `Label` option, you can insert chapter and table or figure numbers. The table and figure counters are tracked separately, so you can have two types of frame captions running through your chapter. Ventura calls these counters *Table* and *Figure*, but in your mind you can call them whatever is applicable—for example, *Graphs* and *Pictures*.

The *label* is the text of the caption and can be up to 60 characters long. Depending on the point size of the caption tag and the size of the frame, the caption may end up being more than one line. Besides chapter, table, and figure numbers, you can insert text attributes as described in Tip 11.2.

If you want to have a caption longer than 60 characters, in Edit mode position the cursor next to the end-of-file marker in the caption frame (the current selection box displays `End of File`). You can now type a caption longer than 60 characters. This new text can have text attributes changed from the FONT SETTING FOR SELECTED TEXT dialog box.

If the text becomes too long for the generated caption frame, you must resize the caption frame just as you would any other frame. Be careful because resizing may change the size of the frame to which the caption is attached. If you have any text or inserts on the Label line of the ANCHORS & CAPTIONS dialog box, when inserting the free-form caption, you may first need to press Enter once or twice to move the insert point past the generated text; otherwise, you risk having the free-form caption obscure the generated text.

11.16 Tip **You can change the tag of the caption just as you would change any other tag.**

Ventura generates a Z_LABEL CAP tag for the text on the Label line and a Z_CAPTION tag for free-form captions. These tags can be changed just like any other tags.

11.17 Tip **You can modify the ruling line above, ruling line below, ruling box around, and frame background and resize generated caption frames.**

You can change the ruling line above, ruling line below, ruling box around, and frame background for the generated caption frame. You also can resize the generated caption frame. Because the caption frame is tied to the frame it is captioning, however, resizing in some directions resizes both frames.

Using Auto-Numbering

One of the most useful and least-used features of Ventura is the program's capacity to number paragraphs automatically.

11.18 Tip **Use the Auto-Numbering command to create lists, generated text, outlines, and section numbers.**

Keep the following points in mind to use automatic numbering successfully:

- ❑ You have to know the exact name of the tag for the paragraphs you want numbered automatically.
- ❑ You can set up to 10 levels of numbers by listing up to 10 different tag names. In an outline or technical manual, for example, you may want numbering to extend down through several levels of detail.
- ❑ You can have the paragraphs numbered in any of the following ways: arabic numerals (1, 2, 3), capital letters (A, B, C), lowercase letters (a, b, c), roman numerals (I, II, III), or lowercase roman numerals (i, ii, iii).

- You need to know the syntax of the automatic numbering bracketed command:

  [*tag name,*1* or *A* or *a* or *I* or *i* for the numbering style,modified starting number if any]

  [*Section head,A,3], for example, means to number all paragraphs tagged with the Section head tag, use capital letters, and begin with the third letter—in this case, *C*.

- You need to know the syntax modifiers of the automatic numbering bracketed command:

  [-] preceding the bracketed command suppresses the preceding level of automatic numbering. The following syntax produces the autonumbering shown:

  Level 1: [*Section head,A]
  Level 2: [*Sec subhead,1]

  A Section Heading
  A1 Section Subheading

  If the Level 2 definition is preceded by [-], the Level 1 number is suppressed at lower levels, as shown:

  Level 2: [-][*Sec subhead,1]

  A Section Heading
  1 Section Subheading

- Tags are created for each level of automatic numbering. These tags are called Z_SEC1, Z_SEC2, Z_SEC3, Z_SEC4, etc. They are separate from the paragraphs they number. These generated tags also are preset to appear on a preceding line. A section number normally appears as follows:

  1
  Section

  If you want the number and the text on the same line, modify the Z_SEC tag to set `Break: Line Break Before` and `Keep With Next: Yes`. The numbered paragraph tag must be changed so that the alignment is set to `Relative Indent: On` and `Indent Width` is set to about 12 points. If you want rules, a ruling line above should be attached to the Z_SEC tag, and a ruling line below should be attached to the numbered paragraph tag. The result of these changes is as follows:

  1 Section

- You can modify the Z_SEC tags just as you would modify any other tags.
- You can insert text attributes (see Tip 11.2).
- You can insert chapter numbers.
- You can include punctuation or text with the numbers, or you can use text alone. In an interview, for example, you can have two tags—one for the question and one for the answer. Set up the automatic numbering levels as follows:

  Level 1: [*Q tag]Question:
  Level 2: [-][*A tag]Answer:

  These level definitions produce the following result:

  Question: Paragraph containing question...
  Answer: Paragraph containing answer...

  Change the alignment to `Relative Indent: Off` and `Indent: 0`; then change the spacing to a figure `In From Left` that is enough to skip the words *Question* and *Answer* and allow both the Q and A tags to line up.
- You can create independently numbered lists by forcing a reset of the numbers. Set Level 1 as [*Body Text]—notice no number follows the tag name. Set Level 2 as [*List,1]. Now any time you have a paragraph of body text interrupting the list tags, the numbers are reset and the next set of List tags begins with the number 1.

Using the Update Counters and Renumber Commands

The counters for numbering chapters, pages, tables, and figures can be linked to counters in other chapters so that when several chapters are joined into a publication, the counters can continue across chapters. This section gives tips for using Ventura's counter and renumber capabilities.

11.19 Tip **Use the UPDATE COUNTERS dialog box to link counters between chapters (in publications) or to modify or reset the counters for chapters, pages, tables, or figures at any point within a chapter.**

To access the UPDATE COUNTERS dialog box, choose Update Counters from the Chapter menu (see fig. 11.5).

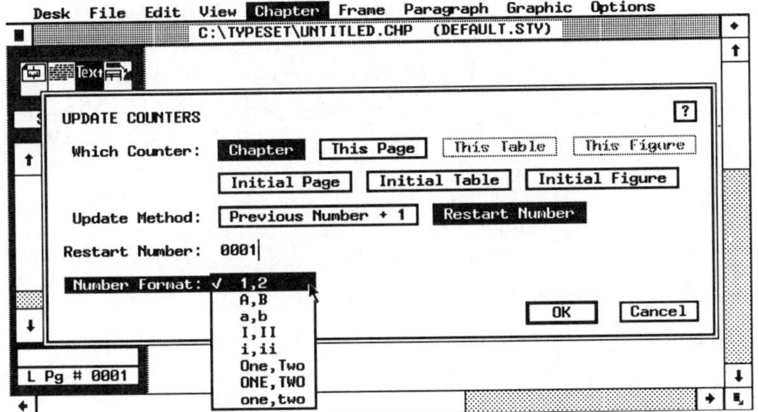

Fig. 11.5.
The UPDATE COUNTERS dialog box.

Table 11.5 shows how counters are affected from the UPDATE COUNTERS dialog box.

Table 11.5
UPDATE COUNTERS Dialog Box Options

Option	*Settings*
Which Counter	For this option, you can choose Chapter, This Page, This Table, This Figure, Initial Page, Initial Table, or Initial Figure. This setting determines which counter is affected by the rest of the settings in the dialog box. Chapter, This Page, This Table, and This Figure affect the chapter from the current page or selected table or figure. The This Table and This Figure buttons are grayed unless the selected frame has been given a table or figure number in the ANCHORS & CAPTIONS dialog box. Initial Page, This Table, and This Figure affect only the current chapter's counters but can be set from anywhere in the chapter.

Table 11.5—*Continued*

Option	*Settings*
Update Method	You can choose either Previous Number + 1 or Restart Number. If you are assembling a multiple-chapter document (a publication), choose Previous Number + 1 to force numbers for pages, tables, figures, and chapters to be carried forward from one chapter to the next. This option requires renumbering to be done from the MULTI-CHAPTER OPERATIONS dialog box. Use Restart Number to start a new chapter or series of pages, tables, or figures; to force numbering for those items to begin with a number of your choice; or to change numbering styles for a table of contents or foreword.
Restart Number	If you choose Restart Number as the Update Method prompt, you can enter a number of your choice.
Number Format	You can choose arabic numbers (1, 2, 3), capital letters (A, B, C), lowercase letters (a, b, c), roman numerals (I, II, III), lowercase roman numerals (i, ii, iii), capitalized word as number (One, Two, Three), all capitals word as number (ONE, TWO, THREE), or lowercase word as number (one, two, three).

Note that if you select a frame and implement a restart number, that frame, if moved, causes renumbering to begin from its new position. Be aware of this when you copy or move a captioned frame.

If you restart numbering on a particular page because that is where the text for a section or chapter ends, editing your text may make the section or chapter end on a different page. Restart Number is keyed to the physical page and not the text. In such a case, you must make changes from the UPDATE COUNTERS dialog box. You can cancel Restart Number by selecting the frame or page again and choosing Previous Number + 1.

To avoid extra work, you should update counters just before you print your final copy. To make possible corrections easier, you should keep notes as to which frames and pages, if any, were set with Restart Number.

11.20 Tip **Use the Renumber Chapter command to update the numbers for automatic numbering.**

To update automatic numbering, either choose Renumber Chapter from the Chapter menu or use the keyboard shortcut Ctrl-B.

Creating Tables of Contents and Indexes

Ventura has the capacity to create indexes and tables of contents. Tables of contents are easily created with text specified by tags. To create a table of contents, you fill in a chart similar to that used in the AUTO-NUMBERING dialog box.

Indexes are difficult to prepare with Ventura. Instead, you should rely on a word processor that can search for and replace text. This section shows you how to create an index with either Ventura or your word processor.

11.21 Tip **Use the GENERATE TABLE OF CONTENTS dialog box to create a table of contents for your publication.**

Because you generate the table of contents by pulling text from specific tags, you must do the following in the planning process before you can create a table of contents:

- ❑ You use headings, subheadings, sub-subheadings, and so forth, for entries in the table of contents. Make a careful note of the exact tag names involved. Make the tag names hierarchical and meaningful.
- ❑ Use the same style sheet throughout the publication so that you don't accidentally have a tag with one spelling in one chapter and another spelling in another chapter.
- ❑ Make your settings with the UPDATE COUNTERS dialog box in each chapter before creating the publication. After opening your publication, select the Renumber command from the MULTI-CHAPTER OPERATIONS dialog box to implement the counters correctly.

To generate a table of contents, first select Multi-Chapter from the Options menu to access the MULTI-CHAPTER OPERATIONS dialog box (see fig. 11.6). Open a publication by clicking Open and then choosing a previously created publication with the ITEM SELECTOR dialog box (see Tip 11.25 to learn how to create a publication). Double-click to choose the item. Or click once and then click OK or press Enter.

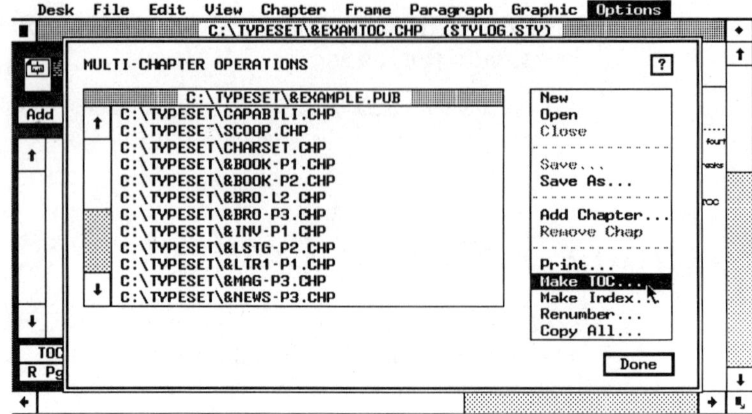

Fig. 11.6.
The MULTI-CHAPTER OPERATIONS dialog box.

Click the Make TOC command to access the GENERATE TABLE OF CONTENTS dialog box (see fig. 11.7).

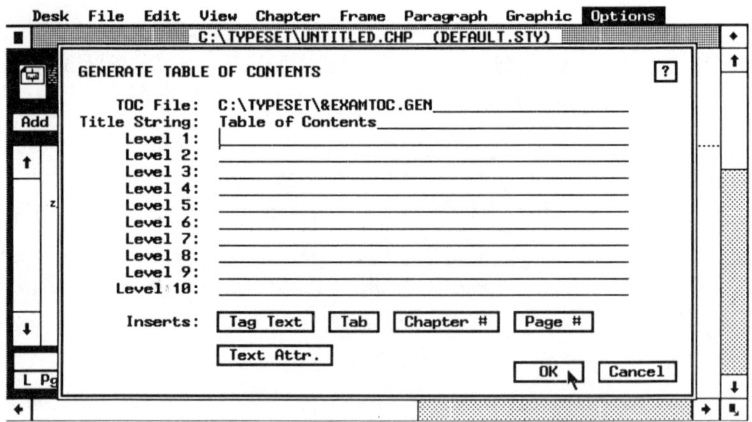

Fig. 11.7.
The GENERATE TABLE OF CONTENTS dialog box.

From the GENERATE TABLE OF CONTENTS dialog box, you can edit the `TOC File` path and file name. You also can edit the `Title String` to something other than *Table of Contents*.

You are allowed up to 10 levels of entries in your table of contents. Unless you are preparing technical manuals, you probably do not use more than two or three levels. Just as in the AUTO-NUMBERING dialog box, you are given templates for entries that you can edit. You generate the following templates by clicking the various `Inserts` buttons:

- Tag Text=[*tag name]. Replace *tag name* with the exact name of the actual tag.
- Tab=→. Inserts a tab stop.
- Chapter #=[C#]; Page #=[P#]. Takes the number from actual chapter and page during table of contents generation. Because these numbers are affected by the UPDATE COUNTERS dialog box, you must remember to renumber from the MULTI-CHAPTER OPERATIONS dialog box before generating the table of contents. Because renumbering a publication can take a long time, save the renumbering step until you are ready to generate all generated files such as the index and table of contents. See Tip 11.25 for more information.
- Text Attr.=<D>. Set these attributes as discussed in Tip 11.2.

You can add your own text and punctuation outside of the command brackets. For example, the command

"[C#]-[P#]."

can produce

"3-1."

Once you are satisfied with your choices, click OK or press Enter to begin generating the table of contents. If you have several long chapters, this process takes a long time because each chapter is loaded into Ventura and examined and the appropriate text is generated. Once complete, the table of contents file is a generated text file (GEN) with the path and file name specified in the GENERATE TABLE OF CONTENTS dialog box. You can load the table of contents file into Ventura and create a style sheet by modifying the generated tags Z_TOC TITLE, Z_TOC LVL 1, Z_TOC LVL 2, Z_TOC LVL 3, etc.

If you save your publication after generating the table of contents, Ventura remembers your table of contents settings.

11.22 Tip Insert index entries from within Ventura.

The index generated by Ventura can be sophisticated. To create an index, Ventura needs to know several things:

- Where is the word or phrase you want indexed?
- Is the word or phrase a primary or secondary entry? That is, should an entry have its own place in the index, or should it be subordinate to another word or phrase?

- Should the phrase be alphabetized as it appears in the primary or secondary entry, or should another key be used (if, for example, the phrase contains unimportant articles like *the* or *an* or a numerical figure like *4* that you want indexed on *four*)?
- Should the word or phrase also point to other entries with *See* and *See Also* references?

To create an index with Ventura, position the cursor on the word or phrase in the text that you want to use as the index entry and choose Ins Special Item from the Edit menu or press the keyboard shortcut Ctrl-C. From the Ins Special Item menu, click Index Entry or press F3 to access the INSERT/EDIT INDEX ENTRY dialog box (see fig. 11.8).

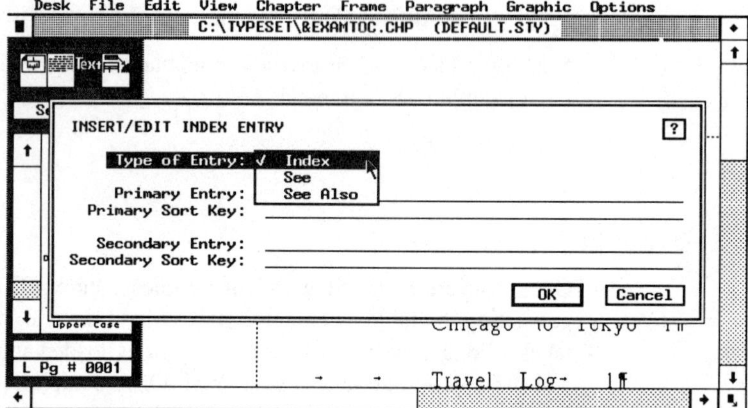

Fig. 11.8.
The INSERT/EDIT INDEX ENTRY dialog box.

At each index insertion point, you can have three types of entries: Index, See, and See Also. You also can index an item as a Primary Entry or as a Secondary Entry. Table 11.6 gives some examples of indexing.

See and *See Also* entries don't have page numbers listed. Therefore, these entries don't need to be in any particular place in the publication. You should enter all the *See* and *See Also* entries at the end of a chapter so that you can easily index and edit them.

Keep notes so that you can use exactly the same primary and secondary entry words and phrases throughout the process of index entry. If you have multiple references, they appear with all page references separated by commas (for example, Honey, 88, 98, 102).

Entries for references that span pages should indicate the page range (for example, Honey, 88-98). To create page ranges, you must have footers or headers using the 1st Match and Last Match feature (see Tip 11.4). You must

Table 11.6
Examples of Indexing

Entry	*Index Example*
Type of Entry: Index Primary Entry: Honey	Honey, 88
Type of Entry: Index Primary Entry: Honey Secondary Entry: African Bees	Honey, 88 African Bees, 122-123
Type of Entry: See (or See Also) Primary Entry: Honey Secondary Entry: Behavior	Honey, 88 See Behavior
Type of Entry: Index Primary Entry: Honey Secondary Entry: 1988 Production Secondary Sort Key: nineteen	Honey, 88 1988 Production, 90*

*This entry is alphabetized on the word *nineteen*.

also insert the index entry into the paragraph tagged to appear as the first match and last match in the footers or headers. When the index is generated, a range is created for those entries that span pages because the index entry code is carried along with the tagged text in the footers or headers.

To edit or delete index entries, position the cursor in front of the degree sign inserted when you created the index entry. (The current selection box displays `Index Entry`; `Index, See`; or `Index, See Also`.) To delete the entry, press the Del key. To edit the entry, hoose Ins Special Item from the Edit menu or press Ctrl-C; from the Ins Special Item menu, click Index Entry or press F3.

11.23 Tip Use your word processor to "pretag" index entries.

Finding and entering index entries for all the words and phrases that you want in an index in Ventura is tedious and tiring work. An easier method is to use your word processor's search-and-replace feature. To create the index entries with your word processor, do the following:

1. Make a list of words and phrases you want indexed, along with the key words you want to search for to create the entries.

2. Load the entire text file used for your publication into your word processor. If the file is large, spanning multiple Ventura chapters, combine the files if possible into one large file (noting and marking chapter break points so that you can later separate the chapters again).

3. Search for the key word and replace with the following:

   <$Iprimary[sort];Secondary[sort]>key word

   Remember to add the key word at the end so that the index entry doesn't simply replace the word you are trying to index.

4. Insert a list of *See* and *See Also* references at the end of the document. Later, when you load the chapter back into Ventura, use the techniques in Tip 11.22 to create index entries for the *See* and *See Also* references.

11.24 Tip Use the MULTI-CHAPTER OPERATIONS dialog box to generate the index.

When you are ready to generate the index, choose Multi-Chapter from the Options menu. From the MULTI-CHAPTER OPERATIONS dialog box, open your publication and click the Make Index command to access the GENERATE INDEX dialog box (see fig. 11.9).

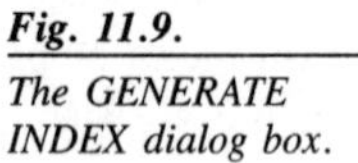

Fig. 11.9.

The GENERATE INDEX dialog box.

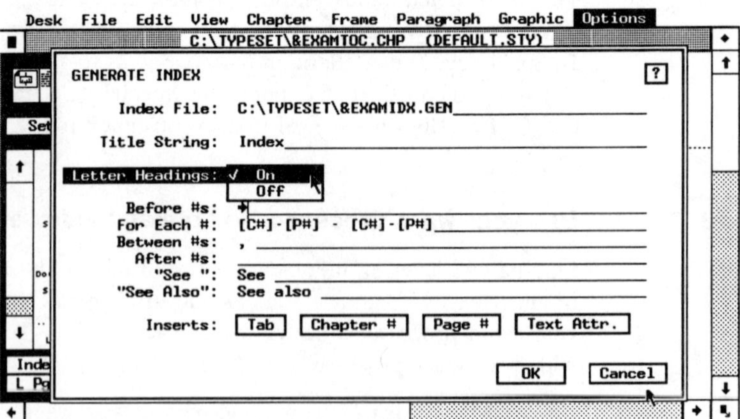

You can edit the `Index File` path and file name as well as the `Title String` to suit your preferences. You can choose from the following options and templates in the GENERATE INDEX dialog box:

- `Letter Headings`: `On` or `Off`. If this option is set to `On`, an *A* is inserted at the beginning of the *A* entries, a *B* at the beginning of the *B* entries, and so forth. An exclamation point is inserted at the beginning of non-alphabetic entries (such as those beginning with numbers or symbols). The default is `Off`.
- `Before #s`. Enter any text you want to appear before page numbers—for example, *pg.*, a comma, or a tab. The default is a tab.
- `For Each #`. Use `[C#]` and `[P#]` templates. You can have chapter or page numbers or both. You also can specify how to display page ranges if you have created any.
- `Between #s`. Enter the punctuation you want between numbers where an index item has multiple entries. The default is "comma space."
- `After #s`. Enter the punctuation you want after numbers. The default is no punctuation.
- `"See"` and `"See Also"`. You can change the text string that introduces these two types of entries.
- `Inserts`. See Tip 11.2 for a discussion of these inserts.

Once you are satisfied with your choices, click OK or press Enter to begin generating the index. If you have several long chapters, this process takes a long time because each chapter is loaded into Ventura and examined and the appropriate text is generated. Once complete, the index file is a generated text file (GEN) with the path and file name specified in the GENERATE INDEX dialog box. You can load the index file into Ventura and create a style sheet by modifying the generated tags Z_INDEX TITLE, Z_INDEX LTR, and Z_INDEX MAIN.

Remember to choose the Renumber command from the MULTI-CHAPTER OPERATIONS dialog box before creating either an index or a table of contents. The Renumber step takes time, so plan to do it only once, just before generating the index or table of contents (see Tip 11.25 for more information).

If you save your publication after generating the index, Ventura remembers your index settings.

Creating and Printing a Publication

Once you have created and indexed all your chapters and set all the counters, you are ready to combine the chapters into a publication, generate your index and table of contents, and print the entire publication.

11.25 Tip **Use the MULTI-CHAPTER OPERATIONS dialog box to create, open, close, save, or rename a publication; to add or delete chapters; and to rearrange the order of chapters before generating an index or table of contents before printing.**

You access the MULTI-CHAPTER OPERATIONS dialog box by choosing Multi-Chapter from the Options menu (refer to fig. 11.6). Use this dialog box if you are combining more than one chapter into a publication.

Ventura calls a group of combined chapters a *publication*. You can create a publication by doing the following:

1. Click New if it is not ''grayed out'' to clear any previously loaded publications or chapters.
2. Click Add Chapter.
3. From the ITEM SELECTOR dialog box, choose the chapters you want included in the publication. You don't need to select the chapters in the order you want them to print.
4. Repeat steps 2 and 3 until all the chapters are added.
5. Arrange the chapters in order by clicking a chapter name and holding the mouse button until a hand appears. Drag the chapter name into its proper place in the list. Release the mouse button and the list is rearranged.
6. Click Save to save the publication with a name of your choice in the ITEM SELECTOR dialog box.
7. Make sure that no chapter names are selected, or the Print, Make TOC, Make Index, and Renumber commands will be grayed out. Click somewhere other than a chapter name or button to deselect any chapters to make the selections available.
8. If you have set counters, click Renumber.
9. If you need to generate an index or table of contents, select those options and proceed as outlined in this chapter.

10. To print the publication, select Print to access the PRINT INFORMATION dialog box. Make your selections as discussed in Chapter 10. If you have chosen to direct output to a file name, you can print the chapters in one large combined file or in separate files by choosing the option under `Multi-Chp. Print Files`.

Chapter Summary

In this chapter, you learned how Ventura keeps track of and numbers chapters, pages, tables, figures, footnotes, and paragraphs.

You learned about the comprehensive header, footer, repeating frames, cross-reference, footnote, frame-caption, and automatic-numbering capabilities of Ventura.

You learned how to create indexes and tables of contents as well as how to combine and generate numbers across the many chapters of a publication. You also learned how to print a publication.

Chapter

12

Using the Professional Extension to Ventura Publisher

With the release of Ventura Publisher 2.0, Xerox added some new capabilities and power—more than could be used easily with only 640K of memory. Instead of adding these enhancements to the regular (base) version of Ventura, requiring users of the base products to upgrade their hardware, Xerox offered an add-on software package called the Professional Extension.

Many of the Professional Extension capabilities are specialized and not needed by every Ventura user. The base program has work-arounds for accomplishing some of the same tasks. If you have the Professional Extension, this chapter helps you learn how to use it most effectively. If you don't have the Professional Extension, this chapter may help you determine whether you need the added capabilities.

To install the Professional Extension, you need 600K of free hard disk space for the files (in addition to what the base Ventura occupies already). To use the hyphenation dictionary, you need 1.2 megabytes of expanded memory and another 1.2 megabytes of disk space for the hyphenation files.

If you want to take advantage of the expanded memory support, you need more than 640K of memory and a driver to install expanded memory (EMS) such as a Lotus/Intel/Microsoft EMS driver (3.0 or later) or a compatible (such as the EEMS driver from AST). Consult your system manuals for memory capacities and installation instructions for the EMS driver.

Assessing the Capabilities of the Professional Extension

The Professional Extension to Ventura Publisher adds seven capabilities, two of which require expanded memory:

- Expansion of memory support using either EMS or EEMS drivers to access memory on your system over 640K. This expansion is necessary for long or complex documents that you cannot create with the base version of Ventura. In addition, many operations run more quickly. If you don't have EMS memory, you can still use most of the other features of the Professional Extension. Use of expanded memory will essentially eliminate the "frame too complex" message that can occur with base Ventura and a frame with more than 725 line elements. The Professional Extension allows up to 12,000 line elements per frame, depending on the amount of memory available.

- Improved accuracy and control of hyphenation with the 130,000-word typesetter's hyphenation dictionary licensed to Xerox by EDCO. This feature requires 1.2 megabytes of EMS memory and 1.2 megabytes of added disk storage. If you don't have EMS memory, you can use most of the other features of the Professional Extension, but you should not install the hyphenation dictionary.

- Composition of complex equations. If you need to create complex equations in your documents, this feature alone merits your purchase of the Professional Extension.

- Forward and backward referencing. With the base product of Ventura, you can insert forward and backward references manually ("continued on page *n*," "see table *n*"), but with the Professional Extension, these references can be generated and updated automatically.

- Use of variables for primitive merges or easy customizing. Most of you are familiar with "mail merging" in word processors. The Professional Extension allows simple variable definition and substitution for customizing standard documents.
- Simplified table and form creation. With the base version of Ventura, tables are created in the Graphic mode. The Professional Extension adds a fifth mode—Table mode—for creating, editing, and modifying tables. You also can import spreadsheet and database files directly into tables.
- Automatic vertical justification for aligning adjacent columns. With the base version of Ventura, you could achieve a similar effect manually with small empty frames.

If you occasionally create tables or sometimes need vertical justification, you can probably get by with the base version of Ventura. You may, however, benefit from the additional capabilities of the Professional Extension for composing equations, cross-referencing and inserting variables, creating tables and forms, vertical justification, or precise hyphenation control.

Installing and Setting Up the Professional Extension

If you have previously installed Ventura, the installation of the Professional Extension will be familiar territory. If not, you may want to read about installing Ventura in Chapter 1.

12.1 Tip **You need the disk set from the base version of Ventura and the disk set from Professional Extension to install the Professional Extension.**

Besides what is required by the base Ventura, another 600K is required by the Professional Extension for its files. If you install the hyphenation dictionary, you need another 1.2 megabytes of disk space for a total of 1.8 megabytes. Remember that Ventura works best with a minimum of 2 megabytes of free disk space for storing temporary files. This means that if you install the Professional Extension with the hyphenation dictionary, you need at least 3.8 megabytes of free disk space to provide for the 2 megabytes of free disk space Ventura likes for its use during operations.

To install the Professional Extension, follow these steps:

1. Insert the Professional Extension Application disk #1 (in either 5 1/4- or 3 1/2-inch disk format) into drive A, type *a:vpprep*, and press Enter.

2. At the prompt `Is your hard disk drive C?`, press Enter if Ventura is already installed or you want it installed on drive C. If you are installing Ventura on another drive, press N and then Enter. Then press the letter of the drive you want Ventura installed on and press Enter.

3. At the prompt `Are you installing this version for the first time?`, press Enter.

   This prompt really should ask, ''Are you installing the Professional Extension for the first time?'' Answer N to this question only if you are reinstalling the Professional Extension to change monitors, mice, or printers.

   Next, Ventura copies the application files from the floppy disk to the hard drive. If you are using 5 1/4-inch disks, you receive prompts to insert the Professional Extension Supplemental Application disk #2 and press Enter to finish copying the application files.

4. At the appropriate prompt, insert the Loadable Filter disk from the base version of Ventura into drive A. Press Enter to continue.

5. You are asked, `Do you wish to install the EXAMPLE FILES?` If you have previously installed the Example files, you do not need to reinstall them. Otherwise, install them. If you choose Y, press Enter and follow the prompts for disk insertion.

   Warning: If you have previously installed the examples and if you choose Y here, your old examples will be overwritten. If you have made changes to example chapters—including style sheets—without renaming them, you will lose those changes.

6. At the next prompt, insert the Utilities disk from the Ventura base product into drive A and press Enter. The utilities are copied onto the hard drive.

7. Select the graphics card and the display your system uses; press the appropriate letter and press Enter.

8. Select the mouse you use by pressing the appropriate letter and pressing Enter. If you choose other than a bus mouse, also choose either COM1 or COM2 as the mouse port.

9. Select the printer you use; press the appropriate letter and press Enter. Choose the printer port used by the printer.

   Note: If you selected one or more printers for base Ventura, you must select each printer again to use it with the Professional Extension.

   Warning: If you have previously installed either a PostScript or HP laser printer and you install it again here, the corresponding CNF file will be copied to your VENTURA directory, and it will overwrite the existing CNF files. If you have modified the CNF files, your changes will be lost. Therefore, make copies of the CNF files before you install the Professional Extension so that you can restore your modified files after installation. See Chapter 10 for more information about CNF files.

10. The next question is `Do you want to select another printer?` If you want to use more than one printer with the Professional Extension, press Y, press Enter, and repeat step 9 to install each additional printer. When you finish selecting printers, press Enter.

11. The next screen summarizes your screen, mouse, and printer choices. If all selections are correct, press Enter. If any selections are incorrect, press N and then press Enter. Repeat steps 7 through 11 as needed.

12. You are asked, `Do you wish to use the dictionary?` If you have at least 1.2 megabytes of EMS memory on your system and want to use the special hyphenation dictionary, press Enter to copy the dictionary to your hard drive. If you don't have the requisite EMS memory or don't want the dictionary installed, press N and press Enter.

13. Depending on the graphic and printer drivers you have chosen, insert the needed disks from the Ventura base disk set.

14. At the prompt, insert the Professional Extension Font disk (#16 for 5 1/4-inch disks and #9 for 3 1/2-inch disks).

15. If you installed the hyphenation dictionary, you are asked to insert the Professional Extension Hyphenation disks (disks #17 through #19 for 5 1/4-inch disks and disk #10 for 3 1/2-inch disks).

16. You are now finished with the installation process. Type *vpprof* to run Ventura with the Professional Extension.

12.2 Tip **You can have the base version of Ventura and the Professional Extension installed at the same time.**

You still can use the base version of Ventura (if it's installed) after installing the Professional Extension. To run Ventura, type *vp* (which invokes the VP.BAT file). To run the Professional Extension, type *vpprof* (which invokes the VPPROF.BAT file).

If you no longer want to use the base version of Ventura, you can free disk space by deleting files not used by the Professional Extension. You can safely delete VP.APP, VP.OVR, VP.RSC, and VP.STR from the VENTURA directory and the VP.BAT file from the root directory.

Supporting Expanded Memory

With the Professional Extension's expanded memory capabilities, you can create larger and more complex documents and speed up certain functions of Ventura.

When PCs were first developed, no one foresaw the need for more than 640K of memory. The first PC microprocessors could not use more than 640K of memory even if it had been available.

Within a short time, the need for more than 640K became apparent. The people most in need of extra memory were those who created huge spreadsheets with 1-2-3. Because 1-2-3 keeps the entire spreadsheet in memory, the spreadsheet could not be made larger when the memory was full. Soon after the release of the AT class of computers, which used the 80286 chip, several companies (Lotus, Intel, and Microsoft) developed a method for applications to use more than 640K of memory.

The Lotus/Intel/Microsoft (LIM) specifications were called EMS. Later, the AST company developed a superset of the LIM specifications called EEMS. The Professional Extension can use either EMS- or EEMS-compatible Versions 3.0 or later.

If you have expanded memory, either your computer or the expanded memory board came with a driver for installing expanded memory. Read the documentation that came with your system or board to learn how to install the EMS or EEMS driver correctly.

Once the EMS driver is correctly installed, the Professional Extension automatically uses the extra memory unless you restrict it (see Tip 12.3).

To see the amount of EMS memory available for documents, choose Publisher Info from the Desk menu. The dialog box that appears tells you how much EMS is used by any applications (SYS) and how much EMS is available for your document (APP).

12.3 Tip

Control the amount of EMS memory used by the Professional Extension with the /E switch in the VPPROF.BAT file.

When you install the Professional Extension, the batch file VPPROF.BAT is created and placed in the root directory of the drive that contains the VENTURA directory.

The command line for loading the Professional Extension is almost the same as for loading the base version of Ventura. Instead of DRVRMRGR VP, the command is DRVRMRGR VPPROF. You may add the same command switches as those described in Chapter 1.

You can use the /E switch to control the amount of EMS memory used. For example, adding /E=144 restricts the amount of EMS memory used by the Professional Extension to 144K. The minimum amount is 144K, so numbers from 1 to 144 cause the Professional Extension to restrict memory to 144K. Numbers from 144 to the amount of actual EMS memory cause the Professional Extension to use whatever amount of memory you specify.

If you don't want any EMS memory occupied by the Professional Extension, set the /E switch to zero (/E=0) and delete the file GEM.EMS from the Ventura directory.

Creating Equations

If you are an engineer, a physicist, a mathematician, or a chemist, or you are involved in any of the physical sciences, you have probably wanted a way to insert equations into Ventura. The Professional Extension has a sophisticated equation composition and editing system built-in.

12.4 Tip

To create and edit equations, use the Ins Special Item feature while in Text mode.

If you learned how to insert fractions in Ventura, creating complex equations uses many of the same skills. Just like with fractions, you create equations by positioning the text cursor where you want the equation to appear. Then follow these steps to create an equation:

1. Choose Ins Special Item from the Edit menu or use the keyboard shortcut Ctrl-C.
2. An expanded version of the Ins Special Item menu appears. Click Equation or press F4 to access the Equation Editing screen.
3. In the Equation Editing screen, enter the equation (see Tip 12.7 for an understanding of equation command words). For examples of some of the most common symbols, either select Choose Equation Text from the Edit menu or use the keyboard shortcut Ctrl-C. A menu of 10 items appears (see fig. 12.1). Click your choice or press one of the 10 function keys assigned to the menu choices.

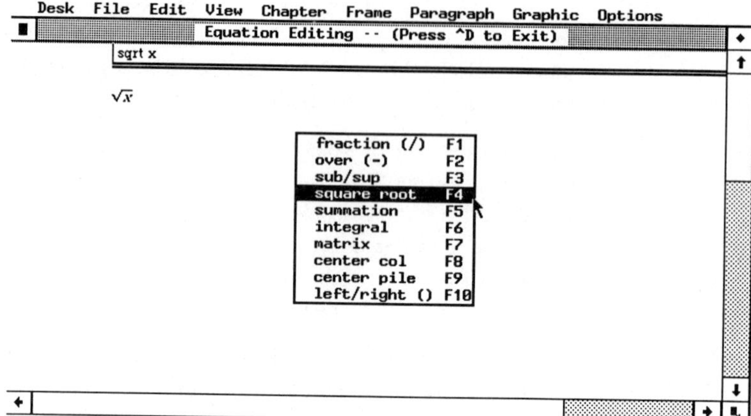

Fig. 12.1.

The Choose Equation Text menu.

A symbol command is inserted above the double editing line, and after a moment, the symbol appears below the line exactly as it will appear in your document. Figure 12.2 gives an example of an inserted square root.

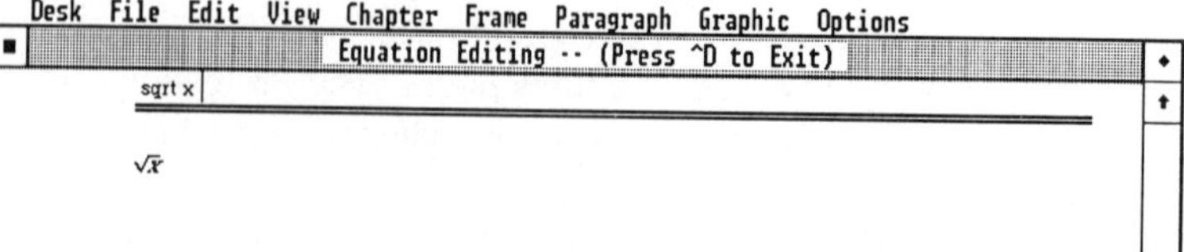

Fig. 12.2.

Equation editing.

4. Delete the incorrect part of the command and enter your data. Add other commands to complete the equation. Figure 12.3 gives an example of replacing *x* with *126* and the resulting change above and below the double editing line.

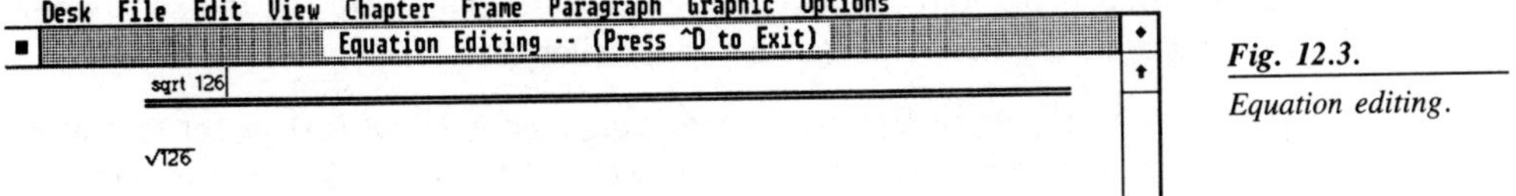

Fig. 12.3.
Equation editing.

5. Choose Exit Equation Editing from the Edit menu or use the keyboard shortcut Ctrl-D.

When your document returns, you see the completed equation. The current selection box displays `Equation`, and a small degree symbol is visible just before the text of the equation. (If you cannot see the degree symbol, press Ctrl-T or choose Show Tabs & Returns from the Options menu.)

You cannot edit an equation directly. You must return to the Equation Editing screen by positioning the cursor before the equation so that the current selection box displays `Equation` and then repeating steps 1 and 2.

12.5 Tip

Set Grow Inter-Line To Fit to On in the TYPOGRAPHY SETTINGS dialog box.

Because equations often extend above or below a normal line of text, before you enter an equation, select the paragraph while in Paragraph mode and choose Paragraph Typography from the Paragraph menu. In the TYPOGRAPHY SETTINGS dialog box, make sure that `Grow Inter-Line To Fit` is set to `On`. Click OK or press Enter.

With `Grow Inter-Line To Fit` set to `On`, the space between lines will expand if the equation you create extends above or below the normal line of text.

You also can select the equation while in Text mode and click Set Font to make changes in the FONT SETTING FOR SELECTED TEXT dialog box. Or, once the text is selected, you can interactively size the equation by holding down the Shift key and pressing the up- or down-arrow keys to increase or decrease the point size, respectively.

12.6 Trap

Because some printers may not have the point size of the subscript or superscript available, incorrect printing of the equation may occur. Use the ATTRIBUTE OVERRIDES dialog box to select correct point sizes.

PostScript printers do not require changes in superscript or subscript size or upward or downward shift to print correctly. Some printers (such as Hewlett-Packard LaserJets or compatibles) may lack the correct font size for superscripts or subscripts, resulting in overlapping characters or incorrect printing of the equation. To avoid this overlap, change the point sizes of the superscript and subscript characters to match your available font selection.

While at the Equation Editing screen, you cannot select text to set text attributes or change font sizes. You can, however, change the superscript and subscript size and upward or downward shift by selecting the paragraph containing the equation while in Paragraph mode and then choosing Attribute Overrides from the Paragraph menu. In the ATTRIBUTE OVERRIDES dialog box, make the necessary changes and then click OK or press Enter.

For correct formatting, avoid using tabs and center and right or decimal alignment in equations.

12.7 Tip

Learn the Professional Extension's language for creating equations.

Once you are at the Equation Editing screen, only the Professional Extension's equation language is understood. The program's developers created this special language because the mathematical symbols used in equations have no keyboard and few ASCII equivalents.

Including complete information about the equation language is beyond the scope of this chapter, but like any language, this one has rules you must follow:

- Certain words are "special" command words and have a significance in the equation language. Whenever you use a command word, you *must* place a space before and after it. If you leave out the surrounding spaces, the Professional Extension will not interpret the word as a command.
- Because spaces are part of command words, in the equation language, you must denote actual spaces with a tilde (~) for a regular space or a caret (^) for a thin space.
- Command words affect the expressions that follow them; diacritical mark commands affect the preceding expressions.
- Expressions can be single characters, groups of characters not separated by a space, special words, and characters inside braces, { }.

In the equation language, there are five classifications of command words:

1. *Symbols*. When you type a symbol word or character, a symbol appears below the double line. For example, "sqrt" is the symbol word for the symbol $\sqrt{\quad}$.

2. *Diacriticals*. Certain words or numbers have special punctuation, like accents or special characters that are placed above words or numbers. For example, ''bar'' is the diacritical command to place a line above an expression.
3. *Text Attributes*. In the equation language, you cannot use the special typographical commands to affect text attributes. For example, <B> will not make text bold. To affect text attributes, you need to learn special command words; the command ''bold'' makes the next expression appear in boldface.
4. *Equations*. When you enter an equation word, a symbol for an equation can change the position of the expression that follows or create an equation symbol.
5. *Normal Text*. If you want a noncommand word to appear as an unitalicized word, precede the word with the word ''roman.'' If the word ''roman'' is omitted and the word entered is not a command word, the word appears in italicized text. If you want a command word to appear as text, surround the word with quotation marks.

12.8 Tip — Create bold brace, bracket, and Greek characters.

Even though your printer probably doesn't have a bold symbol font, you can create a bold effect. Place two braces, brackets, or Greek characters next to each other and then use the Back command, which superimposes the characters, creating a bold effect.

12.9 Tip — Learn all the command words in the equation language that apply to your profession.

The Professional Extension's equation language contains about 94 command words. Documentation for the Professional Extension provides excellent examples for all the command words. Refer to that documentation for examples of the following commands:

- ❑ Symbols and characters: 22 words and symbols
- ❑ Romanized words: 21 words
- ❑ Diacritical commands: 8 commands
- ❑ Font commands: 6 commands
- ❑ Equation commands: 37 commands

See figure 12.4 for an example of a complex command sequence and the equation created by the commands.

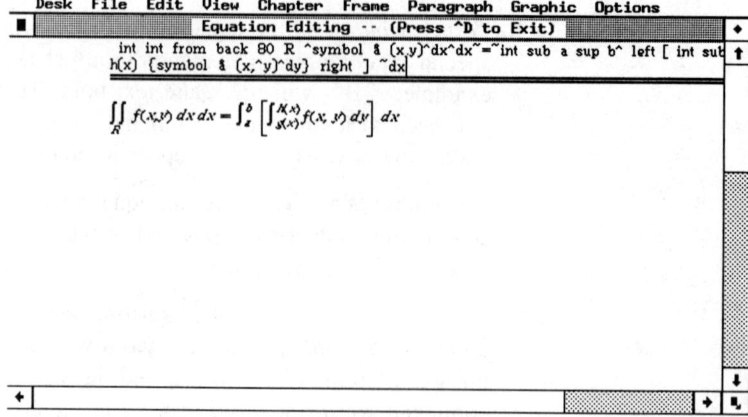

Fig. 12.4.

An equation created with the Professional Extension equation generator.

Using Automatic Cross-Referencing

If you have ever created a document with references to future chapters, pages, sections, tables, or figures, you know the frustration of keeping track of such references and being certain of their accuracy when you prepare to print. With the Professional Extension, you can insert cross-references that can be generated and updated automatically just before printing.

12.10 Tip

Inserting the current page or chapter number with Cross Ref is the same as in the base Ventura program.

With the Professional Extension, inserting the current page or chapter number using the cross-reference feature parallels the procedure in the base version of Ventura. However, the dialog box looks different because it has more cross-referencing capabilities (see fig. 12.5). Chapter 11 provides information on how to insert the current page or chapter number.

For page and chapter number insertion, choose P# or C# and leave the At The Name line blank.

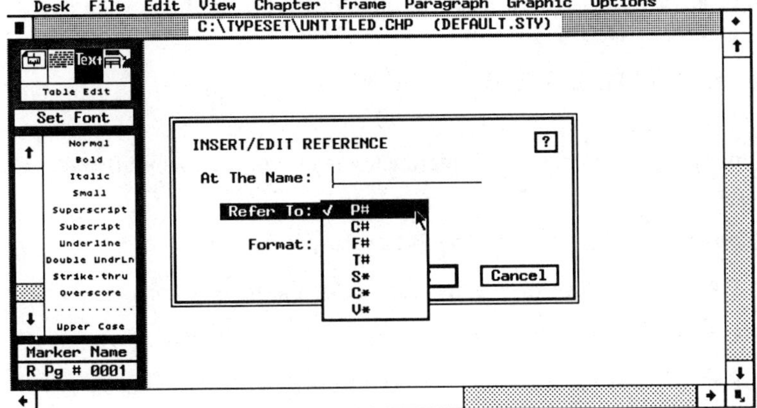

Fig. 12.5.
The INSERT/EDIT REFERENCE dialog box.

12.11 Tip **Creating cross-references requires two steps: first, insert a marker or create an anchor; next, insert a cross-reference.**

To insert a cross-reference marker, place the text cursor where you want to insert the reference and then follow these steps:

1. Choose Ins Special Item from the Edit menu or use the keyboard shortcut Ctrl-C.
2. At the INS SPECIAL ITEM dialog box, click `Marker Name` or press F7.
3. At the INSERT/EDIT MARKER NAME dialog box, enter a marker name. You may mix letters and numbers, but correlating the marker name to the area being marked is best. Letters can be upper- or lowercase. Click OK or press Enter.
4. Make a note about the marker name and location.

In the current selection box, the words `Marker Name` appear. A degree sign in the text designates where you inserted the marker. To edit the marker name, position the text cursor just before the degree symbol and repeat steps 1 through 4. To edit the frame anchor name, change it in the ANCHORS & CAPTIONS dialog box (see Chapter 6).

If you are marking a frame rather than a spot in the text, create an anchor name to serve as a frame marker name (see Chapter 6 for instructions about how to create an anchor name).

To create a reference for the marked places, place the text cursor where you want the cross-reference and follow these steps:

1. Choose Ins Special Item from the Edit menu or use the keyboard shortcut Ctrl-C.
2. At the INS SPECIAL ITEM dialog box, click `Cross Ref` or press F6.
3. Type the *exact* marker or frame anchor name in the blank after `At The Name`.
4. Choose one of the items at the `Refer To` prompt:

   P# or C#—Page or chapter number of the marker name.

   F# or T#—Figure or table number of the frame anchor name.

   S*—Section number that precedes the marker or frame anchor name.

   C*—Caption text (generated, not free-form) from the frame with the referenced frame anchor name.

   V*—Variable text (see Tip 12.12 for information about text variables).
5. For P#, C#, F# or T#, you can choose from eight numbering formats: Arabic numerals; upper- or lowercase letters; upper- or lowercase Roman numerals; initial capital, lowercase, or all capital words. You also can choose Default, which uses the numerical style of the counter you are referencing.
6. Click OK or press Enter.

The word `Reference` appears in the current selection box, and a degree sign appears in the text where you inserted the reference. To edit the reference, position the text cursor just before the degree symbol and repeat steps 1 through 6.

After you create a marker or frame anchor name and a cross-reference, the actual cross-reference is not created until you create or load the publication and choose the Renumber command from the MULTI-CHAPTER OPERATIONS dialog box (see Chapter 11 for details on using this command).

Using Variable Insertion

Ventura is not a word processor and doesn't have the capability of creating a form letter and substituting variables in ''personalized'' letters—like the ones you get promising a million dollars. With the Professional Extension, you can set and replace a number of text variables across all the text files in a publication. Although this capability is welcome, its implementation is rather cumbersome. If you want to print more than a few form letters or documents, you should use your word processor's merge function.

12.12 Tip **Creating variables requires two steps: first, create the text you want substituted; next, insert a cross-reference to a variable.**

To create the variable text, insert the text cursor at the beginning of the chapter (or wherever you want to store the variable's text). Because all the variable text is hidden, put all variable text in one place so you can easily find it at a later date. Then follow these steps:

1. Choose Ins Special Item from the Edit menu or press the keyboard shortcut Ctrl-C.
2. At the INS SPECIAL ITEM dialog box, click `Variable Def` or press F8.
3. Type the variable name and make a note of it.
4. Type up to 54 characters of substitute text for insertion at the variable reference point. Click OK or press Enter.

In the current selection box, you see the words `Variable Def`. A degree sign in the original text marks where you inserted variable text.

To edit the variable text, position the text cursor just before the degree symbol and repeat steps 1 through 4.

To insert a variable reference, place the text cursor where you want it inserted and then follow these steps:

1. Choose Ins Special Item from the Edit menu or use the keyboard shortcut Ctrl-C.
2. At the INS SPECIAL ITEM dialog box, click `Cross Ref` or press F6.
3. In the INSERT/EDIT REFERENCE dialog box on the `At The Name` line, type in the variable name created in step 3 of the preceding section.
4. Set `Refer To` to `V*`. Click OK or press Enter.

In the current selection box, the word `Reference` appears, and a degree sign in the text designates the insertion. To edit the text, position the text cursor just before the degree symbol and repeat steps 1 through 4.

After you create a variable text and the variable reference, the variable text is not inserted until you create or load the publication and choose the Renumber command from the MULTI-CHAPTER OPERATIONS dialog box (see Chapter 11 for details on using this command).

Note: If you create variable references without corresponding variable definitions, an error file tells you about unresolved variable definitions. This error often occurs if you do not insert the *exact* variable definition name on the `At The Name` line.

Creating Tables

With the base Ventura program, you can create tables and forms by using graphics tools like the Box Text and Line drawing tools. With the Professional Extension, you gain a sophisticated table and form layout tool.

12.13 Tip To create a table, change to the fifth mode—Table Edit mode.

After you install the Professional Extension, the Ventura screen doesn't look much different except for the addition of a box that displays `Table Edit` underneath the four mode icons (see fig. 12.6). When you click the Table Edit icon, the addition button changes to display `Ins New Table` and the assignment list displays 10 items that deal with table editing.

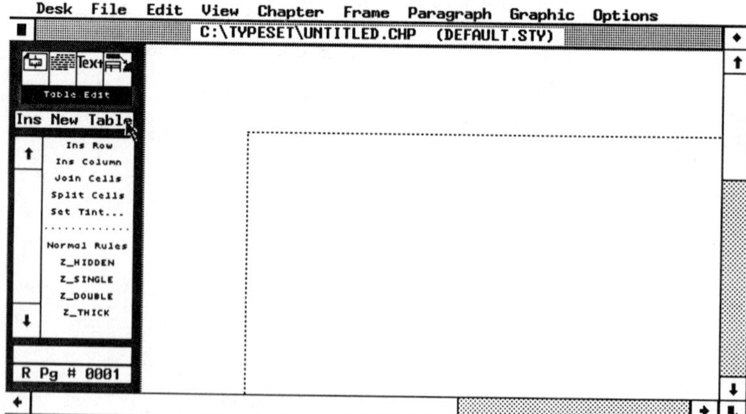

Fig. 12.6.
The five modes with Table Edit mode selected.

Unlike the other modes, Table Edit mode has no specific menu bar. The Edit menu has Set Column Width (or Ctrl-C) and Edit Table Settings (or Ctrl-D) commands available when you are in Table Edit mode and have selected a portion of an existing table. The Edit menu also has commands for cutting, copying, and pasting rows or columns.

To create a new table, follow these steps:

1. Change to Table Edit mode by clicking the Table Edit icon. (No keyboard shortcut exists for switching to Table Edit mode.)
2. The table edit cursor is a small cross. Position the cursor on your document where you plan to insert a table and click. (If you don't set the table insertion point before clicking Ins New Table, you see a warning that tables cannot be positioned in a header, footer, footnote, or another table.)

   Regardless of where in the paragraph you click, a shaded bar appears just before the paragraph to mark the table insertion point. A table can be inserted only *before* a paragraph. The current selection box displays `Before Para`, indicating the table insertion point.
3. Next, click the Ins New Table addition button to access the INSERT/EDIT TABLE dialog box (see fig. 12.7).
4. Modify the settings in the INSERT/EDIT TABLE dialog box (see Tip 12.15).
5. Click OK or press Enter.
6. Change to Text mode to enter text in the table.

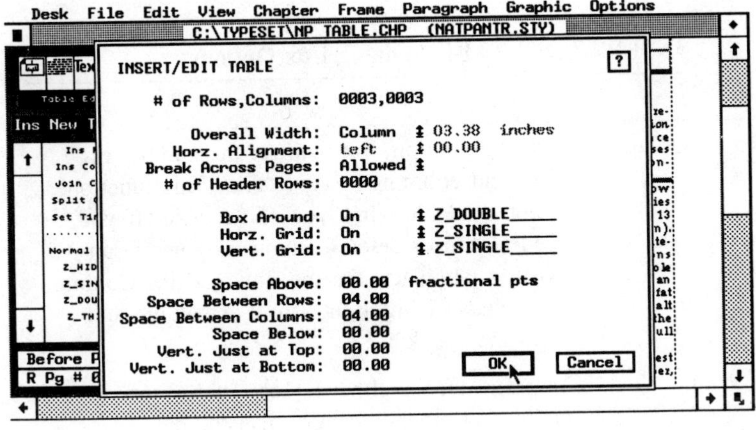

Fig. 12.7.

The INSERT/EDIT TABLE dialog box.

12.14 Tip

You also can create a table while in Text mode by using the Ins Special Item feature.

To create a table while in Text mode, follow these steps:

1. Place the text cursor at the beginning or end of the paragraph, depending on where you want the table to appear. (If you place the cursor at the end, you will see the words `Paragraph End` in the current selection box.)
2. Choose Ins Special Item from the Edit menu or press the keyboard shortcut Ctrl-C.
3. From the Ins Special Item menu, click Table or press F9 to access the INSERT/EDIT TABLE dialog box.
4. Modify the settings in the INSERT/EDIT TABLE dialog box (see Tip 12.15).
5. Click OK or press Enter.
6. Change to Text mode to enter text into the table.

12.15 Tip

Set the specifications for your table by using the INSERT/EDIT TABLE dialog box.

The INSERT/EDIT TABLE dialog box appears when you create a table. Table 12.1 provides descriptions of options in this dialog box.

Table 12.1
INSERT/EDIT TABLE Dialog Box Options

Option	*Result*
# of Rows, Columns	With this option, you can set the number of rows and columns in your table. This function is not available when you edit a table. If you need to add or delete columns or rows in an existing table, use the Ins Row and Ins Column commands or highlight a row or column and press the Del key.
Overall Width	You can choose either `Column` or `Custom`. A table cannot be any wider than the column or frame in which it's placed. The default width of a table is the width of the frame or column, but you can set a custom width of less than the

Table 12.1—*Continued*

Option	*Result*
	column or frame width. If the table spills over into another column of a different width, the table automatically adjusts to the new column's width.
Horz. Alignment	If you set a custom overall width, you can align the table left, center, or right, or you can choose to indent for a specified amount.
Break Across Pages	You can set this option to either `No` or `Allowed`, to allow a table to continue onto the next page, column, or frame if it doesn't fit on the current page, column, or frame. If you choose `No`, the entire table moves to the next page, column, or frame if more room is needed. For short tables, you should choose `No`; for longer tables, choose `Allowed`.
# of Header Rows	If your table continues (breaks) to another page, column, or frame, you will probably want the table headings reproduced at the top of each segment. For this option, enter the number of rows you want repeated each time the table is divided.
Box Around, Horz. Grid, and Vert. Grid	You can set the box around and the grids to one of the default tags provided in the assignment list (`Z_HIDDEN`, `Z_SINGLE`, `Z_DOUBLE`, or `Z_THICK`), or you can develop custom rule settings.
Space Above	This command sets the amount of padding between the top of the table and the preceding paragraph. A good spacing to use is the body text interline spacing.
Space Between Rows and Space Between Columns	These options let you set the spacing between rows and columns.
Space Below	This option sets the amount of space between the bottom of the table and the top of the paragraph that follows. A good spacing to use is the body text interline spacing.

Table 12.1—*Continued*

Option	*Result*
Vert. Just at Top and Vert. Just at Bottom	For these options, you enter a number for the maximum amount of space you want the Professional Extension to add at the top or bottom of a table. This amount is in addition to the Space Above and Space Below values you have already set. If you use different figures for the top and the bottom, then space is added proportionally in the ratio of your settings (see Tip 12.34 for more information about vertical justification).

12.16 Tip

Once a table is created, you can modify any of the settings in the INSERT/EDIT TABLE dialog box except the # of Rows, Columns option.

If you want to make changes in the INSERT/EDIT TABLE dialog box, change to Table Edit mode and click anywhere in the table. Then choose Edit Table Settings from the Edit menu or use the keyboard shortcut Ctrl-D.

When the INSERT/EDIT TABLE dialog box returns, notice that the # of Rows, Columns option is grayed. To increase or decrease the number of rows or columns, use the Ins Row, Ins Column, or Cut Row/Column commands described in Tip 12.20.

12.17 Tip

Change the column widths by holding down the Alt key and moving the vertical column divider with the mouse.

You can change the width of the columns visually or through the TABLE COLUMN WIDTHS dialog box. To change a column visually, follow these steps:

1. Change to Table Edit mode.
2. Press and hold down the Alt key. Position the cursor in the middle of the column you want to change. Press and hold the mouse button. The cursor changes into a four-way arrow cursor (see fig. 12.8). Drag the vertical line to its new position and release the mouse button.
3. If the right boundary of the table changes, repeat the process to reposition the right table boundary.

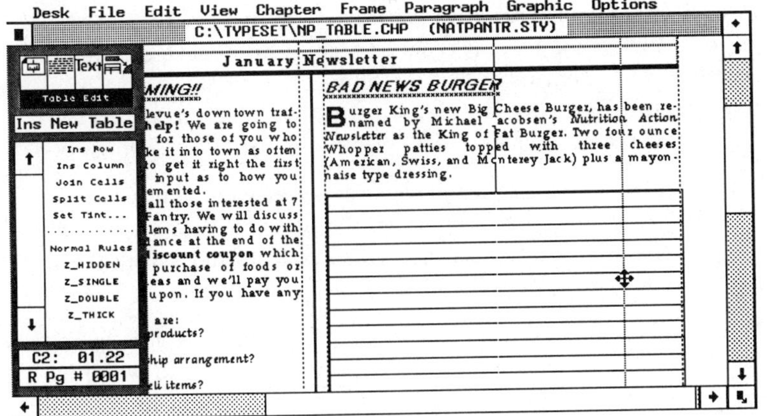

Fig. 12.8.

Visually changing column width.

12.18 Tip

Change the column widths by using the TABLE COLUMN WIDTHS dialog box.

The width of the columns also can be changed through the TABLE COLUMN WIDTHS dialog box. Follow these steps:

1. Change to Table Edit mode.
2. Click anywhere in the column you want to resize. The current selection box gives the grid coordinates of your position (for example, R5C0..R5C1; the left boundary of the table is C0 and the top boundary of the table is R0).
3. Select Set Column Width from the Edit menu or press the keyboard shortcut Ctrl-C to access the TABLE COLUMN WIDTHS dialog box (see fig. 12.9).
4. If you did not click in the column you wanted to change, you need to set the `Column Number` dial by clicking the left arrow for lower numbered columns or the right arrow for higher numbered columns. (You cannot click higher than the actual number of columns.)
5. Set the `Width Setting` to `Fixed` or `Variable`. If you set the `Width Setting` to `Fixed`, the column is fixed at the width entered on the `Fixed Width` line.

   If you set the `Width Setting` to `Variable`, the column is set in one of two ways. One, if some columns are set to a `Fixed Width`, then the `Variable` columns divide automatically as a proportion of the available space left over.

Two, if all columns are set to Variable (and the Overall Width is set to Column), you can set each variable as a percentage of the overall width. (Remember that the sum of the variables must be 100 percent.) You also can set the narrowest column to 1 and set the other columns as integer multiples of the narrowest column.

A three-column table, for example, can be set with widths of 50, 25, and 25, and the first column will be twice the size of the other two columns. Or you can set the widths as 2, 1, and 1 with the same result.

Note: If all columns are set to Fixed and the total width is less than the column width, the table is narrower. If the total width is greater than the column width, the column will overrun its boundaries or you may receive a message about a frame that doesn't fit. In such cases, change the column widths back to appropriate values.

6. Click OK or press Enter.

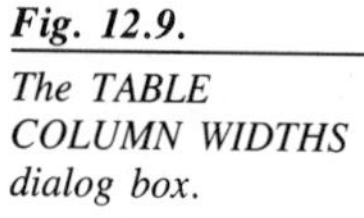

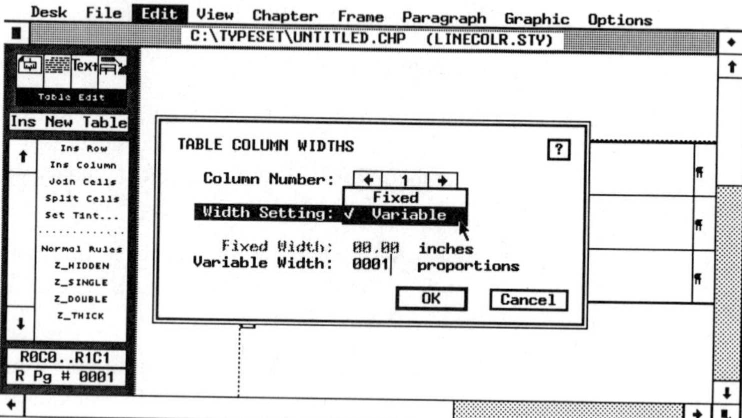

Fig. 12.9.

The TABLE COLUMN WIDTHS dialog box.

12.19 Tip **Change to Text mode to enter data into a table.**

To enter data into the table, change to Text mode. Each intersection of horizontal and vertical grid lines creates a little box called a "cell." If you select Show Tabs & Returns (which you access from the Options menu or by pressing the keyboard shortcut Ctrl-T), you see paragraph markers in each cell of the table—much like Box Text boxes in Graphic mode (see Chapter 8).

Click in your chosen cell and begin entering text. If the text is too long to fit in the cell, *the cell automatically expands* as necessary. You cannot press Enter while entering text in a cell because only one paragraph per cell is permitted. (If you try, you get an error message asking whether you want to insert a new paragraph above or below the table.) You *can* insert a line break by pressing Ctrl-Enter if you need the effect of another paragraph within a cell. Remember, a line break does not actually create another paragraph.

You can move the cursor from cell to cell with the arrow keys. If the cursor is at the end of the paragraph preceding the table, pressing the right arrow or the down arrow moves the cursor into the first cell of the table. If the cursor is at the beginning of the paragraph following the table, pressing the left arrow or the up arrow moves the cursor into the last cell of the table.

All the capabilities you normally expect in Text mode remain available. You can cut, copy, and paste text from the page to a cell, from a cell to the page, or from a cell to another cell.

You can apply tags to the text in cells or modify the default tag created when the table is generated. The default tag is called "Table Text."

12.20 Tip **You can edit table rows or columns by using the addition box and Edit menu commands.**

When you are in Table Edit mode, the addition box has two blocks of commands. The first four commands are Ins Row, Ins Column, Join Cells, and Split Cells. Additional commands on the Edit menu exist for you to cut, copy, and paste rows or columns. Table 12.2 provides more information about each of these options.

Table 12.2
The Table Edit Commands

Option	*Result*
Ins Row and Ins Column	Click the row or column you want the new row or column inserted adjacent to and then click Ins Row or Ins Column. Rows are inserted above and columns are inserted to the left of the selected row or column.
Cut Row/Column	To delete a row or column, click the row or column you want to delete and press the Del key or choose Cut Row/Column from the Edit menu. A dialog box asks whether you want to cut a row or column; click the appropriate box or cancel the command.

Table 12.2—*Continued*

Option	*Result*
Join Cells	To join cells, select the cells you want joined by clicking and dragging the mouse from the upper left to the lower right corner of the block of cells. When the cells are highlighted, click Join Cells. The column and row lines of the selected cells disappear, but the cells still exist and can later be restored if you use the Split Cells command. For purposes of entering text, however, the joined cells act as a single cell.
Split Cells	To split cells, select the cells you joined previously and now want to split by clicking and dragging from the upper left to the lower right corner of the block of cells. When the cells are highlighted, click Split Cells. The column and row lines of the selected cells reappear.
Cut, Copy, and Paste	To cut or copy rows or columns (you cannot move individual cells), select the cells you want to Cut or Copy by clicking and dragging the mouse from the upper left to the lower right corner of the block of cells. When the cells are highlighted, pick the appropriate command from the Edit menu or use a keyboard shortcut. Then you can paste the rows or columns depicted on the Table Clipboard by positioning the table cursor in the table at the point of insertion and pressing Ins. Note that any splitting or joining formatting is lost when rows or columns are retrieved from the Table Clipboard. Prior to each Cut, Copy, or Paste command implementation, you receive an extra prompt to confirm your intentions. Sometimes, you need to specify whether the command pertains to columns or rows. If you select the entire table to cut or copy, the Professional Extension verifies that you want to affect the entire table.

12.21 Tip Highlight different table cells with shading (tint).

With the base Ventura program, you learned to change the frame background (Frame menu), rules (Frame and Paragraph menus), and fill attributes (Graphic menu). For tables, the creators of the Professional Extension introduced another term for setting the color and pattern of an object—tint. Even though the term is new, the command works in a familiar way.

While in Table Edit mode, you can dress up a table with the Set Tint command. To tint a cell or group of contiguous cells, select your choices by clicking and dragging them from the upper left to the lower right corner of the cell or block of cells.

Once the cells are highlighted, click the Set Tint command in the assignment list to access the TABLE CELL TINT dialog box with its choices of eight colors and nine patterns. An example of the color and pattern chosen is shown in the dialog box.

If you have many noncontiguous cells to tint, you have to tint each cell separately because no way is available for you to select multiple nonadjacent cells.

12.22 Tip Change the lines around a cell or around the table by using the tags on the assignment list or in the INSERT/EDIT TABLE dialog box.

When you create a table, you set the default for lines surrounding it (box around) and the horizontal and vertical grid lines in the INSERT/EDIT TABLE dialog box. You can override the defaults by selecting the cells you want to change. Click and drag them from the upper left to the lower right corner of the cell or block of cells. When the cells are highlighted, click in the assignment list on `Z_Hidden` (to hide the lines), `Z_Single`, `Z_Double`, or `Z_Thick` to change to single, double, or thick lines. If you want to restore the defaults set in the INSERT/EDIT TABLE dialog box, click `Normal Rules`.

12.23 Trick Create custom rules for use in the table by creating special tags.

If you don't like the four options for lines around tables or cells, create custom lines by following these steps:

1. Be sure that generated tags show on the assignment list by setting `Generated Tags` to `Shown` on the SET PREFERENCES dialog box, which you access from the Options menu.
2. Create a "dummy paragraph" and, while in Paragraph mode, tag it with the generated Z_ tags (Z_Hidden, Z_Single, Z_Double or Z_Thick) to modify the table rule tags created automatically when

you inserted the table that you want to modify. Or create a new tag to tag the dummy paragraph.

3. From the Paragraph menu, choose Ruling Line Above to access the RULING LINES ABOVE dialog box.

4. Don't change the width setting; keep it set at None. Notice a new option at the bottom of the dialog box: Table Rule List. If Table Rule List is set to Hidden, the ruling line above works as usual. If it is set to Shown, the dialog box sets the tag for table rules and the tag appears in the assignment list when you are in Table Edit mode.

   You *can* change the color, pattern, dashes, and any of the space or height settings to customize the table lines.

5. Click OK or press Enter.

6. Delete the dummy paragraph.

If you modified an existing tag that had already been applied to portions of the table, the table lines will have changed to reflect the modified tag settings. If you created a new, custom tag, you have to apply it to the cells of your choice (see Tip 12.22).

12.24 Trick

You can select a block of cells quickly by using the Shift key.

To select a group of cells quickly, click in the upper left corner of the block; then hold down the Shift key and click in the lower right corner of the block of cells. The entire block is selected.

12.25 Tip

Use the table capabilities to create forms quickly.

Because the fifth mode is called Table Edit, you may think that it's only for tables. The table capabilities of the Professional Extension also help you create forms such as invoices, calendars, and questionnaires with more ease than the graphics tools allow.

12.26 Tip

Use the Professional Extension to import PRN files directly from spreadsheets (such as 1-2-3) and SDF files from databases (such as dBASE III PLUS or dBASE IV) into automatically generated tables.

In Chapter 4, you learned to extract data from other programs such as 1-2-3 and dBASE III PLUS or dBASE IV. The conversion process was somewhat convoluted and was easier with a third-party utility. Printing spreadsheet data was easier with a nonproportional font to ensure that numerical data was properly aligned. Extracting dBASE data involved writing a program.

The Professional Extension adds automatic conversion capabilities for PRN files (produced by spreadsheets like 1-2-3) and SDF files (produced by data base programs like dBASE).

Study your spreadsheet documentation for help in producing a PRN file. In 1-2-3, for example, you print to a file and the file receives the extension PRN automatically.

To produce an SDF (Standard Data Format) with your database program, read over its documentation. In dBASE III PLUS, for example, use your file and then the Copy To file name command. dBASE automatically gives the file a TXT extension. The Copy To command copies *all* records and *all* fields. If you want to copy particular fields or files, use the Report To File function or write custom code. If you are unfamiliar with the Copy To or Report To File commands, consult your dBASE documentation.

To load a PRN or SDF/TXT file, follow these steps:

1. While in Text mode, place the text cursor where you want to place the table.
2. From the File menu, choose Load Text/Picture.
3. From the LOAD TEXT/PICTURE dialog box, choose `Text` and select the `PRN-to-Table` button. (This choice is available only in the Professional Extension.) Click the `Text Cursor` option at the `Destination` prompt. If you prefer, you can put the file in the list of files for later transfer to a page or frame.
4. From the ITEM SELECTOR dialog box, choose the file you want to import. ***Note:*** if the file you are importing has an extension other than PRN, you may have to change the file filter for your file to appear in the selector box.
5. Click OK or press Enter. The converted file is loaded into an automatically created table (see figs. 12.10 and 12.11).

Note: After the Professional Extension converts the PRN or SDF file, your work is not complete. You need to modify the tags, shade areas as desired, and change any line settings to suit your purposes. If too many columns or too much data is in the table, additional editing is required for you to fit everything correctly on the page.

Fig. 12.10.

A 1-2-3 PRN file automatically converted to a table.

Item	Cost	Retail	Margin	Category
Heel lifts	0.60	2.00	70.00%	50
Ice bag	1.39	3.00	53.67%	50
Finger/thumb splint	4.20	8.95	53.07%	50
Elastic elbow support	3.35	6.95	51.80%	50
Elastic ankle support	3.35	6.95	51.80%	50
Elastic knee support	3.35	6.95	51.80%	50
AOA lumbar belt	11.30	22.95	50.76%	50
AOA knee brace	9.95	20.00	50.25%	50
Temp-Aid ice bag	5.30	10.60	50.00%	50
NLife	varies	varies	50.00%	50
Butterfly pillow	10.50	21.00	50.00%	50
Lumbar pillow	11.50	23.00	50.00%	50

Fig. 12.11.

A dBASE III PLUS SDF (TXT) file automatically converted to a table.

Store	Address	City	State/Zip
Abundant Life	90 Kam High-way	Hilo	HI 96720
Aloha Health Foods	1005 Ala Moana	Honolulu	HI 96814
Aloha Village Store	PO Box 709	Kealakekua	HI 96750
Arthur Yamada In-ternational	1327 S. King Street	Honolulu	HI 96814
B-Alive	318-B Kuulei Road	Kailua	HI 96734
Big Island Natural Foods	Parker Ranch Shopping Ctr-Kamuela	Kamuela	HI 96743
Celestial Natural Foods	66-443 Kam Highway	Haleiwa	HI 96712
Crystal Reef	28 Melia Place	Paia	HI 96779
Down to Earth, Honolulu	2525 S. King	Honolulu	HI 96826
Down to Earth, Wailuku	1910 Vineyard	Wailuku, Maui	HI 96793

12.27 Tip **Vertical space in a table row is determined by the spacing of the tag setting of the table cell's text.**

If you want narrower rows, change the above, below, or interline space of the cell text tag from the SPACING dialog box (accessed from the Paragraph menu). If you increase any of these figures, the vertical height of each row is increased. If you set all three figures to zero, the height of the row is only a little bigger than the font size chosen for the tag.

12.28 Trap **If you load a chapter that contains a table into the base Ventura, only codes (not the table) are shown. If you delete any of the codes, you can alter or destroy the table.**

It's a good practice not to load chapters created with the Professional Extension into base Ventura if tables were created and inserted into the chapter. When loaded in base Ventura, a table shows as only a series of codes. These codes define the table and, if deleted, make it impossible for the Professional Extension to later re-create the table correctly.

Using the Hyphenation Dictionary

If you have at least 1.2 megabytes of EMS memory available, you can use the Professional Extension's 130,000-word EDCO hyphenation dictionary. You need the extra memory because the dictionary operates in RAM.

If you installed the Professional Extension and did not install the dictionary, you must reinstall the Professional Extension to use the dictionary.

Using the EDCO hyphenation dictionary rather than the hyphenation algorithm provided with the base Ventura program gives you two primary advantages:

- Dictionary hyphenation is far more accurate than algorithmic hyphenation (hyphenating according to a complex set of rules).
- You have more control over many hyphenation parameters such as how short a word to check, how few characters to allow before or after a hyphen, and whether apostrophes are treated as additional characters or ends of words.

12.29 Tip

To use the hyphenation dictionary, set Hyphenation to USDICT in the ALIGNMENT dialog box.

When in Paragraph mode, select a paragraph and choose Alignment from the Paragraph menu. Set `Hyphenation` to `USDICT`, and the Professional Extension uses the EDCO hyphenation dictionary for all paragraphs with that tag. If the EDCO dictionary isn't loaded, `USDICT` does not appear as an option.

If you want to use only the EDCO hyphenation dictionary and not the algorithm, you can rename the USDICT.DH1 file in the VENTURA directory to USDICT.HY1. Only one file should have the HY1 extension (see Chapter 4 for more information).

12.30 Tip

Use the command line in the VPPROF.BAT file to load the hyphenation dictionary and control hyphenation parameters.

The VPPROF.BAT file loads the EDCO hyphenation dictionary into memory automatically with the following commands:

```
CD \VENTURA\DICT
EDCODICT
drtlcfg -M6 -B2 -E3 -AA -PC:\VENTURA\DICT
dload ENGLISH
```

The first command changes the directory to the \VENTURA\DICT subdirectory where the EDCO dictionary and its files are stored.

The second command loads the EDCODICT memory-resident dictionary controller.

The third command runs DRTLCFG.EXE and sets the −M, −B, −E, −A, and −P switches that control the hyphenation parameters. You can change any parameter. Be sure to include a space before and after each switch, but do not put any spaces within the switch which includes a dash, a letter, and a parameter (for example, −M6). Following is a list of DRTLCFG.EXE parameters and what they do:

- −M sets the minimum number of letters in a word before EDCO tries to hyphenate. The installed setting of −M6 keeps words of less than six characters from being hyphenated.
- −B sets the minimum number of characters before a hyphen. The installed setting of −B2 means no fewer than two letters will precede a hyphen.

- −E sets the minimum number of characters after a hyphen. The installed setting of −E3 means no fewer than three characters will follow a hyphen.
- −A sets whether an apostrophe is treated as another character or as the end of a word. A or E sets the apostrophe as the end of a word; C sets the apostrophe as another character.
- −P sets the path for the DCT file. In the case of the Professional Extension, the dictionary is ENGLISH.DCT.

The fourth command loads the ENGLISH dictionary. Although not mentioned by Xerox, additional hyphenation dictionaries in other languages may be offered at a future date.

12.31 Trick

Add a fifth line to the VPPROF.BAT file to unload the hyphenation dictionary when you quit Ventura.

You should include an additional line at the end of your VPPROF.BAT file to unload the dictionary from memory:

```
\VENTURA\DICT\DLOAD -U
```

The Professional Extension does not do this automatically.

12.32 Tip

Use DUPD.EXE to update the hyphenation dictionary and CHKWORD.EXE to see a word's hyphenation points.

The \VENTURA\DICT subdirectory contains two utilities: CHKWORD.EXE and DUPD.EXE.

Use DUPD.EXE to add or delete words in the hyphenation dictionary or to change hyphenation points for words in the dictionary.

Because the dictionary will be updated, you need enough disk storage space for the old and new versions of the dictionary—about 2.4 megabytes total. To update your dictionary with DUPD.EXE, follow these steps:

1. Create an ASCII file called UPDATE.TXT with the words you want to add, delete, or change hyphen points for. Use +, =, or ! to indicate whether to add, delete, or change the hyphen points, but don't insert spaces after the signs.

   A plus (+) sign before a word means "add this word." (For example, +*lin-ing-er* adds my last name to the dictionary; use hyphens to indicate hyphen points. If I didn't want my name hyphenated, I would use +*lininger* to indicate no hyphen points.)

An exclamation (!) point before a word means "delete this word." (For example, *!loser* deletes the word "loser" from the dictionary.)

An equal (=) sign before a word means "change hyphen points for this word." (For example, *=wal-l-pap-er* changes the hyphen points—incorrectly in this example—for the word "wallpaper.")

2. Load the dictionary into memory by typing the following four lines (press Enter at the end of each line):

   CD \VENTURA\DICT
   EDCODICT
   drtlcfg –M6 –B2 –E3 –AA –PC:\VENTURA\DICT
   dload ENGLISH

   Or if you haven't added the DLOAD –U command to your VPPROF batch file, you can load VPPROF and then quit to load the dictionary into memory.

3. Type *dupd update.txt* to update the dictionary.

You can use CHKWORD.EXE to check the current hyphenation points for a word based on the –M, –B, and –E switches. Run the program by typing *chkword* and entering words you want checked. Hyphenation points are indicated by dashes; because of the –M, –B, or –E switches, unused hyphenation points are indicated by ~.

12.33 Tip **You can add additional suffixes or prefixes to the EDCO dictionaries.**

If a word isn't located in the 130,000-word hyphenation dictionary, the prefix and suffix files are examined by Ventura for matches.

The \VENTURA\DICT subdirectory contains an ENGLISH.PFX (prefix) and ENGLISH.SFX (suffix) file. You can add more prefixes or suffixes with any text editor. Be sure to save the file as plain ASCII. The entries are in alphabetical order, but new entries do not need to be alphabetized.

Using Vertical Justification

Adjacent columns often don't align exactly. Maybe your table has more than one column on a page and the columns contain font variations, frames with text or graphics, gaps created by column or page breaks, or "Keep With Next," "Widows," or "Orphans" (see Chapter 5). Lack of alignment means text from one column is either a bit above or a bit below the text in the column next to it. You can correct this problem somewhat by using empty frames as space fillers to force vertical justification (see Chapter 6). The Professional Extension can accomplish this justification automatically.

With the Vertical Justification feature, the Professional Extension forces text in a frame to fit vertically so that the last sentence reaches the bottom of the frame—no matter how many columns are on the page. Space is added first between frames, then between paragraphs, and, if needed, between individual lines of text.

12.34 Tip **You can control vertical justification from four dialog boxes.**

You can control vertical justification from any of four different dialog boxes (see table 12.3 for each option). Vertical justification can add space between different page elements to accomplish its task (space is never subtracted). Depending on where you want space added, change the settings in the appropriate dialog box. The settings in each of the four dialog boxes are similar but affect different document elements.

Space is added by the "feathering" or "carding" methods. Feathering adds the exact space needed. Carding adds space only in multiples of the interline spacing setting for body text. Feathering is successful in aligning the bottoms of adjacent columns, but the body text does not necessarily align horizontally from column to column. Carding is also successful in forcing perfect alignment of the bottom of adjacent columns. The body text aligns horizontally from column to column, but only if the interline spacing for all paragraph tags was set up as whole number multiples of body text leading as recommended in Chapter 5.

The Professional Extension adds up to the maximum amount of space you set as allowable in attempting vertical justification of a page. If the maximum amount of space is added and the page still does not vertically justify, the Professional Extension adds no space at all. This feature prevents the Professional Extension from vertically justifying a page that only has a few lines, resulting in unsightly white space.

For vertical justification to work, you must set `Vert. Just. Within Frame` to either `Feathering` or `Carding` in the CHAPTER TYPOGRAPHY dialog box. The other three dialog boxes (FRAME TYPOGRAPHY, PARAGRAPH TYPOGRAPHY, and INSERT/EDIT TABLE) are local controls for modifying or overriding the CHAPTER TYPOGRAPHY settings (see fig. 12.12).

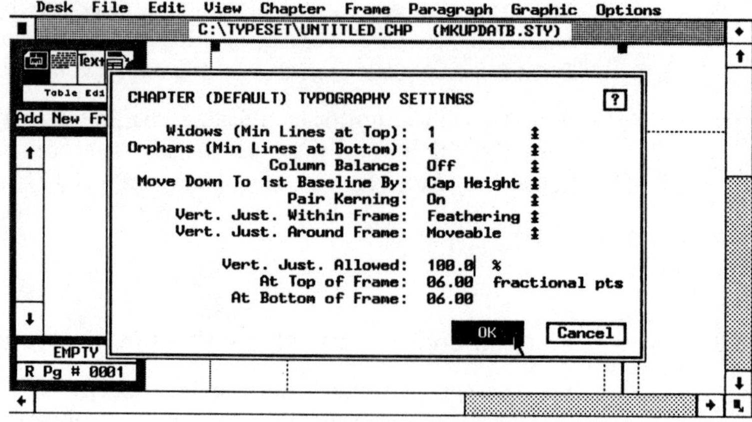

Fig. 12.12. *CHAPTER (DEFAULT) TYPOGRAPHY SETTINGS dialog box with vertical justification settings.*

Table 12.3 explains the options available with the dialog box settings.

Table 12.3
Dialog Box Options for Vertical Justification

Settings	*Options*
CHAPTER TYPOGRAPHY	
Vert. Just. Within Frame	You can set this option to `Off`, `Feathering`, or `Carding`. If you choose `Off`, no vertical justification is available for the chapter even if set from other menus.
Vert. Just. Around Frame	The options available are `Off`, `Fixed`, or `Movable`. If you select `Off`, no vertical justification around frames occurs in the chapter. If you choose `Fixed`, space is added only to page elements that fall below a frame, keeping the frame and the text above it in place. The `Movable` option adds space above and below the frame, perhaps moving the frame.
Vert. Just. Allowed	When you set `Vert. Just. Within Frame` to `Feathering` or `Carding`, you can set the `Vert. Just. Allowed` percentage. The normal setting of 100% adds up to the total of the interline spacing to force vertical justification.

Table 12.3—*Continued*

Settings	*Options*
At Top of Frame and At Bottom of Frame	For these options, you enter an amount for the maximum space the Professional Extension adds at the top or bottom of a frame in addition to the `Vert. Padding` you have already set from the SIZING AND SCALING dialog box. If you use different figures for `At Top` and `At Bottom`, then space is added proportionally in the ratio of your settings.
FRAME TYPOGRAPHY	
	The FRAME TYPOGRAPHY dialog box has the same settings as the CHAPTER TYPOGRAPHY dialog box. For specific frames, you can override the CHAPTER TYPOGRAPHY settings for vertical justification. Keep settings at `Default` for the same settings as CHAPTER TYPOGRAPHY. Set this option to `Off` to keep the Professional Extension from adding space in or around a frame.
PARAGRAPH TYPOGRAPHY	
Vert. Just. At Top of Para, At Bottom of Para, and Between Lines of Para	Enter an amount that sets the maximum space the Professional Extension adds at the top, bottom, or between paragraphs to force vertical justification. Because the figures can be different for each tag, you may want to limit the space that can be added to certain tags and force other tags to bear the bulk of the extra space.

Table 12.3—*Continued*

Settings	*Options*
INSERT/EDIT TABLE	
Vert. Just at Top and Vert. Just at Bottom	Enter an amount for the maximum amount of space the Professional Extension adds at the top or bottom of a table in addition to the Space Above and Space Below values you have already set. If you use different amounts for the top and bottom, space is added proportionally in the ratio of your settings.

Figure 12.13 gives an example of a page without vertical justification. Figure 12.14 has Vert. Just. Within Frame set to Feathering, and Vert. Just. Around Frame set to Movable. (The line at the bottom of the frame was drawn to show text lining up horizontally. Ordinarily, you would not want text overlapping a line.)

Nature's Life • 6703 International Avenue • Cypress, CA 90630 • Spring '88

The Service of Selling, Part 2

It is not the usual thing to get any comments back regarding any items in a company Newsletter. In our last issue of **Nature's Life Update**, we received many calls and several letters of appreciation for Part 1 of this series on "selling." They were very much appreciated. Thank you for your kindness.

As you recall, last time we discussed selling as a service. That is, selling is not something you do to a customer. Rather, it is an act of service you do for a customer. Once you believe that, there are numerous tools to help you sell more effectively—that is, help the customer more effectively.

Selling, like any profession only has a handful of successful practitioners. In the past century, it came to the attention of some observers that people who were successful have certain things in common.

I have recently been privileged to listen to a series of audio tapes by two pioneers in the field of "Success Philosophy." They are Napoleon Hill, who at the behest of Andrew Carnegie, the steel tycoon, interviewed the most successful men of his day in order to determine what it was that made them successful; and W. Clement Stone, a student of Hill's, who rose from poverty to oversee an insurance empire valued at over $6 billion.

The tape series I allude to is called "Success through a Positive Mental Attitude." It is available from the tape publishers Nightingale-Conant (800/323-5552). I highly recommend it. Elsewhere in this **Update** I will list their 17 "Rules of Success" for you and your staff to study.

Last time we dealt with the three axioms of selling:

(1) A confused mind always says NO! (2) No one likes to appear stupid. (3) It is best to offer a "yes or no" choice rather than "multiple choice." This time I'd like to deal with what to offer a customer who asks for advice regarding specific supplements.

Multiples

All one or two-a-day multiple formulas are inadequate in their mineral content. The only minerals that are sometimes up to useful levels are iron, copper and zinc. This is because the useful dose is low enough that too much room is not taken up in the formula. The multiple formula is usually designed for one of the following types of customers:

1) Those who refuse (or have a spouse, friend, son, etc.) who refuse to take "any more of those dang pills."

2) Those who are tired of taking "all those dang pills," and want to know if you have anything they can take that will allow them to eliminate "some of those dang pills."

3) An unsophisticated buyer who knows they need something but doesn't want to end up taking a "bunch of dang pills."

4) Someone going on a trip who doesn't want to cart along all their "dang bottles."

5) A sophisticated buyer who wants a baseline formula from which to build.

Multiples are usually promoted as low, medium, high or ultra high potency. What they are is determined by two factors. (1) The size of the pill (bigger is stronger), and (2) the amount of Vitamin B. The amount of Vitamin A and D will either be 1,000/400 or 25,000/1,000. Some formulas now contain both Vitamin A and Beta-Carotene.

Fig. 12.13.
Newsletter without vertical justification.

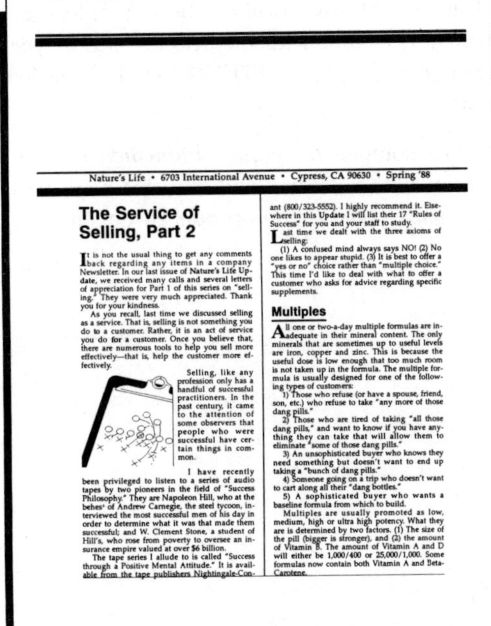

Nature's Life • 6703 International Avenue • Cypress, CA 90630 • Spring '88

The Service of Selling, Part 2

It is not the usual thing to get any comments back regarding any items in a company Newsletter. In our last issue of Nature's Life Update, we received many calls and several letters of appreciation for Part 1 of this series on "selling." They were very much appreciated. Thank you for your kindness.

As you recall, last time we discussed selling as a service. That is, selling is not something you do to a customer. Rather, it is an act of service you do for a customer. Once you believe that, there are numerous tools to help you sell more effectively—that is, help the customer more effectively.

Selling, like any profession only has a handful of successful practitioners. In the past century, it came to the attention of some observers that people who were successful have certain things in common.

I have recently been privileged to listen to a series of audio tapes by two pioneers in the field of "Success Philosophy." They are Napoleon Hill, who at the behes' of Andrew Carnegie, the steel tycoon, interviewed the most successful men of his day in order to determine what it was that made them successful; and W. Clement Stone, a student of Hill's, who rose from poverty to oversee an insurance empire valued at over $6 billion.

The tape series I allude to is called "Success through a Positive Mental Attitude." It is available from the tape publishers Nightingale-Conant (800/323-5552). I highly recommend it. Elsewhere in this Update I will list their 17 "Rules of Success" for you and your staff to study.

Last time we dealt with the three axioms of selling:

(1) A confused mind always says NO! (2) No one likes to appear stupid. (3) It is best to offer a "yes or no" choice rather than "multiple choice." This time I'd like to deal with what to offer a customer who asks for advice regarding specific supplements.

Multiples

All one or two-a-day multiple formulas are inadequate in their mineral content. The only minerals that are sometimes up to useful levels are iron, copper and zinc. This is because the useful dose is low enough that too much room is not taken up in the formula. The multiple formula is usually designed for one of the following types of customers:

1) Those who refuse (or have a spouse, friend, son, etc.) who refuse to take "any more of those dang pills."

2) Those who are tired of taking "all those dang pills," and want to know if you have anything they can take that will allow them to eliminate "some of those dang pills."

3) An unsophisticated buyer who knows they need something but doesn't want to end up taking a "bunch of dang pills."

4) Someone going on a trip who doesn't want to cart along all their "dang bottles."

5) A sophisticated buyer who wants a baseline formula from which to build.

Multiples are usually promoted as low, medium, high or ultra high potency. What they are is determined by two factors. (1) The size of the pill (bigger is stronger), and (2) the amount of Vitamin B. The amount of Vitamin A and D will either be 1,000/400 or 25,000/1,000. Some formulas now contain both Vitamin A and Beta-Carotene.

Fig. 12.14. *Newsletter with vertical justification.*

Chapter Summary

If this chapter seemed difficult, don't worry. The features in the Professional Extension are intended for extensive layout demands. The controls are sophisticated and complex. Xerox wisely omitted these capabilities in the base product because many users don't need them.

If you need the capabilities of the Professional Extension, however, you should have a working knowledge of its hardware requirements and major capabilities.

In this chapter, you learned about expanded memory support using either EMS or EEMS drivers to access memory on your system over 640K. You saw how you can create and edit complex equations. You learned how to use the new forward and backward referencing of variables for primitive merges and referencing of section, caption, page, chapter, and figure numbers.

You also learned table and form creation. You learned how to use the powerful new hyphenation feature with the 130,000-word typesetter's hyphenation dictionary licensed to Xerox by EDCO. Finally, you learned how to use vertical justification.

You have now completed *Ventura Publisher Tips, Tricks, and Traps*. I hope you have enjoyed the journey and that this book will become a useful tool to help you enhance your Ventura-produced documents.

Appendix

A

This appendix contains a listing of suppliers for Ventura-compatible products, instructions for installing Bitstream Fontware, and a table of decimal keyboard codes for various fonts.

Suppliers of Ventura-Compatible Products

This section presents an alphabetized list of suppliers of products that work well with Ventura. These products support or enhance various capabilities to help you produce top-quality documents. Along with a brief description of each product, the vendor's name, address, and telephone number have been included.

3G Graphics

11410 NE 124th Street
Suite 6155
Kirkland, WA 98034
(206) 823-8198

Images with Impact provides terrific EPS images that were originally available only for Macintosh systems. The package provides high quality and good value.

Adobe Systems, Incorporated

1585 Charleston Road
P.O. Box 7900
Mountain View, CA 94039-7900
(800) 833-6687

Adobe Type Library of PostScript fonts are the highest quality PostScript fonts available. They come packaged as individual fonts and in Publishing Pack font collections.

Adobe Illustrator for the PC is a sophisticated, professional graphics program that originally appeared on the Macintosh. It runs under Windows and offers great drawing and font-effects capabilities. Adobe Illustrator comes bundled with Adobe Collector's Edition of PostScript clip art, specialty fonts, and dingbats.

Aristocad, Incorporated

1650 Centre Pointe Drive
Milpitas, CA 95035
(408) 946-2747

The Soft Kicker screen driver allows your EGA or VGA monitor to emulate a full-page monitor. This is a must-have utility for the serious desktop publisher—no more having to use scroll bars to see the rest of the page. You move the cursor, and the page moves with you.

Atech Software

629 South Rancho Santa Fe Road
San Marcos, CA 92069
(619) 438-6883 (order line)

Publisher's Powerpak is the one of the best values in budget fonts. It gives PostScript-like font-scaling capabilities to more than 200 dot-matrix, laser, ink-jet, and bubblejet printers.

Bitstream, Incorporated

Athenaeum House
215 First Street
Cambridge, MA 02142
(800) 522-3668

Fontware fonts for Hewlett-Packard and compatible laser printers and PostScript devices offer a large variety of high-quality fonts. They are available individually or in Fundamental collections. Fontware requires an installation program, which is provided free with Ventura.

Casady & Greene, Incorporated

P.O. Box 223779
Carmel, CA 93922
(408) 624-8716

Fluent Laser Fonts come in 22 volumes of high-quality PostScript fonts. These unusual and versatile fonts are useful when you need display or decorative fonts. They are available individually or in bundled sets.

Vivid Impressions is a collection of EPS clip art with a holiday and fantasy theme.

Central Point Software, Incorporated

15220 NW Greenbrier Parkway
#200
Beaverton, OR 97006
(503) 690-8090

The Deluxe Copy II PC Option Board is an add-on board that connects to your PC's internal 3 1/2-inch drive. Once connected, your drive can read, write, and format Macintosh-compatible disks while retaining its capability to work as a DOS drive. All the transfers made between Macintosh and PC systems during the preparation of this book were done with the Option Board, which offers a flawless and inexpensive way to transfer files between the two platforms.

PC Tools Deluxe is a collection of DOS utilities. Specifically mentioned in this book is the disk caching utility, which is made for Central Point by Multisoft (recently rated the producer of the top disk cache by *PC Magazine*).

Computer Support Corporation

15926 Midway Road
Dallas, TX 75244
(214) 661-8960

Arts & Letters Graphics Composer includes thousands of professionally drawn clip-art images you can modify easily. The package also includes several fonts with which you can create special effects. Arts & Letters Graphics Composer is one of the best values for the nonartist.

Arts & Letters Graphics Editor is a draw program with the same capabilities as the Graphics Composer but offers free-form drawing tools as well. Its clip-art library is not as large, but extra images are available. Both programs run under Windows.

Corel Systems Corporation

1600 Carling Avenue
Ottawa, Ontario K1Z 8RT
(613) 728-8200

Corel Draw is a sophisticated but easy-to-use drawing program that runs under Windows. It is particularly notable for its ease in creating effects with the numerous fonts that are included. Corel Draw is one of the best.

Headline is a non-WYSIWYG program for creating EPS files of special font effects. This package is superseded by Corel Draw, but if you are budget-minded, this program is well worth a look.

Tab-In imports database and spreadsheet data.

New Font is a non-WYSIWYG program for creating specialty PostScript fonts for Ventura based on fonts you have available for your system. It does not create screen fonts. Many of the effects can be created with Corel Draw, although no actual font sets can be created.

Loader lets you download Adobe PostScript fonts to your printer before starting Ventura, letting the fonts act as resident fonts.

Custom Applications, Incorporated

5 Middlesex Technology Center
900 Middlesex Turnpike
Billerica, MA 01821
(508) 667-8585

Freedom Of Press is a software PostScript emulator that supports 19 dot-matrix and non-PostScript laser printers. Remember that PostScript emulators are slow and not compatible with all PostScript fonts.

Digi-Fonts, Incorporated

3000 Youngfield Street
Suite 285
Lakewood, CO 80215
(800) 242-5665

Digi-duit is an inexpensive way to create regular and special effect fonts for Hewlett-Packard LaserJet and compatible laser printers. The special effects available include wide, slant, rotation, flop, and reverse. This package is somewhat difficult to use with a command line interface.

Digital Research, Incorporated

70 Garden Court
Box DRI
Monterey, CA 93942
(800) 443-4200

GEM Artline is a GEM-based draw program with superb capability of creating font effects. It is compatible with Bitstream Fontware.

Dayna Communications, Incorporated

50 South Main Street
Salt Lake City, UT 84144
(801) 531-0600

The DaynaFile is an external disk drive that lets an Apple Macintosh computer read and write to DOS formatted disks. DaynaFile is available as either a 5 1/4-inch, 360K and 1.2M drive, or as a 3 1/2-inch, 720K and 1.4M drive.

Image Club Graphics, Incorporated

1902-1151 SE
Calgary, Canada T2G 3C2
(800) 661-9410

Digit-Art is a large collection of EPS and TIFF clip art. The images are clean, original, and striking. Digit-Art is a good value.

Inner Media, Incorporated

60 Plain Road
Hollis, NH 03049
(603) 465-3216

Collage Plus is a screen-capture and image-management utility that allows editing of screen captured images. You can use this memory-resident program within Ventura to preview pictures before they are loaded.

INSET Systems Incorporated

12 Mill Plain Road
Danbury, CT 06811
(800) 748-0844

InSet is a great utility for capturing and editing screen figures (the screen figures in this book were all created with it). InSet also allows you to include graphics in programs that don't normally allow graphics.

Hijaak is a useful utility for converting various graphics formats. Many formats are supported, and new ones are added frequently. Hijaak can capture but not edit screens.

Keytronic

P.O. Box 14687
Spokane, WA 99214-0687
(509) 928-8000

Keytronic Touchpad Keyboard is for users without a mouse. It allows keyboard shortcuts and mouse movement using a built-in touch pad.

LaserMaster Corporation

7156 Shady Oak Road
Eden Prairie, MN 55344
(612) 944-6069

LC2 Controller allows non-PostScript printers to support scalable fonts. With 2M of memory, it allows all supported printers (including PostScript) to speed output dramatically. The LC2 Controller supports Bitstream Fontware fonts. If you use it with a PostScript printer, PostScript capabilities are lost. The major benefit to using the product is speeding up your printing. This is a great product if it meets your needs.

LaserTools Corporation

3025 Buena Vista Way
Berkeley, CA 94708
(415) 843-2234

LaserTORQ is an essential utility that not only serves as a print spooler, but actually speeds up printer output. It works with both laser and other types of printers. The TORQ program speeds up printer output for only nonlaser printers.

Trading Post allows the baud rate on a serial laser printer to be increased for more rapid throughput. It also allows programs that don't support PostScript to output to a PostScript printer.

Marketing Graphics, Incorporated

4401 Dominion Boulevard
Suite 210
Glen Allen, VA 23060-3379
(804) 747-6991

Publisher's PicturePaks includes three volumes of clip art suited for business use, available in PCX, CGM (WPG), or PIX formats.

Messenger Software, Incorporated

20202 Center Ridge Road
Suite 5
Rocky River, OH 44116
(216) 333-9936

xFer is a utility for transferring files between the PC and Macintosh environments. This system uses programs on both the PC and Macintosh, and a direct connection either via cable or modem accomplishes the linkup. xFer supports five word processor formats and can transfer in MacBinary, AFE, and text modes.

Metro Image Base, Incorporated

18623 Ventura Boulevard
Suite 210
Tarzana, CA 91356
(800) 525-1552

Metro Image Base clip-art libraries contain excellent TIFF or PCX clip art of complex and rich images. The packages are a good value; they contain 100 images per volume, and the graphics are sensibly grouped.

Metroplex Digital Corporation

P.O. Box 815729
Dallas, TX 75381-5729
(214) 242-2612

Pub-Star I helps you tag text files using a word processor. This useful utility can read and list style sheet attributes. It also can define and include custom inserts such as typographical quotes, em dashes, and so forth. If you do extensive tagging in your word processor, this utility is well worth a look.

Mickey turns your left mouse button into an Enter key.

Micrografx

1303 Arapaho
Richardson, TX 75081-2444
(800) 272-3729

Draw Plus and Designer are among the most sophisticated of the professional draw packages currently available for PCs. Rich and complex, these Windows-based programs can create extraordinary pictures.

Headline Typefaces are add-on typefaces for use within Designer or Draw Plus.

Standard and Special Edition Clip-art include incredible electronic clip art created with Micrografx products. The Special Edition series includes maps and anatomy that can be used by professional designers.

Multisoft Corporation

15100 SW Koll Parkway
Suite L
Beaverton, OR 97006
(800) 234-5945

PC-Kwik Power Pak is a collection of DOS utilities that includes a disk cache, screen and keyboard accelerator, and RAM disk. The disk cache is available separately and was recently rated by *PC Magazine* as one of the best caches available.

New Riders Publishing

P.O. Box 4846
Thousand Oaks, CA 91360
(818) 991-5392

Style Sheets for Newsletters, Business Documents, and Technical Documents are a series of book and disk combinations that come with excellent style sheets for various needs. The books cover the layouts and explain how the style sheets were created.

Desktop Manager is a memory-resident utility to help track a Ventura document's history. The package includes catalog, timed-backup, and management capabilities for Ventura. Desktop Manager is essential if more than one person is working on the same document. The automatic timed-backup feature alone is worth the price.

Pecan Software Systems, Incorporated

1410 39th Street
Brooklyn, NY 11218
(800) 637-3226

With Style is a file-management utility that offers powerful style sheet control. With this utility, you can add, delete, copy, modify, merge, and rename tags in style sheets.

ProGraf

P.O. Box 270897
Houston, TX 77277
(713) 840-8098

Drop-Cap PCX files helps you create drop-caps in Ventura. The package is inexpensive and high quality.

Quarterdeck Office Systems

150 Pico Boulevard
Santa Monica, CA 90405
(213) 392-9851

DESQview is a multiple-window operating environment. It is especially useful with 80286 and 80386 systems that have several megabytes of RAM. DESQview allows several programs to run at the same time (you switch between them with a keystroke).

SNA, Incorporated

P.O. Box 3662
Princeton, NJ 08543
(609) 683-1237

VP Toolbox is a powerful utility for cataloging and controlling the various elements of a chapter. It has extensive capabilities for modifying and controlling style sheets. It can tell you which tags are used and which are unused, for example. VP Toolbox is almost essential if you have trouble tracking multiple chapter elements.

SoftCraft, Incorporated

16 North Carroll Street
Suite 500
Madison, WI 53703
(800) 351-0500 (order line)

Font Solution Pack includes a group of programs for creating fonts for Hewlett-Packard LaserJet and compatible printers. The Font Solution Pack was designed with the desktop publisher in mind. It includes WYSIFonts for installing screen fonts, Laser Fonts for installing printer fonts, and Font Effects and Spinfont for creating special font effects. Also included are SoftCraft Font Editor for editing fonts and one Bitstream Fontware typeface. SoftCraft also offers many inexpensive laser fonts from its own collection, but be aware that the interface for SoftCraft programs is difficult and takes some effort to master.

Solutions International

P.O. Box 989
Montpelier, VT 05602
(802) 229-9146

The Curator is a program for translating various Macintosh graphics formats into other Macintosh or PC-compatible graphics formats. This program is indispensable if you do much graphics work and need to translate Macintosh EPS files into DOS EPS files.

SPC Software Publishing Corporation

P.O. Box 7210
1901 Landings Drive
Mountain View, CA 94039-7210
(415) 962-8910

Harvard Graphics is a popular business graphing and charting program. You can create sophisticated charts for inclusion in Ventura. It has a nonwindows graphic interface.

Symantec

Living Videotext Division
117 Easy Street
Mountain View, CA 94043
(800) 441-7234

GrandView is a powerful outlining and management tool. This book was outlined in GrandView before being written.

SymSoft, Incorporated

P.O. Box 4477
Mountain View, CA 94040
(415) 491-1552

Hotshot Graphics is a screen-capture, editing, and image-cataloging program. It can convert to PCX, GEM, TIFF, and EPS formats.

T/Maker Co.

1973 Landings Drive
Mountain View, CA 94043
(415) 962-0195

ClickArt contains EPS, GEM, and PCX formats. The EPS art is great and the GEM and PCX formats are terrific values.

Scrapbook + is a Windows utility to help you track all your graphics files that are in a format Windows supports. Besides text, the program can convert between EPS, TIFF, and Microsoft Paint. This package is essential if you use Windows.

Ventura Publisher Users' Group, Incorporated

7502 Aaron Place
San Jose, CA 95139
(408) 227-5030

This users' group publishes *Ventura Professional!*, the Ventura users' magazine. If you are serious about Ventura, join VPUG for their magazine, electronic bulletin board, and support services. For only $36 per year, it is a good value.

ZSoft Corporation

450 Franklin Road
Suite 100
Marietta, GA 30067
(404) 428-0008

Publisher's Paintbrush, PC Paintbrush Plus, and PC Paintbrush Plus for Windows are the best paint (bit-map) programs for the PC. All these packages can act as front ends for scanners. They are essential for cleaning or editing scanned images before importing them into Ventura.

Publisher's Type Foundry is a font editing and creation tool for serious desktop publishers. With this program, you can create your own PostScript or bit-mapped fonts.

Installing Fonts with Bitstream Fontware

With Ventura, you received a Bitstream Fontware installation kit, which is required to install Bitstream typefaces for use with Ventura. You can use Bitstream fonts with the following printers:

- ❑ AST TurboLaser
- ❑ Apple LaserWriter or LaserWriter Plus
- ❑ Cordata LP300X
- ❑ Epson LQ
- ❑ Epson MX-80 (with Graftrax) or FX-80
- ❑ Hewlett-Packard LaserJet Plus or LaserJet II
- ❑ IBM Graphics or Proprinter
- ❑ NEC P5
- ❑ PostScript-compatible printers
- ❑ Tall Tree JLaser
- ❑ Toshiba 24 wire
- ❑ Xerox 4020 or 4045

If you have a PostScript printer, the sample typefaces provided with Ventura do not work on your printer. Because these faces—Swiss, Dutch, and Symbol—already reside in your printer under the names Helvetica, Times, and Symbol, you don't need the sample typefaces anyway. If, however, you purchase additional fonts from Bitstream, you need the installation kit to install the fonts properly. You also need a minimum of 1.5 megabytes of free disk space to accommodate the installation kit and fonts.

To install fonts using the Bitstream Fontware installation kit, do the following:

1. Place disk 1 of the Fontware kit into drive A, type *fontware* on the DOS command line, and press Enter.

2. After the opening screen appears and after you specify whether you have a color or monochrome system, the main Fontware menu appears. Highlight the Set Up Fontware command and press Enter.

3. Fontware asks on which directory you want to install the Fontware files. If the suggested drive is incorrect, you can change it, but there's no reason to change the name of the directory from FONTWARE. Press Enter.

4. Fontware asks in which directory Ventura is installed. If the suggestion is incorrect, make the correction. Press Enter.

5. Fontware asks for confirmation of the directories you specified. If the directories are wrong, press N and make the corrections; otherwise, press Y. Fontware spends some time copying files to the hard drive. After a minute or so, you are prompted to insert disk 2 of the Fontware kit. Insert the disk and press any key to conclude copying the installation files to your hard drive.

6. You are prompted to select your display monitor. Use the arrow keys to go through the list until you find your monitor. Once your display is highlighted, press Enter.

7. You are next prompted to select the display character set. This is the set of characters used to create screen fonts. Choose either the VP US or VP International character sets. They are similar, but the US set has fewer characters. Do not choose PostScript Outline or VP Symbol; Outline is only for PostScript printer (not display) fonts, and Symbol is only for the Symbol typeface.

8. Choose your printer model.

9. Choose the printer character set. If you have a PostScript printer, you must choose PostScript Outline. For other printers, choose either VP US or VP International (choose the same set selected in step 7). If you are installing Symbol fonts, choose VP Symbol.

10. The directories, display model, display character set, printer model, and printer character set you specified are summarized on the screen. If they are all correct, press F10. Otherwise, press Esc and make any necessary corrections. To stop the process without completing the installation, press Ctrl-Q to exit. Whenever you want to leave the installation program, you can press Ctrl-Q.

11. After you press F10, the Typeface menu appears. Because no typefaces have been installed previously, the panel reads `0 Typefaces Available`. If you have a non-PostScript printer, you can add Swiss, Dutch, or Symbol (if you selected the Symbol display and printer character sets previously). If you have any font packages from Bitstream, you can now add those for any type of printer, including PostScript. Press F3 and insert your font disk into drive A. Press Enter.

12. Fontware lists the fonts available on the disk. Select the desired fonts and styles (Bitstream uses the term *typefaces*) by positioning the highlighted cursor with the arrow keys and pressing Enter. You can deselect a typeface by highlighting it and pressing Enter a second time. Selected typefaces have large arrows next to them on the screen.

13. After selecting the typefaces, press F10 to copy them to your hard drive. This may take a few moments, and you may be asked to insert a second disk. Once copied, the typefaces are listed as available. Repeat steps 11 through 13 to add more typefaces.

14. If you change your mind after adding a typeface, you can delete any typeface by pressing F5, positioning the highlighted cursor using the arrow keys, and pressing Enter. You are asked to confirm the deletion by pressing Y to delete the typeface or N to cancel the deletion.

15. When you are done installing fonts, press F10 to continue.

16. At the Printer Make Fonts screen, choose the fonts you want to create by moving the highlighted cursor to the desired font and pressing Enter; deselect fonts by pressing Enter a second time. If you are creating non-PostScript fonts, you must enter point sizes for the fonts you select; on PostScript systems, you do not enter point sizes. You cannot make fonts smaller than 6 points. You cannot make fonts larger than 40 points for the Xerox 4045, 36 points for the LaserJet Plus, 72 points for the LaserJet II, 99 points for 9-pin dot-matrix printers, and 60 points for 24-pin dot-matrix printers.

17. To make multiple point sizes for the same font, enter a space between the sizes you type: *10 12 36*, for example. Use only whole numbers for the point sizes. Press Enter when done. Use the arrow keys to select point sizes for other typefaces. To enter exactly the same point sizes for one font as the preceding font, select the typeface and press F9.

18. For non-PostScript printers, you can select the same point sizes for screen fonts as you did for printer fonts by positioning the highlighted cursor on the typeface name and pressing F4. A confirming dialog box appears. You also can enter different sizes by pressing F2 to go to the next screen. Because you did not enter printer-font point sizes for PostScript printers, you must enter your choice of point sizes for screen fonts by pressing F2 to go to the Display Make Fonts screen.

19. At the Display Make Fonts screen, select the sizes of the screen fonts you want to make. For non-PostScript printers, the choice is yours whether you want to make screen fonts for all the point sizes of printer fonts you are creating. For PostScript printers, if you select a screen point size of 6, 7, 8, 9, 10, 11, 12, 14, 16, 18, 20, 24, 28, or 36, you will be able to see most font changes even in Reduced or Enlarged View. Each screen font takes up memory and disk space, however, so do not create too many font sizes. (Read the tips in the "Using and Understanding Screen Fonts" section of Chapter 9.)

20. Once you finish selecting printer fonts and printer-font and screen-font point sizes, press F6 for an estimate of how long the font-creation process will take and whether you have enough disk space. If you don't have enough room, you can delete point sizes or fonts until you have enough room; you may have to exit Fontware and make room on your hard drive by deleting some files. Once you have made room, start up again by typing *fontware* at the FONTWARE directory.

21. If the time and space estimates are satisfactory, press F10. Once again, Fontware presents time and space estimates. Press Y to proceed or N to halt the process. Depending on what you are creating, you wait either a short or long time.

22. Complete the installation process by either directing Ventura to use the newly created Fontware printer width table or merging it with an existing font table (see Tips 9.3 and 9.4). The new width table is found in the FONTWARE directory; it has the name of the printer you chose with a WID extension. Make sure that the width table file name is unique before you copy it to the VENTURA directory with your other width tables.

When you are through creating fonts and have copied the width table to the VENTURA directory, delete the FONTWARE subdirectory and all the subdirectories of FONTWARE. If you have enough disk space and think you may create more fonts or font sizes in the future, you can leave the FONTWARE files on your disk. If the files remain on your disk, the next time you load fonts, go to the FONTWARE directory and type *fontware* to load the installation kit.

Decimal Keyboard Codes for Regular (Roman), Symbol, and Zapf Dingbat Fonts

In this table are four columns. You enter the number in the Decimal column by holding down the Alt key and entering the number from the keypad—not the row of numbers along the top of your keyboard. Depending on which font you are using, the corresponding regular (Roman), symbol, or Zapf dingbat (usable with only PostScript printers that have this font available) appears on the screen. If you don't have Zapf dingbat screen fonts, the Roman character appears on the screen, but the dingbat does print correctly.

Table A.1
Decimal Keyboard Codes

Decimal	Roman	Symbol	Dingbat
1-31	unused		
32	space		
33	!	!	✁
34	"	∀	✂
35	#	#	✃
36	$	∃	✄
37	%	%	☎
38	&	&	✆
39	'	∍	✇
40	(	(	✈
41	)	)	✉
42	*	∗	☛
43	+	+	☞
44	,	,	✌
45	-	−	✍
46	.	.	✎
47	/	/	✏
48	0	0	✐
49	1	1	✑
50	2	2	✒
51	3	3	✓
52	4	4	✔
53	5	5	✕
54	6	6	✖
55	7	7	✗
56	8	8	✘
57	9	9	✙
58	:	:	✚
59	;	;	✛
60	<	<	✜
61	=	=	✝
62	>	>	✞
63	?	?	✟
64	@	≅	✠
65	A	Α	✡
66	B	Β	✢
67	C	Χ	✣
68	D	Δ	✤
69	E	Ε	✥
70	F	Φ	✦
71	G	Γ	✧
72	H	Η	★
73	I	Ι	✩
74	J	ϑ	✪
75	K	Κ	✫
76	L	Λ	✬
77	M	Μ	✭
78	N	Ν	✮
79	O	Ο	✯
80	P	Π	✰
81	Q	Θ	✱
82	R	Ρ	✲
83	S	Σ	✳
84	T	Τ	✴
85	U	Υ	✵
86	V	ς	✶
87	W	Ω	✷
88	X	Ξ	✸
89	Y	Ψ	✹
90	Z	Ζ	✺
91	[	[	✻
92	\	∴	✼
93	]	]	✽
94	^	⊥	✾
95	_	_	✿
96	‘		❀
97	a	α	❁
98	b	β	❂
99	c	χ	❃
100	d	δ	❄
101	e	ε	❅
102	f	ϕ	❆
103	g	γ	❇
104	h	η	❈
105	i	ι	❉
106	j	φ	❊
107	k	κ	❋
108	l	λ	●
109	m	μ	❍
110	n	ν	■
111	o	ο	❏
112	p	π	❐
113	q	θ	❑
114	r	ρ	❒
115	s	σ	▲
116	t	τ	▼
117	u	υ	◆
118	v	ϖ	❖
119	w	ω	◗
120	x	ξ	❘
121	y	ψ	❙
122	z	ζ	❚
123	{	{	❛
124	|	|	❜
125	}	}	❝
126	~	~	❞

Table A.1—*Continued*

Decimal	Roman	Symbol	Dingbat
127		unused	
128	Ç	unused	
129	ü	ϒ	❡
130	é	′	❢
131	â	≤	❣
132	ä	⁄	❤
133	à	∞	❥
134	å	ƒ	❦
135	ç	♣	❧
136	ê	♦	♣
137	ë	♥	♦
138	è	♠	♥
139	ï	↔	♠
140	î	←	①
141	ì	↑	②
142	Ä	→	③
143	Å	↓	④
144	É	°	⑤
145	æ	±	⑥
146	Æ	″	⑦
147	ô	≥	⑧
148	ö	×	⑨
149	ò	∝	⑩
150	û	∂	❶
151	ù	•	❷
152	ÿ	÷	❸
153	Ö	≠	❹
154	Ü	≡	❺
155	¢	≈	❻
156	£	…	❼
157	¥	⏐	❽
158	¤	⎯	❾

Decimal	Roman	Symbol	Dingbat
159	ƒ	↵	❿
160	á	ℵ	➀
161	í	ℑ	➁
162	ó	ℜ	➂
163	ú	℘	➃
164	ñ	⊗	➄
165	Ñ	⊕	➅
166	ª	∅	➆
167	º	∩	➇
168	¿	∪	➈
169	“	⊃	➉
170	”	⊇	➊
171	‹	⊄	➋
172	›	⊂	➌
173	¡	⊆	➍
174	«	∈	➎
175	»	∉	➏
176	ã	∠	➐
177	õ	∇	➑
178	Ø	®	➒
179	ø	©	➓
180	œ	™	➔
181	Œ	∏	→
182	À	√	↔
183	Ã	·	↕
184	Õ	¬	➘
185	§	∧	➙
186	‡	∨	➚
187	†	⇔	➛
188	¶	⇐	➜
189	©	⇑	➝
190	®	⇒	➞

Decimal	Roman	Symbol	Dingbat
191	™	⇓	➟
192	„	◊	➠
193	…	〈	➡
194	‰	®	➢
195	•	©	➣
196	–	™	➤
197	—	∑	➥
198	°	⎛	➦
199	Á	⎜	➧
200	Â	⎝	➨
201	È	⎡	➩
202	Ê	⎢	➪
203	Ë	⎣	➫
204	Ì	⎧	➬
205	Í	⎨	➭
206	Î	⎩	➮
207	Ï	⎪	➯
208	Ò		
209	Ó	〉	➱
210	Ô	∫	➲
211	Š	⌠	➳
212	š	⎮	➴
213	Ù	⌡	➵
214	Ú	⎞	➶
215	Û	⎟	➷
216	Ÿ	⎠	➸
217	ß	⎤	➹
218	Ž	⎥	➺
219	ž	⎦	➻
220	⁄	⎫	➼
221		⎬	➽
222		⎭	➾

Index

A

B

C

D

E

F

G

H

I

N

O

S

T

U

V

W

X

Y

Z

More Computer Knowledge from Que

LOTUS SOFTWARE TITLES

1-2-3 QueCards 21.95
1-2-3 QuickStart 21.95
1-2-3 Quick Reference 6.95
1-2-3 for Business, 2nd Edition 22.95
1-2-3 Command Language 21.95
1-2-3 Macro Library, 2nd Edition 21.95
1-2-3 Tips, Tricks, and Traps, 2nd Edition 21.95
Using 1-2-3, Special Edition 24.95
Using 1-2-3 Workbook and Disk, 2nd Edition 29.95
Using Symphony, 2nd Edition 26.95

DATABASE TITLES

dBASE III Plus Handbook, 2nd Edition 22.95
dBASE IV Handbook, 3rd Edition 23.95
dBASE IV Tips, Tricks, and Traps, 2nd Edition 21.95
dBASE IV QueCards 21.95
dBASE IV Quick Reference 6.95
dBASE IV QuickStart 21.95
dBXL and Quicksilver Programming: Beyond dBASE 24.95
R:BASE Solutions: Applications and Resources 19.95
R:BASE User's Guide, 3rd Edition 19.95
Using Clipper 24.95
Using Reflex 19.95
Using Paradox, 2nd Edition 22.95
Using Q & A, 2nd Edition 21.95

MACINTOSH AND APPLE II TITLES

HyperCard QuickStart: A Graphics Approach 21.95
Using AppleWorks, 2nd Edition 21.95
Using dBASE Mac 19.95
Using Dollars and Sense 19.95
Using Excel 21.95
Using HyperCard: From Home to HyperTalk .. 24.95
Using Microsoft Word: Macintosh Version 21.95
Using Microsoft Works 19.95
Using WordPerfect: Macintosh Version 19.95

APPLICATIONS SOFTWARE TITLES

CAD and Desktop Publishing Guide 24.95
Smart Tips, Tricks, and Traps 23.95
Using AutoCAD 29.95
Using DacEasy 21.95
Using Dollars and Sense: IBM Version, 2nd Edition 19.95
Using Enable/OA 23.95
Using Excel: IBM Version 24.95
Using Managing Your Money 19.95
Using Quattro 21.95
Using Smart 22.95
Using SuperCalc4 .... 21.95

HARDWARE AND SYSTEMS TITLES

DOS Programmer's Reference 24.95
DOS QueCards 21.95
DOS Tips, Tricks, and Traps 22.95
DOS Workbook and Disk 29.95
IBM PS/2 Handbook 21.95
Managing Your Hard Disk, 2nd Edition 22.95
MS-DOS Quick Reference 6.95
MS-DOS QuickStart 21.95
MS-DOS User's Guide, 3rd Edition 22.95
Networking IBM PCs, 2nd Edition 19.95
Programming with Windows 22.95
Understanding UNIX: A Conceptual Guide, 2nd Edition 21.95
Upgrading and Repairing PCs 24.95
Using Microsoft Windows 19.95
Using OS/2 .... 22.95
Using PC DOS, 2nd Edition 22.95

WORD-PROCESSING AND DESKTOP PUBLISHING TITLES

Microsoft Word Techniques and Applications 19.95
Microsoft Word Tips, Tricks, and Traps 19.95
Using DisplayWrite 4 .... 19.95
Using Microsoft Word, 2nd Edition 21.95
Using MultiMate Advantage, 2nd Edition 19.95
Using PageMaker IBM Version, 2nd Edition 24.95
Using PFS: First Publisher 22.95
Using Sprint 21.95
Using Ventura Publisher, 2nd Edition 24.95
Using WordPerfect, 3rd Edition 21.95
Using WordPerfect 5 .... 24.95
Using WordPerfect 5 Workbook and Disk 29.95
Using WordStar, 2nd Edition 21.95
WordPerfect Macro Library 21.95
WordPerfect QueCards 21.95
WordPerfect Quick Reference 6.95
WordPerfect QuickStart 21.95
WordPerfect Tips, Tricks, and Traps, 2nd Edition 21.95
WordPerfect 5 Workbook and Disk 29.95
Ventura Publisher Tips, Tricks, and Traps 24.95
Ventura Publisher Techniques and Applications 22.95

PROGRAMMING AND TECHNICAL TITLES

Assembly Language Quick Reference 6.95
C Programming Guide, 3rd Edition 24.95
C Quick Reference 6.95
DOS and BIOS Functions Quick Reference 6.95
QuickBASIC Quick Reference 6.95
Turbo Pascal Quick Reference 6.95
Turbo Pascal Tips, Tricks, and Traps 19.95
Using Assembly Language 24.95
Using QuickBASIC 4 .... 19.95
Using Turbo Pascal 21.95
AutoCAD Quick Reference 6.95

Que Order Line: **1-800-428-5331**

All prices subject to change without notice. Prices and charges are for domestic orders only.
Non-U.S. prices might be higher.

SELECT QUE BOOKS TO INCREASE YOUR PERSONAL COMPUTER PRODUCTIVITY

Using Ventura Publisher, 2nd Edition

by Diane Burns, S. Venit, and Linda Mercer

This is a comprehensive text for all levels of Ventura Publisher users. You will learn both program basics and design fundamentals as you progress step-by-step through this informative text. Dozens of detailed example documents are presented, and the new features of Ventura Publisher 2.0—including the Professional Extension—are highlighted. Learn how to produce professional publications with *Using Ventura Publisher*, 2nd Edition!

MS-DOS User's Guide, 3rd Edition

by Chris DeVoney

This classic guide to MS-DOS is now better than ever! Updated for MS-DOS, Version 3.3, this new edition features several new extended tutorials and a unique new command reference section. The distinctive approach of this text lets you easily reference basic command syntax, while comprehensive tutorial sections present in-depth DOS data. Appendixes provide information specific to users of DOS on COMPAQ, Epson, Zenith, and Leading Edge personal computers. Master your computer's operating system with *MS-DOS User's Guide*, 3rd Edition—the comprehensive tutorial/reference!

Ventura Publisher Techniques and Applications

by Michael Miller

Learn how to produce effective newsletters, business reports, lists, and books with the step-by-step examples presented in this book. Numerous "evolving stylesheets" help your publications progress from rudimentary design to elaborate layouts. Along the way you'll learn the techniques you need to develop your own unique applications. An ideal book for anyone looking to advance beyond basic document preparation.

Using WordPerfect 5

by Charles O. Stewart III, et al.

WordPerfect 5 is the latest version of the popular word processor and Que's new *Using WordPerfect 5* is the perfect WordPerfect guide. This comprehensive text introduces you to WordPerfect basics; helps you learn to use macros, Styles, and other advanced features; presents information on outlining, referencing, and text columns; and shows you how to use WordPerfect for desktop publishing. Also included are numerous Quick Start tutorials, a tear-out command reference card, and an introduction to WordPerfect 5 for 4.2 users. Become a WordPerfect expert with *Using WordPerfect 5*!

ORDER FROM QUE TODAY

Item	Title	Price	Quantity	Extension
940	Using Ventura Publisher, 2nd Edition	$24.95		
948	Ventura Publisher Techniques and Applications	22.95		
838	MS-DOS User's Guide, 3rd Edition	22.95		
843	Using WordPerfect 5	24.95		

Book Subtotal	
Shipping & Handling ($2.50 per item)	
Indiana Residents Add 5% Sales Tax	
GRAND TOTAL	

Method of Payment

☐ Check ☐ VISA ☐ MasterCard ☐ American Express

Card Number ______________________ Exp. Date ______________________

Cardholder's Name ____

Ship to ____

Address ____

City ______________________ State ______________ ZIP ______________

If you can't wait, call **1-800-428-5331** and order TODAY.

All prices subject to change without notice.

FOLD HERE

Place
Stamp
Here

Que Corporation
P.O. Box 90
Carmel, IN 46032

REGISTRATION CARD

Register your copy of *Ventura Publisher Tips, Tricks, and Traps*, and receive information about Que's newest products. Complete this registration card and return it to Que Corporation, P.O. Box 90, Carmel, IN 46032.

Name ____________________ Phone __________

Company ____________________ Title __________

Address ______________________________

City ______________ State _______ ZIP _______

Please check the appropriate answers:

Where did you buy *Ventura Publisher Tips, Tricks, and Traps*?

- ☐ Bookstore (name: ____________________)
- ☐ Computer store (name: ____________________)
- ☐ Catalog (name: ____________________)
- ☐ Direct from Que ____________________
- ☐ Other: ____________________

How many computer books do you buy a year?

- ☐ 1 or less
- ☐ 2–5
- ☐ 6–10
- ☐ More than 10

How many Que books do you own?

- ☐ 1
- ☐ 2–5
- ☐ 6–10
- ☐ More than 10

How long have you been using Ventura Publisher?

- ☐ Less than 6 months
- ☐ 6 months to 1 year
- ☐ 1–3 years
- ☐ More than 3 years

What influenced your purchase of *Ventura Publisher Tips, Tricks, and Traps*?

- ☐ Personal recommendation
- ☐ Advertisement
- ☐ In-store display
- ☐ Price
- ☐ Que catalog
- ☐ Que mailing
- ☐ Que's reputation
- ☐ Other: ____________________

How would you rate the overall content of *Ventura Publisher Tips, Tricks, and Traps*?

- ☐ Very good
- ☐ Good
- ☐ Satisfactory
- ☐ Poor

How would you rate *Part I: Understanding Ventura Basics*?

- ☐ Very good
- ☐ Good
- ☐ Satisfactory
- ☐ Poor

How would you rate *Part IV: Printing Ventura Documents*?

- ☐ Very good
- ☐ Good
- ☐ Satisfactory
- ☐ Poor

How would you rate *Part V: Using Advanced Ventura Applications*?

- ☐ Very good
- ☐ Good
- ☐ Satisfactory
- ☐ Poor

What do you like *best* about *Ventura Publisher Tips, Tricks, and Traps*?

What do you like *least* about *Ventura Publisher Tips, Tricks, and Traps*?

How do you use *Ventura Publisher Tips, Tricks, and Traps*?

What other Que products do you own?

For what other programs would a Que book be helpful?

Please feel free to list any other comments you may have about *Ventura Publisher Tips, Tricks, and Traps*.

____

____

____

____

____

____

FOLD HERE

Place Stamp Here

Que Corporation
P.O. Box 90
Carmel, IN 46032